Building More Effective Organizations

HR management and performance in practice

Organizations today are facing heightened challenges in their efforts to perform effectively. These challenges are reflected in the failure of many long-standing organizations and the shortened tenure of senior-level executives. There is increasing agreement that the unique competitive advantage organizations have today lies in their people, their human resource management practices and their cultures. All other elements of production can be readily obtained, bought or copied. We are now in the era of human capital; to be successful, organizations need to unleash the talents of their people. Fortunately we now have considerable understanding of what high-performing organizations look like. However, a large gap still exists between what we know and what managers actually do. With contributions from a team of leading academics and practitioners, *Building More Effective Organizations* provides an extensive survey of human resource management and the organizational practices associated with the high performance of individuals.

Ronald J. Burke is Professor of Organizational Behaviour at the Schulich School of Business, York University. One of Canada's most prolific researchers and writers, Professor Burke's work has focused on the relationship between individual well-being and the work environment.

Cary L. Cooper is Professor of Organizational Psychology and Health and Pro-Vice Chancellor (External Relations) at Lancaster University. He is the author of over 100 books, Editor-in-Chief of *The Blackwell Encyclopedia of Management* and the editor of *Who's Who in the Management Sciences*. Professor Cooper was awarded a CBE for his contribution to organizational health.

Building More Effective Organizations

HR management and performance in practice

Edited by

Ronald J. Burke

Professor of Organizational Behavior, Schulich School of Business, York University, Toronto, Canada

Cary L. Cooper

Pro-Vice Chancellor (External Relations), Professor of Organizational Psychology and Health, Lancaster University, Lancaster, UK

CAMBRIDGE
UNIVERSITY PRESS

CAMBRIDGE UNIVERSITY PRESS
Cambridge, New York, Melbourne, Madrid, Cape Town, Singapore, São Paulo, Delhi

Cambridge University Press
The Edinburgh Building, Cambridge CB2 8RU, UK

Published in the United States of America by Cambridge University Press, New York

www.cambridge.org
Information on this title: www.cambridge.org/9780521688529

First published 2008

Printed in the United Kingdom at the University Press, Cambridge

A catalogue record for this publication is available from the British Library

Library of Congress Cataloguing in Publication data
Building more effective organizations: HR management and performance in practice / edited by
Ronald J. Burke, Cary L. Cooper.
    p.   cm.
Includes index.
ISBN 978-0-521-86854-9 (hardback) – ISBN 978-0-521-68852-9 (pbk.)
1. Personnel management.   2. Organizational effectiveness.   I. Burke, Ronald J.   II. Cooper, Cary L.
III. Title.
HF5549.B8739   2007
658.3 – dc22   2007032994

ISBN 978-0-521-86854-9 hardback
ISBN 978-0-521-68852-9 paperback

Contents

Part I   Building more effective organizations

Part II   Enhancing individual health and performance

Figures

Tables

Contributors

Yehuda Baruch
Norwich Business School, University of East Anglia, Norwich, UK

John Bessant
Imperial College, London, UK

Ronald J. Burke
Schulich School of Business, York University, Toronto, Canada

James Campbell Quick
Goolsby Leadership Academy, University of Texas at Arlington, Arlington, TX, USA

Sue Caton
Faculty of Health, Social Care and Education, Manchester Metropolitan University, Manchester, UK

Barry Colbert
School of Business, Wilfrid Laurier University, Waterloo, Ontario, Canada

Cary L. Cooper
Lancaster University School of Management, Lancaster University, Lancaster, UK

Dave Francis
Imperial College, London, UK

Alvin L. Gibson
Department of Management and Economics, East Stroudsburg University, USA

Stuart Kennedy
People and Organization Development, Royal Mail, London, UK

Steve Kerr
Chief Learning Officer, Goldman Sachs, New York, NY, USA

Elizabeth Kurucz
Schulich School of Business, York University, Toronto, Ontario, Canada

Steffen Landauer
Vice President, Hewlett-Packard, Palo Alto, CA, USA

Jeong-Yeon Lee
School of Business, University of Kansas, Manhattan, KA, USA

Elise Lelon
Independent Consultant, New York, NY, USA

Suzan Lewis
Middlesex University Business School, London, UK

Tony McCarthy
People and Organization Development,
Royal Mail, London, UK

Michael I. Meltzer
Sirota Survey Intelligence, New York,
NY, USA

Philip Mirvis
Independent Consultant, Bethesda, MD,
USA

Louis A. Mischkind
Sirota Survey Intelligence, New York,
NY, USA

Dennis W. Organ
Kelley School of Business, Indiana
University, Bloomington, IA, USA

Emma Preece
Elpconsulting Company, London, UK

Christine Purcell
Faculty of Health, Special Care and
Education, Manchester Metropolitan
University, Manchester, UK

Ivan T. Robertson
Robertson Cooper Ltd, Manchester,
UK

Susannah Robertson
Robertson Cooper Ltd, Manchester,
UK

Eduardo Salas
Department of Psychology, University of
Central Florida, Orlando, FL, USA

Silvia Salas
College of Business Administration,
Florida International University, Miami,
FL, USA

Val Singh
International Centre for Women
Business Leaders, Cranfield School of
Management, Cranfield University, UK

David Sirota
Sirota Survey Intelligence, New York,
NY, USA

Janet Smithson
School of Law, University of Exeter,
Exeter, UK

Kevin C. Stagl
Department of Psychology, University of
Central Florida, Orlando, FL, USA

Sherry E. Sullivan
Department of Management, College of
Business Administration, Bowling Green
State University, Bowling Green, OH,
USA

Gordon Tinline
Robertson Cooper Ltd, Manchester, UK

Mary Ann Von Glinow
College of Business Administration,
Florida International University, Miami,
FL, USA

David Wheeler, Dean
School of Management, Dalhousie
University, Halifax, Nova Scotia, Canada

Foreword

Building more effective organizations

The literature about organizations seems a growth industry with courses proliferating on the subject in business schools. Academic writing about the subject is only outdone by practitioners of the art of organizational analysis and change. The focal unit in any study of organizations varies depending upon the academic preparation or the experience of the theorist, researcher or practitioner. In the West, studies focused on patterns of growth and development until the middle and late 1970's when declining organizations were also recognized. The key questions have evolved from early descriptive studies of structure to studies of cycles in organizational effectiveness and then to component operations, resource utilization and functioning teams.

The field now includes theorists, researchers or practitioners out of engineering, sociology, political science and behavioral studies, each with their own brand of jargon. In this volume, the focus is on human organizations and the issues that arise from the time the organization is formed to the time it ceases to exist. As with every attempt to understand, study, and improve upon that on which one focuses, the process of analogy is a foundational tool of the writers. When the editors set the writers the task, of collecting innovative ideas about building more effective organizations. Regardless of their own academic discipline they focused on identifying ways to improve qualitative or quantitative performance within an organization's boundaries. Regardless of the orientation or background of the writer, certain characteristics are related to successful functioning.

For example, the concepts of decision taking and control are fundamental to coordination and predictability and must be present for organizational efficiency. If one approaches organizations as institutional entities, one will have to consider the legal and cultural context as it impacts on these activities. If one takes a resource perspective – inanimate or human – it is essential to address how to identify, obtain, preserve and manage valued resources. It is imperative to ensure the flow of these resources between the organization and its relevant environment – this enables an effective transformation process that brings value into the organization.

As organizations operate in environments of increasingly rapid change, the organization shelters, with increasing difficulty, its core internal processes that are used to transform and add value to the raw materials, goods, and services it provides for its constituents. The enormous pressure from competition for raw materials, services, skills, information, technology and customers means that organization builders are constantly adjusting their models of how an organization functions.

One interesting feature that is emerging in today's organizations is the challenge from open-source approaches to issues that, in the past, were under the control of mechanisms inside the boundaries of the organization. Thanks to the almost zero additional cost of data transmission that makes sharing ideas, broadly, rather than trying to control and manage them, some successful organizations, for example Toyota, are experimenting with loosening the internal control mechanisms (see Evans and Wolf from HBR July, 2005).

Thinking of how organizations might operate with lower levels of control and a reduction in the use of power by focal members of the organization and still be able to coordinate and provide predictability seems like a highly desirable goal. Trying to develop alternatives to *control* and *power* in the current, rapidly changing organizational milieu could very well be a useful endeavor as it provides organizations with new vehicles to sustain themselves over time. Power and control mechanisms are more useful for keeping what one already has, but they seem less helpful in gaining what is new and innovative. Measures of organizational efficiency will likely add new dimensions for squeezing out the last bit of value from its current core technology.

It is understandable that concepts such as learning organizations, continuous innovation, blurring of boundaries, end of hierarchy, the role of fundamental values and ethics in organizational exchanges and chaos theory have become increasingly important concepts in organizational studies. One important factor compounding all of these pressures in the West is the aging of the workforce. In time past in human organizations, there was the cadre of seasoned workers who knew how things 'ought to be done.' The unspoken, generally agreed upon, methods and ways of acting, previously passed along by long-time organizational members, helped to maintain an efficient core technology for the organization.

Now with changes to virtually every aspect of internal organizational actions, and with exchanges with the external environment blurred by fewer boundaries and differing cultures, the uncertainty and stress is compounded. Aging organizational members, if maintained as part of the enterprise, must learn new skills and behave in unfamiliar ways. The unavailability of younger, newly trained personnel hampers western organizations in their adaptation. Open source ideas might become useful if applied profitably.

This book addresses a pressing need for practitioners who each must respond to the challenge of rapid, frame-breaking change. It provides a compilation of current knowledge about important topics for researchers and students of action. And the discerning theorist and academic will pick up important clues about what will be future, successful designs for creating effective organizations of the future.

William F. Weitzel
Emeritus Professor of Management
Price College of Business Administration
University of Oklahoma,
Independent Consultant in the Management of Organization
Change and co-author of *Leadership: magic, myth or method* (1992)
New York: AMACOM

Preface

Ronald J. Burke and Cary L. Cooper

Organizations today are facing heightened challenges in their efforts to perform effectively. These include increasing levels of competition, the internationalization of business, accelerating pace of change, technological advances, meeting the needs of an increasingly diverse workforce, more demanding customers and consumers, greater concerns about corporate governance and board transparency and increasing threats and costs of international terrorism and national security. These are very challenging – and exciting – times to be in senior levels of management. These challenges, with their accompanying difficulties, are being reflected in the shortened tenure of senior level executives as they voluntarily or involuntarily leave their positions.

There is increasing agreement that the unique competitive advantage organizations have today lies in their people, their human resource management practices and systems, and their cultures (O'Reilly and Pfeffer, 2000). All other elements of production ((financial, physical plant, technology, products and services) can be readily obtained, bought or copied. We are now in the era of human capital (O'Toole and Lawler, 2006); to be successful organizations need to unleash the talents of their people.

Fortunately the past decade has produced considerable understanding of what high or peak performing organizations look like. But a huge gap still exists between what we know and what managers do – what Pfeffer and Sutton (1999) refer to as the "knowing-doing" gap. There are several reasons for this gap: much of the writing on peak performing organizations is written in academic jargon and difficult to access, many managers have little time for reading given the demands of their jobs, some of the writing does not address the immediate issues that managers are facing, and many of the action strategies require a considerable amount of time to implement, while managers are rewarded for the short term.

There is also a "doing-knowing" gap: managers take action though relatively little may be known about the benefits of these actions, the context in which they best work or how to implement them. Managers often follow fads, the advice of gurus, or copy what seems to have worked in organizations currently getting a lot of publicity, without considering whether their organization is similar to other high profile organizations.

Businesses that people admire are those that deliver the kind of service that one really likes and you can talk with someone who understands your situation and needs. People do not care about the structure of these organizations, their management style or how they set strategy. The former are organizational capabilities, intangible assets that are not on the balance sheet, but make all the difference when it comes to market value. It has been suggested that half the market value of a publicly controlled firm is derived from financial factors and the other half from the expectations and confidence created in the organization's stakeholders: its customers, employees, investors and regulators (Ulrich and Smallwood, 2003).

The "soft stuff" such as leadership, the ability to attract talent, brand development and corporate culture drive market value. The job of the HR department and human resource management practices more broadly is to build organizational capabilities that drive profitability and top-line growth (Lawler, 2003).

Important capabilities include improving overall product and service quality, getting new products to market ahead of the competition, enhancing a firm's cultural brand identity, higher success rates for mergers and acquisitions, creating high productivity and accountability and optimizing flexibility and adaptability relative to threats and opportunities (Burke and Cooper, 2006).

The past decade has produced research evidence supporting the critical role that people play in the success of organizations. This evidence has been generated in a variety of different types of organizational settings including manufacturing, professional services, financial services and health care (Ulrich and Brockbank, 2005; Huselid, Becker and Beatty, 2005).

Sirota, Mischkind and Meltzer (2005) have shown using stock prices, that companies who have more enthusiastic employees (more job satisfied) outperformed the average prices of companies in the same industries by more than two-and-a-half times. In addition, the stock prices of companies with unenthusiastic employees (low job satisfaction) lagged behind their industry competitors' average price by almost five times. The role of management was critical to levels of employee enthusiasm. The management of more enthusiastic employees focused on three goals: achievement – being proud of one's work and employer; camaraderie – having an opportunity for positive, productive relationships at work; and equity – feeling treated justly in relation to basic conditions of employment such as pay, job security and respect.

Why should effective HRM practices increase firm performance? Performance increases because employees work *both harder and smarter*. Employees work harder because of greater job involvement, more peer pressure for results and for the economic gains based on high performance (Lawler, 1992). Employees work smarter because they can use their knowledge and skills acquired through training and development in the jobs themselves in getting the work done. In addition, effective HRM practices are likely to reduce the direct and indirect costs of employee grievances. Finally, performance benefits are seen in the elimination of jobs whose main responsibility is to monitor people whose main job is to monitor other people. The potential benefits for adopting HRM best practices can be substantial. Pfeffer (1998) concludes that the return from utilizing effective HRM practices ranges typically between 30 to 50 percent.

Leslie, Loch and Schaninger (2006) considered the relationship of management practices and performance in 230 businesses around the world. They considered 34 practices in their study under nine outcome categories (e.g., direction, accountability, capabilities, motivation). They collected data from more than 115,000 individual managers and employees. Executives and managers could use a wide variety of these practices to improve the organizational performance of their companies. They drew three major conclusions from this large project. First, managers should avoid simplistic organizational solutions. Organizations were more likely to improve their current performance and underlying (and long-term) health by using a combination of complementary practices. No one practice (e.g., TQM, leadership development, culture change) was likely to make a difference. Second, high performing organizations were generally good (but not necessarily great) at all the management practices studied. Poorly performing organizations were likely to perform badly on at least one of the management practices. Third, managers should focus on a small number of practices that, introduced together, were likely to be successful, (i.e., introducing three or four complementary practices was more likely to lead to improved performance). Interestingly, they found that three management practices were common among many of their high performing organizations. These were: clarifying roles and accountabilities, articulating a compelling direction and vision for the future, and developing a strong performance-oriented culture based on openness and trust. These three practices were both complementary and synergistic.

For organizational change to be successful a high level of motivation must be present. This raises the question of whether organizations need a crisis to make successful transformations. While a crisis may help in some cases, organizations can be successfully transformed without one. If the following conditions are met, the chances for a successful change are increased.

1. Each employee must continue to act and contribute while questioning their actions and contributions.
2. Employees must adopt a new view of their and their organization's future – both why a change is taking place now and where the change is heading – and understand their personal benefits from supporting the change.
3. Employees need to experience the new reality; it must be more than mere words.
4. The change process leaves room, and provides resources, for mistakes and surprises.

For a change to be a success, organizations must come to grips with some central questions. Why does the organization need to do this? Where is the organization headed? How can/will the organization reach its goals?

This collection identifies some of the common challenges facing organizations and reviews relevant research findings as well as offering descriptions of initiatives that have proven successful in addressing them. These challenges are:

- increasing levels of employee engagement and enthusiasm
- satisfying both organizational and employee needs simultaneously
- bringing about organizational change.

We believe the following statements to be valid:

1. People are the only competitive advantage in the long term.
2. We know a lot about the nature of effective HRM practices and their link to high performance.
3. We also know a lot about why these HRM practices have not been more widely adopted by managers.
4. We also know a lot about the ways to change organizations to make them more satisfying and productive.
5. We are also acquiring knowledge as to how best to convey this information to students of management and practicing managers.

Our hope is that readers will close somewhat the "knowing-doing" and "doing-knowing" gaps as a result of our efforts.

Overview of the contents

In the first chapter in Part I, Building more effective organizations, Ronald Burke sets the stage for the chapters that follow. He begins by reviewing the challenges facing organizations today in their efforts to remain competitive and achieve high performance. He then summarizes some suggestions offered by leading thinkers such as Jon Katzenbach, David Sirota, Wayne Cascio, Jim Collins, Jerry Porras and Ed Lawler on the characteristics and qualities of successful organizations. Such organizations need the capacity to adapt and change in response to, and in anticipation of, emerging demands and opportunities. Suggestions for developing the capacity and competencies for change are proposed, based primarily on the work of John Kotter and Ed Lawler. To achieve peak performance we need healthy people and healthy organizations. Fortunately, there is an emerging consensus on how to build more effective organizations. The time is right for managers to assimilate this information and take action. They have little choice if the organizations they lead are to thrive.

Part II, Enhancing individual health and performance, contains four chapters. David Sirota, Louis Mischkind and Michael Meltzer maintain that company performance results from enthusiastic employees – those demonstrating a high level of engagement. They show how management practices diminish employee enthusiasm through policies and procedures used to manage their workforces and in the relationships managers have with employees. Enthusiastic employees have three goals: equity – to be treated fairly; achievement – to take pride in one's achievements, the organization's accomplishments and to be recognized for one's achievements, and camaraderie – to have cooperative relationships with co-workers. They describe four organizational cultures indicating how each meets or does not meet employee goals. Enthusiasm is highest in partnership cultures where employees are treated as allies. They conclude their chapter with concrete proposals for developing partnership cultures.

Dennis Organ and Jay Lee illustrate the value of organizational citizenship behavior (OCB) in the workplace and evaluate the effects of various managerial action strategies on levels of OCB. OCBs have been shown to be associated with clearly valued organizational outcomes. Job satisfaction or morale is a strong predictor of OCB. They suggest that supervisory evaluation of employee performance is the major lever through which OCB is elicited and rewarded.

The supervisor–employee relationship is fundamentally a social exchange relationship with supervisors having many opportunities and ways of influencing employee behaviors.

Alvin Gibson and James Quick offer a set of solutions for the human dilemmas created by stress in the workplace. They consider seven practice areas: supervisory support and executive stress management, job design, scheduling and work flow, communication pathways and information nodes, work and family, positive stress, fairness and justice in the workplace and human resource management systems integrity. Running through these best practices is a recognition of the human side of organizations and the importance of humane leadership in stressful workplaces.

Ivan Robertson, Gordon Tinline and Susannah Robertson argue that organizational performance and enhanced staff well-being go hand-in-hand. Yet many managers see these in opposition to each other. Individual well-being is reduced when workplace stressors are at high levels. They cite emerging evidence which indicates that high levels of workplace stress have associated economic costs resulting from lost productivity. There is also evidence to suggest that levels of psychological well-being are associated with self-reported productivity, the latter was also found to be related to objective indicators of productivity. They describe the use of an organizational diagnostic tool that assesses levels and sources of work stressors to first establish baseline data and then provide feedback for discussion and identification of important problem areas. They conclude with reports of the benefits of such audits carried out in two public sector organizations. As the authors of other chapters also show, data collection, feedback and problem solving remain the central elements in successful organizational change efforts.

Part III, Enhancing organizational health and performance, consists of six chapters. Steve Kerr, Steffen Landauer and Elise Lelon tackle the central and critical issue of leadership development. As this collection maintains, leaders are at the heart of all successful change initiatives. The authors' efforts are informed, in part, by years spent designing, developing and evaluating leadership development initiatives in several organizations noted for their success in this regard. As a result, the chapter is grounded in "reality". It identifies issues that need to be addressed and offers examples of actual company efforts and choices. The chapter is organized around seven questions such as "What is the organization's working definition of leadership and what kind of leadership is it seeking to develop?", "What should the content of the initiative look like?", "Who is to be developed?", and "How should the success of the initiative be evaluated?" Readers interested in leadership development will find much to think about here.

Kevin Stagl and Eduardo Salas consider the use of teams in organizations as one way to leverage human capital. Almost all efforts at organizational transformation involve the use of teams. Although teamwork has advantages, this potential is often unrealized. They discuss what it takes to build more effective teams. Using a team effectiveness framework as a platform, they offer best practices in team leadership, in cross-training to develop skills, and in building more effective teams. Effective teams require considerable care and attention. In their thinking, five conditions are central: establishing a real team, developing a compelling direction, creating an enabling structure, fostering a supportive context, and providing access to expert coaching. These conditions seem to meaningfully apply to larger change and improvement efforts as well.

Yehuda Baruch and Sherry Sullivan first review the nature of the new employee–employer work contract that has resulted from both individual and organizational changes. They then indicate how career management systems have also necessarily changed as a result. The traditional linear career is dying or already dead; non-traditional careers are fast becoming the norm. In recognition of this, career management programs have become more varied and flexible with career patterns and jobs now needing to be more intrinsically satisfying and meaningful. Organizational and life-long learning also needs to be more strongly supported. They propose the Kaleidoscope Career Model as a basis for developing organizational career management programs to better guide the more complex career options of a more diverse workforce, offering concrete suggestions as to the issues that need attention and how these might be addressed.

Silvia Salas and Mary Ann Von Glinow consider factors critical to fostering organizational learning and how organizations can create and maintain a learning culture. Organizations that effectively transfer knowledge between individual, group and the organizational level have a unique competitive advantage. They focus on the relationship and interdependence that exists between leaders, employees, the organizational culture and the knowledge itself in their analysis and recommendations.

Christine Purcell and her colleagues review the effects of European work-family policies on organizational practices and their impact on organizational functioning. Reconciling work and family life has become a major issue in the European Union. They report findings from a seven-European country study of organizational best practices for supporting work-family balance. They found that best practices differed in the various countries: the context mattered. Managers reported access to more best practices than did non-managers. They propose the concept of the "healthy organization" as a new way of looking at the effects of organizational practices on work-family balance. A healthy organization values the role of its employees in contributing to and sustaining performance. Thus individual health and organizational health are interdependent. Healthy organizations abide by statutory regulations, have managerial support for work–family issues, behave with consistency in this area, foster trust and mutual understanding between employees and managers, develop co-worker support for those attempting to achieve work–family balance, offer realistic workloads and strive to create gender equity. They conclude with an examination of flexible work practices such as reduced contractual hours, compressed hours, flexible hours, working from home and arrangements for responding to family emergencies. There is benefit to both organizations and individuals from supporting work–family balance.

Finally, Val Singh reviews current diversity and inclusion management initiatives from leading-edge firms. At their core, these initiatives encompass agendas for strategic change and efforts to engage managers in the change process. These initiatives include recruitment, development, role modeling, reverse mentoring, diversity networks, diversity events, flexible work arrangements and diversity partnering relationships with outside organizations. She also provides concrete examples of these efforts from the firms that she studied.

Part IV, Transforming organizations, contains five chapters. John Bessant and Dave Francis highlight what is known about achieving outstanding performance in manufacturing organizations. This sector has undergone dramatic – some would say traumatic – change as older "rust belt" factories are replaced by state-of-the-art, high tech operations. This sector has also experienced significant staff downsizing. Manufacturing organizations today, like organizations in other sectors, need to be agile, flexible, innovative and achieve high levels of employee involvement. They describe how some manufacturing organizations have achieved high levels of employee involvement in innovation specifically. Manufacturing operations are now also more likely to be virtual and networked. All these initiatives require a new set of managerial skills making education, knowledge and learning increasingly important ingredients for success. In previous times, people were adjuncts to the machinery; today, achieving outstanding performance in manufacturing organizations begins with people.

Emma Preece describes a case study of culture change in Britannia, a large financial services organization in the UK. She outlines the approach and strategies undertaken by Britannia in bringing about the desired culture change and offers early results on employee satisfaction. Britannia was performing well but senior executives realized that changes were needed to respond to events taking place in the financial services sector. She used interviews with key informants to develop her case study. The key purposes of Britannia were first articulated by senior executives, resulting in five core values (e.g., putting our customers first). The CEO was supportive of the change program, and was actively involved as its champion and spokesperson. The senior executive team also applied these values in their own behaviors. Various communication channels were used to convey the changes throughout the organization. Employee attitude surveys were undertaken with an emphasis on "doing something" with the results. She offers recent survey data indicating that the culture change generally had a positive impact on staff perceptions. In addition, assessments by employees of the culture indicated that it had changed in the planned for direction. Coincidently, Britannia achieved record financial performance during this time period as well. In reading this case study, one gets the sense of the key role played by the CEO in bringing about a successful transformation.

Barry Colbert, Elizabeth Kurucz and David Wheeler emphasize the importance of organizations adopting more sustainable business practices. There is an increasing and urgent need to rethink the relationship of business and the broader society. They suggest that developing sustainable organizations will require new ways of viewing how change happens and of developing internal resources and capabilities. In their view, a sustainable organization has four characteristics termed the four C's: connectivity, commitments, culture and capabilities. Three commonalities run across the four C's: a systems perspective that recognizes pluralism, synthesizing various stakeholders' interests, and a focus on value creation and value maximization in several areas. Strategic human resource management practices are central to build capacity on these fronts. Organizational examples they provide make their concepts come alive.

Stuart Kennedy and Tony McCarthy describe "Be in to win", part of an innovative approach by Royal Mail Group to tackle the growing issue of chronic sick absence with the organization. It involved a six-month scheme in which all employees with a 100 percent attendance record were entered into a draw to win one of seventeen brand new Ford cars. Initially seen by some in the media as a gimmick centered on bribery, the "Be in to win" incentive scheme increased attendance at Royal Mail by 18 per cent, resulted in an average of 2000 extra people at work per day and saved the business over 80 million pounds in sick absence payments and lost time. Royal Mail's positive approach to absence management played a large part in helping the organization return to profitability and record the highest levels of quality for over ten years.

In the final chapter, Phil Mirvis describes efforts by organizational leaders to build their companies into communities having a "higher purpose" and to build a community of leaders. One such initiative that he helped organize and facilitate was an annual retreat of 250 leaders of the Asia region of a multinational food's business unit that spent three days in India to learn about community life. In this chapter, he reviews some of the theory behind such large group interventions and describes innovative practices they used to build this large leadership community. Business leaders went in small groups to various places to self-study local communities and were asked to record their observations, feelings and insights about the community they observed. Discussions of their observations and reflections led to a change in their organization's mission and purpose. Many of the leaders did redefine their company's mission to be more reflective of a" higher purpose"; that is a commitment to do something to improve the daily life of others rather than focusing only on the bottom line.

REFERENCES

Burke, R. J. and Cooper, C. L. (2006) *The human resources revolution: Why putting people first matters.* London: Elsevier.

Huselid, M. A., Becker, B. A. and Beatty, R. W. (2005) *The workforce scorecard: Managing human capital to execute strategy.* Boston: Harvard Business School Press.

Lawler, E. E. (1992) *The ultimate advantage: Creating the high involvement organization.*

Lawler, E. E. (2003) *Treat people right.* San Francisco: Jossey-Bass.

Leslie, K., Loch, M. A. and Schaninger, W. (2006) Managing your organization by the evidence. *The McKinsey Quarterly*, 3, 65–75.

O'Reilly, C. A. and Pfeffer, J. (2000) *Hidden value: How great companies achieve extraordinary results with ordinary people.* Boston: Harvard Business School Press.

O'Toole, J. and Lawler, E. E. (2006) *The new American workplace*, New York: Palgrave Macmillan.

Pfeffer, J. (1998) *The human equation: Building profits by putting people first.* Boston: Harvard Business School Press.

Pfeffer, J. and Sutton, R. I. (1999) *The knowing-doing gap.* Boston: Harvard Business School Press.

Sirota, D. Mischkind, L. A. and Meltzer, M. I. (2005) *The enthusiastic employee: How companies profit by giving workers what they want.* Philadelphia: Wharton School Publishing.

Ulrich, D. and Brockbank, W. (2005) *The HR value proposition.* Boston: Harvard Business School Press.

Ulrich, D. and Smallwood, N. (2003) *Why the bottom line isn't: How to build value through people and organization.* New York: John Wiley.

Acknowledgements

I started working during my summer vacations as a teenager. When I had to decide on a major area of concentration for graduate studies in the Department of Psychology at the University of Michigan in 1960 it was a "no brainer". I wanted to learn more about work and organizations as a result of my mainly – but not exclusively – positive experiences during these summers. So I chose organizational psychology. The outstanding faculty there were interested in research findings that could be used to improve organizational effectiveness. These values have shaped most of my work since then. They also influenced my decision to teach in Schools of business and management rather in Departments of Psychology, believing that business schools would be more supportive of applied research.

This collection has its roots in this journey. We know a lot about building organizations that meet the needs of employees, owners and society at large.

Cary Cooper and I have developed a productive friendship and collaboration over the years which is certain to continue. I also thank our international contributors for their fine work.

Support for this initiative was provided in part by the Schulich School of Business. Louise Coutu provided valuable secretarial and administrative support here in Canada, while Gerry Wood did the same in the UK.

Finally, I would like to thank my partner, Susan, who offers encouragement and love.

Ronald Burke
Toronto, Ontario

I would like to thank my old mentor Professor Fred Massarik of UCLA for helping me start my long journey in trying desperately to understand the complexities of organizational behavior.

Cary L. Cooper
Lancaster, UK

Part I

Building more effective organizations

Building more effective organizations: A primer[1]

Ronald J. Burke

This chapter sets the stage for those that follow. We seem to be at a "tipping point" (Burke and Cooper, 2006) in the way organizational leaders are coming to view the importance of people as a key element in their organization's success and are prepared to act on this realization. It first lays out new challenges facing organizations as their employees, competition and business environment changes. In response to these new, and in some cases continuing demands, organizations need involved and engaged employees, need to manage and develop their talent, and to continuously adapt and change to survive. Contributions from some central researchers and writers are thus reviewed to provide a sense of what is known about continued high levels of organizational performance and the emerging consensus of what needs to be done to achieve this.

The new world of work and organization

O'Toole and Lawler (2006), in collaboration with the Society for Human Resource Management, wrote a follow-up to *Work in America*, published in 1973. Using focus groups with HR managers and state-of the art reviews by leading US academics, they identify ways in which workplaces have changed over this time period, why these changes have occurred, the impact of these changes on workers and organizations, and organizational and government policy initiatives necessary for organizations (and American society) to remain competitive. Effective HRM that emphasizes building human capital lie at the center of these efforts.

Too many organizations are wedded to outdated HRM practices that are out of step with the demands of today's business environment.

O'Toole and Lawler (2006) identified several themes in their review. These include:

- insufficient creation of new "good" jobs;
- increased choice and risk now borne by workers;
- increased influence of competitive and economic considerations in managerial decisions;
- increased tension between work and family life;
- increased social stratification based on education;
- changes in the nature of careers;
- a mismatch of skills and business needs – too few highly skilled, skill shortages in science, engineering and mathematics;
- reduction in corporate training;
- less sense of community at work associated with reduced motivation and commitment to organizations;
- the continuing health care crisis characterized by high escalating costs;
- demographic changes leading to a shortage of skilled workers connected with changes in retirement and immigration policies;
- failure to use HRM best practices to build human capital;
- more women at work in professional and managerial jobs; their career patterns and paths becoming increasingly similar;
- most people end up working for several employers during their working life;
- lifelong learning is necessary for continuing success;
- no longer having to retire at 65;
- more people work at home some of the time;
- work intensified – having to work faster and harder – making the home – personal life integration problem a major one for more people;
- talent now available is richer, and more experienced;
- workers have more freedom, responsibility and greater personal accountability;
- employees now less loyal to a given employer;
- shift from manufacturing to service jobs;
- more global operations;
- more use of outsourcing and on-shoring – foreign companies buying companies in a given host country.

The global business environment has forced organizations to reinvent themselves, embrace change, and increase the speed of innovation, change and adaptation.

A need for continual improvement in products, services and business processes.

The age of human capital

Business is a lot more complex today than it was 20 to 30 years ago. Increase in the provision of services by organizations has raised the importance of human capital (Stewart, 1997; 2001). Intangible assets such as the quality of its brand name, business systems and processes, and the quality of its workforce have become critical defining features of organizations.

Organizations have also developed more complex structures in response to the need for speed, global operations, and higher value-added activities. These include changing and flexible job descriptions, global teams, virtual teams, and becoming less bureaucratic. There is also a greater pressure for economic performance, often associated with greater use of downsizing and out-sourcing. There is increasing evidence that people and organizational culture represent the only unique competitive advantage (Pfeffer, 1994; 1998; Ulrich and Brockbank, 2005; Ulrich and Smallwood, 2003).

The "war for talent"

Talented people are critical to the success of a company, therefore the importance of strengthening the firm's talent pool is now heightened.

How to attract, develop, excite and retain highly talented managers.

Why does a war for talent exist today? Michaels, Handfield-Jones and Axelrod (2001) suggest the following.

1. The shift from the industrial age to the information age.
2. Greater demand for high level managerial talent.
3. An increase in the numbers of people changing companies.

Excellent talent management is now a competitive advantage.

Companies that scored in the top quintile on their talent management index earned, on average twenty-two percentage points higher return to shareholders than did their industry peers.

Michaels, Handfield-Jones and Axelrod report that most companies are unfortunately poor in talent management. Only 20 percent believe they have enough talented leaders to meet their current business needs and future opportunities. Only a small percentage of companies indicated strong agreement that their organizations endorsed the following five talent management practices:

bringing in highly talented people – 14%

develops people quickly and effectively – 3%

retains almost all high performers – 8%

removes low performers – 3%

knows who the high and low performers are – 16%

Organizations are facing a new reality:

- companies need people
- talented people are the competitive advantage
- better talent makes a huge difference
- talented people are scarce
- people are mobile and their commitment is short term
- people now demand much more from their organizations.

Organizations, if they are to successfully manage talent, need to embrace a talent mindset, craft a winning employee value proposition (EVP), rebuild their recruiting strategy, weave development into their organization, and differentiate and affirm their people.

Leaders must passionately believe that performance and competitiveness are achieved with better talent – the talent mindset. That is, to be successful you must have great talent. Managers need to create a statement as to why talented managers should join and stay with their organization (provide challenge, development, a great company with great leaders, good pay, and open, performance-oriented culture) in order to make their organization a place where talented people would want to work. Organizations must go out and find great candidates at all levels of the organization and actively market the organization as a great place to work. They need to make development a major part of their organization's initiatives by the use of stretch jobs, coaching and mentoring. They should review performance and differentiate high, middle and low performers. And invest differentially in these individuals. Leaders need to have high standards for talent. They need to spend lots of time in people decisions. They need to instill a talent mind-set in all managers at every level in the organization. They need to provide the necessary resources to attract develop, excite and retain talent. Finally, managers must be held accountable for the talent pools they develop.

Characteristics of effective organizations

What qualities do effective organizations have? What makes them effective? These questions have moved to the forefront in the past decade with some consensus on their qualities. This section reviews some of the most important in this regard.

Jon Katzenbach

Katzenbach (2000) was intrigued by the fact that some organizations "uniquely and consistently fire up the positive emotions within their workforces and channel the extra energy to higher levels of performance than their competition can." (Katzenbach, 2000, p. ix).

He defines higher or peak performance "as any group of employees whose emotional commitment enables them to make or deliver products or services that constitute a sustainable competitive advantage for their employer" (p. x). Peak performance is performance "better than the norm, better than expected, better than the competition and better than similar workforces in other places".

Katzenbach and his research team identified over 25 peak performing organizations, many well-known and highly desirable places to work. They assumed that these organizations would show a pattern consistent with principles of good people management. They undertook detailed case studies of each using available published data and information, studied middle and upper management as well as front-line workers. Each case study took several days and involved intensive interviews, surveys and focus groups. Those companies were specifically selected to represent a diverse set of products, services and industries. They observed five different patterns, termed balanced paths, in the companies studied.

The key to achieving an emotionally committed workforce was maintaining a balance between organizational performance needs and employee fulfillment. Peak performing organizations were disciplined in meeting organizational needs for shareholder return, market share, customer satisfaction, work output and the development of key capabilities. Peak performing organizations were also disciplined in meeting employee needs for decent wages leading to a secure livelihood, direction and structure, identity, purpose and self-worth, belonging and social interaction, and opportunity.

The leaders of peak performing organizations also shared common philosophical beliefs and management practices. They strongly believed in each employee; they engaged their employees emotionally and rationally; they strived for organizational performance goals and worker fulfillment with equal commitment and zeal.

Katzenbach concluded, to his surprise, that good people management (e.g., treating people fairly, providing rewards), by itself, fell short. In addition, most organizations try to implement good people management, with varying degrees of commitment and success. While these efforts were useful, peak performing organizations moved beyond them.

Five paths to peak performance captured all the higher performing organizations studied. Each path represented a different approach for firing up the workforce to achive higher performance. These five paths were: Mission, Vision and Pride (MVP), Process and Metrics (P&M), Entrepreneurial Spirit (ES), Individual Achievement (IA), Recognition and Celebration (R&C).

High performing organizations in all five paths balanced organizational and individual fulfillment needs. Five broad categories of employee needs were addressed.

- *Basic subsistence* – receiving adequate pay, working in a safe and secure work environment.
- *Structure and control* – knowing what was expected, knowing why things happen, knowing where the organization was heading, having some control over one's future.
- *Identity and purpose* – seeing value in one's work, taking pride in one's skills and abilities.
- *Belonging* – being part of a selected group, being part of something special, having feelings of ownership.
- *Opportunity* – having opportunities for challenge, making progress, learning and developing.

Mission, values and pride

These organizations had magnetic leaders, a compelling legacy, and held bold, impossible dreams. Their leaders provided an inspiring vision, made all employees feel valued, and worked hard at selecting the right people. Members of MVP organizations took most pride in the accomplishments and reputation of their organization and the accomplishments of their work units. Employee pride was reinforced by recognition. Company values were strongly held and widely shared by employees.

Process and metrics

These organizations typically had demanding customers and were in dynamic marketplaces. They valued consistent behavior, clear measures of important goals, emphasized continuous improvement, and relied heavily on data and results. The P&M path stressed individual accountability, well-defined successes that translated organizational objectives into individual goals. Organizational and business processes were clear and efficient. These processes also provided individual fulfillment as well. Those employees meeting challenging individual goals were well rewarded.

Entrepreneurial spirit

These organizations were somewhat similar to those pursuing the MVP path in that they had magnetic leaders and bold, impossible dreams. Leaders tended to be hands-off; individual initiative and risk taking was encouraged; meaningful rewards and recognition was provided and opportunity widespread. These organizations worked hard at ensuring they had selected the right people. Employees were rewarded in terms of what they created and the personal risks taken (high risks/high rewards). Leaders tried to get out of the way of talented employees.

Individual achievement

These organizations were similar in some ways to those pursuing the P&M path (e.g., demanding customers, dynamic and fast-changing marketplaces). Their employees were ambitious; individual growth and goal achievement were linked with and led to high levels of organizational performance; there were high rewards to those that met their goals. Employees in these organizations knew what mattered most and the performance-reward links were clear the IA path provided opportunities to grow and develop to employees as individuals. Efforts were made to monitor and reward individual contributors with promotions and growth opportunities. Individuals took responsibility for their own development and being successful.

Recognition and celebration

These organizations resembled both the MVP and ES paths. They had inspiring leaders, a compelling history and legacy, and were in fast-changing market-places. Employees were provided with meaningful recognition and rewards, and were valued for their contribution. The work itself, however, was not intrinsically stimulating, and the workforce was largely unskilled at relatively low pay levels. The R&C path worked best in combination with another path. Individual and group accomplishments were recognized and rewarded in an environment characterized by enthusiasm, fun and excitement.

Several organizations followed more than one path simultaneously. Following more than one path, if the paths are well integrated, can strengthen the organizations and reinforce each other over time. But following more than one path was more likely to be more demanding and complicated. In addition, organizations can follow one or more paths, enact it/them badly, or have their path(s) be unbalanced, and thereby perform at low levels.

Every successful organization pursued a P&M path to some degree. This path is based on concepts of accountability and performance management (clear measures and standards, performance transparency in that employees know how they and others are performing). The P&M path was typically linked with one or more other paths – most commonly with R&C and MVP.

Katzenbach suggests that organizations need to have particular beliefs and skills to succeed in any of these paths. First, they must have knowledge of the need to balance both organizational performance needs and individual fulfill-ment needs. Second, they must be committed to meeting employee fulfillment needs with the same intensity and discipline as meeting organizational perfor-mance needs. Third, organizations must have a willingness and commitment to addressing emotional and rational needs of employees. Fourth, organiza-tions need the skill and discipline to develop the tools and processes that align the organization to the path(s) that meets the employees needs for fulfillment.

Katzenbach observed three powerful sources of energy in the organizations studied: magnetic leaders having a clear, inspiring, and bold vision; being in a dynamic marketplace characterized by unpredictable conditions, aggressive competitors and demanding customers; and having a remarkable history and legacy of accomplishment represented by heroes, legends and martyrs.

There are a variety of ways to create and channel energy. These include the following.

1. Building an image of peak performance and success: showing people they are valued, creating and shaping the big picture of where the organization is heading, and generating collective energy across the unit or organization.
2. Keeping the emphasis on performance: selecting the right people and having demanding standards, clearly articulating what is most important to the organization (its values), developing clear performance measures, and offering meaningful recognition and rewards.
3. Opening up options and opportunity: creating lots of opportunity for development and advancement, distributing leadership opportunities throughout the organization, and making the work more meaningful and interesting.

It is obviously critical to enforce disciplined behavior throughout the organization. This is the only way to ensure a balanced approach in any of the paths undertaken. This discipline can refer to costs, customer service, recruiting and training, accountability and performance management.

Organizations interested in finding the path that best fits their circumstances need to address two key areas. The first is developing a compelling business case. Why would they want a peak performing workforce? Where in the organization is such a workforce most needed? What will it cost to produce such a workforce? What are their performance needs and assumptions with regard to customers, employees and shareholders? How important is their workforce compared to other factors in how their organizations perform? How good a job are they doing in meeting employee needs for support and safety structure and control, identity and self-worth, belonging and trust, and growth and development? The second is to pursue a balanced path (or paths). What sources of energy can they build on? Your company history? What makes their employees proud? Who are the most respected leaders? What process of alignment of employee and organization performance needs should their organization use? Regular or special communication of their efforts? Use of formal management processes? Informal networks? Employee programs? Are their performance achievements known to their employees?

The change to a peak performing organization and a fired up workforce will make new demands of organizational leadership and raise the standards for both front-line workers and managers alike. Leaders will have to be more emotional, becoming more personal, supportive and interactive. Leaders will need to unleash the emotional energy in employees. Everyone will need to become "higher performing" as well. Accountabilities will be clear and pursued vigorously.

Jim Collins and Jerry Porras

Collins and Porras (1994) studied eighteen outstanding and long-lasting companies (outperformed the stock market by a factor of fifteen) comparing them to one of their top competitors. Great companies embraced both extremes on a number of dimensions (e.g., visionary and futuristic/outstanding daily execution). They put profits after people and products. They retained a core ideology while changing practices, products and people. They set challenging and risky goals. They build very strong cultures. They promote from within. They resist the status quo and continually try to do better. They experiment, take action and make things happen. Mistakes are accepted as a necessary cost of doing outstanding business. Finally, they work continually to make sure all parts are as well aligned as is possible.

Visionary companies continue to be outstanding performers over long time periods, several generations of leaders and many product life cycles. Collins and Porras use the term 'visionary companies' to distinguish companies that have been the best performers in their industries for decades.

Collins and Porras used vast amounts of financial data and written information (books, articles, case studies, company publications, video footage) on their 36 companies. The key question was what distinguished the visionary companies from the eighteen comparison companies?

In the visionary companies, the building of the company was the ultimate goal not the building of products. Visionary companies put profits after people. Visionary companies lived with paradox (e.g., low cost and high quality, conservative and bold). Visionary companies retained a core ideology while pursuing programs and change. Visionary companies had "big hairy audacious goals" visionary companies had cult-like cultures. Visionary companies tried lots of things keeping what was useful. Visionary companies invested heavily in management development believing strongly in promotion from within. Visionary companies were never satisfied with being good enough. Finally, visionary companies forged their core ideology and unique approaches to progress and peak performance into all aspects of the organizations and into everything the organization did.

What makes truly outstanding organizations different from other organizations?

Much of the latest management writing can be described as buzzwords and fads trumpeted as new or creative approaches. Most of these buzzwords are not new, having been practiced in outstanding organizations for decades.

In addition, widely-held assumptions about outstanding organizations were found to have questionable value.

Collins and Porras (1994), for example, list twelve shattered myths. These include: it takes a great idea to start a great company, visionary companies require great and charismatic visionary leaders, the most successful companies exist first and foremost to maximize products, and visionary companies are great places to work, for everyone (Collins and Porras, 1994, pp. 7–9).

Jim Collins

Collins (2001) studied fourteen companies that dramatically improved their performance and maintained these results for at least fifteen years. These companies were matched with comparison companies that were unable to move from good to great. Data on these companies included financial information, interviews with many executives in the good to great companies, and published material on these 28 companies.

Similar to the earlier Collins and Porras (1994) study, the good-to-great companies were contrasted with those companies that failed to achieve greatness. As in the 1994 book, Collins found many of the myths were not supported. Thus, strategy did not separate the two groups of companies. Neither technology nor mergers and acquisitions made a difference. Good to great companies were not necessarily in great industries. Finally, bringing in celebrity leaders from the outside reduced the likelihood of moving from good to great.

But some factors did distinguish the two groups of organizations. Senior executives in the good-to-great companies invested in building the company and not themselves. This exhibited high levels of personal humility and professional resolve and fearlessness. Executives in good-to-great companies focused initially on recruiting the right people and removing the wrong people. Then efforts were made to build a superior executive team. Executives in good-to-great companies thrive on truth, dialogue and debate and the facts. Good-to-great companies understood what they could excel at and what they could not. Good-to-great companies had a culture of discipline. Disciplined people engaged in disciplined thought, and then undertook disciplined action. Good-to-great companies used carefully selected technology as an accelerator of momentum. The changes that took place in these good-to-great companies were natural, evolving and cumulative processes over a long period of time. There was no single dramatic defining moment or program.

David Sirota

Sirota, Mischkind and Meltzer (2005) write about enthusiastic workers – workers that go the extra mile for their employers. Too many workers are indifferent to their organizations and their organization's purposes. Indifferent workers are getting their human needs only minimally satisfied by their organizations. They argue for the importance of addressing the sources of employee indifference. This journey begins by understanding what workers want and then giving it to them. Their research and consulting has shown that relatively little conflict exists between the goals of the vast majority of workers and their organizations. Workers have basic human needs that management can and should address; doing this creates enthusiastic employees, and employee enthusiasm provides a large competitive advantage.

Sirota and his colleagues have been asking workers what they want for over 30 years, collecting survey data from over four million workers throughout the world. They identified three primary sets of goals of people at work: equity, achievement and camaraderie. These goals were common across cultures and appear to have changed little over time.

- *Equity*   to be treated justly in relation to the basic conditions of employment (a safe workplace, a reasonable workload, reasonable job security, satisfactory pay and fringe benefits, being treated with respect, and having trustful management), fairness in the way workers are treated.
- *Achievement*   to take pride in one's accomplishments, doing work that matters and doing it well, to be recognized for one's accomplishments, and to take pride in the organization's accomplishments. Achievement stems from the challenge of the work itself, acquiring new skills, having the ability to perform the job (receiving the necessary training, direction, resources, information), receiving recognition for good performance, and working for a company of which one can be proud.
- *Camaraderie*   to have warm, interesting and cooperative relationships with others at work – teamwork, a sense of community, and friendliness.

Satisfying all three goals (equity, achievement, camaraderie) results in high levels of employee enthusiasm. They provide research evidence showing a link between employee enthusiasm and organizational performance. They devote several chapters to each of these three broad goals, indicating specific initiatives for satisfying each of the three goals. For example, they provide suggestions for offering stable employment, using specific company examples.

Sirota and his colleagues advocate flat organizations (minimal hierarchy) and participative management that offers opportunities for mutual manager – employee influence, and the use of self-managed teams. All too often bureaucracy – rules and procedures – get in the way of getting the job done efficiently and well.

They conclude their book with thoughts on how organizations can bring all these elements together in the total organization culture. They advocate the partnership organization as a model – people at all levels working together for common goals. They contrast this type of organization with three other models: the transactional model – workers are treated as commodities; the paternalistic organization – workers are treated as children; and the adversarial organization – workers are treated as enemies.

The partnership organization embodies win–win, basic trust, a long-term perspective, high performance standards, confidence in workers competence, joint decision making, open communication, mutual influence, mutual assistance in helping each other perform, recognition, respectful day-to-day treatment, and sharing of financial gains.

They offer guidance on how to turn partnership theory into partnership practice. This process begins with the senior management team and must be sustained by them. Introducing partnership must begin with the business goals. In addition, introducing change in values and behaviors consistent with partnership principles must be undertaken in line with these principles, placing a high priority on the need to work collaboratively with all stakeholders.

They lay out the following nine step process.

1. What is the business goal?
2. Is the organization ready for this change?
3. What exactly does the organization want to do and why?
4. Where is the organization now?
5. What key aspects of the organization need to be changed to get it from where it is now to where it wants to be?
6. How should the action plan for change be communicated to all parts of the organization?
7. What specific changes need to be made and how should they be undertaken?
8. What training do managers need to equip them for partnership?
9. What metrics do we need to develop to assess the progress and effectiveness of the changes that have been undertaken?

Sirota, Mischkind and Meltzer (2005) provide evidence that engaged employees (they use the term "enthusiastic employees") lead to business success. The solution, for them, is to give employees what they want. Workers want equity, achievement and camaraderie. They describe a range of organizational policies and practices targeted at each. Equity or fair treatment results from justice at work, job security, fair pay and respect. Achievement stems from company pride, resources and support that enables one to do a good job, challenging work and feedback, recognition and rewards. Camaraderie develops from the use of work teams and participative decision making. They offer guidance on how to go about changing an organization's culture to build a partnership between workers and management, emphasizing the fact that senior management support and actions are critical.

Wayne Cascio

A marked increase in organizational downsizing in the 1990s in much of the industrialized world fostered considerable research on how to increase the success of this complex organizational change. Downsizing coupled with mergers and acquisitions are on the rise and, though challenging, it is possible to downsize, or merge, successfully.

Cascio (2002) reports the results of an eighteen-year study of Standard and Poor's 500 firms showing that firms that restructured through downsizing were not more profitable than those that did not and in many cases fared worse. He makes the case for restructuring responsibly, treating employees as assets to be developed so that they can be prepared and able to help the organization be successful.

For most businesses, the bottom line is almost always financial. Yet the human bottom line is critical for reaching organizational goals. Cascio addresses the notion that employees are costs to be cut rather than assets to be developed. There are creative and profitable alternatives to restructuring and cutting costs – termed responsible restructuring by Cascio. All organizations will have their economic ups and downs. Preventative planning distinguishes those organizations that can deal with these in a thoughtful, orderly way and those that respond in a panic reaction of mass layoffs. Many firms have downsized and restructured successfully to improve their productivity. General Electric, under former CEO Jack Welch, is a prime example of this. Responsible restructuring relies on the employees to continue to provide a sustained competitive advantage.

Most organizations see employees as costs to be cut; a smaller group see employees as assets to be developed. The first are the downsizers. For them the key question becomes What is the smallest number of people we need to run the business? The second are the responsible restructurers. For them, the key question is What do we need to do to remain successful and improve our circumstances?

Cascio makes the case for responsible restructuring by building on the research findings from the HRM literature. Particular HR practices have been found in high performing organizations. These include skills training and continuous learning, information sharing, employee participation, flattened organizational hierarchies, rewards linked to performance and innovative labor-management partnerships. These practices create a workplace where management invests in their employees and employees invest in their organization.

Cascio highlights a small number of firms having no-layoff policies showing how employment stability contributes to organizational success in these cases. There are ways to make money in business: you cut costs or increase revenues. And future costs are more predictable than are future revenues, so cost cutting is the most common approach taken. In fact, some costs may actually increase during layoffs (e.g., severance pay, outplacement, reduced productivity, loss of institutional memory). Layoffs carry a large human and financial toll.

Cascio considers many of the myths about downsizing.

- *Downsizing employees boosts profits*   The evidence shows that profitability does not necessarily follow downsizing.
- *Downsizing boosts employee productivity*   Productivity results after downsizing show a mixed picture.
- *Downsizing employees has no effect on the quality of products or services*   For most organizations, downsizing employees does not lead to long-term improvements in the quality of services or products.
- *Downsizing has no adverse effects on those who remain*   Downsizing has had negative effects on the morale, commitment and workload of survivors.
- *The total cost of downsizing is reflected in the costs of the layoff*   In some sectors, the largest cost is the loss of relationships and contacts, business, information and innovation.
- *Sabotage and violence are rare*   These activities are more common than we think.
- *Stress-related diseases are more common among those who have lost their jobs than survivors*   Survivors are just as likely to experience these as those laid off.

Studies have compared various types of employment relationships (e.g., transactional, mutual investment, underinvestment, overinvestment). Using employee survey responses and both peer and supervisory ratings, the mutual investment employee-organizational relationship produced the best outcomes; performance was rated higher and employee attitudes were the most favorable.

Employee attitudes have been shown to affect firm performance in several of the studies. Alternatives to downsizing exist including the following:

- use downsizing as the last resort; focus on new ways of building the business;
- focus attention on managing the survivors well;
- create good will among those laid off;
- redeploy people to other jobs;
- ask for voluntary pay cuts as well as sacrifices from executives and managers; issue company stock in return for these give-backs;
- let employees determine how to cut costs;
- use attrition, workforce planning, and detailed performance reviews to reduce the workforce;
- offer training, counseling and outplacement;
- if layoffs are needed, reduce employees in ways that are consistent with company values.

Cascio offers some guidelines for restructuring based on what has led to positive outcomes for a variety of organizations and their workforces. These are based on two critical elements in a restructuring: justice and communication. Justice involves issues of fairness; fairness of procedures used to make decisions and fairness in the outcomes of these decisions. "Fairness lies in the eyes of the beholder; it is a perception. Fairness produces job satisfaction, lower levels of stress and higher levels of motivation and performance. Fairness also increases cooperative and helping behaviors and better organizational citizenship." (Cascio, 2002)

Communication increases employee understanding and acceptance, builds support for the changes, reduces uncertainty, maintains employee commitment, and sustains organizational performance. Face-to-face communication is particularly important and the CEO must take the lead role. Other guidelines include the following.

1. Build the restructuring plan into the over-all business plan; this facilitates preventative planning.
2. Be clear on the reasons for the restructuring.
3. Consider the benefits of workforce stability.
4. Before making final decisions on restructuring, share concerns with employees and get their input.
5. Avoid downsizing as a quick-fix for major long-term problems.

6. Get employee input on what "perks" should go first.
7. Make sure the processes of staff reduction are fair.
8. Communicate regularly in a number of different ways.
9. Provide surviving employees with a view of the future. This fosters commitment and trust and will contribute to the ongoing success of the organization.
10. Train employees and managers in how to deal with the restructuring changes.
11. Consider the organization's HRM practices and policies in light of the changes being undertaken.

The 4+2 organization

Joyce (2005) and Joyce, Norhia and Robertson (2003) report the results of a long-term study of what really works in achieving and sustaining high levels of financial performance by organizations. He and his research team collected and analyzed ten years of data from 200 firms in 50 sub-industry groupings.

Data were collected via interviews, surveys and archival sources. They identified eight management practices that distinguished successful from unsuccessful organizations. Four practices were seen as essential foundation practices; failing at many was associated with poor financial performance. The other four were complementary: being successful on two of these was associated with financial success, but it could be any combination of two of the four. Hence the 4 + 2 formula.

The critical four were:

1. Strategy – successful performing firms devised and maintained an engaging focused strategy.
2. Excellence – successful performing firms developed and maintained flawless operations and customer focus
3. Culture – successful performing firms developed and maintained a performance-oriented culture
4. Structure – successful performing firms built and maintained a fast, flexible and flat organization.

Complementary practices

1. Talent – successful performing firms held on to talented employees and found others

2. Leadership – successful performing firms held leaders and directors accountable.
3. Innovation – successful performing firms made industry-transforming innovations.
4. Mergers and relationships – successful performing firms grew.

But building the 4 + 2 organization is very difficult – if it was easy every organization would be successful. Joyce identified four types of firms in his sample: winners, losers, climbers and tumblers and compares winners with the other three allowing him to propose ways for the other types to change to become more like the winners. He also identifies key turning points that distinguished losers from climbers (organizations that were improving their financial performance) and between climbers and winners (financially successful organizations).

High involvement organizations

Research on high involvement (HI) organizations has found they often show performance advantages such as higher levels of worker commitment, more teamwork, trust, loyalty, productivity less turnover and absenteeism (Lawler, 1996; Lawler, Mohrman and Benson, 2001). These result in lower labor costs. HI organizations also have some disadvantages (O'Toole and Lawler, 2006) such as employee resistance to change, employee dependence on the organization, and the time needed to create the desired levels of workforce skills.

Why are there so few HI organizations? Managers do not measure or do not know how to measure the intangible benefits of particular HRM efforts. And though HI organizations may lead to better employee health and improved family lives, these elements are difficult to measure.

Characteristics of HI organizations – what needs to be done to achieve HI status

- reduce social distance between workers and leaders;
- design jobs to increase autonomy and influence;
- build jobs into career paths;
- minimal use of outsourcing;
- all workers salaried;
- employees supported to develop their skills;
- use profit sharing and employee stock ownership;

- develop information on costs of turnover and share this with all managers and directors;
- encourage employers to educate workers on their role in limiting their own health-risk factors (diet, exercise, healthy lifestyles);
- make supervisors more supportive;
- encourage and support work–family life balance;
- manage people so as to reduce levels of stress (e.g., clear performance expectations and standards, how rewards are provided, provide adequate resources to do the job);
- create a sense of community – both within and outside the organization through participation, involvement and philanthropy.

Treating people right

The business environment today is more demanding than ever. To succeed, Lawler (2003) believes that organizations need to "treat people right". Treating people right is very difficult however, with organizations and individuals having important roles. Organizations need to motivate and satisfy their employees; employees need to help make their organization effective and peak performing.

For this to work, both people and organizations need to succeed. Organizations need high performing people to be successful; organizations need to be successful to make the conditions that motivate and satisfy their employees. Lawler termed this a "virtuous spiral of success" when both organizations and individuals perform at high levels. The challenge is to develop and implement structures, processes and practices that are desirable for both organizations and individuals.

Some managers see a conflict between what is good for the organization and what is good for employees. This conflict does exist in some cases, but Lawler contends that treating people right reduces the conflict. Treating people right produces long-term gains for both organization and individuals. Organizations that "treat people right" can attract more qualified employees, retain them, and motivate them to perform at higher levels. Employees receive more interesting and challenging work, higher rewards, more varied career options and identify with a winning organization. Organizations take responsibility for introducing programs and processes that reward and develop their employees; employees take responsibility for their knowledge and skills and contribution of high performance. "Treating people right" is a two-way street

(Lawler, 2003, p. xiii). The virtuous spiral of success leads to higher levels of individual and organizational performance and success and rests on sound human resource management practices and organization design principles.

To meet these challenges, organizations need to attract, retain, motivate, organize and manage their people. People are now the source of competitive advantage and organizations must acknowledge the contribution that human capital plays. To be successful organizations need talented employees *and* sound organizational and HRM systems and practices.

Lawler identifies some principles for treating people right and creating a virtuous spiral.

1. Attraction and rentention – identifies the types of workplace they want to be so they can attract and retain the right people.
2. Hiring practices – hire the people that fit their workplace.
3. Training and development – training employees for job success, growth and development.
4. Designing work – designing jobs that are meaningful.
5. Mission strategies and goals – designing and articulating a compelling vision with a company in strategy and goals, that the employee can understand and embrace.
6. Reward systems – designing and implementing rewards that reinforce values and objectives.
7. Leadership – developing leaders who can create a motivating and successful work environment.

Senior managers first need to know what makes organizations effective. These include: strategy, organizational capabilities, core competencies, and the external environment (Lawler, 2003). Senior managers also need to understand what makes people effective. To be effective, people need both knowledge and skills and high levels of motivation.

Is there consensus on what an effective organization looks like?

Kirby (2005) takes a step towards developing a theory of high performing organizations. Peters and Waterman (1982) began this journey with the publication of their groundbreaking *In search of excellence.* Kirby reviews the contribution of ten groups of researchers. Although high performance can reside in individuals, teams, business units or organizations, these researchers focus on the organizational level. Who are the high performing organizations? Most of these researchers used several criteria including financial success, longevity, and CEO expert ratings of success. Researchers then sought to identify keys to success in their high performing organizations. Issues of causality need to be addressed: does talent management lead companies to be successful or do successful companies have the resources to embark on talent management programs? In addition, since researchers typically are looking at predictors of past performance, the question of whether these factors will predict future performance in a different world also must be addressed. Management researchers are not only building on earlier and each other's work, but are beginning to find some agreement.

Organizations continue to be under pressure to change because of the need to reduce costs, improve the quality of products and services, find new areas for growth and to become more productive.

Most attempts to bring about increases in organizational performance – total quality management, reengineering, right sizing, restructuring, culture change, mergers and acquisitions, turnarounds – fail; they fall short of expectations because they do not bring about changes in behavior (Kotter, 1994).

Kotter identifies several common mistakes in failed change efforts. These include:

1. Not making the need for change urgent.
2. Not having a sufficiently powerful guiding coalition.
3. Underestimating the power of vision.
4. Undercommunicating the vision.
5. Letting obstacles block the new vision.
6. Not creating short-term wins.
7. Declaring victory too soon.
8. Not anchoring the changes to the organization's culture.

John Kotter

Kotter and Cohen (2002), building on Kotter's earlier work (Kotter, 1996) address the question of how organizations go beyond talking about change to actually changing people's behavior. They conducted interviews with several hundred people in over 100 organizations that were undergoing or had undergone large scale change. They identified the importance of making employees feel differently as well as thinking differently about the proposed changes. They advocate change approaches directed to the heart instead of the mind, preferring a "see-feel-change" approach as distinct from the more common "analysis-think-change" approach.

In his 1996 book, Kotter examined almost 100 cases of organizational change and concluded that most were not done well. He identified an eight-step change process in case studies based on successful organizations. Kotter and Cohen, using these eight steps, describe what individuals did at each step to achieve desired outcomes.

Their basic premise was that people were more likely to change their behavior "because they are shown a truth that influences their feelings" than "because they are given analysis that shapes their thinking" (Kotter and Cohen, p. 1, italics in original).

Changes included the introduction of new technologies, mergers and acquisitions, restructuring, new strategies, cultural changes, dealing with globalization, and the introduction of internet-based operations. Changes can also take place in the whole organization, an office, a department or a work team.

They developed four broad conclusions from their work. First, organizations that changed successfully often made large changes instead of small improvements, knowing how to overcome resistance. Second, though large scale organizational change was complex, they found support for Kotter's earlier eight-step process. Third, the key was to successfully bring about changes in people's behavior at each step in the change process. Fourth, while both thinking and feeling were important in all organizations, the key to bringing about successful change lay in emotions.

The eight steps or stages of successful large scale change

1. Increase urgency. Employees begin to talk to each other about the need for change. A critical mass of respected and important employees is needed to get others motivated and open to change.
2. Building the guiding team. A group having the power to lead a large scale change is formed and helped to work well together. The guiding team must have the credibility, skills, reputation, connections and formal authority to lead a change.
3. Create the right vision. The guiding team develops the right vision and creates the strategies for the change effort. The guiding team creates a sensible, clear, simple, inspiring vision and strategies (gaining support, detailed plans and budgets).
4. Communicate to all stakeholders for buy-in. Undertake active and widespread communication efforts, employees continue to buy into the change. The importance of simple messages from the heart. This involves actions, the use of symbols, and presentations to employees.

5. Empower all to action. Employees are empowered to act in ways consistent with the vision. Obstacles to change are eliminated building up employee self-confidence.

6. Create short-term wins. As more employees act in ways consistent and supportive of the vision, fewer will resist the changes. Small wins produce credibility, more success, and greater commitment and motivation for even more progress.

7. Be persistent. Employees continue to make the changes until the vision is realized. The guiding team and organization are relentless in talking about and supporting the change.

8. Perpetuating the change. The new behaviors become part of the new culture. The new culture, widely-shared norms of behaviors and values, acts through employee orientation, rewards, promotions and activities that unleash emotions.

The first four steps help to alter the status quo; steps five through seven introduce new ways of doing things, step eight grounds the changes in the corporate culture making them permanent. The introduction of change usually follows this order, but the organization operates in several stages at once. That is, a number of small projects are going on simultaneously. Behavioral change is central at each of the eight steps.

The most meaningful changes resulted from showing employees what the problems were and the ways that these would be resolved. It did not involve data gathering and analysis, the writing of reports and the making of presentations.

Successful change followed a see-feel-change pattern. Employees first see a problem; this creates feelings – positive feelings increase (urgency, optimism) while negative feelings decrease (cynicism, fear, complacency); these new feelings lead to behavior change.

Emotionally charged ideas change behaviors and reinforce the new desired behaviors. Analysis provides employees with information, reports and presentations about problems and solution; this leads to changes in how employees think. These new thoughts change their behavior and reinforces any new behaviors.

Both approaches are needed, but historically, analysis has been the most common approach. Analysis has some major shortcomings. First, intensive analysis may not be needed to identify a problem. Second, analysis may be of limited value in a fast-changing, ambiguous, turbulent environment. Third, while sound analysis may change thinking, it rarely motivates people to do something. Motivation involves feelings not thinking.

Emotions that work against change include anxiety, fear, insecurity, fatigue, cynicism, pessimism, arrogance, and anger. Emotions that support change include optimism, urgency, trust, passion, hope, enthusiasm and excitement.

Kotter and Cohen provide concrete real-life examples of successful efforts taken within change efforts at each of the eight steps. Organizations will continue to be successful in a world characterized by accelerating change only if they are able to create more change leaders at all levels of their organization.

Ed Lawler

Organizations are created to perform effectively but not to change. Lawler and Worley (2006) maintain that to continue to be successful in an increasingly competitive business environment, organizations need to change and change continually. In a nutshell, organizations cannot remain peak performers unless they have the capacity to change.

They identify characteristics of organizations that embrace change:
- They are closely connected to and understand their environments.
- They foster and reward experimentation.
- They learn about and embrace new techniques and technologies.
- They strive for continuous performance improvements.
- They identify short-term competitive advantages.

Organizational leaders need to understand their organization's values, and use them to support needed changes. Leaders also need to build cultures that embrace change.

Some core values support change while others impede it. Organizations need to have a passion for change. Managers also need to design the organization (policies, practices) to support change. This necessarily begins with top leadership. Leaders also must change themselves before they can change their organizations. Thus, leaders need to see themselves as builders not as traditional managers of others.

Surviving is not the same thing as performing at peak levels

There is a high rate of decline in previously high-performing organizations that survive. Organizations need to be both successful and have the capacity for change.

A peak performing organization is about change. Organizations cannot remain effective if they cannot change. They need to continually change what they do well to be successful to fit the demands of a changing business environment.

Organizations can improve their capacity for change. In fact, Lawler and Worley believe that the ultimate competitive advantage for organizations today is the capacity to change.

They need to encourage and support change (experimentation, learning new practices and technologies, continuous improvements, monitoring the environment).

Lawler and Worley created a Built to Change model consisting of possible future business scenarios and three key organizational processes (strategizing, creating value, designing) that contribute to organizational effectiveness. These processes are ways the organization responds to the demands of a changing environment. They are organized around an identity that the organizations wants to create (core values, behaviors, beliefs). These components change over time in response to environmental changes. Rather than finding a single competitive advantage, Lawler and Worley instead suggest that organizations find a series of short-term (temporary) advantages.

The designing of structures and processes helps the organization put the pieces together in reaching its performance goals. When all the pieces come together, a "virtuous performance spiral" is created in which initial success leads to continued success.

Shared leadership works best in supporting change readiness. Shared leadership reduces hierarchy, builds more leaders at various levels, and supports change initiatives.

The time is right

Ivancevich, Duening and Lidwell (2005) suggest that managers today, more than ever before, are open to ideas and programs that can make them and their organizations more effective. In addition, efforts by the research community over the past 50 years have produced a large body of knowledge about the characteristics of effective organizations and how to increase organizational effectiveness that can now be put into practice. Managers are also facing problems today that are complex and difficult to solve. More managers are comfortable with thinking long term rather than searching for a quick fix and more students in business programs such as the MBA are exposed to organizational effectiveness research findings.

A failure to use this information and knowledge is likely to lessen economic performance and satisfaction with working life. The economic health of a country is dependent on how well individuals, teams and organizations are managed and led.

Managers tend to rely either on their own experiences to solve problems or seek answers from gurus, fads and fashion. Ivancevich and his colleagues advocate instead a "more professional and scientifically based approach to management problems and decisions" (2005, p. 1056). They argue for the development of guidelines and standards for the application of organizational behavior research findings, their way of advocating evidence-based practice. The gap between research and practice is smaller in some professions (e.g., medicine, law, engineering) than in management and the organizational sciences.

Evidence-based management

Pfeffer and Sutton (2006a, 2006b) believe that sound ideas for improving organizational effectiveness exist and are known, unfortunately these are too often ignored by managers. Managers are generally unaware of practices that work effectively and seem uninterested in finding out about them.

There are several reasons for this. The evidence is sometimes limited and weak, almost anyone can claim to be an expert in management and organization, there is an incredible number of sources of management advice available to managers, and there is no certainty that what works in one organization will work in another.

Why don't managers use ideas based on the current best evidence of best practice? They typically trust their own experience more than available research evidence. They use what they were exposed to previously even if their current organization is very different from their previous one. Or they prefer to use approaches they believe they are skilled at or have worked for them in the past. Managers often get exposed to the hype and selling of particular ideas by "gurus". Other ideas and practices fit the beliefs of managers; providing contradictory information does not cause them to change their beliefs. In addition, managers often mimic what other organizations which they believe to be successful are doing. This is not always undesirable, but at best they can only become perfect imitations.

Benchmarking is the term used to describe the identification and copying of practices undertaken by leading organizations. Benchmarking has value for managers and their organizations when the logic behind the practices that account for high performance are clearly understood, they know why it works, and what will work in their particular organization.

Pfeffer and Sutton propose that managers should use the best evidence on how companies should be managed and this material should be taught to them.

Key questions that managers need to ask include:
– Is the organization using a particular practice similar to our organization?
– What is the evidence supporting the practice?
– Can we gather even more evidence about this practice? It is important to consider both confirming and disconfirming information – that is, a need to use all the evidence.

Encourage pilot projects, experimentation and trial runs, and encourage and reward learning from these. Emphasize facts surrounding these experiments.

They offer six standards or yardsticks for assessing management knowledge, in the belief that currently used standards are not working well.

1. Acknowledge the heritage of ideas being touted as new; there are not that many truly new ideas.
2. Be critically suspicious of "breakthrough" ideas.
3. Acknowledge that business evidence is developed and accumulated slowly by lots of people building on each other's work rather than by one person working alone.
4. Look for both the benefits and the disadvantages of these ideas and practices.
5. Supplement conclusions based on solid research evidence with stories of both success and failure.
6. Take an open minded position towards new ideas and practices, particularly with regard to one's own biases and beliefs.

We hope this collection provides food for thought to our readers in their quest to both understand and build more effective organizations.

REFERENCES

Burke, R. J. and Cooper, C. L. (2006) *The human resources revolution: Why putting people first matters.* London: Elsevier.

Cascio, W. F. (2002) *Responsible structuring: Creative and profitable alternatives to layoffs.* San Francisco: Berrett-Koehler.

Collins, J. (2001) *Good to great: why some companies make the leap and others don't.* New York: Harper Collins.

Collins, J. C. and Porras, J. I. (1994) *Built to last: successful habits of visionary companies.* New York: Harper Business.

Ivancevich, J. M., Duening, T. N. and Lidwell, W. (2005) Bridging the manager-organizational scientist collaboration gap. *Organizational Dynamics*, 34, 103–17.

Joyce, W. F. (2005) What really works: Building the 4+2 organization. *Organizational Dynamics*, 34, 118–29.

Joyce, W., Nohria, N. and Robertson, B. (2003) *What really works: the 4+2 formula for sustained business success.* New York: Harper Business.

Katzenbach, J. R. (2000) *Peak performance: Aligning the hearts and minds of your employees.* Boston: Harvard Business School Press.

Kirby, J. (2005) Toward a theory of high performance. *Harvard Business Review*, July–August, 30.

Kotter, J. P. (1994) Leading change: Why transformation efforts fail. *Harvard Business Review*, March–April.

Kotter, J. P. (1996) *Leading change.* Boston: Harvard Business School Press.

Kotter, J. P. and Cohen, D. S. (2002) *The heart of change: Real-life stories of how people change their organizations.* Boston: Harvard Business School Press.

Lawler, E. E. (2003) *Treat people right.* San Francisco: Jossey-Bass.

Lawler, E. E. and Worley, C. G. (2006) *Built to change: How to achieve sustained organizational effectiveness.* San Francisco: Jossey-Bass.

Lawler, E. E. (1996) *From the ground up: Six principles for creating new logic organizations.* San Francisco: Jossey-Bass.

Lawler, E. E., Mohrman, S. A. and Benson, S. G. (2001) *Organizing for high performance: Employee involvement, TQM, reengineering and knowledge management in Fortune 1000 companies.* San Francisco: Jossey-Bass.

Michaels, E., Handfield-Jones, H. J. and Axelrod, B. (2001) *The war for talent.* Boston: Harvard Business School Press.

O'Toole, J. and Lawler, E. E. (2006) *The new American workplace.* New York: Palgrave Macmillan.

Peters, T. and Waterman, R. (1982) *In search of excellence.* New York: Harper & Row.

Pfeffer, J. (1994) *Competitive advantage through people.* Boston: Harvard Business School Press.

Pfeffer, J. (1998) *The human equation: Building profits by putting people first.* Boston: Harvard Business School Press.

Pfeffer, J. and Sutton, R. I. (2000) *The knowing-doing gap: How smart companies turn knowledge into action.* Boston: Harvard Business School Press.

(2006a) Evidence-based management. *Harvard Business Review*, January, 63–74.

(2006b) *Hard facts, dangerous half-truths, and total nonsense; Profiting from evidence-based management.* Boston: Harvard Business School Press.

Sirota, D., Mischkind, L. A. and Meltzer, M. I. (2005) *The enthusiastic employee: How companies profit by giving workers what they want.* Philadelphia: Wharton School Publishing.

Stewart, T. A. (1997) *Intellectual capital: The new wealth of organizations.* New York: Double-day/Currency.

Stewart, T. (2001) *The wealth of knowledge: Intellectual capital and the twenty-first century organization.* New York: Doubleday.

Ulrich, D. and Brockbank, W. (2005) *The HR value proposition.* Boston: Harvard Business School Press.

Ulrich, D. and Smallwood, N. (2003) *Why the bottom line isn't: How to build value through people and organization.* New York: John Wiley.

NOTE

1. Preparation of this chapter was supported in part by the Schulich School of Business. Louise Coutu prepared the manuscript.

Part II

Enhancing individual health and performance

2 Enthusiastic employees

David Sirota, Louis A. Mischkind and Michael I. Meltzer

The impact shook everything for blocks. Fire sucked so much oxygen out of the air around the contact zone that windows in nearby buildings blew out as the towers of the World Trade Center began to wither and then collapse. On the thirty-second floor of the World Financial Center, next to the targeted Twin Towers of the World Trade Center in lower Manhattan, the editorial and business offices of *Barron's* magazine were almost instantly reduced to rubble. Yet, on September 11, 2001, *Barron's* employees had already turned their attention to publishing the next issue of their magazine – and *on time*. The idea of not publishing never even came up. The *Barron's* workers – reporters, editors, administrators and support staff – were among the Dow Jones employees who returned to their old quarters in less than a year after the attack, having published their magazine from other locations. They, and their colleagues at *The Wall Street Journal*, never missed an issue.

The people at *Barron's* are what we call enthusiastic employees. In modern parlance, they are also called "engaged," but the exact term does not matter. We know what they are – they *care* – and having employees like them is a prerequisite for long-term business success. Enthusiastic employees outproduce and outperform employees who are not motivated. They step up to do the impossible. They rally each other in tough times.

The waning of enthusiasm

Employee attitude surveys, such as those conducted by Sirota Survey Intelligence®, show clearly that almost all employees are enthusiastic when they're hired: hopeful, ready to work hard, and eager to contribute. In just a few months, however, morale begins to decline sharply. Our surveys of *Barron's* employees – unlike those in the great majority of companies – show them to be enthusiastic throughout their careers.

What happens to dampen employee enthusiasm in most companies? We shall show that the culprit is management and will describe what management does and what it can do differently. Our conclusions and solutions are drawn from our systematic employee attitude surveys and detailed case studies from hundreds of companies that cover millions of employees.

A dollars-and-cents business case can readily be made for high employee morale. The advantages of having enthusiastic employees are that they routinely produce significantly more than the job requires, often working all kinds of hours to get things done, and done right; volunteer for difficult assignments; search for ways to improve things, rather than just reacting to management's requests; and encourage co-workers to high levels of performance and seek ways to help them. In addition, enthusiastic employees welcome, rather than resist, needed change; conduct transactions with external constituencies, such as customers, in ways that bring great credit (and business) to the company, and have much lower absenteeism and turnover rates.

Only about 14 percent of the business units we have surveyed can be characterized as having enthusiastic work forces, which we define as places where more than 75 percent of employees are satisfied with their company and jobs, and where less than 10 percent are dissatisfied. Managers spend a great deal of their time dealing with difficult individual employees. Many think handling troublesome employees is their primary workforce problem. But the reality is far worse. The biggest problem is the vast number of workers who are not openly troublesome, but who have become indifferent to the organization and its goals. At least openly troublesome workers are identified and can be dealt with. The "walking indifferent," however, are silent killers. They give a mere fraction of what they are capable of contributing. The economic cost of this under-utilization to the affected business is enormous.

How does a company tackle this kind of problem? It usually responds in one of two ways: It can pressure employees to do more, or it can treat its workers to a series of rah-rah events, speakers, and programs. Neither approach will do much good – in fact, any attempt to get more out of an employee through pressure will likely exacerbate the problem. Management needs to get to the root of employee indifference, and address it.

First, we must understand what workers want. Then, we must give it to them. This might sound absurd to some, a sure way to insolvency. On the contrary, it is a powerful path to business success.

Many leaders fail to recognize that enthusiasm is the natural state of employees and that, by their own actions, management gradually destroys the enthusiasm that almost all new employees bring to their jobs and companies. (The decline in morale observed in our research would be even greater if many dissatisfied employees had not already left their companies, and so did not participate in the survey.)

How does management diminish the enthusiasm the great majority of people bring to their new companies? The fault lies both in the policies and procedures that companies use in managing their workforces and in the relationships that individual managers establish with their employees.

In most organizations, managements unwittingly de-motivate their employees by treating them as something disposable – like paper clips. Specific attitudes and behaviors that contribute to this negative culture are:

- At the first sign of business difficulty, employees – supposedly a company's "most important asset" – become expendable.
- Many companies treat the vast majority of their employees as lazy and unreasonable in their demands ("they want the world"), instead of addressing just the small percentage of them – about 5 percent – who actually are.
- Employees receive inadequate recognition and reward for their contributions: about half of workers in our surveys report receiving little or no credit, and almost two-thirds say management is much more likely to criticize them for poor performance than praise them for good work.

In addition, employers create obstacles to their workers' performance, such as excessive bureaucracy, more attention to placing blame than solving problems, inconsistent management decisions, insufficient training, failure to communicate, lack of employee input into decision-making, and delays in making decisions.

Why management demotivates employees

Many years of research have established that there is little basic conflict between the goals of management and those of employees. The key question is not how to motivate workers, but how to sustain the motivation that employees initially and naturally bring to their jobs – and prevent management from destroying it. The major reason management continues to go down this errant path is because employers continue to buy into myths about workers.

These myths include:

- *Most people dislike their jobs.* Our data take sharp issue with this notion. Our surveys show that more than 70 percent of workers at all levels like the kind of work they do. Among blue-collar workers, the level is 72 percent.

- *Whether workers should be treated as thinking human beings depends on the type of work they do.* For example, as the myth goes, it is useless – even counterproductive – for employees doing routine, highly standardized work to be involved in decisions about the work. The problem with this bit of "common sense" is that it is contradicted by the legion of extraordinarily participative initiatives in manufacturing plants throughout the world. The fact is that there is no category of employee for whom involving workers in decisions – asking them to help through thinking – is not appropriate.

- *Employees will never be happy with their pay.* On the average, 40 percent of workers rate their pay as good or very good, 23 percent rate it as poor or very poor, and the rest (37 percent) rate their pay as middling. Although there are a number of factors determining satisfaction with pay, the major ones are whether it is competitive and is keeping up with the cost of living.

- *Complimenting employees on a job well done goes to their heads, makes them complacent, and increases their demands for more money.* Recognition by management is one of the most powerful motivators of continued good performance and high morale. It is the lack of recognition that depresses most people's natural desire to want to do a good job.

- *Companies that have no hesitation laying off workers perform better than those that go to great lengths to keep their workers employed.* Research done in the 1990s (Cascio, Young & Morris, 1997) shows that downsizing companies outperformed the 500 leading publicly traded companies in the Standard & Poor's index only slightly during the six months following news of a restructuring, and then lagged badly, netting a negative 24 percent by the end of three years, as measured by profits and returns from stocks. The theory of keeping a company "lean and mean," then, may really only be making it mean.

- *Most employees are lazy and need to be controlled.* Our research definitively shows that overwhelmingly employees are industrious and want to do a good job and be proud of it. We find that only about 5 percent can be described as "allergic" to work.

- *Most employees resist change, whatever it is.* Employees resist changes that they see as harmful to themselves or their organizations, such as speeding up the pace, which hurts work quality. However, they gladly welcome changes they see as helpful, such as new equipment and methods that help them do their jobs better. Employees are also resistant to changes that management secretly develops without their input and springs on them at the last minute.

What workers want: The three-factor theory

Instead of continuing to perpetuate myths about workers, management policies need to be directed toward satisfying the three primary goals that matter most to almost all employees. When companies can meet their employees' goals, the result is not just satisfied employees, but *enthusiastic* employees. Every successful company has to address three crucial employee goals – *all three of them*:

- *Equity.* To be treated justly in relation to the basic conditions of employment, such as fair wages, benefits, job security, safe working conditions and respectful treatment.
- *Achievement.* To take pride in one's accomplishments by doing things that matter, and doing them well; to receive recognition for one's accomplishments; to take pride in the organization's accomplishments.
- *Camaraderie.* To have warm, interesting, and cooperative relationships with others in the workplace.

These fundamental goals – we call it our three-factor theory – are nearly universal and extraordinarily similar in their impact across generational, cultural, occupational, and demographic lines. Elements of the three-factor theory are supported by a large body of theoretical and empirical research (Maslow, 1971, McClelland, 1985, Deci and Ryan, 2000).

Our own research shows that employees are four times more enthusiastic about their jobs when all three elements that contribute to employee enthusiasm are present in the workplace, rather than only two of these. Employees are fifteen times more enthusiastic when equity, achievement, and camaraderie are all present in the workplace than when only one factor is present.

Employee enthusiasm results in enormous competitive advantages for those companies with the strength of leadership to manage for real long-term results. The effects are on many different aspects of performance, ranging from on-the-job benchmarks such as productivity, quality, sales and customer satisfaction, to overall company profitability and stock market performance.

Consider stock market performance. Year after year, our research demonstrates that strong employee morale pays off in higher stock valuations. In our study of 2005 stock market performance, for example, the stock prices of fourteen high-morale companies (as measured by our surveys) increased an average of 16 percent, while those of other companies in the same industries increased by an average of only 6 percent, an advantage of more than $2\frac{1}{2}$ to 1. The stock prices of fourteen medium-morale and low-morale companies increased by 11.7 percent, while those of others in their same industries climbed by an average of 19.8 percent, a negative difference of more than $1\frac{1}{2}$ to 1.

Morale is a direct consequence of companies satisfying the three basic goals of employees, and employees return this "gift" of good treatment with higher productivity and work quality, lower turnover (which reduces recruiting and training costs), a decrease in workers shirking their duties, and a superior pool of job applicants. These gains translate directly into higher company profitability.

Further, satisfied employees lead to satisfied customers, which results in higher sales. Satisfied customers and higher sales, in turn, result in more satisfied employees who can enjoy the sense of achievement and the material benefits that come from working for a successful company. It's a "virtuous circle" (the opposite of a vicious cycle), the best of all worlds.

While our three-factor theory may seem obvious and just common-sense, the fact is that popular theories of what employees want can be quite different than what we propose and these theories change continually. For example, we are led to believe that there are large differences in goals among different "generations" of workers: baby boomers, Gen X, Gen Y, etc. There is absolutely no systematic evidence for this!

In our research, we correlated the satisfaction with each of the three goals with overall morale and found that the correlations were almost identical across generations. Further, they were nearly identical for male and female employees, employees of different racial and ethnic groups, management and non-management personnel, professionals and non-professionals, and employees in different parts of the world. The great similarity of correlations means that these employee groups do not differ in the extent to which the three goals drive morale (Sirota, Mischkind and Meltzer, 2005). When an organization works to satisfy these goals, the result is high workforce morale and performance.

One goal cannot be substituted for another. Improved recognition of employees' contributions, for example, cannot replace better pay, while money cannot substitute for taking pride in a job well done, and pride alone will not pay the mortgage. It is impossible to get employees excited about a company that gives them challenging work to do when they have a basic sense of inequity as to how they are treated with regard to pay, benefits, and the like. In fact, more challenging work can increase employees' sense of inequity when it widens the gap between what employees are contributing and what they are getting for their contribution. A great company for employees is one that meets all of the three goals.

The three-factor theory provides a positive view of the nature of the great majority of people at work and the essentials of human motivation have changed very little over time. It is management that has been acting differently and it is reaping the consequences. As an example, if you treat workers like disposable commodities – which began to happen with the downsizings of recent decades – you should not be surprised that workers are no longer loyal. Why should they be? It would be irrational for people to be loyal to organizations that show no interest in them other than as, essentially, temporary "hands" to get the work done.

Nothing is very complicated about this perspective. The performance improvement methods we recommend and that will be described shortly are the mainstays of an enlightened management: enlightened in its understanding that what the overwhelming majority of people seek from work does not conflict with management's objectives and, in fact, usually strongly supports them. If these methods are implemented, the results will be outstanding.

Which aspects of work do we find not correlated with overall employee morale? They tend to be about what might be termed the "frills" of work. Although senior management often spends much time on them, they do not really touch on workers' basic goals. These include the physical aesthetics of the work environment (such as wall color), recreational activities (such as holiday parties), various formal programs (such as suggestion programs), and formal communication mechanisms (such as a company newsletter). It is not that employees do not care about these at all, but that they matter much less than other more fundamental concerns. It matters much less to them, for example, that there is a well-designed company newsletter, or a suggestion program, than that their immediate supervisors communicate and listen to them.

We are in no way suggesting that the frills be dropped – almost everyone likes a holiday party – but that they be seen as supplements to, not substitutes for, the more basic policies and practices.

Four cultures

There are four broad types of employee relations cultures relevant to the satisfaction of worker goals:
• *Paternalistic*, where employees are treated as children;
• *Adversarial*, where employees are treated as enemies;
• *Transactional*, where employees are treated as ciphers;
• *Partnership*, where employees are treated as allies.

A partnership culture – by far the most effective of the four – is characteristic of organizations that do best in satisfying the three basic goals of workers. Partnership is a business relationship *plus*. The plus is the human dimension – the trust and goodwill that cause people to go beyond what is required by strictly monetary calculations, formal contracts, and short-term interests. It is a culture of mutual respect and loyalty.

There are those who contend that employee loyalty to organizations is dead because new economic conditions have rendered untenable lifetime employment with caring companies. There will never be a return to old-fashioned paternalistic management. But this need not be replaced by a neutral "transactional" management system, where employees are viewed as faceless commodities that can be removed at a moment's notice.

A transactional relationship would seem to be the most efficient method of management. After all, little or nothing is owed employees beyond a paycheck for the work they have performed ("We've paid you, now we're even."). But the financial gains from this relationship are usually temporary because such organizations receive little from their workers beyond what is absolutely required and can be easily monitored. For example, can a company expect its employees to treat customers with individual care and concern – the kind that create loyal customers – when workers are treated as invisible, interchangeable and expendable parts? A transactional relationship is, therefore, often a prescription for short-term success and long-term mediocrity.

The loyalty in a partnership relationship is not the same as the loyalty parents and children have to each other. Instead, it involves the bonds that develop among adults working collaboratively toward common, long-term goals, and having a genuine concern for each other's interests and needs.

The major components of a successful partnership are:

- *Win-win.* The parties recognize that they have key business goals in common, and that the success of one party depends on the success of the other.
- *Basic trust.* The parties trust each other's intentions.
- *Long-term perspective.* The parties are committed to a relationship that survives the short-term vicissitudes of business.
- *Excellence.* The parties set high performance standards for themselves and each other.
- *Competence.* The parties have confidence in each other's competence.
- *Joint decision making.* The parties make key decisions jointly on matters that affect each of them.
- *Open communication.* The parties communicate fully with each other.
- *Mutual influence.* The parties listen to and are influenced by each other.

- *Mutual assistance.* The parties help each other perform.
- *Recognition.* The parties recognize each other for their contributions.
- *Day-to-day treatment.* The parties routinely treat each other with consideration and respect.
- *Financial sharing.* To the extent that the collaboration is designed to generate improved financial results, the parties share equitably in those results.

These criteria can be applied to any business relationship: between employees and management (including employee unions), between work units, and also to relationships with external business entities, such as suppliers.

Recommendations for specific policies and practices

We come now to management *action.* It is one thing to conduct research and spin broad theories but quite another to recommend specific policies and practices that achieve the desired ends and are practical. Here is a small sampling of the policies and practices that we have found most effective for creating a partnership organization where employee enthusiasm is the norm rather than the exception. The key questions for any employee-related action designed to enhance partnership must be:

- What is the impact on employees' sense of fair treatment?
- What is its impact on their pride in their jobs and organization?
- What is its impact on productive social interaction among employees?

Enhancing job security

The specific policies and practices that facilitate employee enthusiasm begin with equity – the degree to which people believe their employer treats them with fairness. A sense of fair treatment is fundamental and there is nothing more fundamental for most employees than job security. As noted, a major characteristic of the "transactional" management that has emerged over the last two or three decades is to treat employees as faceless, interchangeable, and disposable objects. This management attitude includes ordering layoffs even when a company is doing *well.* What message does management send through these and similar actions? It might be an encouraging (albeit short-term) message to the investment community, but to workers, it is simply this: "Forget all that talk about you being an asset to the company: You are really a cost and a disposable commodity. And we will keep our costs down!" Workers in such situations experience layoffs not as prudent business stewardship, but rather as base inequitable treatment.

The way many American companies now seem to operate – by essentially using downsizing as a strategic maneuver, rather than as a last resort compelled by economic necessity – is largely misguided and self-defeating. It violates a fundamental need of workers and, in doing so, severely damages the sense of equity that is necessary for effective organizations. It is equally momentous when a company makes a decision *not* to downsize even though other companies in the industry take that path. The alternative philosophy was articulated by F. Kenneth Iverson (Iverson and Varian, 1997), the late chairman of Nucor, an extraordinarily successful US steel company:

"Painsharing" has helped us get through the tough times without ever laying off a single employee or closing a single facility for lack of work, even when the industry overall was shedding thousands of jobs. But, our history of no layoffs is not noble, altruistic or paternalistic. It's not even a company policy. We've told our employees time and again, "Nothing's written in stone. We'll lay people off if it is a matter of survival." The question is: When is laying people off the practical and sensible thing to do? To compete over the long term, a company needs loyal, motivated employees. Can management expect employees to be loyal and motivated if we lay them off at every dip of the economy, while we go on padding our own pockets? (*F. Kenneth Iverson, former Chairman, Nucor*)

The policy represented in Mr. Iverson's view isn't just humanitarian – *it is the policy that is best for the business.* Layoffs are not good for a company in the ordinary course. Although a layoff often results in a short-term spike in a company's stock price, the impact on the long term can be quite different. A mountain of evidence casts doubt on the efficacy of downsizing for many companies as a cost-reduction strategy. As noted earlier, research conducted in the mid-1990s found that *over the long term*, the performance of downsizing companies lags badly.

In most companies, downsizing the work force is frequently a short-term solution with little or no long-term benefits. Lester Thurow of MIT writes:

Layoffs are painful and costly. There are innumerable reasons they should be avoided if possible: Severance payments must be made. Higher training costs lie ahead. The skilled members of the team whom a firm has laid off will not be there to be rehired when times get better. Morale suffers among the remaining workers, and fewer will be willing to make personal sacrifices to help the company while it needs it most. (Thurow, 2001).

Organizations with enthusiastic employees downsize only as a last resort, developing "rings of defense" to cushion the blow of poor business conditions, such as implementing hiring freezes, retraining surplus employees for other jobs in the company, and reducing or eliminating the use of temporary employees.

Another step is accepting a temporary hit to profits and stock prices. For example, Southwest Airlines – another extraordinarily successful company – has never had a layoff, even after 9/11, which hit the airline business particularly hard. Said James Parker, CEO of Southwest at that time: "We are willing to suffer some damage, even to our stock price, to protect the jobs of our people" (Parker, 2001). As the passengers of Southwest will attest, the company has a highly enthusiastic workforce.

The companies that are genuinely committed to providing their employees with stable employment follow these specific practices:

- Exhaust all possible alternatives before laying off people.
- When layoffs cannot be avoided, first ask for volunteers.
- When layoffs cannot be avoided and there are not enough volunteers, act generously and decently. From an organizational standpoint, you are not doing it just for those who are let go, but for those who will stay.
- Communicate honestly, fully and regularly throughout the entire process and start the communications early.
- Recognize the impact of what you are doing on the survivors, and take steps to minimize the negative impact.

Do not confuse providing employment stability with tolerance for unsatisfactory employee performance. Organizations must distinguish between conditions over which employees have no control – such as a market downturn or the introduction of labor-saving technology – and those where an individual simply chooses not to perform.

Sharing in the financial gain

How about the upside, that is, how are employees treated when a company is doing well? In a profit-making organization, it is difficult to talk about true partnership without policies and practices that assure that employees can share in the financial achievements of their company. There are countless plans for doing this – such as profit sharing, stock ownership distribution, and merit pay schemes. However, the system that has been shown to have the greatest positive impact on employee attitudes and performance is "gainsharing." As the name says, it is a method for sharing gains with employees – the gains that the employees themselves, as a group, achieve for the organization. Although a number of gainsharing plans exist – the most common are the Scanlon Plan, the Rucker Plan, and Improshare – they have the following characteristics in common:

- They are used in relatively small organizations, most successfully when the number of employees is below 500.
- The performance is an operational measure, such as productivity or costs, rather than a financial measure such as profitability. Only employee-controllable performance is used.
- The organization establishes a historical base period of performance for a group.
- Performance improvement over the base creates a bonus pool, which is the savings that the improvement has generated. Typically, about half of the pool is paid to employees, usually as a percentage of their base pay, with all participating employees receiving the same percentage. The bonuses are usually paid on a monthly or quarterly basis, the idea being that they should be paid as closely as possible to the performance that is being rewarded.
- If there has been no gain, there is no pool.
- Almost all gainsharing plans include the heavy involvement of employees in developing and implementing ideas for improving performance.

Although gainsharing was once employed mostly in small manufacturing concerns, it has spread recently to service organizations, including hotels, restaurants, insurers, hospitals, and banks. Estimates vary, but a good guess is that about 20 percent of American companies have gainsharing plans. In most cases, however, it is applied to just a minority of the workforce, such as those in a concern's manufacturing facility.

A review of the research on gainsharing shows significant improvement in productivity in the large majority of organizations that use the plan. The range of improvement is wide, as low as 5 percent and as high as 78 percent, with the average being about 25 percent. This shows that the results can be substantial. "The most important thing we know about gainsharing plans is that they work," says Edward Lawler, probably the most prominent organization psychologist studying compensation systems and their effects (Lawler, 1992).

In an example of how a simple gainsharing plan might work, the average monthly sales in a base period, usually the previous year or eighteen months, are calculated. For our example, we will put this at $1 million. The average monthly wage costs over the same base period are calculated, and we will use $200,000 in our example, which makes wages account for 20 percent of sales. If sales in the first month of the gainsharing period reach $1.2 million, the application of the 20 percent guideline produces a figure of $240,000. If the actual wage costs for that month are $210,000, that shows a gain of $30,000, which is split 50–50 between the employees and the company.

This is a simple plan, that focuses on just one performance measure, the ratio of wage costs to sales. Other plans include a number of factors, such as quality and delivery performance, with each factor given a weight in the calculation of the gain to be shared. Other than individual piecework (a system beset by numerous problems), gainsharing provides the clearest linkage between what employees do and the performance measure that determines the payment.

Creating a compelling vision

Research shows a strong correlation between pride in the organization and the overall satisfaction of workers with that organization. There are four main sources of employee pride in this respect, all of which reflect different facets of a single attribute – excellence:

- Excellence of the organization's financial performance.
- Excellence of the efficiency with which the work of the organization gets done.
- Excellence of the characteristics of the organization's products such as their usefulness, distinctness, and quality.
- Excellence of the organization's moral character.

The first two of these factors relate to doing well, and the second two relate to doing good. These four aspects of excellence are, of course, interrelated. It is difficult to produce excellent long-term financial results without providing value to customers, or to succeed for long with unethical business practices. But as determinants of pride, each of the four is distinct and important. Thus, the desire of employees that their company act ethically and produce high-quality products is important in and of itself, not just because ethical behavior and quality are good for business.

People want to work for an organization that does well, but also does good. Companies that "do good" tend to show superior long-term performance. The most impressive study done in this respect was by Collins and Porras, summarized in their book *Built to Last* (Collins and Porras, 1997). The authors sought to determine the factors that distinguish the best companies from the merely satisfactory. They refer to the best as "visionary" because among their key distinguishing features is an emphasis on a vision that is "more than profits":

Contrary to business school doctrine, we did not find "maximizing shareholder wealth" or "profit maximization" as the dominant driving force or primary objective through the history of most of the visionary companies. They have tended to pursue a cluster of objectives, of which making money is only one – and not necessarily the primary one. Indeed, for many of the visionary companies, business has historically been more than an economic activity, more than just a way to make money.

It follows from our argument that a critical condition for employee enthusiasm is a clear, credible and inspiring organizational purpose, in effect, a "reason for being" that translates for workers into a "reason for being *there*" that goes above and beyond money. This purpose is often expressed in a "vision statement." An effective vision or values statement is simple and clear. It is relevant to the business and not so general and filled with platitudes as to be virtually meaningless. And it is inspirational – it appeals to values that employees hold above and beyond profits, especially the usefulness and quality of the product or service for customers. It encourages excellence in the achievement of those values, and promotes a feeling of being special, noticeably different from others. Here are some good examples:

The way I see it, leadership does not begin with power, but rather with a compelling vision or goal of excellence. (*Frederick W. Smith, Founder, Federal Express*)

I want to . . . express the principles which we in our company have endeavored to live up to. . . . Here is how it sums up: We try to remember that medicine is for the patient. We try never to forget that medicine is for the people. It is not for the profits. The profits follow, and if we have remembered that, they have never failed to appear. The better we have remembered that, the larger they have been. (*George Merck II, Former CEO, Merck & Co.*)

Benefits are about people. It's not whether you have the forms filled in or whether the checks are written. It's whether people are cared for when they're in trouble. (*A Three-Person Benefits Department*)

The last statement, from the three-person benefits department, is particularly impressive because it was composed in a very small organization and is devoid of the high-powered executive attention and professional wordsmithing that usually accompanies the process. It was created in the type of department normally known for its fixation on bureaucratic rules and procedures. It is a statement truly from the heart, with the focus in the right place: on the ends (people) rather than the means (completing forms).

A major issue with many vision statements is their credibility: Our surveys reveal that employees in many organizations see large gaps between what management says and what it does. The following are necessary for turning noble-sounding words of a vision/values statement into day-to-day reality:

- Strong and visible top-management support, especially the top person's support.
- Clear, enforceable and enforced policies that support the vision.
- Internal processes that enable the policies to be carried out.
- Full communication to the workforce of the policies and their rationale.
- Training of workers in implementing the policies on their own jobs.
- Tools that the workforce needs to carry out the policies, including authority.
- The workforce's participation in developing the methods used to carry out the policies.
- Measurement of the results, including upward feedback mechanisms (surveys, etc.) to help management determine where and in what way the vision is seen by employees as being fulfilled.
- A reward system geared to the results.

Fostering employee involvement

There is an enormous amount to be gained by involving the workforce in organization improvement. They have much to contribute, especially about improvements in their own jobs and work areas. They are motivated to make work the changes that *they* have initiated. Involvement – treating them as intelligent and dedicated employees – is a sign of respect for them that boosts their morale and commitment. This is true at *all* organization levels.

Managers often confuse participative management with a lack of leadership and chaos. This confusion is especially true in blue-collar settings and in "white-collar factories" (such as call centers). But participative leadership is an active style that stimulates involvement. In an effective, participative organization, no one is in doubt as to who is in charge. But that person expects employees to think, to exercise creative judgment, and not just do. That is the environment in which impediments to getting a job done can be removed and in which employee enthusiasm can flourish.

Research demonstrates repeatedly the superiority of participative management for performance (Pfeffer, 1994). And evidence gathered over decades shows that the value of participative management is not limited to societies with a long history of democratic institutions. Companies in Japan and Germany have, since the Second World War, been at the forefront in establishing participative management systems.

Central to a discussion of participative management is the matter of "steep" vs. "flat" organizations. Organizations that workers feel to be excessively bureaucratic are typically steep: There are many layers in the management hierarchy. A flat organization is the opposite – there are fewer layers in the management hierarchy and, generally, a larger number of employees report to each level. Companies with records of outstanding long-term performance frequently have extraordinarily flat structures. For example, the Nucor Corporation has four management layers (foreman, department head, general manager, and chairman) and the Dana Corporation, which once had fifteen management layers – and was barely profitable – went to five layers and much greater profitability.

The process is circular: Organizations with committed and enthusiastic work forces require fewer controls and the fewer of those controls, the greater the commitment and enthusiasm. A major reason companies with enthusiastic work forces are more successful is simply that it costs much less to manage them.

A goal of every organization should be to flatten its structure as much as possible, probably to somewhere from five to seven levels for the total organization, and just three levels in any facility. Flat organizations lend themselves to decentralized decision making. The decentralization that allows for effective flattening of an organization – not just head chopping – is best accomplished by establishing self-managed teams (often known by the acronym SMTs). SMTs are teams of workers who, with their supervisors, have delegated to them various functions and the authority and resources needed to carry them out. Ideally, the team does the "whole thing," builds a whole product or provides all the services for a defined customer or set of customers.

Increasing control by, not of, employees is the essence of the SMT approach to management. This self control is a product of less need to obtain management's approval for many decisions because these have been delegated to the team ("vertical" autonomy) and less need for the group to interact with other units to obtain their assent to decisions because so many functions – traditionally distributed among a number of departments – are performed within the team and, therefore, under control of the team ("horizontal" autonomy).

Performance is further enhanced in well-run SMTs by the emergence of "group norms," in which members exert a strong influence on each other's behavior. This is especially pronounced in the case of non-productive employees who are subjected to internal group pressure to perform, thus reducing the need for management's intervention.

There is considerable variability in the number and kinds of management tasks delegated to the teams. Any SMT worthy of its name will have a great deal of say over work methods, work scheduling, production goals, quality assurance, and relationships with the team's customers (external or internal). But, some organizations have gone considerably further and delegate human resources decisions, such as hiring employees, to the teams.

A review of the research on SMTs shows that the ideal SMT is one that:

- Produces the whole thing for an identified customer or set of customers with whom the team interacts.
- Has clear goals for which it is accountable.
- Contains within it all the skills needed to get the job done.
- Has access to the information and has control over the resources it needs to complete the job.
- Receives rewards based on team performance (such as through gainsharing).

In other words, under ideal circumstances, the team operates like a small business whose members are highly involved in its management and in the sharing of its rewards. In addition to satisfying employees' achievement and equity needs, SMTs obviously go a long way towards satisfying their need for camaraderie. For all of these reasons, research has repeatedly demonstrated the superiority of this approach to organization. (For more on SMTs see Yeatts and Hyten, 1997.)

Providing recognition

Managers should be certain that all employee contributions, both large and small, are recognized. The motto of many managers seems to be, "Why would I need to thank someone for doing something he's paid to do?" Workers repeatedly tell us on our surveys, and with great feeling, how much they appreciate a compliment. They also report how distressed they are when no one takes the time to thank them for a job well done, but are criticized for making mistakes.

Receiving recognition for achievements is one of the most fundamental of human needs. It is not childish and, rather than making employees complacent, reinforces their accomplishments, helping ensure there will be more of them. Effective recognition should take place both day-to-day and through formal programs: Both are important. A pat on the back, simply saying "good going," a dinner for two, a note from one's boss's boss, some schedule flexibility, a paid day off, or even a flower on a desk with a thank-you note are a few of the hundreds of ways managers and companies can show their appreciation for good work. It works wonders if this is sincere, sensitively done, and undergirded by fair and competitive pay – not considered a substitute for it.

The good news is that, for most managers, training in a few simple principles plus practice can be extraordinarily effective. The key principles of effective recognition are:

- *Be specific about what is being recognized.* The employee needs to be praised for concrete achievements. This both reinforces the particular behaviors that the manager wants to see repeated and, in the eyes of the employee, increases the sincerity of the praise.
- *Do it in person.* Recognition by long distance or proxy is not nearly as effective as face-to-face recognition.
- *Be timely.* Give recognition as soon as possible after the desired behavior. By and large, the more time between the completion of a behavior and the delivery of a reinforcing consequence, the less effective is the reinforcement. This advice is wonderfully summarized in the phrase "catch them at being good." Catching people in the act, as it were, is usually reserved for misdeeds, but applying the same principle to good performance is exactly what managers should do.
- *Be sincere.* This is an odd piece of advice; after all, a manager either means praise sincerely or he doesn't. But even managers who are sincere in their praise provide it in a way that seems insincere to their employees. They might be so general in what they say or so tardy in when they say it that expressing appreciation seems to employees like something a manager feels he has to do rather than something he genuinely wants to do. Or, they might give mixed messages about an employee's performance, such as, "You did well on that, but . . .," or "Thank goodness you finally got that right." A manager might undermine the effect with "humor", saying something like, "You've done such a good job, you would never know that you had an MBA," or, "He's so loyal to the company, he hasn't seen his family in months." Managers can overdo it, exaggerating the achievement with meaningless flattery. Although much of the advice about how to give recognition might seem trite and even corny, be assured that recognition is vitally important to employees and that employees listen carefully to every word that is said when it is given. The simpler and more direct the compliment the better, such as, "You did a great job on . . . and I want you to know that. I especially liked . . . Thank you very much." If the praise is exaggerated or too flowery, it won't be believable. If it is a mixed message, the employee mostly remembers the negative comment or implication, even if the manager finishes on a positive note. People want

honest and deserved acknowledgment of their contributions and, when received, it is greatly appreciated.

Establishing an open communication culture

One of the most counterproductive rules in business is to distribute information on the basis of "need to know." It is usually a way of severely, unnecessarily, and destructively restricting the flow of information in an organization.

Workers' frustrations with an absence of adequate communication are among the most negative findings of employee attitude surveys. What employees need to do their jobs and what makes them feel respected and included dictate that very few restrictions be placed by managers on the flow of information. Hold nothing back of interest to employees except those very few items that are absolutely confidential.

Most managers must discipline themselves to communicate regularly because it's not a natural instinct for them. Schedule regular employee meetings that have no purpose other than two-way communication. Meetings among management should conclude with a specific plan for communicating the results of the meetings to employees.

A straightforward communications approach is best. Many employees are quite skeptical about management's motives and can quickly see through "spin." Tell it like it is. Get continual feedback on how well you and the company are communicating. One of the biggest communication problems is the automatic assumption that a message has been understood. Follow-up often finds that messages are unclear or misunderstood.

We find in our surveys that companies and managers who communicate in the ways we describe reap large gains in employee morale. Full and open communication not only helps employees do their jobs: it is also an important sign of respect for them.

Demonstrating respect

It's not particularly noteworthy that people in organizations are "respectful" of their bosses and that the higher in the hierarchy a person is, the more deference he or she receives. Whether or not appreciation is genuinely felt by their subordinates, bosses receive lots of thank yous, and they rarely receive any verbal abuse or even sharp disagreement. We put this type of respect in quotes because this is not the kind of respect we address in this chapter.

The kind of respect that we have in mind – and that has such profound implications for worker morale – does not come from deference to power or the expectation of reward, but from a sense of the intrinsic worth of human beings – *all* human beings. We define the equity need as the desire to be treated justly in relation to the basic conditions of employment. These conditions are expected simply by virtue of being employed and derive from generally accepted ethical and community standards. The three major financial components of equity are job security, pay, and benefits. The major non-financial component is respect.

Equality is at the heart of respect – the treatment of each individual as important and unique without regard to any other characteristics, such as gender, race, income, or even perceived performance or contribution to the organization. Does equality mean that it is inherently disrespectful for some people to earn more than others, or for some to have more power than others? That is the view only in extreme forms of egalitarian ideology. The rest of us *expect* differentiation in income according to responsibilities and would find an organization with no differentiation in power as ludicrous and dysfunctional.

The core issue is how people at legitimately higher income or power levels *treat* those at lower levels (that is, how they use their power).

To take a simple-minded example, do passengers on a plane see it as illegitimate for a pilot and crew to be in command and give orders? Of course not. But, in manner and attitude, how are passengers treated by the crew? Do they feel themselves treated as welcome guests of the airline, or rudely, as necessary evils, or, perhaps most commonly, indifferently, as "seats?"

How customers are treated has a large impact on their willingness to continue doing business with a company; the impact is no smaller on employees and their willingness to perform at high levels. Here, we are dealing with a fundamental human need that, although it might sound trivial and corny – such as wanting to work for a boss with a friendly manner – has major consequences for human behavior and the effectiveness of organizations.

Lest we be misunderstood, we reiterate here that respectful treatment is terribly important to people, but it is not a substitute for money. Both needs are *independently* important. In fact, respectful treatment and other aspects of good "human relations" are viewed as a sham if employees feel that they are at the same time being economically exploited. "Human relations" should not be treated as "public relations" in the sense of a friendly facade masking basic inequities.

Key elements of respectful treatment include:
- Warmly welcoming employees into the organization.
- Physical working conditions "fit for human beings."
- Open communications.
- Elimination of unnecessary status distinctions.
- Trust in employees to use their judgment as to how to do their jobs and involvement of them in work-related decisions.
- Day-to-day courtesies and civil behavior.

Conclusion

As we have noted, the essence of the system and culture described here is a "partnership" relationship between employers and their employees. A partnership has both psychological and economic components, for example, employees' confidence that they make significant contributions to the organization's success and that they also share in the financial gains for that contribution. It is a high-involvement model: involvement in what the workers give to an organization, and in what they receive from it.

A partnership culture is the surest path to a high-performance organization. Partnership works because it harnesses the natural motivation and enthusiasm that is characteristic of the overwhelming majority of workers. Other management modes dampen – even destroy – that motivation and enthusiasm. A partnership organization works because it assumes that the great majority of workers *are* motivated.

Many partnership organizations did not have to change to that form: They started that way with a visionary founder and CEO who strongly believed that was the way people should be managed. Frederick Smith of Federal Express and Herb Kelleher of Southwest Airlines are good examples of this. But other organizations that have long operated with an entirely different management mode have consciously and deliberately undergone profound culture change to a partnership pattern. Good examples include Gordon Bethune's changes at Continental Airlines and F. Kenneth Iverson's highly successful efforts at Nucor. A major lesson from these examples is that action must begin with, and be sustained by, senior management.

It is ironic that among the most satisfying aspects of life in an organization – as of life in general – are those that can be achieved only by hard work. This is especially true of attempts to change relationships: how people treat one another in their pursuit of earning a living. The overwhelming majority of people in organizations want to act in simple pursuit of equitable treatment, a sense of achievement, and camaraderie.

But as we have pointed out, the vagaries of organizational life often cause people to act in ways not in their better nature. They have to deal with a combination of daily on-the-job frustrations; management that treat them as sources of problems, costs and resistance rather than as assets; and the behavior of the tiny, often highly visible minority of employees who really don't care, and reinforce management's pessimistic view of the workplace. As a result, the simple pursuit of basic goals often becomes a hopeless quest.

Partnership organizations emerge when senior leadership – in most cases, it has been the CEO – has the foresight to see what can be, and not just what is. This requires not only insight into human nature (especially that people want to do good for a good organization), and not just eloquence in communicating the partnership philosophy, but also perseverance and hard work over a period of years to translate the philosophy into specific and daily management policies. It requires seeing and treating employees as genuine allies in achieving change.

REFERENCES

Cascio, W. F., Young, C. E. and Morris, J. R. (1997) Financial consequences of employment-change decisions in major U.S. corporations. *Academy of Management Journal, 40, No. 5,* 1175–89.

Collins, J. C. and Porras, J. I. (1997) *Built to last.* New York: Harper Collins.

Deci, E. L. and Ryan, R. M. (2000) The "what" and "why" of goal pursuits: Human needs and the self-determination of behavior. *Psychological Inquiry, 11,* 227–68.

Iverson, K. and Varian, T. (1997) *Plain talk: lessons from a business maverick.* New York: John Wiley and Sons.

Lawler, E. E. III (1992) *The ultimate advantage.* San Francisco: Jossey-Bass.

Maslow, A. (1971) *The farther reaches of human nature.* New York: Viking Press.

McClelland, D. (1985) *Human motivation.* Glenville: Scott Foresman.

Parker, J. (2001) Where layoffs are a last resort. *BusinessWeek Online,* October 8, 2001.

Pfeffer, J. (1994) *Competitive advantage through people.* Boston: Harvard Business School Press.

Sirota, D., Mischkind, L. A. and Meltzer, M. I. (2005) *The enthusiastic employee.* Upper Saddle River: Wharton School Publishing.

Thurow, L. (2001) *USA Today.* March 21, 2001, p. 15A.

Yeatts, D. E. and Hyten, C. (1997) *High-performing self-managed work teams.* Thousand Oaks: Sage Publications.

Organizational citizenship behavior, transaction cost economics, and the flat world hypothesis

Dennis W. Organ and Jeong-Yeon Lee

Introduction

A substantial literature has developed regarding the nature, antecedents, and consequences of "organizational citizenship behavior" (OCB), or the discretionary non-task contributions rendered by participants to organizational viability and effectiveness (Organ, 1988; Podsakoff *et al.*, 2000; Organ, Podsakoff, and Mackenzie, 2006). The empirical record indicates that individual perceptions and attitudes (e.g., job satisfaction, perceived fairness) or generalized "morale," once regarded as determinants of "productivity," actually better predict OCB (or, as some prefer, "contextual performance," a form of contribution operationally measured in much the same terms as OCB, although defined somewhat differently as a formal construct; Borman and Motowidlo, 1997). More recently, at the organizational level, there is research evidence indicating that indeed operational measures of various forms of OCB are associated with superior group and organizational performance in terms of criteria such as efficiency, quality of output, and customer satisfaction (Podsakoff and Mackenzie, 1997; Walz and Niehoff, 2000; Koys, 2001).

What has remained elusive to date is the identification of an instructive framework of organization theory in which to fit OCB. Initial attempts to anchor OCB (e.g., Organ, 1988) within a "macro" context were not at all systematic, nor were they couched in any coherent theory, but rather took the form of some speculation as to why certain forms of OCB (such as helping coworkers or exhibiting yeoman-like levels of compliance to organizational rules and standards) could plausibly, *ceteris paribus*, contribute to higher levels of efficiency and effectiveness. More recently, Bolino, Turnley, and Bloodgood (2002) have interpreted the positive effects of OCB in terms of "social capital," and Organ (2006) has elaborated upon the potentially positive links between OCB and organizational effectiveness.

However, while it is probably useful to think of specific linkages between OCB and organizational effectiveness, the most that such an exercise can yield is a list of commonsense explanations for why OCB is of some benefit to organizations. No doubt there are many practices that, at the margin, can make an organization a bit more effective by one criterion or another. Ideally, a theoretical scheme is desired that would go far towards establishing the *necessity*, not simply the desirability, for OCB. In other words, if OCB could be shown to fill a "logical gap" in a theory about the necessary and sufficient conditions for organizational viability, then perhaps OCB could fulfill some of the hopes that it could connect "macro" with "micro" phenomena in a tractable and compelling framework.

We believe that Transaction Costs Economics (TCE), particularly as articulated by Williamson (1975, 1991), Williamson, Wachter, and Harris (1975), and Ouchi (1980), offers a promising theory of organizations within which to interpret the significance of OCB. Moreover, we believe that TCE implicitly requires some construct such as OCB. In particular, inclusion of OCB seems necessary in order for Williamson's "internal labor market" (ILM) to offer a viable alternative to markets. In turn, Williamson's treatment of "high-powered" versus "low-powered" incentives goes far toward establishing the logical and theoretical status of OCB. However, like Husted and Folger (2004), we also believe that TCE needs a more thorough, explicit, and nuanced treatment of organizational justice in order for TCE, OCB, and the ILM to fit coherently with each other.

Having developed the linkages between concepts of TCE, OCB, the ILM, and the relevance of fairness issues, we take note of some compelling evidence suggesting that the emergence of a "flat-world" (Friedman, 2005) threatens the survival of the ILM as we have known it in the US and perhaps elsewhere as well. The global system glimpsed by Friedman and others seems, at first glance, to have no obvious means of evoking and strengthening OCB. Thus, questions arise as to whether OCB will be very important in future economic organizations, and if so, what factors would sustain it.

First, we need to review the key concepts in TCE as they pertain to OCB.

Market failures

Briefly, TCE contends that hierarchical organizations arise because of market failures under the convergence of certain conditions. When parties to the exchange are few in number (e.g., two), when bounded rationality is insufficient to predict complex and uncertain contingencies, and information impactedness (the asymmetry of knowledge by exchange partners as to the state or value of the object of exchange) gives rise to opportunism, the costs of market transactions become prohibitive. Each party would require inordinate investments in research, monitoring, and haggling in order to have confidence that a "fair exchange" occurred. Neither party has recourse to a price set by competitive bidders. Because neither party can foresee future states of nature, neither simple nor contingent-claims contracts are feasible.

In Williamson's analysis, asset specificity is a major complication in market-mediated exchange. As applied to the exchange of labor for money, asset specificity takes the form of tacit knowledge more or less unique to a specific context of work, defined not only by the technology and task design of the work but also the relationships with coworkers, customers, and other parties interdependent with each other. Because the value of the laborer is specific to a particular workplace, no independent market forces can determine fair terms of exchange once this asset specificity has occurred. Thus, not only are contingent claims contracts not feasible, neither is sequential contracting. Information impactedness means that the laborer has more knowledge about the extent and value of his or her contributions than anyone else, and given an inclination to opportunism, might dissimulate about those contributions. The purchaser of that labor thus could not take the laborer's assessment at face value, and then haggling raises transaction costs to an excessive level. On the other hand, the buyer of the labor might resort to monitoring ("metering," in Williamson's terms), but this can be taken only so far before the costs again become prohibitive.

To some extent, both Barnard (1938) and Simon (1961) had foreseen these limitations to market contracting. Barnard's solution was the authority relationship (thus introducing hierarchy). This arrangement took the form of an exchange of wage payment for the buyer's right to make future demands upon the laborer within the "zone of [the laborer's] indifference" as to whether to perform or not perform a particular action. Simon suggested that the buyer of labor would actually pay added compensation if unable to specify in advance the optimum specification of behaviors within that zone of indifference i.e., a premium for the possibility that the demands made might be onerous, aversive, or costly in effort for the laborer.

Williamson, *et al.* agree that the authority relationship gets around the problem of trying to devise complex contracts when future states of nature are uncertain. However, they argue that neither Barnard's nor Simon's analyses explain why hierarchy is superior to either contingent claims contracting or sequential spot contracting, both of which allow for adaptability to changing circumstances. Rather, it is the convergence of asset specificity, information impactedness, bounded rationality, and opportunism that give rise to prohibitive transaction costs, even for spot contracting.

Williamson *et al.* propose the "internal labor market" (ILM) as the preferred arrangement for economizing on transactions costs. The defining properties of the ILM are: (1) wage rates attach to jobs, rather than workers (much in the manner of job analysis and job evaluation programs as designed and administered by human resource management experts) and flexibility for adjusting to unforeseeable contingencies is provided by a contract couched in general and open-ended terms; (2) external recruitment draws new workers into the system at the lowest levels of the organization; (3) promotion to higher levels is from within the system, thus providing incentives for long-term involvement in the system, which in turn enables accumulation of site-specific, often tacit, knowledge; and (4) a labor arbitration system provides a mechanism for resolving exceptional and contentious issues. While much of what Williamson, *et al.* describe sounds like a company with a union, and indeed they suggest that unionization facilitates these arrangements, they suggest that a union is not "strictly necessary, especially in small organizations" (Williamson *et al.*, 1975).

Perfunctory versus consummate cooperation

Williamson *et al.* recognize that "acceding to authority on matters that fall within the zone of acceptance merely requires that the employee respond in a minimally acceptable, even perfunctory way," which might suffice for "tasks that are reasonably well-structured." However, for work characterized by long-term accumulation of site-specific, tacit knowledge, something more like "consummate cooperation" is needed. One means of eliciting consummate cooperation is to devise incentive payments on a transaction-specific basis. But Williamson *et al.* reject such a plan, because this would "violate the non-individualistic wage bargaining attributes of internal labor markets." Rather, individuals who display such consummate cooperation over the long term will become recognized, directly or indirectly, by superiors, and those individuals will have higher probabilities and rates of promotion. Thus, Williamson *et al.* reject the "high powered incentives of markets," which are "unavoidably compromised by internal organization," in favor of "flat or low-powered" internal incentives of hierarchies" (Williamson, 1991, p. 275).

Clearly, the notion of "consummate cooperation" is evocative of something like OCB. Worker performance limited to the most specific terms described in the job description – which amounts to the "incomplete contract" in the ILM and complies in the main with core task requirements – provides only "perfunctory cooperation." Moreover, cooperation at this level is often susceptible to "metering" in generally low-cost terms, as with measures or indicators of objective results. Performance that goes beyond that level, to "fill in the gaps" of the contract, includes contributions that do not qualify for "high-powered incentives," in part because such contributions resist metering, also in part because, lacking such metering and absent clear and specific directives, those contributions can be usually withheld with more or less impunity. Thus, with respect to those contributions that distinguish consummate from perfunctory cooperation, ". . . changes in effort expended have little or no immediate effect on compensation" (Williamson, 1991, p. 275). As we shall soon see, the adjective "immediate" here is critical to the link between TCE and OCB.

The authority relation and transactions costs

The authority relation as an incomplete contract, to be filled in as needed in order to adjust to changing conditions, is insufficient to evoke more than perfunctory cooperation. Indeed, beyond some point, the very attempt to exercise authority becomes essentially another exchange that generates serious transactions costs.

Barnard's and Simon's concept of a zone of indifference or zone of acceptance, as an incomplete contract in which the worker "doesn't care very much" which action within that zone is specified at any given time, gives the misleading impression that such a zone is well-defined. It is more likely the case that for either party, relatively few actions reside unambiguously in that zone, quite a few are unambiguously beyond that zone, and many others lie in a broad twilight zone that might or might not have been foreseen in intent or implication at the time of the employment contract. To the extent that the authority figure "pushes the envelope" of this twilight zone, attempting to test the viability of authority with respect to ill-defined expectations, there is likely to be resistance on the part of the worker. Arguments will ensue as to whether a specified behavior is "part of the job" or "what I get paid to do." Short of overt recalcitrance, the worker will experience psychological reactance (Brehm, 1966, 1972), defined as an aversive affective state consequent to the loss of a degree of behavioral freedom and a subsequent motivation to restore that loss of freedom. The worker might comply for the moment, but actively refrain from enacting the specified behavior when unmonitored. On the other hand, systematic monitoring once again generates transaction costs.

Furthermore, even if the supervisor – whether on the basis of formal authority as *per* the employment contract, or perhaps on some additional base of influence – were able to "piece out" the incomplete contract by gradually "stretching" the zone of indifference, this capability would accomplish little if it were necessary for the supervisor to be always on the spot to notice the need for a previously unspecified behavior and actively to instruct the worker as to what should be done. To maintain this different kind of monitoring – monitoring the need for specific worker actions, as opposed to monitoring whether the worker carries out previously given directives – again incurs substantial transaction costs. The point is that any sort of directive is a "transaction," and to the extent that a dominating presence or intrusive monitoring is necessary to induce the appropriate and constructive response to the directive, transaction costs mount.

To be sure, many formal job descriptions and employment interviews specify something about desired employee characteristics and behaviors. The job specification part of a job description often states something about the importance of "cooperation," "initiative," "can-do attitude," and "good team player." However, it is most unlikely that these personal attributes or behavior styles are ever defined in operational terms. What is really important is not just "cooperation," but cooperation in specific terms, in specific contexts, at particular times, for certain purposes. Both employer and employee might well agree that cooperation and team playing are important, but in the real-time exigencies that arise in the workplace, supervisor and employee might have very different notions as to what forms that cooperation should take, how long it should last, and how often it should be rendered.

Borman and Motowidlo (1997) note that "contextual performance," or OCB, is a part of performance that is *general* or *common* to all jobs in collective endeavors, while task performance is specific to a single job or class of jobs. This commonality is at a high level of abstraction – otherwise, it could hardly be common to vastly unlike jobs. What remains is for the specific forms, times, and manners of contextual performance to be played out. Virtually never can more than a small portion of the needed cooperative behaviors be spelled out in advance. Absent such specification, absent intrusive monitoring, and failing a real-time incentive scheme, authority persons must inevitably experience some uncertainty as to what forms of cooperation, team play, and initiative can be commanded, and as we have stated above, probing these uncertain bounds of the zone of indifference gives rise to transactions costs of its own.

Thus, it becomes clear that transaction costs are minimized to the extent that the worker, not the supervisor, is the one who "stretches" the zone of indifference. Or, phrased differently, the worker "fills in the gaps" between what could be specified *a priori* in the employment contract and what later becomes a "reasonable" correlated obligation on the part of the worker. Then, as the worker accumulates site-specific knowledge of the work and its context, the worker responds to the need for "consummate cooperation" when he or she recognizes that need and does not have to be directed or monitored.

There is persuasive evidence that people on the same job differ in what their "perception" of their job obligations include (Morrison, 1994), and related evidence that people who render more of the unspecified or incompletely specified contributions tend to have a broader concept of the job definition. Whether some people bring to the job a tendency to define obligations of the job in broader terms than other people, or people broaden (or conceivably narrow) these definitions as a function of experience on the job, is not clear from the data. We suspect that both factors are involved, but in the remainder of this discussion we proceed on the assumption that at least some of the variance in "perceived job breadth" is attributable to experience on the job and how that experience affects people's concept or image of the organization.

Performance appraisal

In Williamson *et al.*'s (1975) ILM model, internal promotion is the mechanism by which the long-term, but "flat or low-powered incentives" work to induce varying degrees of consummate cooperation. Indeed, evidence supports the proposition that supervisory ratings of participants' OCB or Contextual Performance are reliably correlated with ratings of the participants' "promotability" (Shore, Barksdale and Cross, 1995; Van Scotter, Motowidlo and Cross, 2000). However, the evidence is weak and mixed as to the effect of OCB ratings on actual promotion (Van Scotter *et al.*, 2000). The studies that have examined the correlation between OCB rating and subsequent promotion might not have allowed sufficient time for promotions to occur. But that in itself suggests a limitation in the effect of promotion prospects to motivate OCB and "consummate cooperation": there might not be a sufficient number of promotion opportunities, except over multi-year intervals, to offer compensation for meritorious contributions.

We suggest that the performance appraisal actually constitutes a more viable mechanism for the ILM to reward consummate cooperation. Appraisals occur more frequently and afford more flexibility in recognizing and rewarding varying levels of consummate cooperation. Whether at intervals of six months, a year, or two years, there is a long enough stretch for reputational effects of OCB to become known, directly or indirectly, to some authority figure, yet the occasions are not over intervals so long that individuals cannot make a connection between previous behavior patterns and eventual outcomes. Of course, the incentive is necessarily "flat and low-powered," because there is no one-to-one correspondence between specific acts of consummate cooperation, day in and day out, and eventual recompense. Moreover, some degree of observer error necessarily enters into the equation, because the authority figure's rating (whether explicit or implicitly and judgmentally factored into an "overall" rating) is the product not only of direct observation, which itself might be limited, but also hear-say and inference. But to the extent that supervisors have some basis, or even think they have such a basis, for making even a rough estimate of a person's relative OCB, they will likely use that estimate in performance evaluation.

Abundant evidence is at hand to support the hypothesis that supervisory performance evaluations are influenced by beliefs about individuals' OCB (see e.g., Podsakoff, Mackenzie and Hui, 1993; Podsakoff *et al.*, 2000). There is also evidence that supervisors attach monetary significance to OCB (Orr *et al.*, 1989) and that salary and reward recommendations are reliably correlated with assessments of OCB, accounting for unique variance in such recommendations beyond the effect of task performance (e.g., Park, 1986; Allen and Rush, 1998; Kiker and Motowidlo, 1999). Thus, it seems more plausible that, for most participants, striving towards consummate cooperation is more likely to be sustained by the processes of periodic performance appraisal and wage/salary adjustments, rather than the prospect of progressive promotions to higher rank.

Low – versus high-powered incentives

A pervasive and consistent theme in management textbooks, consulting, and periodicals is the preoccupation with the "reward system," and that usually means the methods by which pay is determined. The basic assumption seems to be that if a particular behavior is in short supply, you can make it more prevalent by promising (or threatening) to make at least part of the paycheck contingent on how often and how well the rank and file display that behavior. If you really want employees to be more productive, then define and measure productivity precisely and map out a one-to-one relationship between differences in productivity and differences in pay. If a university seeks a reputation for excellence, it should make salary strongly dependent on publications in a codified list of "A" journals. When a company comes under fire for its lackluster record in promoting minority employees, one solution suggested by external critics and in-house executives alike is to yoke managers' pay to their records in developing and advancing minority careers.

The common theme in such prescriptions is the assumption that "high-powered incentives," especially as applied to the pay envelope, are needed to "send a message," "get people's attention," and rouse the motivation to achieve the goal in question. What makes an incentive high-powered? One element is the specificity of the outcome or the behavior in question. There is a lot of power difference between a reward system that states "pay depends on performance" and one that bases pay increases entirely on meeting a few specific quantitative goals, such as those that measure units of output, percentage of defects, or number of customer complaints. Another component of high-powered incentives is the subjective probability that the effort expended to achieve some particular and precise goal will actually lead to attainment of the specific proffered reward. A third component is the differential magnitude of gain when the specified behavior or outcome is enacted and/or the loss when such outcomes do not obtain – steep gradients of reward are thought to motivate more strongly, thus do human resource management textbooks advise the would-be manager to put more "teeth" into merit pay plans by distinguishing more levels of performance, rewarding accordingly. If the goal is objectively defined and precisely measured, if there is a straightforward, one-to-one relationship between effort and goal attainment, and if goal attainment really is rewarded as promised along a path of steep gradation, then presumably motivation to exert strong efforts towards those goals is ensured.

The problems with such incentives go well beyond the fact that managers constrained by bounded rationality cannot foresee all of the relevant behaviors needed for organizational effectiveness, and that even if they could, the enumeration of all such behaviors and the design of requisite measuring systems would generate excessive metering costs. Frequent, heavy-handed resort to, and emphasis upon, hard monetary contingencies can have serious side-effects that must be reckoned with.

A substantial body of work (Deci, 1975; Lepper and Greene, 1978) has demonstrated the negative effect that "salient" extrinsic rewards can have on "intrinsic motivation." What Deci described as "salient" sounds much like the "high-powered" terminology of Williamson – a strong contingency between a very specific behavior, or outcome of behavior, and a reward in the form of a pay increase (whether the latter be a bonus or increase in base salary). Deci found that such contingencies do indeed act as powerful motivators of specific behaviors, but at the expense of any pre-existing intrinsic motivation, not in addition to it. Some critics have countered Deci's findings with the observations that much work is not intrinsically motivating, that there is a long-standing norm of monetary compensation for labor rendered, and that in any the case the loss of motivation in studies by Deci and others became apparent only when the contingency was not in effect e.g., during intervals when the naïve subjects were ostensibly waiting idly for the experimenter to return and could have been engaged in the task "just for fun" if so inclined. Nonetheless, we should keep in mind that, even though people certainly expect to be paid for the work they do, they can be paid according to arrangements that differ enormously in the "salience" of the pay and the contingencies that govern the workplace, and second, few contingencies are or can be in effect continuously in the work environment. A system that drives worker pay by steeply progressive incentives keyed to a small number of specific quantitative results would plausibly loom more "salient" to employees than subjective supervisory assessments of overall performance over the course of a year. Furthermore, if for any reason metering systems (which could take the form of the supervisor's watchful gaze, as well as more sophisticated methods) are disrupted or are otherwise not in operation, the result is much like the experimenter's "time out," and the effect on intrinsic motivation would theoretically take the form of "shirking."

Data long since gathered from experimental psychology demonstrate other adverse effects of high-powered incentives, even on the very outcomes they might be intended to encourage. Controlled studies of creative problem-solving have found that salient extrinsic rewards based on solving the problem result in smaller percentages of subjects finding the solution, compared to the condition in which pay was not at risk (Glucksberg, 1962; McGraw and McCullers, 1979). One possible explanation for this finding is that strong pay incentives tend to narrow an individual's perceptual span, rendering important peripheral stimuli less detectable. Also, a strong extrinsic reward incentive is said to increase an individual's drive or activation level, which in turn makes "dominant" – i.e., strong, familiar, obvious – responses increasingly likely, while creative responses usually require responses that are weaker or "less obvious" (Easterbrook, 1959; Zajonc, 1965). In addition, strong incentives for specific task goals have the effect of reducing incidental learning (Bahrick, Fitts and Rankin, 1952; Bahrick, 1954) i.e., learning unrelated to the central or specific task, and arguably much of what we call "tacit knowledge," an important dimension of human capital, is derived precisely by learning that is incidental to the immediate tasks at hand.

More to the central point of this paper is an instructive laboratory experiment conducted by Wright *et al.* (1993). In this study, the experimenters manipulated the presence versus absence of goal-setting, the difficulty of the goals that were set, and the contingency between pay and goal-achievement on a specific task. During the course of the experiment, a confederate of the researchers played the role of an apparent subject who arrived late for the experimental session. Of interest to the researchers was the effect of goals and incentives on the degree of help given to the confederate by the "real" subjects. As predicted, the greater the difficulty of the task goals, and the greater the contingency of pay on meeting those goals, the less aid was given to the confederate. Moreover, the very least incidence of help occurred among those subjects who reported the highest degree of "acceptance" of the goals and payment conditions.

If we could imagine organizations whose effectiveness and success depended entirely on each individual participant allocating the full measure of his or her aptitude, training, attention, and effort on a small number of tasks, utterly without regard to what their coworkers were doing, and if there were no advantage to incidental learning or creative approaches to the task, then perhaps the results of the studies cited above should not occasion much concern. However, we find it difficult to believe that such conditions pertain to organizations characterized by even modest degrees of complexity, task interdependence, environmental change and uncertainty, need to innovate, specialized knowledge, team-based operations, and customer focus. Rather, it occurs to us that such realistic conditions as these are better suited to Williamson's "low-powered incentives," which apply within the context of a supervisor's subjective performance evaluation, typically conducted on an annual basis, in which the evaluation takes account of both task and non-task contributions.

To be sure, supervisory evaluations, dependent as they are upon recall and impressions over the course of the year, are necessarily rough and imprecise at best. This means that a coworker who has spent a half-hour or more at work helping me with a problem today, might not get any "credit" several months later for such service. The coworker probably realizes as much. What we signify by this observation is that no strong or "high powered incentive" has prompted that service, because a direct connection from that one incident to future pay can hardly be assumed with any confidence. Not the least in the implication of this thinking is that the coworker is free to attribute "internal causes" for the help. Such attributions can take the form of thinking e.g., "I'm the kind of person who likes to help others when I can," or "I enjoy the challenge of trying to help somebody solve a problem," or "I do these things because I care about how my colleagues regard me." These attributions stand in contrast to experimental findings that subjects tend to assume that productivity attained under known supervisory surveillance is attributable to external causes (Strickland, 1958), and one suspects that those under such surveillance arrive at similar attributions. Absent such forms of surveillance and high-powered incentives, many forms of contributions are rendered for other reasons. A survey by Watson Wyatt (cited in Pfeffer and Sutton, 2006), of 1,700 high-performing employees from sixteen organizations gave "positive reputation" as the major motive for how they worked. If their stellar performance were not under the influence of high-powered incentives and surveillance, they had ample cause to believe that something more generalized, such as reputation within the profession or among colleagues, guided their efforts.

Also, the low-powered incentive in the form of annual performance appraisals means that work behavior is not constrained by tunnel vision focused on a few compelling statistics and the narrowly defined behaviors that drive those statistics. Rather, participants are free to let broadened perceptual spans pursue peripheral stimuli, enabling them to notice subtle indicators of potential problems or non-obvious cues for how operations could be improved. Employees could go quickly to the aid of a coworker without pondering whether doing so takes something out of their own paychecks.

Supervisory evaluations as social exchange

Textbook discussions of the validity of performance appraisals focus overwhelmingly on how accurately the appraisal captures past contributions. The implicit assumption is that the appraisal provides the mechanism for distributing rewards according to past performance. However, thinking about appraisals only in such historical terms seems unduly limiting. Appraisals are really as much about the future as they are about the past, especially if we consider the appraisal, and any pay increase thereby determined, as a carrier of social exchange.

Blau (1964) has delineated the essential attributes that distinguish economic (or contractual) exchange from social exchange. While granting that many of the transactions that people engage in are not pure economic or pure social exchange but lie on a continuum of mixed forms of exchange, Blau notes that economic exchange specifies the precise terms of the objects being exchanged e.g., a set price for an article of clothing, and also specifies the timing of exchange – a deadline for receipt of a service or commodity and correlated deadline for payment. Either an exact price is set by markets or the parties to the exchange negotiate the fixed terms of the exchange. Furthermore, recourse can be made to external authorities, such as those provided by the legal and judicial systems, for enforcing the terms of the contract. Finally, in economic exchange the value of what is exchanged is independent of the identity of the parties to the exchange (except, of course, for impersonal criteria such as age, expertise, accreditation, and other attributes that legitimize the party's role within the exchange). In other words, you do not have to like the person from whom you buy a car, nor must you respect someone who pays you for income tax preparation services.

Social exchange, by contrast, pointedly avoids any specification of the terms of the exchange – especially when the exchange involves expressions of sentiment, but also when services (helping someone change a flat tire) or even commodities (giving a roommate an extra razor or ballpoint pen that you don't need) are the elements in the exchange. Indeed, there usually is no mention of any *quid pro quo* at all – only a felt obligation on the part of the recipient of the exchange to appreciate what has been rendered, and a tacit understanding that should the appropriate occasion arise, to render something in return. Thus, timing of reciprocation also is not specified. In contrast to economic exchange, which can be enforced by third parties, social exchange depends on trust. However, we speak here, not of "trust" to do anything in particular, but trust that the relationship is genuine and earnest on both sides, that exchange will continue into the future, and that over the long run, the dynamic will tend towards some rough balance – reciprocity or "fairness"–in the exchange. Lastly, in social exchange, the affective value of what is exchanged does depend to some degree on who is party to the exchange. Recognition, positive feedback, and praise have more value coming from a supervisor whom one likes, admires, and respects. Agreement by others with your political opinions matters more when expressed by people reputed to be quite knowledgeable and sophisticated in such areas.

We must emphasize that people engage in social exchange, as described by Blau, for the benefits that such exchange is expected to bring and in fact often does bring to the principals i.e., self-interest enters into the kinds of social exchange that we initiate and in which we persevere. The benefits, of course, tend to be diffuse. They include the material means of solving the problem at hand or meeting some material needs, but also elements of esteem, affection, and even the pleasures afforded by very process of engaging in the exchange. Williamson (1975) has noted:

The power of economics, in relation to the other social sciences, is to be traced in no small part to its unremitting emphasis on net benefit analysis. Care must be taken, however, lest problems be construed too narrowly. This will occur if net benefits are calculated in transaction-specific terms, when in fact there are interaction effects to be taken into account. . . . However, it may be more accurate, and sometimes even essential, to regard the exchange process itself as an object of value. Concern for atmosphere tends to raise such systems issues; supplying a satisfying exchange relation is made part of the economic problem, broadly construed. (Williamson, 1975, pp. 37–38).

Williamson's references to "atmosphere" and "the exchange process itself as an object of value" sound very much like Blau's social exchange. In social exchange there is "attitudinal spillover" that substitutes, at least in part, for "metering."

As Levitt and Dubner (2005) have reminded us, "there are three basic flavors of incentive: economic, social, and moral," and that "very often a single incentive scheme will include all three varieties" (p. 21). Economist Williamson had pointed this out thirty years previously, that "distinctions between calculative and quasimoral involvements are relevant" (Williamson, 1975, p. 38).

Blau's "social exchange" appears to capture what Williamson termed "quasimoral involvement" and what others describe as "commitment." Organizations disengage from pure economic exchange when bounded rationality, asset specificity, and opportunism render transaction costs excessive. This is not, of course, to assert that economic organizations fall back upon friendship or simple favor-doing as a means of managing. Obviously any employer sets forth some terms of exchange in the relationship with employees – starting salary (which is disciplined at least in part by external labor markets) and certain benefits, in exchange for specified hours of work, requisite qualifications for performing core job function, or at least trainability for those functions. However, bounded rationality sets limitations on what can be specified as part of the exchange thereafter. Much of the exchange must be worked out in recurring interactions between employee and supervisor and among colleagues.

The position taken here is that, to varying degrees, the employee–supervisor relationship generates a process of social exchange. Part of this exchange pertains personally to the supervisor, insofar as the exchange involves expressions of sentiment, and part of the exchange involves the supervisor as agent or mediator of the formal organization's resources and aims. The process and manner in which this evolves go far to lessen transactions costs. Neither party has to specify rigorously what has to be done by the other to "balance the books" or to "fulfill the terms of the contract." Thus, one need not calibrate the validity of the performance appraisal and subsequent pay or benefit increases in terms of how closely they mirror all contributions by the employee. The appraisal and salary increase might well be insufficient recompense for all that the employee contributed in the previous year – the supervisor might even admit as much – but the relationship will continue and in the fullness of time some additional reciprocation, in one form or another, will occur. The appraisal results could also be "too generous," if regarded only in terms of payment for hard measures of accomplishments, but here again the relationship continues, and numerous occasions are likely to arise in which the "over-rewarded" party reciprocates with a sort of commitment to show "good faith" in the relationship. Settoon, Bennett and Liden (1996) and Rhoades and Eisenberger (2002) have reported the empirical connections among employee perceptions of organizational support, leader-member exchange, and OCB.

Yet, as noted above, subjective assessments of OCB inevitably contain some component of error, and it is probably substantial. We might note as well that some degree of "opportunism" probably abounds. It has been plausibly suggested that individuals can resort to "impression management" by strategic and calculated instances of OCB so as to mislead authority figures as to the degree of consummate cooperation that is characteristic of those individuals (e.g., Bolino, 1999). Thus, some errors will occur, however well-intended and conscientious the appraisers might be, and no doubt in some cases these errors will be compounded over some repeated intervals, at times injurious to the employee's interests. When this occurs, some individuals will understandably sense that something is amiss and that the system of which he or she is a part is not fair.

Fairness and transaction costs

Husted and Folger (2004) have argued that transaction costs arise largely due to the difficulty in evaluating the fairness of a specific exchange of goods and services. They seem to imply that a concern for justice is lacking in institutional economic models of the firm. However, Williamson's (1975, 1991) discussion of transaction costs does involve concepts of fairness. Prices set by competitive markets with numerous suppliers and bidders would certainly be described as "fair" by some participants; i.e., the market, given certain conditions, is one particular impersonal and objective arbiter of what is "fair." However, small numbers bargaining, asset specificity, and information asymmetry converge in such a way as to preclude such objectivity about fair exchange. Indeed, that is what the haggling, search, monitoring, and enforcement are all about – costs of reckoning what is a fair exchange, in the absence of competitive markets. No matter that opportunism, "self-interest with guile," lurks as a further complication. This is not to say, as economists are accused of saying, that all behavior is motivated by a narrowly egoistic "self-interest," so much as it is a recognition that self-interest demonstrably colors some of our conceptions of fairness. As social psychologist Gerald Leventhal (1980) has argued, in realistic contexts there are usually competing criteria for fairness, and the weights one attaches to them for some overall justice standard are plausibly tilted towards the criterion that is to one's benefit.

Williamson quotes from Doeringer and Piore (1971) in characterizing the internal labor market as one that develops due process rules that "are thought to effectuate standards of equity that a competitive market cannot or does not respect" (Doeringer and Piore, 1971, p. 29). In other words, the ILM comes into existence precisely because otherwise fairness is either not attainable on one side or the other or because the strenuous efforts required to attain such fairness would generate excessive transactions costs.

Furthermore, one of the defining characteristics of Williamson's (1991) ILM is the intra-firm machinery for resolving enduring, important, and nettlesome issues about fairness. In Williamson's schema, such machinery works to the extent that it is not abused and is reserved for exceptional cases. If a union is present, the union rather than the individual determines which disagreements should be addressed by higher councils.

Husted and Folger's (2004) larger point, however, is well taken, as it concerns not simply a set of objective attributes of arbitration machinery, but the perception on the part of individuals that such structural devices actually do enact fairness in outcomes. Ultimately, it would appear that what participants require, in order to confidently contribute consummate cooperation on a sustained basis for eventual compensation, is something much like Lerner's (1977, 1980) "belief in a just world," or more precisely, the belief that the organization approaches a microcosm of a just world in which deep currents tend toward fairness. Such a belief does not depend on absolute fairness at any moment. Indeed, given the many competing criteria for fairness in varied categories of outcomes, coupled with finite resources available to any firm, fairness for one or a subset of participants, as that person or group perceives it, guarantees that others do not receive what they regard as fair exchange. Furthermore, one could well imagine that those in a position to dispense tangible outcomes do not even attempt to do so in terms of any "pure" criterion of fairness, but rather arrive at some tolerable compromise among different criteria – perhaps not completely satisfying anybody at the time, but effecting an outcome that most if not all can "live with." What matters is the perception by participants that authority figures are making an attempt towards fairness, that they are aware when unavoidable exigencies have occasioned unfairness in the short run, and that, given time, they will take measures to correct inequities.

Husted and Folger (2004) cite the importance of not only distributive justice and procedural justice, but also interactional justice – treating participants with consideration and recognizing their right to dignity – as requisite to a fair system. They refer to persuasive evidence that procedural and interactional justice are particularly important when individuals perceive that distributive justice has not obtained. Here, then, would seem to lie the basis for the ILM adjudication system to address those instances in which faith in the organization as a "just world" has been challenged and to restore that faith among the rank and file. So long as the adjudication system is not overburdened and the outcomes enable a "common law" of fairness to evolve, the savings in transaction costs would seem to make this approach far superior to one in which "high powered incentives" are relied upon for eliciting all forms of constructive contributions.

Friedman's flat-world hypothesis

Our reading of Thomas Friedman's *The World is Flat*, especially when coupled with his previous book, *The Lexus and the Olive Tree*, leads us to believe that ILM-type organizations now face enormous challenges to survival. Friedman asserts that the world has recently entered what he dubs "Globalization 3.0." The first long, gradual stage of globalization – in which countries sought resources on a world stage – lasted for three centuries, roughly 1500–1800. The second stage, with brief interruptions due to war, developed as companies reached out to global markets during 1800–2000, with rapid acceleration of this process occurring during the last two decades of the previous century. What we have now, becoming recognizable roughly with Y2K, is globalization at the level of small groups and individuals. This dimension of globalization comes about as a result of the "convergence" of ten "flattening" (or leveling) forces, which include the entry into the global economic game of three billion new participants (China, India, Russia, and Latin America), the massive over-investment in fiber-optic cable during the dot-com bubble, and worldwide common standards for software and software protocol. WalMart and UPS demonstrated how these developments could be leveraged for worldwide supply chains and logistics, outsourcing and insourcing. Ultimately, what all of these developments lead to is a global market for the talents and skills for a key resource: knowledge workers. The electrical engineer trained and living in the Middle West of the US now competes in the labor market with highly trained technical personnel (and there are many, many of them among the new three billion entrants, because one point of excellence among the educational systems of formerly closed economies was the rigorously meritocratic institutions for scientific and technical training) who do not have to leave Bangalore, Beijing, or St. Petersburg.

Globalization 3.0 will, it is predicted, multiply the effects of previous stages of globalization. One such effect, noted in detail in Friedman's earlier book, is inequality in pay. The prospect is that quite subtle differences in talent will command substantial premiums in salary and perquisites, just as we have already witnessed in professional sports – average pay rises, and the lowest-paid players today are clearly better off than those of previous years, but average pay varies more across teams, and on any one team, the ratio of highest-paid to lowest-paid players is much greater than used to be the case. Rosen (1991) observed that, while "external labor market competition disciplines a firm's internal labor market with respect to overall wages and working conditions, it leaves some slack at the micro-transactions level of precise worker interactions." One wonders how much "slack" will be left as Globalization 3.0 moves apace. A global external labor market will not only dictate what an individual is paid upon being hired, but also what level of pay will be necessary to keep that individual – because there will be little in the way of barriers or "friction" for high-priced talent to move to another firm, regardless of where the other firm is headquartered.

Note that we have referred to the differential pay commanded by differences in talent. While talent is seldom measurable in solely objective terms, meaningful differences can be discerned with some consensus among expert observers by studying a person's background of achievement, training, and reputation within specialized communities. This is not to say that those individuals whose talent is appraised and priced at the highest levels at one point in time are necessarily the most productive or creative participants at some other later time – sports fans can easily point to instances in which an all-star athlete goes to the highest bidder with a mega-bucks contract and fails to deliver the expected results – but rich information about talent is what bidders are willing to bet on.

Established economic indices of inequality reveal that disparity in wealth is, in fact, still less in the US than in the early years of the twentieth century. From 1913 until about 1980, the general trend was toward less variance in income share. From 1980 through the next decade, inequality increased, affecting mainly those groups at the bottom of the scale with less formal education. The increasing income disparity since 1990 appears to affect more of the middle class, which includes many of the knowledge workers in the labor force. What is different about the inequality gradient of today versus that of 1913 is that the wealthy elites of that era enjoyed accumulated wealth of family fortunes (*The Economist*, 2006). In 2006, most of the inequality is due to variance in salaries of the "working rich." And it appears that increasing globalization of factors of production, including labor, have much to do with this phenomenon, with accentuation of this effect likely in the flat world.

So, in such a scenario, what scope remains for OCB? The high-powered incentive for talent-in-use would appear to leave little "slack" for recognizing more subtle, discretionary contributions that resist measurement and documentation.

We have some basis for thinking that inequality *per se*, beyond some point, inhibits OCB. A study by Cowherd and Levine (1992) of more than 100 manufacturing firms found that inequality in pay within the firm correlated with lower levels of quality, as perceived by customers. The researchers did not measure OCB, but suggested that the effect of skewness in the distribution of pay relates to effects on quality by way of the effects on spontaneous contributions to quality among the rank and file. Other studies, in groups as varied as top management teams (Siegel and Hambrick, 2000), professional baseball players (Bloom, 1999), and college professors (Pfeffer and Langton, 1993) have noted the inverse association between inequality and criteria (financial performance, winning percentage, research productivity) of organizational effectiveness.

The relationship between pay disparity and collective performance is certainly not absolute, it is quite unlikely to be linear, and no doubt there are some contexts in which extreme disparities might maximize the motivation *for individual* task performance. In the US, with its emphasis on individualism and meritocracy and the American dream of starting poor and making it rich, no doubt greater differences in pay are accepted without a shrug, if not outright applauded. Most cultures endorse a premium in rewards (although such rewards do not always take the form of pay) for those individuals who bring a rare order of talent to bear upon critical exigencies faced by a group or organization. The apparent consensus of those who have studied this issue is that steep differentials in pay become problems to the extent that interdependence among participants is pervasive and essential to high levels of organizational functioning.

Put another way, pay disparity militates against what Williamson (1975) referred to as "atmosphere," in which the exchange process itself is an object of value, and which enhances the role of "quasi-moral" involvement in the group enterprise. To the extent that such involvement occurs, less "metering" is needed to elicit non-specified contributions to group and organizational effectiveness. Some degree of continued association and interaction of participants is a necessary, but not sufficient, condition for the cultivation of quasi-moral involvement; highly skewed pay distributions can retard or suppress such involvement, to the extent that they breach some threshold of unfairness.

The first author has found in classes of undergraduate and graduate students that they readily endorse the core idea in Adams's (1965) equity theory i.e., that fairness in pay is defined by the equality of ratios of individual pay to individual contributions. More interesting is how these same students responded when the following dilemma is posed to them: Which of the following situations do you find it easier to accept, even though according to equity theory neither is considered fair – situation A, in which your pay is the same as a comparison coworker, even though you have no doubt that your contributions, taken altogether, are clearly greater than that of the coworkers; or situation B, in which your pay is less than that of the coworker, but all reasonable evidence suggests that your contributions are equal to those of the coworker? Repeatedly, 90 percent or more of students report that they have less of a problem with situation A. Given the difficulty of measuring and comparing all forms of contributions that employees might make to the collective effort, one now understands why many supervisors prefer to err on the conservative side when deciding the differential in individual pay increases.

The problem looming in Friedman's Flat World is that supervisors might not have the latitude for constraining pay inequality. If global labor markets bid up base pay rates sharply for the best and the brightest, and if it becomes necessary to bid those rates up even higher to hold talented knowledge workers, all of the funds available for pay increases might have to go to a small number of star task performers.

Considering Williamson's emphasis on the importance of the asset specificity of much human capital i.e., site-specific knowledge, much of it tacit and acquired from experience, market-induced skewness of pay outcomes presents a particularly regrettable effect on those with long tenure in a firm. Such employees, even if highly educated, have likely come to depend on firm-specific knowledge for rendering their contributions, as their formal technical education has become outdated. Their contributions might be estimable, but command no value in the external market place. As their employer competes in the global marketplace for younger knowledge workers with cutting-edge technical skills, the natural temptation for managers with budget constraints is to match the going rate for the most talented of those with the requisite skills, making up the difference by putting the squeeze on the longer-tenured people who command much less in the marketplace. After all, "where can they go?"

Indeed, the long-tenured ranks cannot and probably prefer not to go anywhere. Not only are their contributions primarily limited to the specific firm, by dint of tenure they probably are very much "embedded" (Lee, *et al.*, 1996) by a web of professional, personal, and family ties to the community. "Exit" (Hirschman, 1970) is not a viable option. But "voice" is likely to be unavailing of redress, either. "Loyalty," in the sense of full psychological involvement in and support of the company, would be difficult to maintain. The only option left is, according to Withey and Cooper (1989), "neglect" – which we would translate, not as diminished core task contributions, but the inclination to demonstrate more "perfunctory cooperation" or less OCB.

Another feature posed by the Flat World, with its global demand for talented knowledge people, is what Rousseau (2001) calls the "idiosyncratic deal." The manager, dependent on these knowledge workers and trying to retain them, must negotiate with them about the definition of their roles. The organization, created in order to minimize transaction costs, finds such costs reappearing, with the attendant haggling and potential for opportunistic behavior. To the extent that such idiosyncratic deals culminate in substantial differences in the treatment of subordinates, some sense of citizenship probably is vitiated, and with it the quality, frequency, and spontaneity of discretionary contributions.

In the Flat World, membership in organizations is expected to be brief for many participants. Global labor markets will pay premiums to entice talented stars from one firm to another. Those with insufficient talent to command even the minimum comparative pay needed or expected will try to retool and redefine their occupational identities. More functions of organizations will be outsourced or spun off; even organizations themselves will come and go in a revved-up cycle. As a result, fewer employees will attain the levels of tenure and mutual association among themselves that makes "atmosphere" and "quasi-moral involvement" possible. Social exchange, that form of quasi-moral involvement that induces non-specified contributions, requires the expectation of an indefinite future for exchanges to occur. If someone anticipates that tenure will be brief, there will be little opportunity for present contributions to meet with ample recompense.

Finally, at least in the US, the mechanisms for adjudication of felt unfairness in organizations must find some sponsor other than labor organizations. Less than 15 percent of the US civilian labor force now belongs to a union, down from about 40 percent in 1955. Moreover, much of the present unionized labor force is employed in large-scale manufacturing, where the outlook is for far fewer jobs in the Flat World; much of the remainder of labor unions is concentrated in low-paid services. Such downsizing of labor organizations has not occurred in Western Europe, and in Germany and some Northern European countries, a strong role for worker representation in corporate governance is mandated by national law. However, the US, according to Friedman, is farthest along in the process of globalization, thus the first to reckon with these institutional changes, and the cultural norms in such countries as the Netherlands, Germany, Denmark, Sweden, Norway, Finland, not to mention Japan, have historically acted as a brake against steep differentials in pay.

How might OCB be sustained in the Flat World?

Rosen (1991) notes, in his essay on transaction costs and how they are minimized in the internal labor market, that *reputation* plays an important role. That is to say, the community has a collective memory that translates into reputations concerning individuals, the nature and extent of their non-task contributions, and the general character of their involvement in the enterprise. Intrusive metering is not needed to discourage "shirking," because shirking has an adverse effect on reputation, just as it does in commercial dealings in the community.

Conceivably, reputational effects could transcend the organization. The career movements of highly mobile and talented performers will likely occur within closely connected networks (many of which could be "virtual") of persons, professions, and firms around the world. The same technologies that create the Flat World also render such a world highly interconnected.

We suspect that these interconnections enable much exchange of information that goes beyond the purely technical dimensions of work. Academics who regularly attend their specialized conferences know that the halls are rife with talk about the personality, character, and "colleagueship" of the celebrated performers (whether in scholarship, teaching, or administration) in their fields. In a globally connected grid, we might well find that reputational effects about OCB become commonplace. If so, and if talented knowledge workers are mindful of this, such performers will seek to establish their reputations for cooperation and other forms of OCB much as they solidify their reputation for intellect and skill.

During a televised pro basketball game some years ago, the announcer commented that Boston Celtic center Bill Cowens was highly regarded by his peers and pro hoops community, not because of his talent, but his effort. Color commentator Bill Russell, himself a legendary center for Boston, said, "Well, they're wrong, because effort *is a talent*, and it's the most important one you can have." Could such comments become routine in global communications about individuals in their fields of endeavor?

Indeed, in the Flat World, in which an employee might live in India while employed by a firm in Western Europe or North America, we might well come to understand the importance of something like "virtual OCB." If much of the work is performed and coordinated in the virtual dimension, we see no reason why OCB cannot also take upon itself a virtual character. Cooperation, helping, encouragement, conscientiousness, recognition of coworker contributions, can certainly take digitized forms.

Furthermore, even as organized labor becomes less of a direct factor in the structures and systems of organization, we hear more in recent years about how some non-union settings have taken a page from labor contracts and put in place offices and procedures for addressing member concerns about fair treatment and due process. Cigna and Federal Express have perhaps the best known programs of non-union companies that have adopted some features of union grievance procedures to promote *procedural fairness* (Ewing, 1989). Indeed, there might now be more employees with access to grievance channels in non-union firms than in companies with unions, a development that Ewing (1989) predicted almost two decades ago.

If the economic flattening of the world renders the internal labor market as an increasingly fragile institution, questions that arise are: (1) Does such a world really require OCB, as we now define it? (2) Does such a world present near frictionless transactional processes, such that transaction costs that formerly were burdensome become negligible? (3) If some forms of OCB will always be essential to organizational effectiveness, might the Flat World itself provide new structural devices for valuing and sustaining OCB? and (4) If OCB remains important and cannot be sensed by impersonal market forces, is it conceivable that societies will, to one degree or another, gradually evolve cultural norms (such as those of Scandinavia) about inequality in pay and status that will inhibit the steepness of market differentials?

REFERENCES

Adams, J. S. (1965) Inequity in social exchange. In L. Berkowitz (ed.), *Advances in experimental psychology* (Vol. 2). New York: Academic Press.

Allen, T. D. and Rush, M. C. (1998) The effects of organizational citizenship behavior on performance judgments: A field study and a laboratory experiment. *Journal of Applied Psychology*, *31*(*12*), 2561–87.

Bahrick, H. P. (1954) Incidental learning under two incentive conditions. *Journal of Experimental Psychology*, *47*, 170–72.

Bahrick, H. P., Fitts, P. M. and Rankin, R. E. (1952) Effects of incentives upon reactions to peripheral stimuli. *Journal of Experimental Psychology*, *44*, 400–6.

Barnard, C. I. (1938) *The functions of the executive.* Cambridge: Harvard University Press.

Blau, P. M. (1964) *Exchange and power in social life.* New York: Wiley.

Bloom, M. (1999) The performance effects of pay dispersion on individuals and organizations. *Academy of Management Journal*, *42*, 25–40.

Bolino, M. C. (1999) Citizenship and impression management: Good soldiers or good actors? *Academy of Management Review*, *24*, 82–98.

Bolino, M. C., Turnley, W. H. and Bloodgood, J. M. (2002) Citizenship behavior and the creation of social capital in organizations. *Academy of Management Review*, *27*(*4*), 505–22.

Borman, W. C. and Motowidlo, S. J. (1997) Task performance and contextual performance: The meaning for personnel selection research. *Human Performance*, *10*, 99–109.

Brehm, J. W. (1966) *A theory of psychological reactance.* New York: Academic Press.

Brehm, J. W. (1972) *Responses to loss of freedom: A theory of psychological reactance.* Morristown: General Learning Press.

Cowherd, D. M. and Levine, D. I. (1992) Product quality and pay equity between lower-level employees and top management: An investigation of distributive justice theory. *Administrative Science Quarterly*, *37*, 302–20.

Deci, E. L. (1975) Intrinsic Motivation. New York: Plenum Press.

Doeringer, P. and Piore, M. (1971) *Internal labor markets and manpower analysis.* Lexington: Heath.

Easterbrook, J. A. (1959) The effect of emotion on cue utilization and the organization of behavior. *Psychological Review*, *66*(*3*), 183–201.

The Economist: "The rich, the poor, and the growing gap between them." June 17, 2006.

Ewing, D. W. (1989) *Justice on the job: Resolving grievances in the nonunion workplace.* Boston: Harvard Business School Press.

Friedman, T. L. (1999) *The Lexus and the olive tree.* New York: Farrar, Straus and Giroux.

  (2005) *The world is flat: A brief history of the twenty-first century.* New York: Farrar, Straus and Giroux.

Glucksberg, S. (1962) The influence of strength of drive on functional fixedness and perceptual recognition. *Journal of Experimental Psychology, 63,* 36–41.

Hirschman, A. O. (1970) *Exit, voice, and loyalty: Responses to decline in firms, organizations, and states.* Cambridge: Harvard University Press.

Husted, B. W. and Folger, R. (2004) Fairness and transaction costs: The contribution of organizational justice theory to an integrative model of economic organization. *Organization Science, 15(6),* 719–29.

Kiker, D. S. and Motowidlo, S. J. (1999) Main and interaction effects of task and contextual performance on supervisory reward decisions. *Journal of Applied Psychology, 84(4),* 602–9.

Koys, D. J. (2001) The effects of employee satisfaction, organizational citizenship behavior, and turnover on organizational effectiveness: A unit-level, longitudinal study. *Personnel Psychology, 54(1),* 101–14.

Lee, T. W., Mitchell, T. R., Wise, L. and Fireman, S. (1996) An unfolding model of voluntary employee turnover. *Academy of Management Journal, 39,* 5–36.

Lepper, M. R. and Greene, D. (eds.) (1978) *The hidden costs of reward.* Hillsdale: Erlbaum.

Lerner, M. J. (1977) The justice motive: Some hypotheses as to its origins and forms. *Journal of Personality, 45,* 1–52.

  (1980) *The belief in a just world: A fundamental delusion.* New York: Plenum Press.

Leventhal, G. S. (1980) What should be done with equity theory? New approaches to the study of fairness in social relationships. In K. G. Gergen, M. S. Greenberg and R. H. Willis (eds.), *Social exchange: Advances in theory and research.* New York: Plenum Press.

Levitt, S. D. and Dubner, S. J. (2005) *Freakonomics: A rogue economist explores the hidden side of everything.* New York: William Morrow.

McGraw, K. O. and McCullers, J. C. (1979) Evidence of a detrimental effect of extrinsic incentives on breaking a mental set. *Journal of Experimental Social Psychology, 15,* 285–94.

Morrison, E. W. (1994) Role definitions and organizational citizenship behavior: The importance of the employee's perspective. *Academy of Management Journal, 37(6),* 1543–67.

Organ, D. W. (1988) *Organizational citizenship behavior: The good soldier syndrome.* Lexington: Lexington Books.

Organ, D. W. and Paine, J. B. (2000) Contingent and marginal employment, commitment, and discretionary contributions. In Hodson, R. (ed.), *Research in the sociology of work, vol. 9,* pp. 253–70. Stamford: JAI Press.

Organ, D. W., Podsakoff, P. M. and MacKenzie, S. B. (2006) *Organizational citizenship behavior: Its nature, antecedents, and consequences.* Thousand Oaks: Sage Publications.

Orr, J. M., Sackett, P. R. and Mercer, M. (1989) The role of prescribed and nonprescribed behaviors in estimating the dollar value of performance. *Journal of Applied Psychology, 74,* 34–40.

Ouchi, W. G. (1980) Markets, bureaucracies, and clans. *Administrative Science Quarterly, 25,* 129–41.

Park, O. S. (1986) *Beyond cognition in leadership: Prosocial behavior and affect in managerial judgment*. Unpublished doctoral dissertation, Pennsylvania State University, State College.

Pfeffer, J. and Langton, N. (1993) The effect of wage dispersion on satisfaction, productivity, and working collaboratively: Evidence from college and university faculty. *Administrative Science Quarterly*, 38, 382–407.

Pfeffer, J. and Sutton, R. I. (2006) *Hard facts, dangerous half-truths, and total nonsense*. Boston: Harvard Business School Press.

Podsakoff, P. M. and MacKenzie, S. B. (1997) Impact of organizational citizenship behavior on organizational performance: A review and suggestions for future research. *Human Performance*, 10(2), 133–51.

Podsakoff, P. M., MacKenzie, S. B. and Hui, C. (1993) Organizational citizenship behaviors and managerial evaluations of employee performance: A review and suggestions for future research. In G. R. Ferris and K. M. Rowland (eds.), *Research in personnel and human resources management (Vol. 11)*. Greenwich: JAI Press.

Podsakoff, P. M., MacKenzie, S. B., Paine, J. B. and Bachrach, D. G. (2000) Organizational citizenship behaviors: A critical review of the theoretical and empirical literature and suggestions for future research. *Journal of Management*, 26(3), 513–63.

Rhoades, L. and Eisenberger, R. (2002) Perceived organizational support: A review of the literature. *Journal of Applied Psychology*, 87(4), 698–714.

Rosen, S. (1991) Transaction costs and internal labor markets. In Williamson, O. E. and Winter, S. G. (eds.), *The nature of the firm: Origins, evolution, and development*. New York: Oxford University Press.

Rousseau, D. M. (2001) The idiosyncratic deal: Flexibility versus fairness? *Organizational Dynamics*, 29, 260–73.

Scholl, R. W. (1981) Differentiating organizational commitment from expectancy as a motivating force. *Academy of Management Review*, 6, 589–99.

Settoon, R. P., Bennett, N. and Liden, R. C. (1996) Social exchange in organizations: Perceived organizational support, leader-member exchange, and employee reciprocity. *Journal of Applied Psychology*, 81, 219–27.

Shore, L. M., Barksdale, K. and Cross, T. H. (1995) Managerial perceptions of employee commitment to the organization. *Academy of Management Journal*, 38(6), 1593–1615.

Siegel, P. A. and Hambrick, D. C. (2005) Pay disparities within top management groups: Evidence of harmful effects on performance of high-technology firms. *Organization Science*, 16, 259–74.

Simon, H. (1961) *Administrative behavior*. New York: Macmillan.

Strickland, L. H. (1958) Surveillance and trust. *Journal of Personality*, 26, 200–15.

Van Scotter, J. R., Motowidlo, S. J. and Cross, T. C. (2000) Effects of task performance and contextual performance on systemic rewards. *Journal of Applied Psychology*, 85(4), 526–35.

Walz, S. M. and Niehoff, B. P. (2000) Organizational citizenship behaviors: Their relationship to organizational effectiveness. *Journal of Hospitality and Tourism Research*, 24, 301–19.

Williamson, O. E (1975) *Markets and hierarchies: Analysis and antitrust implications*. New York: Free Press.

Williamson, O. E. (1991) *The nature of the firm: Origins, evolution, and development*. New York: Oxford University Press.

Williamson, O. E., Wachter, M. and Harris, J. (1975) Understanding the employment relation: The analysis of idiosyncratic exchange. *6 Bell Journal of Economics*, 250–80.

Whithey, M. J. and Cooper, W. H. (1989) Predicting exit, voice, loyalty, and neglect. *Administrative Science Quarterly*, *34*, 521–39.

Wright, P. M., George, J. M., Farnsworth, S. R. and McMahan, G. C. (1993) Productivity and extra-role behavior: The effects of goals and incentives on spontaneous helping. *Journal of Applied Psychology*, *78*, 374–81.

Zajonc, R. B. (1965) Social facilitation. *Science*, *39*, 269–74.

4　Best practices for work stress and well-being

Solutions for human dilemmas in organizations

Alvin L. Gibson and James Campbell Quick

According to the American Institute of Stress, work stress may well have reached epidemic proportions in the United States, the United Kingdom, and other industrialized nations. Therefore, work stress clearly qualifies as a significant organizational challenge for workers, for their leaders, and for their executives. No one is immune in the twenty-first century workplace. While this both chronic and epidemic problem is a true human dilemma for everyone in organizations, it is just that: a problem. As such, it has one or more solutions. We aim to offer a set of solutions for the human dilemmas that proceed from the challenge created by work stress with the intention to enhance the well-being of workers. The best practice solutions offered in this chapter are based on sound theory and research, on the one hand, and practical relevance and applicability on the other. We address seven best practice areas: supervisory support and executive stress management; job design, scheduling and work flow; communication pathways and information modes; work and family; positive stress (eustress); fairness and organizational justice and HRM systems integrity. We conclude with an emphasis on the human side of the enterprise and the critical importance of humane leadership in highly stressful workplaces.

"You can't let a corporation turn into a labor camp."
Lee Iacocca, from Iacocca

While we are living longer, we may be suffering more. This has been called the Age of Anxiety based in part on a one standard deviation increase in anxiety levels within the US population during the period 1952–1993. Anxiety disorders, one of the two most common presenting complaints for stress, affect one in every six people in the US and one in every five employed people in the UK (Cooper and Quick, 1999). The American Institute of Stress calls job stress a health epidemic based on a set of indicators, including self-report surveys, unscheduled absence data, violent incidents at work, and job loss numbers (Rosch, 2001). The 2001 Labor Day survey by The Marlin Company in collaboration with the American Institute of Stress found 35 percent of employees report that their jobs are harming their physical and emotional health. In addition, 50 percent of employees reported a more demanding workload than a year earlier and 42 percent say job pressures are interfering with their personal relationships.

As early as 1980, NIOSH identified stress and psychological disorders in the workplace as one of the top ten occupational health hazards in America (Millar, 1984). Layoffs and downsizing continued through the 1990s, with their adverse effects on employee, managerial, and executive stress (Morris, Cascio and Young, 1999). Epidemic means "upon the people" when literally translated from the Greek (Tyler and Last, 1998). Epidemiology is the basic science and most fundamental practice of public health and preventive medicine. Epidemics of infection are often assessed on three indicators which are: (1) the percent of the population affected by the disease, (2) the rate of spread of the disease, and (3) the intensity of the adverse impact of the disease. While the ancients often lacked adequate knowledge to do little more than observe victims and record mortality, the evolution of preventive medicine from the mid-1800s affords greater power to stop epidemics (Wallace and Doebbeling, 1998). Treatment alone is rarely effective in the management of epidemics.

Work stress creates significant human dilemmas for people in organizations because it is ubiquitous and because it is not an acute problem with a single cause. Rather, stress is a chronic problem with multiple causes in the workplace. In addition, there are significant individual differences in terms of both the causes and consequences of work stress. What one worker sees as stressful another worker may well see as a challenge. Thus, we have mapped the domain of the work environment in organizations and identified nine areas which may be key sources of stress for workers. These seven well-being and stress best practice areas are:
• supervisory support and executive stress management;
• job design, scheduling and work flow;
• communication pathways and information modes;
• work and family;
• positive stress (eustress);
• fairness and organizational justice;
• HRM systems integrity.

Supervisory support and executive stress management

Managers, from supervisors to executives, have multiple support roles concerning stress. These are critical roles for them to fulfill if they are to help others avert distress while minimizing and managing stress risks. One example of such a role is offering support in various ways to employees. Another is easing the path and playing a triage function for outside sources, such as HR and Occupational Health, to help them. Although managers are not expected to be counselors, they are expected to use compassion and good communication skills when dealing with stress-related circumstances (Boyatzis, Smith and Blaize, 2006; Lait and Wallace, 2002).

A greater consistency of approach is needed from managers in dealing with stress. There is a need for mandatory and relevant training for supervisory through executive level managers, including at senior levels of government as done by Cary L. Cooper for cabinet ministers through the Sunnydale Institute. This is provided to help bring along and keep current the skills and knowledge needed for them to implement organizational policies, including stress-reduction programs. This training will include topics of stress and mental health problems at work, work stress monitoring, and ways of acting to lessen stress-related problems at work (Ornelas and Kleiner, 2003). Overall it should be targeted to help them identify stress-related circumstances and minimize stress risks to individuals, teams, and the organization.

Supervisory support

Supervisory support regarding absences often includes referral of employees to relevant support services. Increased absence may indicate underlying stress problems either at work or at home. Employees' poor performance and attendance due to stress should be managed to prevent unnecessary pressures on colleagues in teams. As part of this, at team meetings supervisors should facilitate open discussion of stress-related issues. It is good to remember that adopting an "open-door" policy will enable managers to be more approachable and help them to identify stress problems at an early stage.

Organizational justice is the extent to which employees are treated fairly in their workplace settings. Its two components are procedural justice, which refers to the fairness of workplace rules and policies, and relational justice, which is related to "the polite and considerate treatment of individuals by supervisors" (Kivimaki *et al.*, 2003, p. 27). The level of employee justice has been shown to impact employee health, stress, and depression (Kivimaki *et al.*, 2003).

Supervisor behavior was found to be an influential variable in predicting psychosocial work conditions beyond that explained by other variables. These results indicated that if employees rated their supervisor's behavior above average, the probability was 63 percent that their psychological well-being score would also be above average (Gilbreath and Benson, 2004). Separately, supervisor supportiveness was found to be related to subordinates' psychological well-being, and abusive supervision was associated with psychological distress (Tepper, 2000).

Executives and stress

Executives need special support for their work-related well being. A major reason for this is that these persons are called upon in open-ended ways to serve other employees and the organization. They often have fewer support people and financial resources than in a previous era, yet are called upon to achieve higher levels of performance. Because these persons are essential to the organization's status quo, special resources should be devoted to limiting their stress levels to moderate levels. Often managers are expected to delegate more authority to others, yet the ultimate accountability remains with them. This creates a potentially nightmare situation. However, preoccupation with their own stress levels should not be an excuse for executives to become out-of-touch with the stress-related problems of their employees (DeFrank and Ivancevich, 1998).

One possibly extreme set of circumstances to be reckoned with in the workplace involves executives whose age, lack of education, or both become a potential liability to top management. These executives may be viewed as incapable, too poorly trained, or insufficiently flexible to move forward with the organization. As a result top management must decide whether to replace these executives with younger, college graduates. Making these decisions is indeed stressful, not only for the executives but also for the entire organization (DeFrank and Ivancevich, 1998).

Best practice statement

Excellence in leadership and supervision displays high, clear expectations of people coupled with support, care, and concern for the individual's well-being.

Job design, scheduling and work flow

The conditions under which employees actually work may need to be explored and addressed before there can be lasting success from initiatives to reduce excessive employee stress. Simply employing stress counseling, Employee Assistance Programs, or flexible work policies may not get at the root of the problem (Caudron, 1998). Problems with supervision, a lack of resources, or understaffing are likely to require decisions that improve the employee's work setting before circumstances are markedly improved.

Increases in organizational flexibility have led to a decrease in worker flexibility and an increase in stress. Examples are lengthened work hours to service customers and expanded responsibilities after layoffs. This zero-sum relationship occurs when time or labor is a major flexibility variable, and less when technology helps the organization to operate with fewer employees. The reverse may occur as well. That is, job sharing, work-at-home practices, and flexible hours can lessen an organization's scheduling latitude while reducing worker stress (Harenstam, 2005). Extreme decreases in worker flexibility can lead to employee turnover, while corresponding organizational flexibility decreases may lead to plant relocation. Best-practices organization initially seek to avoid setting up such zero-sum circumstances. Failing that, they find the best balance for both their employees and the organization, while exploring more effective ways to handle the underlying issues involved.

The use of teams may have one of several net effects on stress, including reducing or magnifying work stress or eustress. Some factors that affect stress are the type of team (e.g., cross-functional, self-managed, ad hoc); relationship fits of individuals within the team; team homogeneity or heterogeneity; the nature of the team's mission; and the team's level of autonomy (Geurts and Grundemann, 1999). Additionally, the purpose of the team is a strong factor in the amount of stress generated. If a team exists to create and make feasible a product that is expected to be vital to the organization, the potential for high amounts of stress is greater than if the team's formation was for the purpose of finding the best location for a new company parking lot. Organizations that do most to help their teams handle stress will document and chronicle the stress conditions for each of their teams. This step is necessary for understanding to evolve.

More specifically, team-related stress may increase for one of the following reasons (DeFrank and Ivancevich, 1998), all which should be documented and understood but some of which may not be cost-effective to address:

- some employees simply function far better as individuals than they do in group settings;
- some employees have no interest in learning team processes or structures;
- employees may have insufficient preparation, training, or compensation;
- empowerment and greater responsibility may not appeal to employees with low growth-need strength.

A classic of increase in stress occurs with uncertainty or the employee has a situation that results in increased stress levels with conflicting job expectations. For example, this may occur when an employee has more than one supervisor, customer expectations clash with organizational regulations or capabilities; or responsibilities within the work unit are poorly delineated (Ornelas and Kleiner, 2003). These cause role conflict or role ambiguity. Often fellow employees do not notice a problem until a similar circumstance occurs that directly involves them. Supervisors tend to focus on work process and output and may, unless trained to consider work stress, never consider asking the employee about the stress implications of their current situation. Best-practice organizations catch these problems before they occur, or are in the very early stages of formation, and use open two-way communication to smoothly implement effective corrective actions.

"Rapid and abrupt" changes in culture and technology within our workplaces and lifestyles may bring about frequent and intense stress (DeFrank and Ivancevich, 1998, p. 55). For this reason it is advisable to consider how changes in the workplace alter the culture, whether initiated by the organization or not. An example of a change with cultural and other implications not initiated by the organization is change brought about by the events of September 11, 2001. When it is possible, either the changes themselves or their effects may need to be altered by speeding them up, slowing them down, neutralizing or canceling them. The end result is to optimally balance corporate goals, including those of holding worker stress to acceptable levels.

To control the effects of rapid changes when introducing technology, modern practices often introduce new technologies by initially using the old worker control interfaces. Over time the interfaces are altered in a gradual manner that drastically reduces worker stress and uncertainty. In some cases the interfaces only need to be altered a little. As a result worker stress is minimized, turnover due to the changes is low, morale is usually maintained or improved, and the desired organizational productivity and other improvements are able to be realized, often on schedule (Michailidis and E-ali Elwkai, 2003).

Best practice statement

Superior collection and compilation of source, or independent variable, data on stress states and causal stress elements throughout the organization's work settings affords the chance to begin real understanding of the organization's most stressful work circumstances.

Communication pathways and information modes

This is probably the most potent of all the topic areas, and is certainly the most comprehensive. Communication is a significant component of every other stress reduction issue. Communication patterns that reduce stress throughout the organization are likely to have a holistic and beneficial impact. Best-practice organizations realize that the level of efficiency of an organization's communication is inevitably linked to its major success outcomes, including goal effectiveness, lowering distress and increasing eustress, and helping employees to thrive.

Office hostility is a common problem in many workplaces. From initial impressions and widely disseminated media descriptions, offices appear as admirably genteel settings. But those inside these organizations have become familiar with behavior such as (Johnson and Indvik, 2001):

- negative eye contact such as "dirty looks";
- insults and yelling;
- public reprimands;
- demeaning comments;
- disruption of meetings.

Work stress can be either a cause or an effect of office hostility. As a cause, those suffering from stress treat others poorly, mirroring how they themselves have been treated. For example, supervisors suffering under extremely demanding work directives may be overbearing and demeaning to their employees, lowering morale and increasing negative behavior among workers (Johnson and Indvik, 2001). As an effect, stress is often a product of communication problems that occur during transformations such as downsizings, acquisitions, and mergers. During these circumstances some give-and-take between employees is often common. This is associated with a hostile climate of anger, withdrawal, and impulsiveness.

Some steps that can be taken to remedy the above are as follows (Johnson and Indvik, 2001):

- eliminate the belief that damaging stress is an essential by-product of operating one's organization;
- fit people to jobs better – in jobs with the most unavoidable stress place people for whom the stress level of those jobs is not excessive;
- know, understand, and act to change the organization's climate where propensities exist for sabotage, bullying, depression, lack of loyalty, sexual harassment, discrimination, and other stress-related factors that harm communication within the organization;
- ensure that top management behaves in a highly facilitating and friendly manner, thus modeling the behaviors it wishes to see in the workplace.

The way that an organization chooses to communicate important events affects employee stress. With acquisitions or mergers, workers who had a high level of satisfaction with the way the organization communicated the event were shown to have fewer sources of stress (Lotz and Donald, 2006). Organizations that are the most effective in reducing stress carefully manage contacts with employees regarding important events will control the framing of important issues in advance; anticipate and adequately respond to employee concerns; keep lines of contact open and create new ones in advance; and monitor employees' levels of suspicion and misgivings (Li-Ping Tang and Fuller, 1995).

Communication during restructuring

When implementing stress-reducing work restructuring of core goods or service processes, it is essential that for best-practice stress reduction, facile communication lines become established and remain open (Moretz, 1989). These lines start to be created during the stages of negotiating and planning the restructuring. They are fully actualized as the new work roles, technology and other changes come into being. Once the new goods or services processes are up and running, the ability to communicate effectively will be essential during the period that the processes are being optimized. A reduction in stress arises from the ability of all parties to fully express themselves during all phases of the restructuring. This allows them to integrate who they are as people with what they are as occupation holders (Henderson and Argyle, 1985).

Employees directly involved in the core processes for best-practice stress-reducing organizations first obtain an early understanding of the benefits of restructuring for them and their firm. Second, management views them, or a representative subset of them, as a partner in the restructuring planning alongside other involved parties such as consultants and specialists. Third, as the changes actually occur there is a mutual willingness between employees and managers to share uncertainties about previously-agreed upon items or plans. This is an indicator of a healthy communication process and should lead to a better overall implementation. This is linked to cultural maturity (Nytro *et al.*, 2000), a concept that points to the importance of worker empowerment as an indicator of organizational capability in managing a change process.

Organizations that are most successful in their efforts to reduce work stress realize that social support from fellow workers has the potential to be a strong possible stress-reduction force. These organizations work to formalize organizationally approved or created social support forms that have been shown to be effective in reducing work stress. Social support can be one of the most potent stress-reducing communication forms because fellow workers have a greater sensitivity to fellow employees' individual tendencies regarding stress. The same situation may be highly stressful for one employee, relaxing for another (Michailidis and Georgiou, 2005); they are typically more willing and able to communicate stress more fully with each other because of their similar status; and they often are more receptive to fellow workers' solutions. Consistently providing social support is an indicator of a management culture that supports worker health (Lyons, 2002).

Based on Fairbrother and Warn's (2003) notions of stress and teamwork, we propose the concept of "stress matching". This is a process of matching workers with critical stress issues with workers who have successfully resolved these same issues. For example, a panel of workers would administer a survey to identify: (1) which critical work stress issues each worker is currently facing, using carefully selected issues; and (2) which of these critical work stress issues each worker had successfully resolved. A select panel of workers would then engage in a mapping and matching process, depicted in Figure 4.1, so as to match workers for stress resolution. A six or twelve-month follow-up would be conducted to assess the effectiveness of this "stress matching" effort.

Organizations should ensure that all workers have access to initiatives and services that may be beneficial to them, such as counselling (Shain and Kramer, 2004). The authors have entitled this "the principle of convenience". These initiatives or services should be certain to look for, among others, employees at their earliest possible state of readiness; those who may have high need for

1. Pool of Workers With Critical Stress Issues

Issue A	Issue B	Issue C
Worker 1	Worker 3	Worker 5
Issue D	Issue E	Issue F
Worker 7	Worker 9	Worker 11

2. Pool of Workers Who Resolved Critical Stress Issues

Issue A	Issue B	Issue C
Worker 2	Worker 4	Worker 6
Issue D	Issue E	Issue F
Worker 8	Worker 10	Worker 12

2. Matching Workers With Needs to Workers with Solutions

Issue A	Issue B	Issue C
Worker 1 with	Worker 3 with	Worker 5 with
Worker 2	Worker 4	Worker 6
Issue D	Issue E	Issue F
Worker 7 with	Worker 9 with	Worker 11 with
Worker 8	Worker 10	Worker 12

Figure 4.1   Stress matching: Pairing workers for critical stress issue resolution

the services but low motivation to go after them; workers who are receiving inadequate or even negative support; and those who are in occupational circumstances associated with a high need for the services, such as employees who work consistently long hours.

Best practice statement

Positive and open communication patterns nurture workers and the organization's culture, helping both to thrive.

Work and family

Organizations with the best stress reduction practices realize that an employee's work can have a positive psychological effect on his or her home life, and that home life can positively support work (DeFrank and Ivancevich, 1998). The most effective programs use work and family to support each other. Work can support family, making it easier for family to support work, by allowing time off for family concerns; letting family members communicate (within reason) while one is on the job; providing resources to help take care of infants and elderly relatives; and providing excellent health care insurance to provide for families' needs. In addition to lower work and home stress, the introduction of such programs has resulted in lower absenteeism, increased retention, elevated employee morale, lowered health care costs, greater commitment, and an increase in productivity.

Initiatives

Work and family conflict has been related to employee well-being (Grant-Vallone and Donaldson, 2001). Typical initiatives provided by firms to address work and family concerns include the following:
- liberalized policies on medical leave, and maternity and paternity leave that go beyond federally-mandated guidelines;
- family leave, including leave for adoption, foster care and, family care;
- options for elder and dependent care;
- sabbaticals for employees;
- flexible work schedules with options on such factors as daily hours worked, days worked per week, daily start and finish times (DeFrank and Ivancevich, 1998).

Demand and feasibility

Before work and family programs are implemented, best practice organizations determine how much their employees actually want them and the projected participation rate for each program. There should also be an investigation of the probability that the projected benefits of the programs will indeed be achieved. Projected benefits for both the organization and employees should be investigated in this regard (Mulcahy, 2003).

The issue of employees who, for one reason or another, do not use work and family programs should also be explored. These employees often do not appreciate the value of the benefits that their fellow employees are receiving. Many are young employees, do not have children, or have no elder or family care concerns. While their fellow employees are receiving time off, they are left to mind the shop. While work stress is decreasing among the favored groups, those left out may experience increased stress due to feelings of resentment and an increased workload (DeFrank and Ivancevich, 1998).

Cost effectiveness of Work–Family programs

Can work and family programs be cost effective? One reason they are increasingly popular in the face of tight budgets, layoffs, and overall cuts in health and retirement benefits is that these programs typically save money. They save workers time, greatly lower their preoccupation with non-work factors while on the job, and can drastically lower costs related to family care. Because they ameliorate some of their greatest potential concerns, work and family programs are associated with reduced stress and greater worker satisfaction (Lyons, 2002; Walls, Capella and Greene, 2001). In turn, organizations are able to operate with greater stability, higher productivity, less turnover, and become perceived as first-choice organizations by prospective jobseekers (Mulcahy, 2003).

Work vs family dichotomies

The best stress-management programs are able to deal with dichotomies. It cannot be denied that there are some inherent zero-sum relationships between work versus family. A major one is time. It is almost impossible, to be simultaneously engaged in intense work while one is wholly devoted to a family activity. Another zero-sum area is occupational skills and up-to-date experience. Leaving work to devote oneself wholly to family life results in a steady loss of these skills and represents a cost to the individual and, by some accounts, to society. A third is, possibly, interaction time. Individuals who experience "interaction fatigue" on the job may shun interaction in family settings (Abdel-Halim, 1981). A fourth is rewards for dedication and exemplary performance. Job-related recognition and status does not usually translate to recognition and status in the family, and vice versa. These zero-sum relationships are important to work stress because, when one devotes oneself greatly to work, the lack of balance with home life mentioned above may become a cause of heightened family stress. A child, for example, may experience few opportunities to be with a parent because of that parent's work schedule. Best-practice organizations realize these zero-sum circumstances occur commonly and effectively find ways to limit the employee's work involvement (subject to that individual's volition) without overly limiting the worker's career path. Employees who minimize their work involvement for the sake of family life are still valued, but usually lose the opportunity for an optimized career life (Walls, Capella and Greene, 2001).

Best practice statement

Work and family programs continue to expand because organizations find them profitable and employees find them necessary to reduce stress and care for their loved ones.

Positive stress (Eustress)

Organizational initiatives to increase eustress

Since eustress is "good stress", organizations should seek to maximize its presence and to minimize "distress", or bad stress. Best-practice organizations consciously employ resources in recognition of this. For example, facilitating communication between employees new to a task and those with the greatest experience on that task will reduce the inexperienced employees' distress and promote eustress.

Examples of work events that may generate eustress necessarily overlap greatly with those that produce distress. Selection- and placement-related circumstances such as employee entry into the organization; promotion; demotion; or transfer often produce both negative and positive stress (LePine, LePine and Jackson, 2004). Singling out employees for rewards, discipline, or other circumstances are further examples of events that produce both. Circumstances that occur universally such as performance appraisal; entry or removal of a person who is or was highly meaningful to a particular employee; and impacts of organizational change do much in this regard.

Before an organization can move strongly to help increase eustress, it has to get past the view that workers are completely responsible for their reactions to organization-set tasks and goals. It is true that an identical work event may be a source of distress in one person and eustress in another (Rothmann, Steyn and Mostert, 2005). One person experiences it as the high point of the day while another has a bad day because of it. Eustress and distress, then, are largely, and perhaps ultimately, products of individual perception. It is to be remembered, however, that these perceptions occur as reactions to and within a defined work environment. Thus, although the individual owns the perceptions and eustress or distress, the work environment owns the work process and product. As a result, despite the fact that individual response differences to stressors do exist, best-practice organizations search for the full locus of possibilities available for them to help their employees experience positive challenges on the job.

Organizations stand to benefit in several ways by increasing eustress (Townsend, 2001). Cost savings from less absence, fewer medications, and reduced health care needs would be realized if employees experienced greater positive stress and less negative stress (Ornelas and Kleiner, 2003). Productivity increases can result from more efficient usage of cognitive energies, particularly when knowledge work is involved. Best-practice stress reduction organizations strive for communication that is less centered on issues perceived to be insurmountable or overwhelming and more focused on attaining organizational goals. A final benefit is that a work–family balance is more easily attained by employees who focus more exclusively on their home lives when not at work.

Leadership and eustress

To maximize eustress, best-practice organizations exert leadership influence when assigning new tasks or goals and communicate clearly regarding existing employee goals. Goals that are difficult but attainable for each employee represent the best fits. Each employee has a somewhat different mix of skill sets, preferences, experiences, and tolerance for ambiguity. The best stress-reducing organizations do not "stretch" employees beyond their capabilities, but do increase their comfort zones in knowledge, skills, and abilities. This requires optimistic leadership (Peterson and Luthans, 2003). It is a key role of organizational leaders to maximize the output of employees, and best-practice leaders carefully ponder the effects of their actions on stress levels (Lines *et al.*, 2005).

Given the importance of initial goal communication to employees (Ornelas and Kleiner, 2003), executives in best-practice organizations realize their supervisors need to consider the tactics and procedures they use when introducing new goals and initiatives. Top management may wish to provide general guidelines that emphasize the desired outcome of this communication. One of the ends in view will be emphasizing a positive process for the employee (Gilbreath and Benson, 2004).

Knowledge exchange and eustress

Efficient sharing of knowledge within the organization is a major issue in our information–critical work environments. A substantive and ongoing communication process itself can be a major source of positive stress (Townsend, 2001). This process first requires requests for information from elsewhere in the organization to be consistently honored. Second, it calls for increases in a work unit's organizational knowledge, often acquired through painstaking experience, to be made available to the organization generally rather than hoarded for selective future use by the work team or business-unit level manager. Third, being a best-practice organization presupposes a communications base between work units that informs them of the most pressing knowledge needs of the others. This facilitates a culture that is marked by the proactive sending of information by one work unit to another.

Organizational culture and eustress

The organization's shared values, norms, and goals can promote eustress. Best-practice organizations possess a culture that promotes positive communication, sharing of resources, and clearly defined goals at all levels (Lines *et al.*, 2005). This allows employees to stay focused on salient processes and anticipated events (Ornelas and Kleiner, 2005). Eustress is a form of controlled stress – Table 4.1 shows eustress promotion during project states. A work environment that is under control will help many employees to avoid stress overload and thus to enhance their performance in activities.

Best practice statement

High eustress and controlled distress in a work setting is definitive evidence that finesse and high performance are the order of the day.

Fairness and organizational justice

Jerald Greenberg and his colleagues have extensively explored the link between fairness, organizational justice and workplace stress (Greenberg and Colquitt, 2005). The evidence is becoming clear and overwhelming that a fair and just work environment for all concerned is an essential ingredient to the healthy management of stress. Greenberg and his colleagues explore three key forms of organizational justice: procedural justice, distributive justice, and interactive justice. These are forms of fair treatment at work. The basic ideas in justice theories are that employee perceptions of fair procedures, fair distribution of outcomes, and fairness in interpersonal treatment all influence stress, motivation and behavior. Justice and fairness satisfy the basic human need to be treated with dignity and respect. Justice and fairness influence people's

Table 4.1 Organizational eustress promotion during project stages

No.	Stage and item	How item promotes eustress
	Stage I – Project assignment	
1.	In general terms, accurately describe and delineate overall task	A carefully-executed project orientation reduces misunderstandings; empowers management to "sell" project to employee; gives employee opportunity for initial and realistic "excitement" that can carry throughout the process
2.	Propose realistic general timetable, justify it, allow employee time for input	Reduces or eliminates need for "emergency" psychological footing; establishes reasonably quick pace to encourage challenge element
3.	Employ sufficient personnel on task	Minimizes issues of recurring employee overload expectations, intermittent overload is expected and unavoidable
4.	Open intranet access to relevant information nodes	Some privileged information needed by employee on ad hoc basis; access to this before it is needed sends a strong positive signal
5.	Designate subject matter experts (some external to the firm) such as advisors, innovators, professors, and specialists; allow employee to participate in selecting; establish formal connection of each with employee, these will be needed when difficult-to-find understanding is required during familiarization and implementation	This allows employee to be entrepreneurial and cast a wider net for process and solution possibilities; interaction with experts can help maintain high energy level
	Stage II – Project familiarization	
1.	Initial support sessions or brief training	Necessary if project is a "carryover" or continuation; helpful in any event if they are available; sets employee off to a strong implementation
2.	As-needed consultation with employees or supervisors who have prior experience with similar project; also needed for implementation	A vital source of organizational support; promotes persistence through discussion and resolution of perceived inequities and irregularities as they arise.

(cont.)

Table 4.1 (*cont.*)

No.	Stage and item	How item promotes eustress
3.	Establish clear daily, weekly, critical, and other near-term objectives, modifiable as change needs arise – Project charting possibly needed for this	Clear and modifiable (through established procedure) objectives promote psychological stability; communication of project progress is enhanced by referral to a reliable timetable.
	Stage III – Project implementation	
1.	Effective feedback and controls in place to ensure progression toward resource conservation and overall goals are satisfactory	Necessary to avoid actual or false perceptions of lack of progress or resource wastage
2.	Projects commonly have more than one supervisor; ensure that use of multiple supervisors is not creating role conflict or role ambiguity issues; supervisors to corrdinate and communicate; one supervisor to openly accept employee role conflict descriptions	Reduces possibility of project derailment due to assignment of impossible task demands
	Stage IV – Post-task project evaluation	
1.	Compare actual with envisioned project in terms of parameters such as goal attainment, resource use, and organizational benefit	Accurate depiction of how project benefits organization will dispel employee illusions and "inoculate" employee from erroneous explanations
2.	Smoothly move employee from former project into appropriate new one, consideration of change of work location, peers, employee status, and additional factors	Reduce change stress, promote eustress in new role

emotions, their sense of trust and control, and their moral sense of right and wrong.

While organizational justice research has a long history, a recent review of the research on justice perceptions has shown employee perceptions of fairness are linked to their work performance, to organizational citizenship behaviors, and to work attitudes (Colquitt and Greenberg, 2003; Latham and Pinder, 2005). Greenberg (1988) found that a person's organizational position influences self-imposed performance expectations. Specifically, a two-level move up in an organization with no additional pay creates a higher self-imposed performance expectation than a one-level move up with modest additional pay. Similarly, a two-level move down in an organization with no reduction in pay creates a lower self-imposed performance expectation than a one-level move down with a modest decrease in pay. This suggests that organizational position may be more important than pay in determining the level of a person's performance expectations.

Justice and fair treatment at work are positive and important because they create a sense of psychological security, predictability, and stability with regard to procedures, outcomes, and interpersonal relationships. The absence of justice and the presence of injustice as well as the absence of fairness and the presence of unfairness can have both unintended and negative consequences. All managers, from supervisors through the senior executive ranks, must be sensitive to these issues. In 2006, the unfair, unjust, and even illegal treatment of its own members by the Hewlett-Packard Board of Directors led to significant public outcry and turmoil, including the resignation of Patricia Dunn as chair and member of the Board in September of that year. Hence, the public at large as well as employees and leaders alike are increasingly sensitive to issues of fairness and justice.

Unintentional final consequences of injustice and unfair treatment

When people experience injustice and unfair treatment at work, there can be a variety of unintended, negative consequences. Greenberg (2004) has summarized the relationship between organizational justice and stress in the Justice Salience Hierarchy (JSH) shown in Figure 4.2. The highest levels of stress reactions occur when there is distributive injustice, procedural injustice, and interactional injustice while the lowest levels of stress occur when there is distributive, procedural, and interactive justice. Trip, Bies, and Aquino (2002) found that revenge resulted from the experience of unfair treatment at work. Greenberg (2002, 2006) himself has linked the experience of unfair treatment to employee theft as well as to insomnia in the case of payment inequity. In still another study, Ambrose, Seabright, and Schminke (2002) linked injustice to sabotage behavior on the part of employees.

These forms of dysfunctional behavior (i.e., revenge, employee theft, insomnia, and sabotage) are among the unintentional consequences of injustice and unfair treatment at work. Aggressive reactions or other forms of violent and deviant behavior that do harm to both individuals and the organization are the more extreme forms of dysfunctional behavior. Fortunately, Greenberg

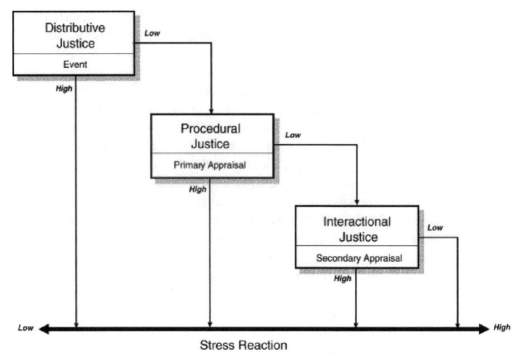

Figure 4.2   The Justice Salience Hierarchy (JSH)
Source: J. Greenberg, "Stress Fairness to Fare No Stress: Managing Workplace Stress by Promoting Organizational Justice," *Organizational Dynamics*, 33, 4, 2004, p. 358. [Figure (c) 2004, Jerald Greenberg. Reproduced with permission.

and Alge (1988) found that only a small number of individuals respond to such unfairness through dysfunctional behavior.

Managerial actions: Best practices to address this human dilemma

Managerial actions can make a positive impact on the experience of justice and fairness at work. For example, Greenberg (2006) found in his study of insomniac reactions to underpayment inequity mentioned above that supervisory training in interactional justice significantly reduced insomnia for the nurses. Thus, when managers are sensitive to the feelings and emotions of their employees, employees feel appreciated and supported. Further, this experience of appreciation and support appears to compensate for problems of procedural injustice or distributive injustice, or at least to cushion the blow.

Interactional justice has stress-relieving benefits because it affords the manager the opportunity to provide social support to employees. Elsewhere, Greenberg and Cropanzano (2001) suggest that managers can employ just and fair procedures to help bridge the cultural and individual differences in a diverse workplace. When organizational procedures and processes are just, open, transparent, and fair, employees are able to see that different groups or different individuals are treated the same. In one way or another, justice appears to be a universal concern among people across cultures. Managerial training can lead to positive managerial actions with positive benefits for all in the workplace. Greenberg and Colquitt (2005) suggest that managerial training in justice and fair treatment may include explanations of justice concepts, case studies, directed role-playing exercises, and carefully guided group discussions.

Best practice statement

The fair and just workplace is one in which people are treated with dignity, integrity, and equality.

HRM systems integrity

Human Resource Management (HRM) practices have a significant effect on organizational and employee performance and health outcomes, as well as on the long-term viability of the firm (Browne, 2000). These can greatly affect work stress, and involve a combination of functions such as selection, recruiting, and training that are necessary for organizational continuity, and others, including Employee Assistance Programs (EAPs) and certain employee benefits, that enhance the effectiveness of employees. HRM is also involved in implementing temporary projects and in organization change (Mroczek *et al.*, 2005). Managing these systems with integrity requires honesty of intent as well as delivery. It means that a fair-minded outsider with comprehensive knowledge of the specific HR system involved would see the system as striking a balance of fairness, openness, and high ethical standards.

Performance appraisal

In this area, organizations with best-practice work stress reduction practices generate a minimum of stress. This ongoing set of conditions is achieved by using fair and open standards that are linked to the organization's goals at all levels. Performance appraisals focus centrally on task standards and on work behaviors, not on personality, personal values, or individual attributes (Nelson and Quick, 2006). A key and important distinction is made between the person, the person's values, beliefs, and core attributes that define the person as a human being and the person's behaviors, actions, and work performances which may be modified or altered for the mutual interest of the individual and the organization. Therefore, it is critical in the performance appraisal process to affirm the individual and speak honestly and critically about the person's work behaviors and performance. That critical distinction sometimes gets confused or lost, leading to personalized conflicts and accusations in what should be a learning event.

Employee assistance programs

Employee Assistance Programs (EAPs) are used in many workplaces, and offer a potentially valuable range of services. They have been of great value regarding personal issues such as childcare, eldercare, legal issues, financial problems, and some health-related issues (e.g., encouraging an employee to visit the doctor rather than "living with" a symptom). However, even well-managed EAPs are generally limited in value for managing organizational stress since they can usually only address the symptoms of work stress rather than its causes (Clawson, 2005).

One manner in which an EAP can help resolve causes of work stess is if it results in better employee recognition of problem causes, which can then be referred to his or her supervisor. This can be augmented if HR managers receive data from the whole organization (no confidential data) on the kinds of personal problems being reported by the EAP's. This can then be used as a diagnostic tool to help identify issues in the workplace (Clawson, 2005).

Training

Effective training systems help reduce employee stress because they keep worker knowledge, skills, and abilities current in their jobs and reduce perceptions of occupational inadequacy. Training is one of the major unspoken ways that employers can let their workers know that they are meaningful. When this increases it can reduce stress. Although the training paradox exists that employees who are well-trained are then more marketable for seeking positions elsewhere, best-practice firms do not reactively stand still when it comes to training for teams, quality and continuous improvement, development for promotion, and promoting general educational skills (Nygaard and Dahlstrom, 2002).

If the workplace changes rapidly, the importance of employee training comes to the fore. Employee skills must be updated to meet the new requirements placed upon them. Without training, current employee knowledge becomes obsolete and fails to be replaced by more cutting edge knowledge. As a result such employees rapidly move towards functional incompetence (DeFrank and Ivancevich, 1998).

For adequate training to help most in reducing stress not only is there a need to learn new technologies and systems, but employees must also do the following (DeFrank and Ivancevich, 1998):

- gain communication skills, learn new communicating modalities, and assimilate new terminology and concepts;
- alter and improve their decision making;
- keep up with changes in customer preferences and customer-generated technological requirements;
- improve their ability to cope with stress;
- continue to expand team and coworker interaction skills;
- continue to respond to common organizational goals as these are modified.

Executive training is also necessary to reduce stress. The increased accountability combined with lessened control that is an increasingly common lot of managers calls for ongoing exposure of executives to effective techniques for handling these difficult circumstances. To help keep down excessive stress, it is preferable that this exposure begins before the circumstances arise (DeFrank and Ivancevich, 1998).

Best practice statement

Design a set of HRM systems which expect and support the best work performance from all employees, serving both employees and the organization.

Conclusion

Nearly fifty years ago Douglas McGregor focused our attention on the human side of enterprise. Cutcher-Gershenfeld has brought our attention back to McGregor's seminal work and provided insightful, annotated commentary on this great management thinker who was deeply concerned with people (McGregor and Cutcher-Gershenfeld, 2005). In this best practices chapter on work stress and well-being, we too have concerned ourselves with the human side of enterprise and attempted to articulate some solutions for human dilemmas in organizations. McGregor's thinking had important implications for nurturing leadership; the management of the entire enterprise; management teams; providing better performance feedback; achieving high levels of performance without losing concern for the individual; and cultivating a value-driven workplace.

Since the Golden Age of management thought and practice in the America of the 1950s when McGregor lived and taught, we have learned significantly more about stress and strain in organizations and for individuals. We have learned about the threats which pose health risks for workers and leaders alike. The best practices framework that we have set forth is couched in the context of humane leadership. McGregor originally referred to the assumptions about people contained in his Theory Y. This is not soft-minded leadership or country club leadership. Rather, humane leadership is leadership that expects the best out of people and is willing to support, nurture, and bring forth the best the individual has to offer. McGregor well understood, as do we, that organizations are not welfare systems that foster dependency but rather product and service delivery systems in which individuals take responsibility and are self-motivated. These systems deserve and demand humane leaders who care for the individual, provide challenge and opportunity coupled with care, support, and concern. Without these attributes of the humane leadership, the organization may well turn into a labor camp.

REFERENCES

Abdel-Halim, A. (1981) Effects of role stress-job design-technology interaction on employee work satisfaction. *Academy of Management Journal, 24*(2), 260–73.

Ambrose, M. L., Seabright, M. A. and Schminke, M. (2002) Sabotage in the workplace: The role of organizational justice. *Organizational Behavior and Human Decision Processes, 89,* 947–65.

Boyatzis, R. E., Smith, M. L. and Blaize, N. (2006) Developing sustainable leaders through coaching and compassion. *Academy of Management Learning and Education, 5,* 8–24.

Browne, J. (2000) Benchmarking HRM practices in healthy work organizations. *American Business Review, 18*(2), 54–61.

Caudron, S. (1998) Job stress is in job design. *Workforce, 77*(9), 21–3.

Clawson, T. (2005) Are EAPs the answer to stress? *Human Resources,* October, 56.

Colquitt, J. and Greenberg, J. (2003) Organizational justice: A fair assessment of the state of the literature. In J. Greenberg (ed.), *Organizational Behavior: The State of the Science,* 2nd edn: Mahwah: Erlbaum Associates.

Cooper, C. L. and Quick, J. C. (1999) *FAST FACTS: Stress and strain* (clinical monograph). Oxford, England: Health Press.

DeFrank, R. and Ivancevich, J. (1998) Stress on the job: An executive update. *Academy of Management Executive, 12*(*3*), 55–66.

Fairbrother, K. and Warn, J. (2003) Workplace dimensions, stress, and job satisfaction. *Journal of Managerial Psychology, 18*, 8–21.

Geurts, S. and Grundemann, R. (1999) Workplace stress and stress prevention in Europe. Chapter 2, pp. 9–31, in Michiel Kompier and Cary Cooper, *Preventing stress, improving productivity: European case studies in the workplace*. New York: Routledge.

Gilbreath, B. and Benson, P. (2004) The contribution of supervisor behavior to employee psychological well-being. *Work and Stress, 18*(*3*), 255–66.

Grant-Vallone, E. and Donaldson, S. (2001) Consequences of work–family conflict on employee well-being over time. *Work & Stress, 15*(*3*), 214–26.

Greenberg, J. (1988) Equity and workplace status: A field experiment. *Journal of Applied Psychology, 73*, 606–13.

(2002) Who stole the money, and when? Individual and situational determinants of employee theft. *Organizational Behavior and Human Decision Processes, 89*, 985–1003.

(2004) Stress Fairness to Fare No Stress: Managing Workplace Stress by Promoting Organizational Justice, *Organizational Dynamics, 33*, 352–65.

(2006) Losing sleep over organizational justice: Attenuating insomniac reactions to underpayment inequity with supervisory training in interactional justice. *Journal of Applied Psychology, 91*, 38–69.

Greenberg, J. and Cropanzano, R. S. (2001) *Advances in Organizational Justice*. Palo Alto: Stanford University Press.

Greenberg, J. S. and Colquitt, J. (2005) *Handbook of Organizational Justice*. Mahwah: Erlbaum Associates.

Harenstam, A. (2005) Different development trends in working life and increasing occupational stress require new work environment strategies. *Work, 24*, 261–77.

Henderson, M. and Argyle, M. (1985) Social support by four categories of work colleagues: Relationships between activities, stress and satisfaction. *Journal of Occupational Behavior, 6*(*3*), 229–39.

Iacocca, L. with Novak, W. (1986) *Iacocca, an autobiography*. New York: Bantam Books.

Johnson, P. and Indvik, J. (2001) Rudeness at Work: Impulse over restraint. *Public Personnel Management, 30*(*4*), 457–65.

Kivimaki, M., Elovainio, M., Vahtera, J. and Ferrie, J. (2003) Organizational justice and health of employees; prospective cohort study. *Occupational and Environmental Medicine, 60*, 27–34.

Lait, J. and Wallace, J. (2002) Stress at work: A study of organizational-professional conflict and unmet expectations. *Relations Industrielles/Industrial Relations, 57*, 463–87.

Latham, G. P. and Pinder, C. C. (2005) Work motivation theory and research at the dawn of the twenty-first century. *Annual Review of Psychology, 56*, 485–516.

LePine, J., LePine, M. and Jackson, C. (2004) Challenge and hindrance stress: Relationships with exhaustion, motivation to learn, and learning performance. *Journal of Applied Psychology, 89*(*5*), 883–91.

Lines, R., Selart, M., Espedal, B. and Johansen, S. (2005) The production of trust during organizational change. *Journal of Change Management, 5*(*2*), 221–45.

Li-Ping Tang, T. and Fuller, R. (1995) Corporate downsizing: What managers can do to lessen the negative effects of layoffs. *S.A.M. Advanced Management Journal*, 60(4), 12–31.

Lotz, T. and Donald, F. (2006) Stress and communication across job levels after an acquisition. *South African Journal of Business Management*, 37(1), 1–8.

Lyons, E. (2002) Psychosocial factors related to job stress and women in management. *Work*, 18, 89–93.

McGregor, D. and Cutcher-Gershenfeld, J. (2005) *The human side of enterprise, annotated edition*. New York: McGraw-Hill (Original work published in 1960).

Michailidis, M. and E-ali Elwkai, M. (2003) Factors contributing to occupational stress experienced by individuals employed in the fast food industry. *Work*, 21, 125–40.

Michailidis, M. and Georgiou, Y. (2005) Employee occupational stress in banking. *Work*, 24, 123–37.

Millar, J. D. (1984) The NIOSH-suggested list of the ten leading work-related diseases and injuries. *Journal of Occupational Medicine*, 26, 340–41.

Moretz, S. (1989) Stress requires correctives, cosmetics won't do. *Occupational Hazards*, 51(4), 49–51.

Morris, J. R., Cascio, W. F. and Young, C. E. (1999) Downsizing after all these years. *Organizational Dynamics*, Winter Issue, 78–87.

Mroczek, J., Mikitarian, G., Vieira, E. and Rotarius, T. (2005) Hospital design and staff perceptions: An exploratory analysis. *The Health Care Manager*, 24(3), 233–44.

Mulcahy, W. (2003) Work/life benefits keep small- and medium-sized businesses competitive. *Employee Benefit Plan Review*, 57(8), 24–6.

Nelson, D. L. and Quick, J. C. (2006) *Organizational behavior: foundations, realities & challenges*, 5th edn. Mason: Thompson/Southwestern.

Nytro, K., Saksvik, O., Mikkelsen, A., Bohle, P. and Quinlan, M. (2000) An appraisal of key factors in the implementation of occupational stress interventions. *Work and Stress*, 14(3), 213–25.

Nygaard, A. and Dahlstrom, R. (2002) Role stress and effectiveness in horizontal alliances. *Journal of Marketing*, 66, 61–82.

Ornelas, S. and Kleiner, B. (2003) New developments in managing job stress. *Equal Opportunities International*, 22(5), 64–70.

Peterson, S. and Luthans, F. (2003) The positive impact and development of hopeful leaders. *Leadership and Organization Development Journal*, 24, 26–31.

Quick, J. C., Cooper, C. L., Nelson, D. L., Quick, J. D. and Gavin, J. H. (2003) Stress, Health, and Well-Being at Work. In J. Greenberg (ed.), *Organizational behavior: The state of the art*, 2nd edn. Mahwah and London: Erlbaum Associates.

Rosch, P. J. (2001) The quandary of job stress compensation. *Health and Stress*, 3, 1–4.

Rothmann, S., Steyn, L. and Mostert, K. (2005) Job stress, sense of coherence and work wellness in an electricity supply organization. *South African Journal of Business Management*, 36(1), 55–63.

Shain, M. and Kramer, D. (2004) Health promotion in the workplace: Framing the concept; Reviewing the evidence. *Occupational and Environmental Medicine*, 61, 643–46.

Tepper, B. (2000) Consequenses of abusive supervision. *Academy of Management Journal*, 43, 178–90.

Townsend, J. (2001) Get tough with stress. *Management*, *26*, 24–5.

Trip, T. M., Bies, R. J. and Aquino, K. (2002) Poetic justice or petty jealousy? The aesthetics of revenge. *Organizational Behavior and Human Decision Processes*, *89*, 966–84.

Tyler, C. W. Jr. and Last, J. M. (1998) Epidemiology. In R. B. Wallace and B. N. Doebbeling (eds.) *Maxcy-Rosenau-Last public health & preventive medicine*, 14th edn: 5–33. Stamford: Appleton & Lange.

Wallace, R. B. and Doebbeling, B. N. (1998) *Maxcy-Rosenau-Last public health & preventive medicine*, 14th edn. Stamford: Appleton & Lange.

Walls, G., Capella, L. and Greene, W. (2001) Toward a source stressors model of conflict between work and family. *Review of Business*, *22*, 86–91.

5 Enhancing staff well-being for organisational effectiveness

Ivan T. Robertson, Gordon Tinline and Susannah Robertson

Early to bed, early to rise Work like hell and advertise

Ted Turner

The European Protestant work ethic in combination with the American gift for self-promotion, captured well by Ted Turner, seems to define what the typical CEO would consider the key ingredients for high performance in their organisation. The idea that they should be concerned with the well-being and health of their staff, as a business or organisational performance issue, still seems to be a curious notion to many. This is most likely to be true for businesses with Boards that believe that anything that is outside a narrow definition of shareholder value or Return On Investment (ROI) should not be their concern. This chapter argues that staff well-being should be considered as an essential determinant and metric of organisational and business effectiveness.

The healthy, happy, productive worker is a well established new notion. However, in our work – helping organisations improve staff well-being – we keep being asked for its business case. In our experience the assumption among business managers is often that you can attend to staff happiness and well-being, as a "touchy feely" HR issue, or you can drive high performance and productivity, but it is not usually possible to reconcile these twin aims.

In fact, this distinction between issues that relate to high performing workforces versus issues concerned with improving the well-being of workforces is purely academic – in the worst sense of the word! It does not reflect the realities of organisational life. The problems that confront practitioners, on a day-to-day basis, are not neatly segregated in this way. Absenteeism, for instance, provides a good example of a problem that transcends this artificial distinction and relates to both productivity and well-being. Progressive employers are beginning to recognise the important issues involved here. The remainder of this chapter examines the issues, and signposts a progressive way ahead for employers and HR practitioners.

Well-being and motivation

Psychologists know a great deal about the factors that influence motivation and well-being in the workplace and there is a substantial amount of supporting research.

The factors that influence well-being and motivation can be grouped into one of two broad categories – Person factors and Situation factors. This approach is derived from Albert Bandura's concept of "Reciprocal Determinism" (Bandura, 1977). Bandura was the first to provide a coherent model that combined the influences of person and situation factors in a convincing way. His theory proposes that both internal psychological factors, as well as external situational factors, have a role in controlling behaviour. Stable, internal psychological factors can have a noticeable impact on work-related emotional factors, such as job satisfaction and well-being. Indeed it has been known for some time, since the ground-breaking work of Richard Arvey and his colleagues (1991), that job satisfaction has a demonstrable genetic component – probably working via the heritability of negative affectivity. Organisations can do little to influence stable psychological (person) factors, even though they are important determinants of people's emotional experience of work. Organisations can however, have an impact on the key situational factors.

Stress and well-being

The most significant dangers to psychological well-being in the workplace are generally categorised under the heading of work-related stressors – which lead to the experience of stress and may significantly damage well-being.

Lazarus (1966) explored the stressor–strain relationship and, in particular, how the transaction from stressor to strain occurs. Lazarus found that individuals' cognitive appraisals moderate the stressor–strain relationship. Only if an individual interprets it to be threatening or harmful will it cause them strain or stress.

Lazarus and Folkman (1984) developed the notion of appraisal or perception, as a stressor–strain mediator. They suggest that the individual appraises the stressor (primary appraisal) and appraises their own ability to cope with it (secondary appraisal). Only when both appraisals are negative, when the stressor is perceived to be harmful and the individual feels that they do not have the resources to cope with it, will they suffer stress. In other words, a stressor has to be perceived and recognised by the individual as overwhelming their ability to cope, to be felt. It is in the "eye of the beholder". This discussion suggests that put simply:

When individuals perceive that the demands made upon them exceed their ability to cope then they have entered the stress arena.

Perhaps one of the most important definitional issues is the qualitative distinction between pressure and stress. There is nothing wrong with pressure, indeed it can stimulate us to action and enhance our performance. Only when *the demands made upon someone exceed their ability to cope* does pressure become damaging and produce stress and its consequential negative effects.

Over time, excessive stress is harmful to health. The way in which individuals cope with stress (e.g. excessive smoking, increased alcohol consumption) can also carry significant health risks. We know also from research that people under stress are more likely to have accidents and take longer to recover from illness. As organisations have increasingly recognised that stress is a serious problem and an important health and safety issue, the diagnosis and measurement of workplace stress and health has gained prominence. Growing research evidence suggests that the most effective way in which organisations can reduce workplace stress is by eliminating or modifying the sources of stress inherent in the work environment. This concern for monitoring and modifying sources of stress has emphasised the need to develop an appropriate organisational tool to objectively identify those sources to which employees are exposed at work.

Well-being and performance/productivity

There is clear recognition and evidence for the existence of a relationship between workplace stressors and mental and physical health outcomes. While this strong body of work helps with our understanding, there are further management issues that have been less well addressed.

The established link between work stressors and employee well-being places a clear moral obligation on employers to provide healthy working environments (Patterson *et al.*, 1997). In addition to this moral obligation, it has also been argued that employers should be aware of the impact of reduced well-being and ill-health in monetary terms. For example, Kessler *et al.* (1999) estimated that in terms of depression, monthly productivity losses of approximately $200 to $400 were experienced by each worker, and Greenberg *et al.* (1993) estimated that lost productivity due to depression cost American corporations $12.1 billion in 1990 alone. Furthermore, the impact of mental ill-health on absenteeism has already been established in a number of studies (e.g., Pflanz and Heidel, 2003).

In practice, research in several areas supports an approach that developing employee well-being is not only good for the employees – but also good for the business. The areas providing good support for the positive impact of improved well-being include work on well-being and individual performance, well-being and productivity and well-being and customer satisfaction.

For example, there is a powerful, emerging body of evidence to support the links between individual performance and well-being (e.g., Cropanzano and Wright 1999, Wright and Cropanzano, 2004, Efraty and Sirgy, 1990).

In addition to work linking individual performance and well-being there is research that examines the effects of stressors and health outcomes and their impact on productivity, including evidence of the stress and productivity relationship. For example, Yeh, Lester and Tauber's (1986) study on real estate agents (n = 62) revealed a negative relationship between stress and productivity using a self-report measure of stress. They were reluctant, however, to draw strong conclusions from their findings due to issues such as the small sample size and application within only one occupation.

More recent work by Donald et al. (2005) found that both employee perceptions of commitment from their organisation and psychological well-being were significant predictors of self-reported productivity. It is worth noting that research indicates a high level of correlation between self-reported productivity and objective productivity measures (Meerding et al., 2005; Hurst et al., 1996). This was one of the first large scale studies to support the relationship between mental well-being and productivity. Earlier studies had found links between burnout and performance (e.g., Singh, Goolsby and Rhoads, 1994), but this new research suggests that productivity is actually affected earlier in the stress experience (i.e. before burnout). The implications for organisations are clear – by addressing perceptions of commitment and psychological well-being, bottom-line, business benefits can be realised. The large sample size (n = 16,000) and mix of occupations in this research gives confidence in generalising the findings.

Work on customer satisfaction and employee satisfaction also provides impressive evidence of the business benefits of building employee well-being. If employees are satisfied with their job, work environment, and working relationships etc. then this will be 'reflected' in satisfied customers, via good customer service/service quality. Studies have linked employee attitudes to customer satisfaction (Fosam et al., 1998); employee working environment and employee satisfaction to customer satisfaction (Wiley, 1991); and employee self-efficacy and job satisfaction to perceived customer service quality, (Hartline and Ferrell, 1996). The prevalence of stress has also been found to be negatively correlated with customer satisfaction (King and Garey, 1997). The findings in this area are so consistent that one researcher declared that: 'The relationship between customer satisfaction and employee satisfaction is the one relationship that does not seem to yield conflicting results' (Bernhardt *et al.*, 2000).

In fact, the integration of the areas of well-being and performance is very much in keeping with the spirit of the times – i.e. an increased emphasis on work – life balance, coupled with a need for greater competitiveness – and could lead to a revolution in organisational dynamics and the working lives of the people within them.

So, in practice, what can organisations actually do? Narrow approaches are unlikely to be successful, as the complex interaction of factors needs to be understood and taken into account. For example, if you offer one group of staff the opportunity of flexible working, this may have a detrimental affect on another group of staff. Similarly, giving more control to employees in an attempt to make their jobs more interesting and fulfilling, may produce the reaction that they have too much responsibility and feel unable to cope. In short, a holistic approach to managing well-being needs to be adopted by organisations, in order to account for the interaction of different factors in the workplace.

To improve the well-being of their employees and to gain the bottom-line benefits, there is a clear need for organisations to obtain a baseline picture of well-being and to measure key bottom-line indicators such as absenteeism and performance figures. An evidence-based action plan should then be developed to address any issues/areas of concern identified regarding well-being. Essentially, a measurement tool is needed, to enable organisations to assess all of the interconnected factors in the workplace, to monitor them over time and to cross-reference the findings against bottom-line indicators.

One such measurement tool is ASSET (Cartwright and Cooper, 2002), a validated and reliable organisational stress screening survey designed to be used as part of a broader audit approach. The first stage of the ASSET audit approach is for the organisation to plan and promote the audit internally, so that employees are aware that it is taking place, the importance of the process and the potential benefits for them of taking part. Secondly, the survey itself must be conducted either online or in paper and pencil format to collect the relevant data. Stress 'hotspots' (i.e. organisational subgroups where stress levels are particularly high) can then be identified and further investigative

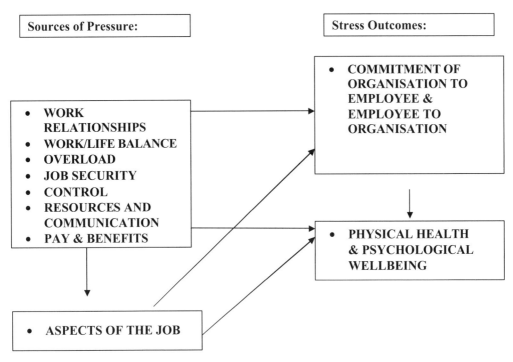

Figure 5.1   The ASSET model

work with staff from these groups carried out. This would be in the form of 'Solutions Groups', where the results from the survey would be explored in more detail with the relevant staff and realistic solutions and improvements would also be discussed. The findings from the audit with recommended interventions would then be fed back to key stakeholders within the organisation and ultimately the recommendations would be formulated into a detailed action plan to take forward.

To further illustrate the approach, the ASSET model (Cartwright and Cooper, 2002) will be used:

The ASSET model

The design of ASSET is based upon the proposed model above. This has been influenced by existing and established models of stress (e.g., Cooper and Marshall, 1978). However, it recognises that factors such as overall job satisfaction (measured by 'aspects of the job') and organisational commitment, usually conceptualised as being the outcome of stress, may also be sources of

Table 5.1 The function of the ASSET questionnaire sections.

Section	Source of pressure	Stress outcome	Other
1. Perceptions of your job	Work relationships		
	Work/life balance		
	Overload		
	Job security		
	Control		
	Resources and communication		
	Pay and benefits		
	Aspects of the job	Aspects of the job	
2. Attitudes towards your organisation		Perceived commitment of organisation to employee	
		Perceived commitment of employee to organisation	
3. Employee health		Physical health	
		Psychological wellbeing	
4. Supplementary			Biographical

stress in themselves. For some occupational groups, high levels of commitment and job satisfaction may moderate the effects of stress.

The design of the ASSET survey

ASSET is divided into four sections. The first three relate to the ASSET model above and together assess the respondent's perceptions of the sources of pressure and the outcomes of work-related stress. The final 'supplementary' section collects biographical information. Stylistically, the questions are brief and respondents simply circle (on the paper and pencil version) and 'click' (on the online version) to indicate their answer. This means that no unnecessary demands are made on respondents' time.

Table 5.1 above displays the elements of the stress model measured by the different sections of the questionnaire. A description of each of these together with their respective subscales as well as some related research follows.

Perceptions of the job

This section of the questionnaire measures a range of possible sources of workplace stress and job pressure. It also includes some questions relating to home and social life-related pressures. This part of the questionnaire comprises 37 items loading on to eight subscales, which collectively assess the eight sources of pressure identified by the ASSET model. Each of these eight sub-scales are briefly commented on below.

Work relationships

Most jobs demand a great deal of contact with other people at work. Poor or unsupportive relationships with colleagues and/or superiors, isolation (a perceived lack of adequate relationships) and unfair treatment can all be potential sources of stress. Kahn *et al.*'s (1964) study of poor working relations found that mistrust of colleagues can create role ambiguity, which can lead to psychological strain. Conversely, good relationships can help individuals to cope with stress. Most of the HR and personnel specialists included in the Industrial Society survey (2001) saw supportive managers (95%) and supportive colleagues (74%) as the two factors in the workplace that are most likely to help employees cope with stress. This ASSET subscale measures the extent to which work relationships are a source of stress.

Work/life balance

The demands of work have the potential to spill over and interfere with individuals' personal and home lives. This can put a strain on relationships outside work and can impact upon the level of stress (Confederation of British Industry, 1998), health and commitment experienced. Balancing the differing demands of home and work is, according to the Industrial Society survey (2001), perceived as the primary cause of occupational stress. ASSET's work–life balance subscale measures the extent to which difficulty maintaining a satisfactory balance between work responsibilities and personal/home life is a source of stress.

Overload

Unmanageable workloads and time pressures can be a source of stress. TUC's survey (2000), for example, identified high workloads as the main cause of stress for employees. In addition, the Industrial Society survey (2001) cited unrealistic deadlines/constant time pressures as the second most influential cause of stress. Furthermore, French and Caplan (1973) found that overload can produce symptoms of psychological stress. This subscale of the

ASSET questionnaire measures the extent to which such overload is a source of stress.

Job security

Whilst significantly fewer employees now expect a 'job for life', the fear of job loss or obsolescence still remains a major potential source of stress. Indeed, job insecurity has been identified as one of the most salient sources of stress for employees today (O'Driscoll and Cooper, 1996). For example, a quarter of the Industrial Society survey respondents rated job insecurity as one of the six most common causes of occupational stress. This subscale of the questionnaire measures the extent to which job insecurity and job changes are a source of stress.

Control

The experience of stress is strongly linked to perceptions of control. Lack of influence in the way in which work is organised and performed can be a potential source of stress. Indeed, individuals who perceive that they can control their environment are less likely to suffer stress than those who do not (Makin, Cooper and Cox, 2000). This subscale measures the extent to which a lack of control is perceived by individuals to be a source of stress. Control is often found to be the most crucial factor in determining stress levels.

Resources and communication

To perform their job effectively, individuals need to feel they have the appropriate training, equipment and resources. They also need to feel that they are adequately informed and that they are valued. A number of sources (e.g., NIOSH, 1999; HSE, 2005; Industrial Society, 2001) have associated all or some of these factors with stress. Furthermore, poor communications were found to be the third most highly rated stressor (in terms of its commonality) in the British Industrial Society report referred to earlier.

Pay and benefits

The financial rewards that work brings are obviously important in that they determine the type of lifestyle that an individual can lead. In addition, they often influence an individual's feelings of self worth and perception of their value to the organisation. This single item scale measures the extent to which pay and benefits are a source of stress.

Aspects of the job

This ASSET subscale measures the potential sources of stress that relate to the fundamental nature of the job itself. Factors such as physical working conditions, type of tasks and the amount of satisfaction derived from the job itself are all included. This subscale correlates highly with established measures of job satisfaction. As already highlighted, job dissatisfaction can be the outcome of work-related stress or can be a source of stress in its own right. When job dissatisfaction is a reflection of reality, for example, if an individual is dissatisfied because they have outgrown their job, it is likely to be a cause of stress rather than an effect (Lyne *et al.*, 1994).

Attitudes towards the organisation

This second major section of the questionnaire is concerned with the measurement of organisational commitment. It consists of nine items divided into two scales: commitment of the organisation to the employee and commitment of the employee to the organisation. This section reflects the non-economic reciprocal obligations that exist between employer and employee.

In terms of the ASSET model, these subscales of the questionnaire measure an effect of stress. However, it must be noted that other factors aside from workplace stress may also affect the level of commitment that a respondent reports (i.e. from the employee and perceived by the employee of the organisation). For example industrial action, such as a threatened union strike, may affect employees' perceived commitment to their organisation.

Commitment of the organisation to the employee

Employees expect to be trusted and respected and want to feel that it is worth 'going the extra mile' for their organisation. This subscale measures the extent to which individuals feel that their organisation is committed to them.

Commitment of the employee to organisation

Employers expect their employees to do their job as best they can and expect them to be loyal and dedicated to the organisation. This subscale measures the extent to which this commitment exists.

Employee health

This third section of the questionnaire assesses respondents' state of health. It consists of seventeen items arranged on two subscales: physical health and psychological well-being. According to the ASSET model and the large body of research on which it is based, poor employee health can be indicative of excessive workplace pressure and experienced stress. Thus, poor health is an outcome of stress, which can be used to ascertain if workplace pressures have positive and motivating, or negative and damaging, effects. However, as with commitment, it must be noted that poor health may not necessarily be indicative of workplace stress. Individuals may, for example, be unwell because they choose not to lead a healthy lifestyle or may be unaware of how to do so. Stressors outside the workplace such as the break-up of a relationship or bereavement are also likely to impact upon a person's health.

Physical health

All items on this subscale relate to physical symptoms of stress. The role of this subscale is to give an insight into physical health, not an in-depth clinical diagnosis.

Psychological well-being

The items listed on this subscale are symptoms of stress-induced psychological ill health. As with the physical health subscale, the role of this subscale is to give an insight into psychological health, not an in-depth clinical diagnosis.

Evidence for the benefits of the audit approach

There is growing evidence of the benefits of adopting a structured and thorough risk assessment approach to well-being in the workplace. For example, in the UK, Somerset County Council (HSE, 2005) adopted a three-pronged approach to assessing and managing workplace stress: they audited the stress levels of all employees using ASSET, they put in place a preventative individual level stress risk assessment process (i.e. to detect stress before it occurs) as well as a reactive individual level stress risk assessment process (i.e., rehabilitation from stress-related illness). Somerset County Council committed to a number of actions based on the evidence from the stress audit and in terms of bottom-line benefits, they saved almost £2 m per year in reduced absences. In 2001 the British Government set a target of 9.1 days per employee for 'casual' sickness absences and required local authorities to achieve this within five years. Somerset cut its average rates from 10.75 days in 2001–2 to 8.29 in 2003–4, nearly a day inside the target in two years. Although the survey behind the reforms was commissioned because of the cost of sickness absence, there was more to it than simply meeting government targets. Somerset Council had a genuine desire to put in place a holistic programme of measures that would ensure the well-being of its workforce and, by doing so, boost productivity.

The City of London (UK) police force adopted a similar approach and again reaped the rewards – they audited 'quality of working life' using ASSET across the force in 2003 and used the findings to construct an action plan to address the issues identified. Listed below are some of the actions the force undertook. It:

- reviewed and established ongoing monitoring of resources available to front line staff;
- undertook a new round of performance development reviews (PDRs), reviewed the quality of completed PDR documentation and related it to role profiles;
- put in place a staff suggestion scheme to increase participation and consultation.

After considerable time and effort carrying out a number of targeted actions, the force re-audited in 2005, using the same survey tool to measure the impact of the interventions put in place. The force's investment in well-being was rewarded when the survey results showed major improvements compared with the 2003 audit. For example, significant reductions in perceived risks to physical health and psychological well-being were reported, as well as significant increases in organisational commitment. Every source of pressure measured was reported as being less of an issue than in 2003. In terms of bottom-line indicators, reductions in sickness absence levels for police officers were identified over the intervention period.

These practical examples reinforce the argument that it is best to audit and then develop an action plan that takes all of the factors relating to well-being into account, rather than just focussing on one, such as work overload or work–life balance. Seeking to improve well-being will be good for the business – as evidenced, employers no longer just face a moral obligation to provide healthy working environments, it is clear that it also makes good business sense to do so.

Overall, this chapter has argued that organisations will get real business benefits from an initial audit, followed by the strategic and systematic implementation of policies and practices that support and develop employee well-being in the workplace. Such policies are not a 'perk' for employees. The strong links between well-being and bottom-line performance factors such as absenteeism and productivity mean that supporting employee well-being is good for the organisation as well as the employee.

REFERENCES

Arvey, R. D., Carter, G. W. and Buerkley, D. K. (1991) Job satisfaction: dispositional and situational influences. In Cooper, C. L. and Robertson, I. T. (eds.) *International review of industrial and organizational psychology*, Chichester: John Wiley & Sons.

Bandura, A. (1977) *Social learning theory*. Englewood Cliffs: Prentice Hall.

Bernhardt, J. M. M., Donthu, N. and Kennett, P. A. (2000) A longitudinal analysis of satisfaction and profitability. *Journal of Business Research*, *47*(*2*), 161–71.

Cartwright, S. and Cooper, C. L. (2002) *ASSET: Management guide*. UK: Robertson Cooper.

Confederation of British Industry (1998) Life on the edge. *Confederation of British Industry Magazine*, July–August.

Cooper, C. L and Marshall, J. (1978) *Understanding executive stress*. London: Macmillan.

Cropanzano, R and Wright, T. A. (1999) A five-year study of change in the relationship between well-being and job performance. *Consulting Psychology Journal: Practice and Research*, *51*(*4*) pp. 252–65.

Donald, I., Taylor, P., Johnson, S., Cooper, C., Cartwright, S. and Robertson, S. (2005) Work environments, stress and productivity: An examination using ASSET. *International Journal of Stress Management*, *12*(*4*).

Efraty, D. and Sirgy, M. J. (1990) The effects of quality of working life (QWL) on employee behavioral responses. *Social Indicators Research*, *22*(*1*) pp. 31–47.

Fosam, E. B., Grimley, M. F. J. and Wisher, S. J. (1998) Exploring models for employee satisfaction: with particular reference to a police force. *Total Quality Management*, *9*, (*2&3*), 235–47.

French, J. R. P. and Caplan, R. D. (1973) Organizational stress and individual strain. In Marrow, A. J. (ed.) *The failure of success*. New York: AMACOM.

Greenberg, P. E., Stiglin, L. E., Finkelstein, S. N. and Bernott, E. R. (1993) The economic burden of depression in 1990 *Journal of Clinical Psychiatry*, *54*, 405–18. In Langlieb, A. M. and Kahn, J. P. (eds.) *Mental health and productivity in the workplace: A handbook for organizations and clinicians* San Francisco: Jossey-Bass.

Hartline, M. D., Ferrell, O. C. (1996) The management of customer-contact service employees: An empirical investigation. *Journal of Marketing*, *60*(*4*), 52–70.

HSE (2005) Case Study: Establishing the business case for investing in stress prevention activities and evaluating their impact on sickness absence levels. *Contract research report RR295*. Available at: www.hse.gov.uk/research/rrhtm/rr295.htm

Hurst, N., Young, S., Donald, I., Gibson, H. and Muyselaar, A. (1996) Measures of safety management performance and attitudes to safety at major hazard sites. *Journal of Loss: Prevention in the: Process Industries*, *9*, 161–72.

Industrial Society (2001) Managing best practice. *Occupational stress*, No. 83, 4–23.

Kahn, R. L., Wolfe, D. M., Quinn, R. P., Snoek, J. D., Rosenthal, R. A. (1964) *Organizational stress*. New York: Wiley.

Kessler, R., Bauber, C., Birnbaum, H. G., Frank, R. G., Greenberg, P. E., Rose, R. M., Simon, G. E. and Wang, P. (1999) Depression in the workplace: Effects on short-term disability *Health Affair*, *18*, 163–71.

King, C. A. and Garey, J. G. (1997) Relational quality in service encounters. *International Journal of Hospitality Management*, *16*(*1*), 39–63.

Lazarus, R. S. (1966) *Psychological stress and the coping process.* New York: McGraw-Hill.

Lazarus, R. S. and Folkman, S. (1984) *Stress, appraisal, and coping.* New York: Springer.

Lyne, K. D., Barrett, P. T., Williams, C. and Coley, K. (1994) A psychometric evaluation of the occupational stress indicator. *Journal of Occupational and Organizational Psychology, 73(2),* 195–27.

Makin, P. J., Cooper, C. L. and Cox, C. (2000) *Organizations and the psychological contract,* Leicester: British Psychological Society Books.

Meerding, W. J., Jzelenberg, W., Koopmanschap, M. A., Severns, J. L. and Burdorf, A. (2005) Health problems lead to considerable productivity loss at work among workers with high physical load jobs. *Journal of Clinical Epidemiology, 58,* 517–23.

NIOSH – Sauter, S., Murphy, L., Colligan, M., Hurrel, J., Scharf, F., Sinclair, R., Grubb, Goldenhar, L., Alterman, T., Johnston, J., Hamilton, A., Tisdale, J. (1999) *Stress at work.* www.cdc.gov/niosh/stresswk.html

O'Driscoll, M. P. and Cooper, C. L. (1996) Sources and management of excessive stress and burnout. In Warr, P. (ed.) *Psychology at work.* London: Penguin.

Patterson, M. G., West, M. A., Lawthom, R. and Nickell, S. (1997) Issues in people management: Impact of people management practices on business performance *Institute of Personnel and Development.*

Pflanz, S. E. and Heidel, S. H. (2003) Psychiatric causes of workplace problems. In Langlieb, A. M., and J. P. Kahn (eds.) *Mental health and productivity in the workplace: A handbook for organizations and clinicians* San Francisco: Jossey-Bass.

Singh, J., Goolsby, J. R. and Rhoads, G. K. (1994) Behavioral and psychological consequences of boundary spanning burnout for customer service representatives *Journal of Marketing Research, 31,* 558–69.

TUC (2000) *Stress at work tops safety poll.* www.tuc.org.uk/h_and_s/tuc-2390-f0.cfm

Wiley, J. W. (1991) Customer satisfaction: a supportive work environment and its financial cost. *Human Resource Planning, 14(2),* 117–27.

Wright, T. A. and Cropanzano, R. (2004) Psychological well-being and job satisfaction as predictors of job performance. *Journal of Occupational Health Psychology, 5(1),* 84–94.

Yeh, B. Y., Lester, D. and Tauber, D. L. (1986) Subjective stress and productivity in real estate sales people *Psychological Reports, 58,* 981–2.

Part III

Enhancing organizational health and performance

6 Maximizing the value of leadership development: key questions (and some answers)

Steve Kerr, Steffen Landauer and Elise Lelon

The purpose of this chapter is to identify, summarize current thinking and best practices about, and provide some answers to the most important questions organizations must resolve as they attempt to systematically develop their current and future leaders. Some of these are obvious, while others are seldom considered in advance, so are usually answered by default. These questions need to be addressed by any organization that is serious about formulating a competent leadership development initiative:

1. What is the organization's working definition of "leadership," and what kind of leadership is it seeking to develop?
2. What are the objectives of the leadership development initiative?
3. What should the content of the initiative look like?
4. Who is to be developed?
5. Who should be the faculty?
6. How should the success of the initiative be evaluated?
7. How should the leadership development group be organized?

What is the organization's working definition of leadership, and what kind of leadership is it seeking to develop?

During the last twenty years, as it has gained momentum and resonance in the business world, the term "leadership development" has been generalized to such an extent that it's not always clear what it means. One reason for the ambiguity surrounding the term is that, instead of being a one-size-fits-all, canned solution, the leadership development initiative of any organization needs to be specifically aligned with its mission, objectives, strategy and business model. Research shows that top companies connect their leadership strategy to their business strategies rather than to touted leadership practices du jour. Depending on an organization's history, culture, the quality and maturity of its work force, the competitive challenges it faces, and a number of additional factors, a firm may require a leadership skill set that is quite different from those of other firms even in the same industry. This suggests that, in order for a leadership development program to be successful, organizations need to do more than simply identify, recruit and train for the standard leadership qualities that are so prevalent in today's management textbooks. As rudimentary as this sounds, many firms fail to keep it in mind when they devise and conduct their development efforts. Therefore, it is worth underscoring the point that before organizations can hope to develop successful leaders, they need to clearly identify the kind of leaders they need to have if they are to succeed.

Although the ability to customize a leadership development initiative begins with an understanding of a company's mission and strategy, arriving at a definition that truly fits the organization requires self-awareness and some self-diagnosis on the part of top management and the board. The process of leadership definition can be conducted wholly internally, or with the assistance of outside consultants. Either way, research shows that the more actively involved CEOs and Boards of Directors are in developing leadership talent, the better are their business results. For example, in one survey of more than 350 public and private US companies, 83 percent of the top-quartile performers reported that their CEOs and Board of Directors were active participants in their firm's leadership development effort. (Hewitt Associates, 2005)

As a precursor to identifying specific leadership attributes, it may be helpful to think about the fit between broad categories of leadership and particular organization needs. Organizations seeking to get the most out of their leadership development effort need to ask themselves such questions as: Is the company in need of visionary, entrepreneurial leaders who will invent new products and markets and get people working on things that no one ever considered before? Or is what's needed a leader who is primarily a "manager," a value maximizer who will reduce costs, identify synergies, and make the most out of something that already exists? Or is the primary need for a charismatic leader who, through the force of his personality, can inspire people to work tirelessly in pursuit of the organization's objectives? (Mayo and Nohria, 2005) A component of this self-assessment exercise is to determine the organization's competitive advantage – what it can contribute to the world that no other institution can. This ongoing discovery, nurturance and redefinition of the company's uniqueness, then, need to become vital parts of the leader's job.

In the same vein, for a development program to shape leaders who are up to that task, the program must be tailored to the company's singularity. In the most effective organizations this becomes a self-perpetuating, virtuous cycle of differentiated achievement – identifying, developing, and appointing leaders whose attributes are highly congruent with the organization's particular needs, strategies, and business model.

Leadership competencies

Once an organization's unique competitive advantages are established, along with a general sense of the type of leader needed, a systematic identification of germane leadership attributes can begin. In *The Leadership Machine*, Lombardo and Eichinger defined sixty-seven competencies, derived from twelve years' worth of data on 6,000 people from more than 140 companies. These competencies fell into six broad categories: Strategic skills, operating skills, courage, energy and drive, organizational positioning skills, and personal and interpersonal skills. (Lombardo and Eichinger, 2000) Many other sets of competencies exist, including those designed by Hay-McBer, the Center for Creative Leadership and DDI, to name just a few.

While they can be helpful in organizing one's thinking about desirable characteristics, a frequent limitation of such competency models is that they become so all-encompassing that they lose their definitional value. One way to test the utility of a particular competency initiative is to ask employees who have not participated in the initiative to look at the list of competencies, then guess which organizational position is being described. In cases where they cannot make an accurate guess, it can be argued that a leadership definition with sixty-seven competencies is no more useful than one with zero. As mentioned earlier, the way to prevent this from occurring is to relate back to the organization's self-analysis and proceed from the vantage point of the company's singular mission, guiding values, and present challenges. From this individualized set of truths, it should be possible to devise a valuable profile of requisite leadership attributes.

The next question to be faced is how stable these attributes are likely to be over time. Lombardo and Eichinger have noted that, despite the dramatic changes in the business environment over the last century, the fundamentals that are generally required of leaders have not changed all that much. Because the business environment *has* changed so drastically, however, a critically important principle is that effective leadership requires not only capability but "copeabilty" – the ability to competently cope with the changes and challenges that come along, however dramatic these may be. The more drastic the changes, the more likely it is that, over the course of a leader's tenure, he will be called upon to make use of very different skills at different times. Therefore, a key component of effective leadership development programs is to identify and develop leadership attributes that are non-static and highly adaptive, and include the ability to lead and manage in an increasingly turbulent world.

Implicit in the discussion to date is the notion that, to be an effective leader, one has to be able to navigate through a number of paradoxes, including: Pursuing stability during times of rapid change; dealing simultaneously with urgent, pressing decisions and longer-term emerging needs; and combining a bias towards action with one of reflection and self-assessment (Chatterjee, 1998). While these pairings may strike the reader as over-polarized, false dichotomies, most leaders do have to attend to them simultaneously. Although some theoretical reconciliation may be possible, it feels to many leaders as though making progress towards one can only occur at the expense of another. They know that it is necessary to continuously change with the times, yet stable structures to control and enable the changes, and consistent and cohesive values and objectives, also seem to be necessary. Today's urgent to-do's are required for making the payroll and being legally compliant and countering competitor initiatives, but it is also critically important to start right now to prepare for future changes that will be required because of shifts in demographics, technology, geopolitics and numerous other factors. It is no small feat to grapple simultaneously with the questions "who are we now?" and "how do we redefine ourselves for the future?" (When Peter Drucker was once asked, during a Q and A session, which of his ideas he would "de-publish" if he could, he thought for a minute and then replied: "I used to think that you could put the same people in charge of today who are responsible for tomorrow.")

What are the objectives of the leadership development initiative?

The obvious response to this question, rebutted by almost no one, is that the primary purpose of any leadership development initiative is to develop the organization's present and future leaders. This answer is true as far as it goes, but it doesn't go very far. Most firms fail to consider, so reject by default, the potential use of their leadership development effort (a) as a "bully pulpit" from which to project the mission, goals and values, either to reinforce the organization's culture or signal a new beginning; (b) as a vehicle for leader assessment, not just development; and (c) as an effective way to engage with clients and other external constituencies, thus adding commercial value.

Using the leadership development initiative as a "bully pulpit"

Jack Welch regularly utilized his leadership development center, Crotonville, as a platform to launch important corporate initiatives. Work-Out, CAP, and many other initiatives were introduced to GE within the structure of the leadership development effort. Even Six-Sigma, whose statistical tools were taught within the GE businesses or at outside vendor locations, was launched at the officer's meeting in Crotonville and was reinforced at every leadership class subsequently held there. By the time he retired Welch had perfected not only the rhetoric of a MAJOR NEW INITIATIVE, but the pomp and ceremony that went along with it. Crotonville would be informed that the Chairman's helicopter was about to arrive. The students (GE executives) would take their assigned seats. Jack's helicopter would descend, like Moses from the mountain, with the sun glistening off the rotors. (By Westchester county ordinance, the skies had to be clear when Welch was in the air.) The effect of his dramatic arrival, coupled with his impassioned advocacy of the new initiative, was to make it clear to everyone that this was something really important, that it was here to stay, and that everyone in GE had to do it, and do it well.

In Goldman Sachs, the Pine St leadership development group has participated in a number of activities aimed at preserving its culture after the firm went public in 1999, and during its rapid, global growth since then. For example, the group has developed orientation programs for new managing directors and partners that are focused largely on cultural content. The group has also developed a set of actionable guidelines for managers who seek to strengthen the culture of their groups. These guidelines pertain to the most important components of the firm's culture, including performance review and feedback techniques, the use of non-financial rewards, how to lead teams and foster teamwork, and ways to establish and maintain strong meritocracies within Goldman's divisions and departments. As a final example, former Goldman Sachs CEO Hank Paulson involved Pine St in a series of nearly thirty "Chairman's" Forums, "each of which was attended by Hank and forty or fifty of the firm's managing directors. The central learning points of these sessions, captured in an "ethical compass" of Paulson's own design, were that (a) the most important asset the firm has is its reputation; (b) a firm's reputation can be lost in an instant by the actions of only one or a few people, and once lost it is extremely difficult to get back; and (c) the only way to establish and preserve an exemplary reputation is to go well beyond the minimum legal requirements for acceptable business behavior.

Using the leadership development initiative as a vehicle for leader assessment

Among the most fundamental choices every parent, teacher, and manager needs to make is the balance between control and development. Most experts agree that, for learning and development to be maximized, participants should be placed in a nurturing environment in which it is safe to take risks, make mistakes, and ask naïve questions. To provide a maximally safe leadership development experience: (a) test results should go only to the student, never to the student's boss; (b) the same should be true for any documentation of mistakes made, or poor judgment displayed, in business games, simulations, role plays and case studies; (c) information gathered from peers and teammates about an individual's strengths and weaknesses should be communicated informally, and not be made part of a permanent record; (d) "developmental" performance reviews should also be conveyed only to the focal person and not memorialized in a paper trail.

The dilemma, of course, is that the information described in (a) through (d) above is often extremely useful in assessing candidates' potential and readiness for increased responsibility and higher level leadership. Given the high cost of putting the wrong people into important jobs, it takes considerable discipline on the part of those responsible for selecting and promoting talent to keep their hands off the data.

Unlike many of the subjects discussed in this chapter, the control vs development question has no right answer, nor even an agreed upon set of best practices to guide the decision. One thing that is clear, however, is that if a leadership program is to assess as well as develop its people, ethical practice requires that participants be told, in advance, that this is the case.

Using the leadership development initiative to include clients and add commercial value

The most direct and impactful way for a leadership development effort to add commercial value is by inviting clients to attend events and classes jointly with internal employees. Goldman Sachs, for example, has developed a robust suite of leadership programs and consulting services that can be accessed by the firm's external clients. This effort will be elaborated upon later in the chapter. Pine St also seeks to add commercial value through its internal leadership programs, by including content focused on commercial excellence, often taught by members of the firm who are known to be extremely effective at fostering client relationships and converting these relationships into outsized financial returns for Goldman as well as their clients. Topics addressed in these sessions typically include such things as: sizing business opportunities, relationship management, assessing risks versus rewards, and managing one's own time in the most-productive manner.

Another example of a company seeking to utilize its leadership development initiative to advance the firm's core business objectives is provided by Hewlett Packard. Each session of its two-day flagship leadership program is focused on the business operating framework of HP, encompassing such topics as customer focus, operational efficiency, and financial and human capital.

What should the content of the initiative look like?

Effective learning can take place in classrooms, boardrooms, or on the assembly line. The teacher can be an educational professional, one's boss, or another senior leader. The method of instruction can be any combination of books, videos, lectures and seminars, and can occur on the job or through replications of real-world experiences such as simulations, role-plays, business games, debates, and case studies.

Although research suggests that the most-effective way to develop leaders is to do all of the above, these tools are not all equally effective. According to many long-term research studies, the optimal mix of learning methodologies to develop skills required to become an effective leader or manager is something in the neighborhood of:
- from work experiences – 70%
- from other people – 20%
- from coursework – 10%.

Learning from work experiences

"Tell me and I'll forget. Show me and I may remember.
Involve me and I'll understand." (old Chinese proverb).

The evidence is clear that most leadership development occurs through what is variously referred to as action learning, experiential learning, on-the-job learning, or learning by doing.

To illustrate this point at the outset of various seminars he was teaching on leadership development, one of the authors of this chapter would ask participants to write down the most important developmental experience of their careers. He would then ask participants, who were senior managers from many different countries and types of organizations, a number of questions about what they had written. Here are a few of these questions, along with responses:

- How many of you wrote down some kind of formal course, conference or program? (typically two or three people out of forty-five)
- In how many cases was it the organization's intention to provide you with a developmental opportunity? (between five and eight people out of forty-five)
- Was the experience you described a "one-off," i.e., a unique event, or one that could be replicated or, if not replicated, simulated? (again, between five and eight people)

The same response pattern was obtained from a poll of 1,450 managers from a dozen global companies, which concluded that, by a wide margin, the best teacher for leadership is experience. (Ready, 1994)

A voluminous body of literature on adult learning and corporate leadership development concludes that people learn best when they are involved in the action of learning. It's easier to learn something new when it is linked to existing knowledge and experience that you already have. When this occurs, the lesson fits into a larger backdrop and has contextual meaning. McCall *et al.* found that executives who had exposure to and practiced a wide array of managerial roles were more effective than those without that breadth of experience (McCall, Lombardo and Morrison, 1988). These roles included such things as new business initiatives, business turnarounds, moves from line to staff, and roles with P&L responsibility. Even in cases where a person's job remains the same, the range of experience can be expanded by allowing the job to be done in another country, launching a new product in a different way, implementing a new recruitment or evaluation system, or instituting a new quality improvement program. Another means of allowing employees to experience a change in role is to flatten the organization. With fewer bureaucratic layers, individuals are usually able to take on more responsibility in a way that ultimately increases their skill set.

The practice of "learning by doing," as embodied in the apprenticeship systems of the guilds, is perhaps the oldest known approach to learning and human development. Among its earliest advocates as a structured system of learning was John Dewey (Dewey, 1910). Today, under the banner of experiential, on-the-job, or action learning, this concept has spawned a management development philosophy and practice that is used in various ways by a multitude of corporations and trainers. Action learning "puts the learning where the work is" by using real-life problems in people's work lives as opportunities to develop skills rather than merely impart knowledge. We made the point earlier that among the most important leadership attributes are adaptability and the reconciliation of paradoxes. There is probably no better way to develop these qualities than through the challenges and contradictions of actual, true-life experiences.

GE's popcorn stands

Learning by doing can be implemented in many ways. One powerful example is provided by GE's use of "popcorn stands," whose name reflects the fact that in nearly all for-profit organizations, approximately 80 percent of the revenue comes from 20 percent of the operations. It is essential that units generating most of the money be led by experienced leaders of proven competence. In the other units, however (the popcorn stands), less experienced, high potential leaders can hone their skills, try out new business models and strategies, and perfect their leadership styles. If they fail, they fail – without adverse consequences for the overall organization. If they succeed, they can be moved to a popcorn stand that provides a different kind of leadership experience – from a long-cycle to a short-cycle business, for example, or from a defense to a consumer business, or from a healthy to a distressed business, or to an out-of-home-country assignment. Inherent in the belief in experiential learning is the idea that the best predictor of leadership is leadership. GE believes that the best way to develop leaders is to provide them with opportunities to lead, and the best way to determine whether the firm has potential CEOs or division heads on its hands is to scrutinize them closely as they carry out their leadership responsibilities. GE's popcorn stands are both an excellent vehicle for leadership development and a great way to assess the capability and cope-ability of its potential future leaders. GE benefits by acquiring deep, subtle knowledge about the leadership capabilities of its rising stars, by observing their responses in a live laboratory to various kinds of stretch assignments and stressful situations. The firm learns how its potential future leaders handle success, and how they cope with failure, in settings where failure isn't costly. By the time a graduate of the popcorn stands is put in charge of a business whose results really matter, she has had the benefit of a superior leadership education, and the likelihood that her performance will disappoint is low.

The individuals also benefit from this approach to leadership development, by affording them an opportunity to figure out what they are good at, and what they like to do. They also become more sensitized to the kind of working conditions that enable them to flourish instead of flounder.

It should be noted that many organizations follow GE's practice of grooming potential leaders by putting them in charge of smaller, relatively unimportant operations and promoting them as they demonstrate their worth. What makes GE unusual is the self-consciousness with which the firm carries out the process – from the creation of "road maps" of experiences to be acquired, to the establishment of evaluation and feedback mechanisms that ensure that the learning, for both the individual and GE, is maximized. This process – called Session C – will be discussed in more detail later in the chapter.

Before leaving this topic, one additional point seems worth mentioning. Numerous organizations visit Crotonville each year to learn more about GE's approach to leadership development, and are usually taken with the concept of the popcorn stands and the role they play in developing GE's leaders. Invariably, the smaller firms point out that, while it is clearly possible for a firm the size of GE to make use of this concept, it seems impractical for much smaller companies. There is some truth to this observation, but two things need to be kept in mind. First, while it is true that smaller organizations have fewer popcorn stands, they also have fewer people who need to be developed. Second, it is *not* necessary that all the popcorn stands be located within the person's own organization. Consider, for example, how universities solve this problem – by arranging internships for their students, and sabbaticals for their faculty. As a corporate example, GE got tremendous benefit (from both an employee development and client relations standpoint) from their "at the customer, for the customer" initiative, in which a number of GE employees spent a period of time working out of the offices of an important customer. While clients may or may not eagerly support such an idea, suppliers often will, and spending some time in the environment of a firm's third-party provider can sometimes be an excellent place to learn and develop new skills.

A further example of a rich opportunity for away-from-the-home-office development comes from the world of social sector, not-for-profit organizations. Goldman Sachs' utilization of this opportunity will be described shortly.

Other approaches to experiential learning

Another approach to action learning is a structured process that involves a problem, client, action, learning set, facilitator, and sponsor. (Revans, 1982)

Whether the process concerns an individual or a team project, the problem is a business or organizational challenge that is confronted by the leader in real time. The client is the leader, the owner of the problem. The action learning set is the heart of the program, where people responsible for solving the problem meet to discuss their respective experiences. This is where the leader and others are able to question their processes, and challenge and encourage each other. The facilitator assists in the learning process by clarifying what the participants are doing and saying, supporting them, asking questions, and challenging decisions. The sponsor is the senior manager who is responsible for the corporate leadership development program.

An important distinction between the approaches of GE and Revans's approach to action learning is that GE places extensive reliance on moving its people into a variety of ongoing work situations. Action learning prefers, but does not require, that the learning be based on actual real world experiences. The question is worth asking: Why, in view of the demonstrated benefits of leadership development through employee mobility, do many firms rely primarily on contrived rather than truly on-the-job action learning experiences? A number of answers to this question exist, but at the heart of the decision to emphasize true on-the-job vs manufactured experiences is a belief by senior leadership in the relative importance of leadership and management skills, as opposed to commercial and technical skills, as the principal basis for hierarchical advancement. At GE, an extremely important criterion for reward and career advancement is one's skill at leading and managing. Identifying synergies, reducing costs, creating compatible systems and processes, and efficiently converting inputs into outputs, are honored and rewarded. Extensive knowledge of the intricacies of the business, though respected, is not a promotional requirement. To make this point, Chuck Okosky, GE's former VP of Executive Development, advises firms to "bet on the . . . people who have demonstrated the ability to assemble and excite a high-quality team, and the intensity to do a tough job well. Don't be afraid to promote stars without specifically relevant experience, seemingly over their heads. Generally you will be surprised at how well they do." (Olofsky, 2002) To make the same point – that outstanding leadership does not require deep product and process knowledge – former CEO Jack Welch would tell GE's future leaders at Crotonville: "At the end of the day, I don't know how to build a jet engine. I'm a chemical engineer. If I built the engine, would you get on the plane? *I* wouldn't get on the plane!"

In contrast, the primary basis for rewards and advancement in most Wall Street firms is a person's industry knowledge, product skills, and commercial track record. Good leadership and management skills, though respected, are not a promotional requirement. The most valued employees in financial service firms are the "producer-leaders", who have extensive knowledge of their industry and possess the technical skills needed to be successful. In many companies, these people are chosen to lead their businesses. The underlying assumption is that technical knowledge and, in the client-facing businesses, commercial skills, are the necessary and sufficient basis for promotion to senior executive positions. In these firms, very few people are encouraged or permitted to be "just" managers. These firms do not consider it essential for promising candidates to be moved around the firm as their careers evolve, to add dimensionality to their experience base across a variety of the firm's business functions and locations. What *is* considered essential is for producer-leaders, up to and including the CEO, to retain and personally service their clients as they advance in their careers.

There are huge advantages to this model, but one consequence is that these people tend to get better and better at their specialties rather than expand their repertoire of skills and experience. In a number of cases, Wall Street firms have promoted their best research analysts, who excel at applying their outstanding analytical skills within a particular industry, into director of research and even CEO positions. Such individuals, though they have deep knowledge of their chosen industry's firms and markets, are sometimes poor leaders of others, and are often unable to benefit from learning-by-doing developmental opportunities because their "producer" roles not only take immense amounts of time, but require them to remain at the cutting edge of their specialty. This frequently prevents them from accepting a mobility assignment that takes them away from their areas of expertise.

Fortunately, in situations where employee mobility is limited, organizations can do a number of things to make use of experiential learning opportunities that do not require taking people away from their desks and out of their areas of expertise for long periods of time. One enjoyable, easy to organize and effective example is the "shadowing" technique popularized by Hewlett Packard. This approach pairs one senior executive with one more junior (the shadow) who, as the name suggests, accompanies the shadowee to various events and meetings that have been carefully selected to provide the shadow with experiences she would not otherwise get. The length of the shadowing assignment varies, and need not be continuous. Some meetings may be too sensitive (or too boring) for the shadow to attend. Provided the offices of both parties are in close proximity, the shadow can spread eight to twelve hours of experience across several days, or even weeks.

A more substantial way to give people on-the-job experiences without taking them away from their day jobs is through the use of special projects. GE, Goldman Sachs and Hewlett Packard all make extensive use of this approach. In all three organizations, timely, important projects are identified by the CEO and others in the executive office. Although the projects are highly tailored to reflect current organizational challenges, opportunities, and priorities, some patterns are evident in the kinds of projects that are selected. Country analyses, for example, are popular with both the executive office and program participants. These projects are usually based around such questions as: Should we invest more (or employ more, or do more business) in Russia, or in India, or in Eastern Europe? Another oft-selected project relates to a competitive analysis, e.g., what products is ___ offering that we aren't? What markets are they in, that we're not? What do our joint customers and/or suppliers say about their service, relative to ours?

At Hewlett Packard, the Office of Strategy and Corporate Development is a key resource in surfacing these projects. Criteria used at HP in selecting projects include: (1) Is the issue important for HP to solve? (2) Is the size appropriate, that is, complex enough to challenge a group of strong leaders, yet sufficiently bounded so that a group of leaders can make significant progress in a limited time frame? (3) Is an engaged project sponsor available? (4) Does the project call for teams to venture outside the bounds of HP to gather data (consistent with the program's objective to broaden the perspectives of participating leaders)?

One way to increase the intensity of the learning experience and heighten the sense of importance, is by having the participants report their findings and recommendations to a very senior audience. In GE, participants meet with the top thirty executives in the company, including the CEO, for a two-hour, no-holds-barred discussion. In Goldman Sachs, participants present their recommendations to the firm's board of directors, one of whom is the CEO.

A final Goldman Sachs, Pine St example of away-from-the-office, experiential learning involves approximately forty of the firm's managing directors who were not on any non-profit board, but wanted to be. Pine St, in collaboration with the Goldman Sachs Foundation, identified and placed these people onto boards that were appropriate for and receptive to someone from Goldman joining. The next step was to structure an arrangement with the Harvard Business School, which agreed to host the new board members from Goldman Sachs, as well as the chairperson of each of the boards they were joining, at a two-day conference at Harvard on the topic of (new) board member effectiveness. The response was extremely positive. The board chairpeople found the experience to be valuable and the Goldman participants even more so, because they received excellent information that they could immediately apply, and also because they got to hang around for two days with the heads of the boards they were joining. Benefits to Goldman included the satisfaction of witnessing a large number of their executives having a positive impact in their communities, as well as some favorable press coverage. To Pine St came the more selfish benefit that, through their activities on non-profit boards, the managing directors received a wealth of experiences – how to motivate through the use of non-financial rewards, for example, how to influence people over whom you lack formal authority, and how to retain valuable workers without being able to promote them – that would have been impossible to come by in the course of their day-to-day jobs.

Adversity as a developmental tool

It has been said that "experience is an unfair teacher because the test comes first, then the lessons follow." It is undeniably true that hardship plays an important role in learning. Probably all of us can recall times in our lives when mistakes or misfortune challenged our confidence and our capabilities. Yet it is often those very struggles that provided us with our most meaningful and powerful developmental experiences. This is no less true of leaders than of other human beings. An important benefit of learning while doing the job is that the process quite often creates meaningful adversity. McCall, Lombardo, and Morrison (1988) found that leaders often identify periods of "derailment" as having had a major impact upon their development. Offering leaders opportunities to learn while they are working at their jobs, rather than removing them from their jobs to learn in a classroom, allows for victories and defeats that may well make a difference in business results. Because these on-the-job experiences have bottom line impact rather than merely being of theoretical interest, they have the potential to powerfully shape leaders' self awareness and problem solving skills. Sometimes, leaders aren't the only ones who gain something along the way. It has been argued that subordinates can learn a lot more from a bad leader than a good one – provided one survives the experience!

Kolb's model

David Kolb has devised a four-stage learning model that can be used to explain how challenging assignments can be of use in developing leadership qualities (1983). To illustrate what happens to people in situations of real-time stretch learning, let's consider the hypothetical example of Melanie Yia, a Managing Director at a biotech venture firm. Melanie is given the opportunity to head up the task force on diversity, which is replete with confusion and controversy, in light of recent events that have occurred at her firm. She knows no one on the task force, and has had no experience with diversity issues from an organizational perspective. However, her boss has confidence in Melanie's ability to solve complex problems, and wants her to develop her interpersonal, group management, and communication skills.

In the first stage of Kolb's model, the individual benefits from concrete experience of doing – of taking action. In this stage, Melanie has her very first meeting as head of the task force. In the second stage, the individual observes the consequences of her action and is able to reflect upon it. In our scenario, Melanie reviews how she handled the meeting and realizes that she failed to seek input from other members. In the third stage, she is able to form general conclusions that are based on her reflection. She analyzes her own observations, sees patterns in her behavior, and begins to internalize the concepts that she has observed. She notices, for example, that she has a habit of cutting people off when they begin to talk, at work and at home. She comes to realize that her reluctance to let others speak is because of her fear that they might point out something she hasn't considered. Finally, in the fourth stage, she is able to test the implications of that insight in new situations, experimenting with her newfound understanding to see if it holds up.

In the next task force meeting, Melanie begins by opening the floor to the group and encouraging people to express their views on the highest priority agenda items for the week. The meeting flows much more smoothly this time around. People are engaged in the conversation and seem to be invested in the outcomes. Melanie returns to her office and concludes that soliciting input, listening rather than just talking, generated a number of insightful suggestions from other task force members. She ends her day by considering how to incorporate these suggestions into the action plan she will present next week.

A number of tools exist to systematize the practice of giving stretch assignments to high-potential employees like Melanie. One of these, devised by Lombardo and Eichinger, is an assignment management matrix that delineates a list of general and specific jobs and projects that will flesh out an individual's experience and exposure (2000). The list of assignments constitutes the left side of the matrix. Across the top are the skills that will be needed to successfully complete these assignments. This graphic can serve as a useful road map for leaders-in-training.

Learning from other people

Typically, the goal of coaching is to enhance mobility. Coaches are goal-directed. They set out performance objectives and help the individual achieve them. Coaching often enables the learning of specific skill or techniques that can be mastered and measured. Some coaches are the coachees' bosses, or people of higher level within the organization. Other coaches are external parties – usually consultants or academics, who provide an impartial perspective aimed at helping the individual to change behavior and become more effective.

Coaching can be short or long term. Short-term coaching is often provided as a stopgap measure to enable individuals to acquire skills they need to be successful in a particular position or circumstance. Longer-term coaching is typically used for the purpose of addressing more substantial developmental goals.

Coaching may also be classified into two general types: Formal and informal. Formal coaching makes use of a customized program, created by the coach to help the individual achieve some explicit objectives. Research suggests that more than 65 percent of Global 1000 companies use some form of formal coaching (Hicks and Peterson, 1998). Although coaching is more labor intensive and, therefore, more costly than most other approaches to leadership development, well designed coaching programs have been found to produce three times more behavioral changes than traditional training approaches. One year after the coaching programs end, most of the desired behavioral changes have been found to remain in place. (Peterson, 2002)

Mentors bear resemblance to coaches, but differ in several important ways. The mentor relationship is more often of a personal nature, and frequently develops between a protege and someone who is two to four organizational levels his senior. However, in many cases mentors have no formal relationship with the firm. While mentoring, like coaching, can be built around specific developmental goals, it is common for less experienced people to seek general career advice or a fresh perspective about office politics or boss–subordinate relationships. Whether one of coaching or mentoring, for the relationship to be successful, honesty and trust must be mutual, the mentor and protégé must meet regularly, and the feedback must be timely.

Arrow Electronics is an example of a best practice company that has successfully institutionalized mentoring. The impetus to do so starts from the top, a worldwide mentoring program focuses on top managers, and all Arrow units devise their own mentoring programs. Mentors are assigned centrally, with careful attention paid to the pairings. The company guidelines are that mentors should meet monthly, things discussed must be kept confidential, and specific subject matter should be identified. Mentoring is deeply rooted in the culture of the firm, and mentors see their role as a vital part of their job. As one dramatic example, B. J. Scheihing, a vice president who is responsible for Worldwide Operations, said of his role, "I once traveled from London to Denmark just to have dinner with someone I was mentoring. He couldn't believe the only reason for that leg of the trip was to spend time with him and I told him, 'You bet it is, and here's why: The next time you're having one of those days – when quitting seems like a pretty good idea – I want you to remember that you are important enough to Arrow that I made a special trip to Denmark to have dinner with you. Instead of quitting, I want you to pick up the phone and call me and together we'll figure out what to do." (Michaels, Handfield-Jones and Axelrod, 2001)

In a more typical example, another Arrow executive, Harriet Green, who is president of the Contract Manufacturing Services Group, has regular breakfasts with her mentees, planned a year in advance. She also has a marker in her Palm Pilot that alerts her when she hasn't heard from her mentees in a long time, in which case she contacts them.

A good example of a well-administered executive coaching program is that of Goldman Sachs, which offers highly structured, intense, individualized development to approximately fifty-five partners, managing directors and vice presidents, all of whom are nominated by the firm's senior leadership. The coaches, too, are carefully selected, thoroughly vetted, and exhaustively briefed about the firm.

A number of factors contribute to the success of the initiative, but three are particularly noteworthy.

1. It is considered prestigious to have a coach. This is in sharp contrast to the stigma that is attached to the coaching program in some firms, and the embarrassment many managers feel at being assigned a coach. Most organizations have, by now, learned "the message" they are supposed to use when informing the coachee of his nomination. ("As you know, all great athletes have coaches . . . blah blah blah . . . You should feel good that the firm has elected to invest in your future . . ., blah blah blah . . . etc. But the only part of "the message" most recipients seem to hear is: "They say I need a coach!") In Goldman Sachs, however, the most senior executives have coaches, and proudly introduce them in conversations and show them off at meetings. The firm has found that, by starting at the very top, with people who are clearly at ease with the assignment and seem to consider it valuable, other people tend to want one as well.

2. The process is open, and people are candid. To establish some degree of trust, many firms find it necessary to create conditions of confidentialty. The coach can speak with the coachee, of course, but not with the coachee's boss; the coach is also denied access to performance reviews and other "sensitive" data about the person being coached, so must figure out on his own, or take the coachee's word for, which developmental needs to work on. In Goldman Sachs, however, people trust the process enough so that the coach *can* access sensitive data and talk with the boss, and the boss comfortably shares her aspirations and concerns about the coachee. The boss might say, for example: "I would love to give Louis an Asian assignment, but his cultural awareness and listening skills are so poor that I don't dare. If you could do something about those particular developmental needs, Louis could have a great career here." Louis sees his coach talking to his boss and doesn't get upset, and the boss shares her views about Louis with his coach, without concern that the information will be inappropriately used.

3. The coaching assignment is managed as any other assignment should be managed. That is to say, the program is closely overseen by the firm's leadership development group; there is a limited (nine-month) time horizon for every coaching assignment; and explicit, written objectives exist, against which the coachee (and implictly, his coach) are assessed at the end of the program.

A majority of firms today probably have some kind of coaching and/or mentoring program. In even the best of these programs, the typical role of the coach–mentor is as a kind of Jimminy Cricket – dispensing sage, benign advice, but without getting directly involved. Within Goldman Sachs's Pine St organization, a different set of rules applies. Specifically, every team member below the rank of vice president is required to select a member of the senior staff as his or her "advocate." Advocates may be thought of as "mentors on steroids," i.e., people who not only dispense advice, but proactively interact on their mentee's behalf with the mentee's boss and, as necessary, with other members of senior management.

Here are two examples of "advocates" in action. The first concerns a member of the Pine St team who was so good at organizing and running orientation programs that he was being overused in that capacity. His advocate came to the team leader with the observation that "I fear we are excessively using *XXX* on these programs. For the sake of his professional development (and his sanity), he should be doing other things." Perhaps the advocate came up with this observation on his own, or perhaps the individual got fed up with doing orientations and asked his advocate to intervene. The team leader had no way of knowing, because Pine St's running rules forbid him from asking.

The purpose of this rule, of course, is to make it safe for team members to be candid with their advocates. If the observation is considered valid, the boss bargains with the advocate in the manner of a team owner negotiating with an athlete's agent. In this case, the team leader asked:: "How about if I use *XXX* for next month's orientation program, because I don't have anyone else, but after that I promise I'll give him a one-year moratorium on orientations so he can do other things? The advocate agreed, and the deal was struck.

The second example concerns two secretaries, one a pleasure to work with, the other so surly and uncooperative that she scared everyone away. The "good secretary's" advocate confronted the team leader, pointing out that the secretaries' workloads had become so unbalanced as to be both inefficient and unfair, and demanded that the leader do something about it. The leader admitted that he was aware of the problem, but was himself scared to approach the other secretary, so had not taken action. Under pressure from the advocate, however, he screwed up his courage and resolved the issue.

Learning from coursework

Although coursework comprises only 10% of the 70–20–10, many organizations focus the bulk of their time and energy on getting this part right. Great attention is spent deriving answers to such questions as: Should we invest in bricks and mortar? Should we create our own curriculum or contract with an outside vendor? If the latter, should we sign a contract with the local university, or use consultants, or employ our own, in-house faculty. What is all too often overlooked by these organizations is the most fundamental question of all, namely: "What should we teach?"

The easiest way to avoid this question is to concentrate instead upon which populations to herd into the classroom – picking off employees by organizational level, for example, or title, or years of service, or by department or division. Although commonly done, this is not an effective way to structure a leadership training curriculum. The best development programs organize their courses around leadership transitions, usually starting with a new manager course, and continuing through a customized set of offerings that reflects the particular challenges faced by organizational leaders as they advance in their careers. Courses may be offered, for example, to leaders who are for the first time overseeing multiple organizational levels, or managing across national boundaries and time zones, or working with a co-head.

There are a number of benefits to creating a curriculum that is based upon transitions. Among the most important are:

1. By inviting people to participate immediately prior to or just after assuming their new roles, participants tend to be particularly receptive to the information conveyed.
2. Content can be targeted to the particular needs of the participants, and experts and role models can be brought in who have successfully done what the attendees have to do to be successful in their new roles.
3. Participants have an immediate opportunity to put into practice what they have learned.
4. Course attendees remain in contact with one another after the program. After almost every successful course, students do huggies, swap calling cards, and promise to call each other "real soon" – but seldom do. Because the participants in a transition-based course have similar back-home concerns and challenges, however, they tend to stay in touch, and often become important sources of advice and support to each other.

As noted above, for a transition-based curriculum to be maximally effective, students must receive the information they need when, or soon after, they assume their new role. An important advantage of the "leaders-teaching-leaders" model (to be discussed in more detail shortly), is that expensive speaker fees are not being paid so classes can be smaller, and therefore more frequent. In some cases, however, whether driven by cost, time urgency, or the nature of the subject matter, we have found "executive briefings" to be a more effective teaching tool than classes. A briefing usually takes the form of a sixty or ninety-minute discussion between a teacher/expert and a "student." The briefing can be held at the perfect time from the student's standpoint, and the information can be maximally tailored to the particular transition.

Usually the dialogue involves the teacher and a single student, but occasionally more than one student participates. For example, when two individuals are made division or department "co-heads," the teacher gets together with each person separately, then meets with both at the same time. One purpose of these meetings is to communicate information about best practice do's and don'ts, garnered from interviews with many of the firm's most effective co-heads. Another purpose is to provide an opportunity for each co-head to share whatever concerns he may have about his new assignment or his partner with the teacher and, if there is sufficient trust, with his co-head.

GE's "Session C"

For clarity's sake, we have offered explanations and illustrations of the "70," the "20" and the "10" as though they were independent approaches to leadership development. However, as noted earlier, considerable evidence suggests that the most effective way to develop leaders is to combine these in an integrated and orchestrated manner. Also as noted earlier, for maximal impact the complete leadership development initiative – including the learning assumptions, content, and delivery – needs to be consistent with and grounded in the context and culture of the particular organization, and must be specifically aligned with the firm's mission, objectives, strategy and business model.

A good example of a thoroughly aligned and integrated leadership development effort is General Electric's "Session C," which blends job-based learning, coaching, and formal classroom training in a way that systematically prepares, and assesses the readiness of, GE's current and future executives for broader leadership responsibilities. Because of the nature of its products and markets, GE seeks to have its candidates for higher office gain experience in a global business, a high tech business, a long- and a short-cycle business, a consumer and a defense business, and other settings that are appropriate to the firm's business models and strategies. Then, as openings arise in one or another of these kinds of businesses, the resumés of GE's potential future leaders are reviewed to permit people to be matched to those assignments that are most value-added. If the opening is in a business that GE depends upon for operating results and profitability, the assignment will normally go to someone who, based on her track record, is very likely to succeed in that position. On the other hand, if the opening is in one of the "popcorn stands," i.e., a business that is not currently a strong contributor to GE's financial results, an individual will probably be selected for whom the experience fulfills an important developmental need.

While a critical component of the Session C process is on job-related, experiential learning (the "70" in 70–20–10), careful attention is also paid to the various ways that the developmental needs of each individual might be addressed via coaching-mentoring and/or classroom training, whether at Crotonville, in one of the GE businesses, or outside GE.

Who is to be developed?

A key strategic question of any leadership development initiative is: Who is the target population? The core audience normally consists of those holding leadership responsibilities, although the categorization of these responsibilities (along with the definition of leadership itself, as noted earlier) should be organization-specific. In some organizations the magnitude of leadership responsibility corresponds quite closely to job title, but usually it does not, so the designation of program participants should not be solely based on title.

Another important decision pertains to the tradeoff between breadth and depth. Organizations must consider whether it is of greater value to offer intensive developmental opportunities to a small group of present and future leaders, or less intensive offerings to some broader group. Of course it is not necessary to be at either extreme. Even the most elitist firms will usually make training opportunities available to new managers, for example, and provide some kind of orientation to all new employees.

Another important, though often overlooked, potential audience for leadership development programs is the organization's clients and other external constituencies. Discussions are broadened and enriched by the inclusion of outsiders, and the strengthened relationships that result from learning side-by-side with one's customers can generate strong commercial benefits.

Defining leadership responsibility

In most organizations, the initial level of leadership responsibility occurs when a person manages others for the first time. As one makes the transition from individual production to getting work done through others, a number of skills become critical, including delegation, motivation, and establishing and communicating business unit strategies. Many organizations define subsequent leadership transitions in terms of span of control (i.e., number of people managed), numbers of organizational levels above and below, and whether direct reports are co-located with the leader or are geographically dispersed. As noted earlier, however defined, developmental opportunities should be offered immediately prior to or soon after the transition rather than waiting until the leader has been in the role for a long time.

Breadth vs depth

Many organizations offer leadership development opportunities to leaders at all levels, and there are sound reasons for doing so. Goldman Sachs, for example, starts early, by including modules on leadership in its orientation program for new analysts who are joining the firm from college. For organizations seeking to hire large numbers of younger employees, the opportunity for early professional development can be an important part of the value proposition, serving as an important recruiting advantage.

However, it is also true that every organization has roles that are unusually important to the firm's success, and has a specified set of individuals who are in these roles or are considered to be "high potentials." Initiatives that strategically target these key people for rich, intense development opportunities are essential to gain maximal returns on the leadership development investment. Being labeled a key contributor, and participating with other leaders and high-potentials in the developmental opportunities that go with the label, can be powerful motivating forces, and can catalyze constructive discussions between individuals and their managers about what action steps are required to make the list. To make this point, Goldman Sachs' CEO once said to a group of his leaders about the firm's high potential program, "If your people are upset about not being in the program, tell them there's another train coming, and let them know exactly what they need to do to get a seat on that train." In the same vein, former CEO Jack Welch used to tell GE's managers: "If your boss tells you you're a high-pot, and you've been with the company for eight years and haven't been to MDC (a course for high potentials), he"s lying to you, and you should go ask him what you need to do to be nominated."

Development in natural work teams

While many leadership programs mix participants from different departments and functions, some topics lend themselves particularly well to business-specific programs. For example, when learning about strategy and business planning, participants benefit when they can share the experience with their teammates and apply what they learn to specific conditions and challenges in their own business. Teamwork is another topic that is often best taught when the relevant parties are in the room together. Finally, as was previously noted, circumstances sometimes arise where highly individualized learning is required, as between co-heads who need to establish a strong working relationship.

Including customers and other external constituencies

For several reasons, external customers may be well worth including in an organization's leadership development initiative. First, discussions are often more interesting when participants and best practices from other organizations are included. For example, teamwork is considered within Goldman Sachs to be the centerpiece of its culture. In preparation for one of the joint Goldman-client courses, clients were asked to submit in advance a copy of their firms' values, principles or mission statements, which were informally content analyzed. Then in class the instructor said: "As most of you know, Goldman considers teamwork to be at the heart of everything it does. Yet we have observed that *seven* of the (more than thirty) clients in this room never even mention teamwork among its core principles and values. Can we talk about this, please? Is it that you seven have embedded teamwork in your actions and attitudes so thoroughly that you don"t need to mention it? Or does your firm believe that friendly competition, or some other model, is a more effective way to conduct business?"

Needless to say, the resultant discussion was far more illuminating and useful than would have been a reaffirmation of teamwork by a classroom full of Goldman Sachs people who had all "drunk the Kool-aid."

A second benefit of including external clients is that the motivation of internal leaders to attend and fully participate in leadership development programs tends to sharply increase when their clients are present. The value of spending time with clients is well understood and, added to the leadership development opportunity, can create a compelling case for attendance. A third advantage, perhaps most obvious but sometimes extremely important, is that client relationships are inevitaby strengthened during the course of the program, which sometimes translates into meaningful commercial dividends down the road.

Client initiatives have been an important part of Goldman Sachs' leadership development activities. The firm's relationship managers host their clients at one- to two-day leadership programs that are held regularly in New York, London, and Hong Kong. Reactions from both clients and Goldman's managers have been extremely positive.

Programs have also been customized for various Goldman Sachs businesses and client groups. These customized programs afford the opportunity to add industry-specific content to more general leadership content. Several programs for hedge fund clients, for example, included sessions on different compensation models that are prevalent in the hedge fund industry, as well as key infrastructure issues entailed in running a hedge fund.

Including other external stakeholders as participants can also produce important benefits to all the parties. The Wharton School, for example, got tremendous mileage from a series of business briefings it ran for members of the business media. In many cases these were people whose training and expertise were not in business, and who were grateful for the opportunity to ask naive questions and develop their expertise in a safe, professional environment. Among the benefits to Wharton was that, as a result of the relationships established during these programs, the Wharton faculty began to receive a lot of requests from the media for quotes and opinions. As another example, GE invited a number of US regulators – among them the NRC, the FAA, the Customs Bureau and the IRS – to attend programs at Crotonville (GE's leadership development center) alongside GE managers from the appropriate businesses. An obvious benefit is that the programs enhanced participants' management and leadership skills. (It has been noted, only half in jest, that the only thing more problematic than a competent regulator is an incompetent regulator.) Additionally, participants acquired a valuable, broadened perspective from being exposed to "the other side's" point of view. The programs also put a human face on GE, providing regulators with an actual person to call (and GE with a chance to respond) if something seemed amiss or confusing.

Who should serve as faculty?

Most organizations employ external experts as faculty in their leadership development programs. These experts can make a strong contribution by serving as an important source of new ideas, and by bringing to the programs a depth and diversity of experience that internal leaders are unlikely to have.

These strengths notwithstanding, we believe that instruction by outside experts should be limited to no more than a third of the curriculum. The primary faculty, in our opinion, should be based on a model of "leaders teaching leaders."

As discussed earlier, the most useful definition of leadership for any organization is one that is grounded in its own culture and reflective of its business model. Consistent with this belief, the people with the deepest knowledge of a firm's businesses and culture are likely to be those who have lived in and experienced them first-hand, and have specific experiences to relate.

For example, as noted previously, many professional services firms utilize a "producer-leader" model, whereby most senior leaders retain significant client and/or execution responsibilities. Successfully balancing their client and leadership responsibilities is a major challenge for leaders in these organizations, and is a key component of their leadership programs. This content is most effectively and, by a wide margin, most credibly delivered by leaders who can offer specific best practices pertaining to these challenges, who can discuss their own criteria for involvement in client or execution matters, and who can relate stories of their own success and lessons learned from their failures.

Many other topics – for example, time management, delegating downward and managing upward, and managing the firm's performance assessment and review process – contain considerable organization-specific content that is often best addressed by insiders who are respected for having solved these problems.

Hewlett Packard provides a good example of an organization that is realigning its leadership development efforts so as to make increased use of internal line faculty. In its 2007 two-day flagship "Leading for Results" program for the firm's top leaders, more than 90 percent of the content is taught by HP leaders, including CEO Mark Hurd and a number of his key deputies on the HP Executive Committee. Another important benefit of the leaders–teaching–leaders model is suggested by the old saying: "If you really want to understand something, try teaching it." Communicating their concepts and beliefs about leadership can be highly developmental for the faculty, forcing them to reflect more deeply on their own roles as leaders and creating heightened self-awareness and building their mastery of the ideas they convey. The preparation for, and act of, teaching also tends to make them better coaches with their own people, and better speakers when interacting with their clients, the press, and other external and internal constituencies.

Another, oft-stated benefit of using internal faculty is to avoid the high *per diems* and speaker fees of prominent professors and consultants. This benefit, while probably real, is often smaller than anticipated. For one thing, most people fail to calculate the opportunity costs of having such senior people occupied in the classroom (though, as mentioned above, the benefits of their involvement may outweigh these costs). Another expense derives from the fact that a robust leaders–teaching–leaders model demands top-flight content expertise and support from the leadership development group. Their challenge is to provide sufficient content, structure, coaching and support to minimize the leaders' time, while maximizing the leaders' own learning and satisfaction from the experience. Although some organizations seek to provide formal recognition and rewards for those who teach, internal faculty generally comprise an all-volunteer army, and the role of the internal leadership specialists is critical to maximizing their impact and keeping them engaged and motivated.

Another solution for delivering training is to employ full-time internal faculty. This approach usually results in lower costs than an external faculty model, while requiring less senior executive time than does the leaders–teaching–leaders model. However, the best subject-matter experts and teachers usually prefer to be outside consultants, finding a diversity of clients more interesting – and more lucrative – than working for a single employer. Furthermore, the half-life of many topics typically taught in leadership development programs tends to be short, so even when competent in-house experts are available, the question remains as to how long their expertise will remain current.

A final difficulty is that, whereas universities can offer training to their students on a June-to-September steady state basis, most corporate and public service employees' availability for training is highly variable. This is due to seasonal and cyclical fluctuations in the demand for their firms' products and services, and also because of the time demands of various internal processes. (Try scheduling a training program in most organizations during performance review season, for example, or just before the end-of-year closing.) It is easy to accomodate such volatility in demand by using external faculty; keeping in-house faculty busy all year, but not too busy, is a more difficult challenge.

A variety of other potential sources of faculty exist, including external clients, the firm's retired executives, members of the board of directors, and people who keep track of the organization for a living, such as Wall Street analysts and members of the press. These people are often fascinating, highly credible instructors, and organizations such as GE and Goldman Sachs use them regularly, but less often, than internal leaders, external consultants, and academics.

How should the success of the initiative be evaluated?

Thick books have been written about ways to calculate the ROI (return on investment) of leadership development. The interested reader is encouraged to consult one of those, as he'll find nothing about that here. We'll get to useful ways to measure the effectiveness of training and development shortly, but want to emphasize at the outset the most immutable truth about leadership development that we know, which is this: The costs of development are up front, and quantifiable. The benefits, inherently and inevitably, are downstream and intangible. It's true that some leadership skills are susceptible to ROI calculations – improvements in cycletime and inventory turns, for example, and six sigma-induced cost reductions – but judgment is not, nor is decision making, nor inspiring others, nor formulating a strategic vision for the enterprise. In the final analysis, an act of faith is required about the costs and benefits of committing resources to developing an organization's current and future leaders, because it cannot be shown that, as a result of training, people are making 9 percent better decisions, for example, or have added 13 percent to the bottom line. Such reasoning may be possible in the world of duplicate bridge, but in the real world there are no control groups, and changes to the bottom line stemming from training and development are indistinguishable from, and may be swamped by, changes because the yen went up, or the Euro went down, or somebody invaded somebody else, or a competitor has entered or left the scene.

Some CEOs understand this point very well. Jack Welch, when he headed GE, had deep respect and affection for leadership development. These feelings in no way immunized Crotonville (GE's leadership development center) from rigorous controls and tough questions about money and headcount, but the questions were never reduced to rote calculations about ROI. Welch would always said: "In tough times you need training more, not less." He prohibited the businesses from cutting their training (or research) budgets to meet his cost-reduction targets. Less fortunate was the head of another prestigious corporate leadership development center, who was constantly asked to produce quantitative evidence that the expenditures he proposed would generate the required rate of return. The reader can probably guess how he solved this problem – by working the math from the bottom up, calculating the number of dollars needed for the proposed expenditure to be approved, then claiming that figure as the expected ROI for the investment. (Since his boss couldn't figure out the ROI of leadership development any more than can anyone else, the forecasted figures were invariably accepted, and were never subsequently discredited.)

Kirkpatrick's measures of training effectiveness

Level four, the most rigorous way to measure the effectiveness of a learning event, according to Kirkpatrick, involves the calculation of output measures such as ROI – which we have already rejected. (Kirkpatrick and Kirkpatrick, 2005) The least rigorous method, level one, is to ask participants whether they benefited from the experience. Research has shown that this method is of limited usefulness. High scores predict whether the respondent will come to another event and would recommend it to others – but that's about it. Whereas level one asks whether participants liked it, level two asks whether they've learned it. This approach is used extensively in schools, of course, where midterms, final exams, pop quizzes and the like are common. Some corporate training, aimed at improving particular skills – e.g., analysis of variance or derivatives mathematics – also makes use of examinations, but most of the subject matter of leadership development cannot be captured in yes–no or right–wrong answers. Although more complex and time consuming, Kirkpatrick's level three is usually the best way to assess the impact of leadership training and development. The question posed at this level is: Are participants using it? To answer this question requires employment of the following steps:

1. Prior to the course, the instructor and/or course designer identifies the behaviors, skills, competencies, etc. that participants can be expected to get better at if the training is successful. This step has a number of uses. It requires people to articulate, in very specific terms, what each module is intended to accomplish. By so doing, it surfaces any differences that exist about the purpose of a course or its desired impact – differences that otherwise may be concealed by the flowery language of the course description. This step is also useful in "outing" instructors whose educational objectives run to things like "heightened awareness" and "shared understanding," and who are offended by being told that they are expected to impart useful knowledge, and will be held accountable for improving participants' skills and behaviors.

2. Once the specific skills and behaviors to be improved by training are identified, a short questionnaire is prepared that inquires into how frequently (always, often, sometimes, seldom, never) the focal person does these things now.

3. Five or six copies of the survey are then given to each participant, shortly before the class or program is to commence, who is instructed to distribute the surveys to a cross-section of people who are in a position to observe his on-the-job performance. This typically includes some combination of participants' bosses, peers, subordinates, and in some cases clients, who complete and return the forms to someone in the leadership development group. The data are not shown to participants, and everyone is given to understand that this is not a critique of the participants, but will be used to assess the effectiveness of the training experience.

4. Sometime after the course is completed, the same questionnaire is re-administered, ideally to the same people, and the pre- and post-course data are compared. Obviously, the appropriate interval between course completion and re-administration of the survey depends on what is being taught. The trick is to allow enough time to elapse for the focal person to display her new skills and for respondents to observe her doing so, without waiting so long that some respondents lose contact with the participant, or events occur within the organization that make it harder to attribute changes in participants' behavior to the learning experience.

Because these data are correlational, they do not permit true cause–effect conclusions and couldn't be published in a first-rate journal. Nevertheless, if the results show that participants have improved their skills and behaviors on the dimensions the initiative was aiming to improve, the development group is happy to take credit. Conversely, if respondents cannot detect any changes in participants' on-the-job behavior, or if observed changes are in the wrong direction, the initiative will be judged to have been a failure.

The authors of this chapter have used this approach in a wide variety of educational experiences, from short, one-time classes to developmental initiatives that occurred over weeks and even months. Provided that respondents to the questionnaire take it seriously and trust that the data they provide will be treated confidentially, and provided that there is enough stability in the workforce so that (most of) the people who respond prior to the course are still around, and are still in regular contact with the focal person a month or two after the program ends, we believe this approach to be a credible, effective way to evaluate the effectiveness of training and development.

One additional point seems worth making with respect to an organization's ability to measure the results of its leadership development effort. The techniques recommended here do not work in a vacuum, but rather are effective within the context of the total developmental initiative. We are not talking here about assessing the effectiveness of some factory in the middle of nowhere, for which formulaic metrics are required because no one above plant manager level ever gets out there. The best leadership development efforts, as noted earlier in this chapter, are partnerships between the training-development staff, the executive office, and many line leaders. The most senior executives in the firm should be actively participating in the initiative – as hosts, faculty, determiners of program content, and as the governing body of the leadership development organization. As they carry out these roles, they will find themselves in constant contact with the trainers as well as those who are being trained. Under such circumstances, the senior executives will find that, while the information they are getting on a day-to-day basis is not as rigorous as the quantitative metrics they are used to receiving from other parts of the business, it is far more informative and actionable.

How should the leadership group be organized?

This important question is seldom given the attention it deserves. A useful first principle is that any group charged with designing and implementing leadership initiatives should seek to exemplify the principles it recommends to others. If a key training module offers techniques for providing speedy, responsive client service, for example, and the group responsible for the training is known to be ponderous, unresponsive and bureaucratic, the odds are good that the trainers will not be credible, and the strength of the message will be impaired.

In an attempt to be faithful to this principle, Goldman's Pine St group developed a set of "running rules" that sought to mirror key pillars of its leadership curriculum as well as to reflect – and in a few cases, modify – the culture of the organization. (See Exhibit A.) For example, because of the firm's deep respect for technical expertise, team members are strongly encouraged to develop their own area of expertise within the field of leadership development.

This boosts their credibility and puts them in good position to work with line leaders who are teaching a session in the Pine St member's area of expertise. (In an entertaining illustration of the effectiveness of this practice, one of this chapter's authors witnessed a senior group of senior Goldman executives – including the head of one of the divisions – sitting around making small talk because the "expert" on the topic to be discussed, a young associate on the Pine St team, was coming to the meeting from another building and was a few minutes late.) The group has measured itself every year against these running rules, and has revised them as necessary to reflect the firm's evolving strategy and Pine St's suite of offerings.

A second principle of organizational design, closely related to success, is to ensure that there is a strong connection between the leadership development group and the leaders it serves. This connection can be built in a number of different ways. Some groups have a reporting line into business leadership, while others establish boards of directors, or advisory councils, made up of line leaders. Many leadership development groups house some team members in the business units, alongside the leaders they serve. A final, obvious point is that the leaders–teaching–leaders model goes a long way toward building connectivity with the executive office and with the businesses.

A final principle is that all group members should be encouraged to assume and demonstrate leadership within their own domain. (See running rules 5, 6 and 8 in Exhibit A.) This sense of empowerment and shared accountability for the group's success is considered by the team to be essential to maximizing Pine St's contribution within the organization.

Exhibit A: Pine St running rules

1. We work very hard to practice what we teach. In particular, we seek to operate smoothly across boundaries (divisional, regional, business unit, firm/client) and in a non-hierarchical manner.

2. We never slow a project down, except when necessary to improve the quality. If our client wants to do something tomorrow, that's when we do it. We regularly seek input to improve the quality of our work, but we make every effort to avoid excessive meetings, postings, and consensus-building. (We keep in mind that sometimes "consensus" means: disagree and commit.)

3. We never refuse requests to help. When it doesn't make sense for us to do something, we help identify someone who can do the job.

4. We search for opportunities to work with individuals from other parts of the firm. Sometimes this takes the form of a formal partnership, but we also benefit from "resources in place" i.e., people whose primary responsibilities lie outside Pine St, but who care enough about some Pine St project to work with us on it. We also welcome opportunities to run pilot sessions of our programs within one division or region before rolling them out firmwide.

5. Each of us spends nearly all his/her time working on projects and programs. We have a very flat organization and strongly believe in empowering people – giving them considerable operating freedom and expecting them to ask for help when they need it. All of our team members lead projects. Senior people regularly work for, and report to, more junior team members.

6. Any member of the team can speak for Pine St and can commit Pine St to a project or a completion date, and that commitment will always be honored.

7. We support and encourage all team members, regardless of their level or years of service, to develop a particular area of expertise.

8. We seek to balance the tendency to leverage each person's expertise with our effort to expose team members to new products and interests. We believe that most people have the good sense to sign up for things they are capable of doing and have the time for, and ask for help when needed.

9. We share credit. When someone leaves a voicemail about a completed piece of work, it is usually to give credit to another team member for a job well done. We also see to it that whoever does the work gets formal recognition for that work (and gets to make the presentation, no matter to whom).

10. We work hard to develop each other both formally through an advocate structure and less formally from on-going apprenticeship, feedback from the team, and the advice of the broader Goldman Sachs community.

REFERENCES

Chatterjee, D. (1998) *Leading consciously.* Woburn, Massachusetts: Butterworth-Heinemann.

Dewey, J. (1910) *How we think.* Reprinted in 2004 by Kila: Kessinger Publishing.

Hewitt Associates (2005) *Top Companies for Leaders.* New York: Hewitt Associates.

Hicks, M. D. and Peterson, D. B. (1998) *The Art and Practice of Executive Coaching.* Minneapolis, Minnesota. Presented at Minnesota Psychological Association's First Friday Lecture Series.

Kirkpatrick, D. L. and Kirkpatrick, J. D. (2005) *Transferring Learning to Behavior: Using the Four Levels to Improve Performance.* San Francisco: Berrett-Koehler Publishers.

Kolb, D. A. (1983) *Experiential Learning: Experience as the Source of Learning and Development.* London: Financial Times/Prentice Hall.

Lombardo, M. M. and Eichinger, R. W. (2000) *The Leadership Machine: Architecture to Develop Leaders for any Future.* New York: Lominger.

Mayo, A. J. and Nohria, N. (2005) *In Their Time: The Greatest Business Leaders of the 20th Century.* Boston: Harvard Business School Press.

McCall, M., Lombardo, M. M. and Morrison, A. M. (1988) *The Lessons of Experience: How Successful Executives Develop on the* Job. New York: Lexington Books.

Michaels, E., Handfield-Jones, H. and Axelrod, B. (2001) *The War For Talent.* Boston: Mckinsey and Company/HBS Publishing.

Olofsky, C. (2002) Personal conversation.

Peterson, D. B. (2002) *Management development: Coaching and Mentoring Programs.* In K. Kraiger (ed.) *Creating, Implementing, and Managing Effective Training and Development,* San Francisco: Jossey-Bass.

Ready, D. (1994) *Champions of Change.* Lexington, Massachusetts: International Consortium for Executive Development Research, pp. 26–8.

Revans, R. (1982) What is action learning, *Journal of Management Development, 1*(3), 64–75.

7 Best practices in building more effective teams

Kevin C. Stagl and Eduardo Salas

The ongoing technological revolution and democratization of capital markets around the globe continue to redefine what is possible for humankind to achieve. At the intersection of capability and opportunity, human ingenuity has produced unprecedented advances in areas such as robotics, fusion-based energy, space-flight propulsion, nanotechnology, genomic-testing, and synthetic biology. Unfortunately, the current on-demand business environment is also characterized by hyper-competition, rapidly evolving ambiguous situations, imperfect solutions, information overload, and intense time pressure (Orasanu and Salas, 1993). Organizations must acknowledge and navigate these challenges in order to fulfill the promise of their mission.

The almost unlimited upside of modern operations in conjunction with the severe consequences of error in this environment have prompted a renewed focus on leveraging human capital as a sustainable source of competitive advantage. One manifestation of the emphasis on maximizing the value of talent can be seen in the increasing use of teams as a performance arrangement to structure work. Organizations rely upon teams to navigate their complex challenges because collectives can draw upon a wider range of capabilities and social networks to be more adaptive, productive, and safer than individuals (Stagl *et al.*, 2006).

Despite the inherent advantages of teamwork, teams of experts often fail to evolve into expert teams (Salas *et al.*, 1997). It is thus meaningful to consider the conditions, processes, and practices that can be instituted to cultivate effective team performance and thereby organizational profitability and viability. This chapter meets this need by leveraging current theory and practice to discuss what it takes to build more effective teams. We begin by defining core constructs and concepts that, in turn, serve as platform for identifying levers of change for building more effective teams. Specific levers are then discussed in greater detail.

The nature of teams

Teams are complex entities, comprised of two or more individuals, who interact socially, dynamically, episodically, and adaptively (Stagl, Salas and Burke, 2007). The vast majority of teams are hierarchically structured and have a limited life-span for their operations. The members of teams have distributed roles, share common valued goals, and hold meaningful but fluctuating levels of task, feedback, and goal interdependencies (Salas *et al.*, 1992). Teams and their members are embedded within an organizational/environmental context that shapes and is shaped by enacted competencies and processes, emergent cognitive and affective states, performance outcomes, and stakeholder judgments of their effectiveness (Salas *et al.*, in press).

Teams engage in teamwork, which consists of enacted processes or behavioral and cognitive acts that are undertaken to transform inputs such as raw materials and information into goods and services. Many initiatives have been launched to identify the competencies teams execute, most have identified similar processes (see Cannon-Bowers *et al.*, 1995; Salas and Cannon-Bowers, 2000; Smith-Jentsch *et al.*, 1998). One recent effort undertaken to illuminate the key skill competencies teams rely upon has classified these actions into performance phases (see Table 7.1) (Marks, Mathieu and Zaccaro, 2001). More attention is given to these performance phases later in this subsection, as our discussion unfolds to describe how teamwork contributes to effective team performance.

It should be noted from the outset that a distinction can be made between taskwork and teamwork processes. Taskwork refers to "a team's interactions with tasks, tools, machines, and systems" (Bowers, Braun and Morgan, 1997, p. 90). For example, the taskwork of a scuba diving instructor consists, in part, of recruiting a small group of new students, providing formal training to those students, and arranging excursions to exotic locales for dive trips. In addition to these core taskwork duties, however, an instructor also assumes responsibility as a team leader when his/her students take the plunge. Once immersed, divers working in dyads, and dive instructors acting as team leaders, engage in teamwork processes by continuously monitoring (i.e., mutual performance monitoring) and helping (i.e., backup behavior) those students that are struggling in their new aquatic playground. Instructors also keep their students aware of unfolding situational contingencies (i.e., meaning ascription) such as the occasional hammerhead shark gliding by overhead. This latter set of interpersonal activities speaks to the core of teamwork.

Table 7.1 Team skill competencies Adapted from (Marks, Mathieu and Zaccaro, 2001)

Processes/skills	Definition
Transition processes	
Mission analysis formulation and planning	Interpretation and evaluation of the team's mission, including identification of its main tasks as well as the operative environmental conditions and team resources available for mission execution
Goal specification	Identification and prioritization of goals and subgoals for mission accomplishment
Strategy formulation	Development of alternative courses of action for mission accomplishment
Action processes	
Monitoring progress toward goals	Tracking task and progress toward mission accomplishment, interpreting system information in terms of what needs to be accomplished for goal attainment, and transmitting progress to team members
Systems monitoring	Tracking team resources and environmental conditions as they relate to mission accomplishment, which involves (1) internal systems monitoring (tracking team resources such as personnel, equipment and (2) environmental monitoring (tracking the environmental condition relevant to the team)
Team monitoring and backup behavior	Assisting team members to perform their tasks. Assistance may occur by (1) providing a teammate verbal feedback or coaching (2) helping a teammate behaviorally in carrying out actions or (3) assuming and completing a task for a teammate
Coordination	Orchestrating the sequence and timing of interdependent actions
Interpersonal processes	
Conflict management	Preemptive conflict management involves establishing conditions to prevent, control, or guide team conflict before it occurs. Reactive conflict management involves working through task and interpersonal disagreements among team members
Motivation and confidence building	Generating and preserving a sense of collective confidence, motivation and task-based cohesion with regard to mission accomplishment
Affect management	Regulating member emotions during mission accomplishment, including (but not limited to) social cohesion, frustration, and excitement

Essentially, teamwork is a set of adaptively enacted cognitive and behavioral processes that are executed by both individual team members (e.g., backup behavior, mutual performance monitoring, peer leadership) and entire teams (e.g., coordination, dynamic reallocation of resources) (Salas *et al.*, in press). Of note, however, some teamwork processes can be conceptualized at either the individual or team levels of analysis (e.g., decision making, situation assessment, plan formulation, plan execution) (Burke *et al.*, 2006). The cognitive and behavioral processes comprising teamwork are enacted *for* a fellow team member (e.g., pointing out a faulty o-ring) or *with* fellow members (e.g., the coordination of the movement of several divers through a small, poorly illuminated cavern). Thus, as compared to taskwork processes which deal with task and system interactions, teamwork processes have a distinctly interpersonal nature, albeit both sets of processes are essential for team performance.

Teams and their members enact the above-noted teamwork and taskwork processes during the performance episodes that they complete as part of their ongoing operations. A performance episode is a "distinguishable period of time over which performance accrues and feedback becomes available" (Marks *et al.*, 2001, p. 359). During a given performance episode, a team typically completes several input–throughput–output (ITO) cycles. For example, a recent attempt to model the cyclical nature of adaptive team performance suggested that team members draw upon individual characteristics such as their mental models and cognitive abilities (i.e., inputs) to scan their environment (i.e., process) for cues signaling the need for change (Burke *et al.*, 2006). Once detected, a plan is formulated and executed (i.e., processes) and if a given modification or innovation is determined to be functional, team adaptation has ensued (i.e., output). An actual example can be seen in a football team's quarterback and wide receivers noticing a defensive shift, the quarterback calling an audible, and completing a long touchdown pass in lieu of the running play that had originally been called by the coaching staff. This example illustrates a single reactive adaptation I–T–O loop. As the play concludes, the offensive unit shifts to a transition phase where it returns to the huddle and plans for the next play. Although this sports example is relatively simple, several I–T–O cycles typically unfold within a given performance episode and several episodes may be handled concurrently by a given team.

In the above example, the members of a football team individually noticed a defensive scheme, interpreted that stream of cues in light of their individual experiences and capacities (cognitive abilities, mental models) and shared cognitive frameworks (team mental models, shared situation awareness), felt potent about their capability to adapt (potency), felt comfortable in taking a risk by changing the play their coaches called (psychological safety), and then coordinated for a score. This speaks to a fundamental difference between pure teamwork processes and the broader concepts of both team performance and adaptive team performance. In order to flexibly execute teamwork and taskwork processes during a performance episode, teams and their members leverage their individual capabilities (e.g., mental models, cognitive abilities, personality characteristics), emergent cognitive states (e.g., team mental models, shared situation awareness), and emergent affective states (e.g., collective efficacy, potency, psychological safety) in order to understand what processes are required, when they should be executed, and how their enactment contributes to the broader goals of their team and organization.

When a team engages in a performance episode, a variety of stakeholders who are either directly or indirectly vested in the team's success form and revise impressions about the team's effectiveness. Team members, team leaders, senior organizational stakeholders, strategic partners, and clientele all evaluate a team's enacted processes and achieved outcomes against objective and subjective standards. Via the application of these standards, they gauge the effectiveness of the actions undertaken and results produced by the team. In order to form effectiveness judgments, concerned parties often use several criteria, including: (1) whether a team's product or service meets or exceeds the standards of the team's clientele; (2) whether the social dynamic arising from team performance strengthened the capability of its members to work together in the future; and (3) whether team members learned and had their needs fulfilled (Hackman, 1987). Each of these three criteria are important indices of team effectiveness.

Fostering effective teams

In the previous section, we defined teams, teamwork, team performance, and team effectiveness in order to provide insight about what we mean when we use these terms throughout the chapter and to briefly communicate a sense of what it is that effective teams do and how they do it. The issues addressed in the previous section, although just a small sample, are varied and complex. Fortunately, prior research undertaken to frame many of the variables that contribute to producing effective teams provides a convenient means of quickly sizing up some of these issues. The team effectiveness model (see Figure 7.1), includes many of the most pertinent inputs, processes, and outputs that make up the I–T–O cycles teams engage in during their performance episodes (Tannenbaum, Beard and Salas, 1992).

Tannenbaum and colleagues' (1992) framework of team effectiveness also depicts a few of the myriad of interventions that can be leveraged to foster more effective teams including: individual training, team training, and team building. In addition to these organizationally administered developmental opportunities, there are a host of other resources stakeholders must leverage to build more effective teams. For example, a staffing system provides a means of securing much needed talent and can be used to actively manage the mixture of competencies in a team. Properly configured reward systems serve to motivate team members to subjugate their own self-interests to those of their collective and to persist in these coordinated exchanges over the long-run. Team coaching can serve to motivate, facilitate, and educate effective teams. Thus, effective teams are the product of many people, systems, and interventions working in unison.

Given that effective teams require considerable care and attention, the question becomes who is attending to these matters? Certainly, team leaders have considerable influence over the effectiveness of their teams. In fact, team leadership has often been conceptualized as an ongoing process of influence whereby leaders sway team members and teams via the use of a sequenced combination of proactive influence tactics (Yukl, 2007). This perspective suggests team leaders influence the task objectives and strategies of a team, team members to implement team strategies and achieve team objectives, team maintenance and identification, and team culture (Yukl and Van Fleet, 1992). A wide variety of influence tactics exist which can be leveraged to promote team effectiveness (Yukl, 2007).

In order to influence teams and their members, some team leaders spend a majority of their time "fighting fires" or directly intervening in team performance to provide solutions to a team's everyday challenges. This kind of problem driven activity can be conducive to achieving valued team outcomes in the short term; but a more encompassing and long-term perspective suggests that effective team leaders spend a majority of their time influencing teams and their members by instituting a set of mutually reinforcing conditions (Hackman, 2002). Once established, these conditions serve to shape a team's tasks, performance strategies, team member and team actions, and interventions undertaken by key stakeholders to build effective teams before, during, and after performance episodes.

Team leaders influence the attainment of objectives by instituting and sustaining five conditions including: (1) establishing a real team, (2) that has a compelling direction, (3) an enabling structure, (4) a supportive context, and (5) access to expert coaching (Hackman, 2002). These five conditions, in turn, influence how team members perceive the relationships between themselves and their teammates, between themselves and their team, between their team and its broader organizational context, and between their team and their

Table 7.2 Best practices in team leadership (adapted from Stagl, Salas and Burke 2007)

• **Best practice 1:**	Define and create team interdependencies
• **Best practice 2:**	Reinforce task interdependencies with congruent goals and feedback
• **Best practice 3:**	Think twice before using teams as a performance arrangement
• **Best practice 4:**	Identify who is currently responsible and accountable for team outcomes
• **Best practice 5:**	Designate the decision-making authority a team has for its work
• **Best practice 6:**	Strive to keep teams intact
• **Best practice 7:**	Exercise authority to establish a compelling direction for the team
• **Best practice 8:**	Stimulate and inspire teams by challenging the status quo
• **Best practice 9:**	Instill collective aspirations by communicating a common mission
• **Best practice 10:**	Provide consequential direction to fully engage a team's talents
• **Best practice 11:**	Promote self-goal setting, self-observation, and self-reward
• **Best practice 12:**	Establish norms for how the team scans its environment for opportunities and what teams must and cannot do to seize opportunities
• **Best practice 13:**	Allocate the optimal number and mix of personnel to a team
• **Best practice 14:**	Implement team-based performance-contingent rewards
• **Best practice 15:**	Institutionalize multitiered reward systems
• **Best practice 16:**	Ensure the information provided to a team is performance targeted
• **Best practice 17:**	Negotiate with senior stakeholders to secure access to sensitive information if it facilitates a team's planning and selection of performance strategies
• **Best practice 18:**	Provide and secure developmental opportunities for teams
• **Best practice 19:**	Train intact teams to promote the development of performance-enhancing team resources
• **Best practice 20:**	Use pre-briefings to instill shared affect, cognition, and behavior
• **Best practice 21:**	Offer novel task performance strategies
• **Best practice 22:**	Engage teams in a two-way discussion of lessons learned and how they can be utilized to address upcoming challenges

organization's operational environment (Stagl, Salas and Burke, 2007). This more encompassing position is consistent with the assertions advanced in our prior work (see Burke *et al.*, 2007; Stagl *et al.*, 2007) and that of Hackman (2002). In fact, the first author and his colleagues have advanced twenty two best practices team leaders can leverage to facilitate team effectiveness (see Table 7.2) (Stagl *et al.*, 2007). The current chapter seeks to reinforce this position with additional techniques, tools, and tips that can be utilized by team leaders and other concerned stakeholders to help build more effective teams.

It should be noted, that the approach to building more effective teams as described above involves the ongoing dedication and coordinated efforts of

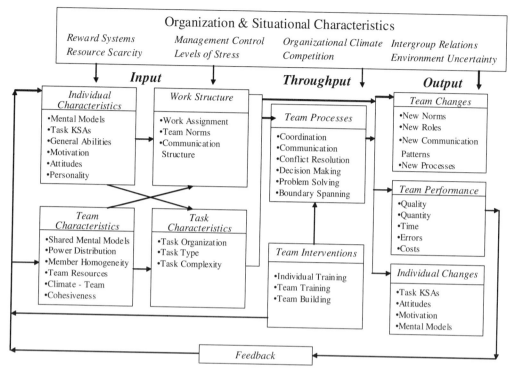

Figure 7.1   Team effectiveness framework adapted from (Tannenbaum, Beard and Salas, 1992)

multiple parties both internal and external to a given team. Regardless of whether it is a team's reward systems that senior stakeholders must tweak to reinforce team performance, its educational system which is largely designed by external vendors, or its information systems that internal programmers work to develop and maintain, the core issue remains one of aligning the efforts of everyone involved to help collectives fulfill their promise. We discuss some of what is known about synchronizing these efforts to help foster the five noted conditions above and, when possible, link identified interventions to the team effectiveness framework depicted in Figure 7.1. Specific actions leaders enact to create these five conditions, and thereby build more effective teams, are provided.

Creating teams

Teams are not small groups of individuals with limited, if any, task, goal, and feedback interdependencies; such as is the case with task forces, committees, councils, and juries (Kozlowski *et al.*, 1996). In contrast, teams perform team tasks and have differentiated but complementary roles, congruent goals and feedback, mutual accountabilities, delimited authority, and stable membership (Hackman, 2002). Most of these characteristics are reflected in Tannenbaum *et al.*'s (1992) team effectiveness framework as depicted in Figure 7.1. For example, team tasks (task characteristics) and complementary roles (work structure) are depicted as inputs. Similarly, delimited authority (management control) is also illustrated in the framework. Moreover, the feedback that is generated from ongoing I–T–O cycles is also modeled in Figure 7.1.

In regard to team tasks, there are several steps practitioners can take to define and create team interdependencies. For example, a team task analysis can be conducted to identify existing interdependencies or to vision the codependencies that will be inherent to a new team (Burke, 2005). This process consists of a requirements analysis that is conducted to identify the tasks that compose the target job. Current teamwork taxonomies (see Fleishman and Quaintance, 1984; Fleishman and Zaccaro, 1992) can be utilized to guide this process. Once an appropriate team task taxonomy is located, a coordination demand analysis is conducted to determine taskwork and teamwork tasks. Interdependent tasks are subsequently linked to team and team member knowledge, skills, attitudes, and other characteristics (KSAOs) for later use in talent staffing, selection, development, appraisal, and retention initiatives.

Best practice 1: *Conduct a team task analysis*
In order to further capitalize on the codependences that make teams an adaptive and effective performance arrangement, complementary roles can be created via job design initiatives. Each team member can fulfill a single role, but more typically, every member is either assigned or forges multiple roles. Sometimes roles are exchanged amongst members fluidly, as is the case when a shared leadership system is instituted. To help create complementary roles, a staffing solution can be utilized which includes the individual assessment of potential team members for the purpose of matching candidates to available roles.

Best practice 2: *Create complementary and clear roles and responsibilities*
Once established, it is important to reinforce task interdependencies and mutual accountabilities with congruent goals and feedback. Goals and goal feedback are required to regulate the allocation of effort and selection of task strategies during team member and team performance (DeShon *et al.*, 2004). Superordinate goals and shared outcomes send the message that team level rather than just individual performance is organizationally valued. By setting mutually agreed upon, specific, and difficult team goals, rather than ambiguous goals, or just individual goals, stakeholders provide teams and their members with the benchmarks they need to regulate their

allocation of resources during performance episodes (Locke and Latham, 1990). Delivering feedback about how well the team is executing its performance strategies, rather than only directing members' attention towards their own performance, also helps members adjust their efforts accordingly, as well as become increasingly accountable for their actions (Rutkowski and Steelman, 2005).

> **Best practice 3:** *Set mutually agreed upon, specific, and increasingly difficult team-based goals for teams and their members*

> **Best practice 4:** *Deliver feedback about both team member and team performance*

Teams also understand who is currently responsible and accountable for team outcomes. In order to foster accountability, stakeholders can hold preliminary meetings to create common ground about a team's purposes and membership. Membership rosters are useful for differentiating core team members from those members who fulfill a support function and for reinforcing who will participate in performance episodes and at what times. Team web pages that include calendars of events, blogs, chat rooms, and digital avatars, provide an easily accessible location for members to send, receive, and exchange information about new or existing team issues such as expected changes in an organization's production schedule that will likely affect team performance strategies.

> **Best practice 5:** *Reinforce mutual accountabilities with preliminary meetings, membership rosters, and team web pages*

Key stakeholders must also designate the decision-making authority a team has for its work, if their aim is to ultimately create real teams that are effective over the long run. In order to determine who is best suited to handle the functions a team fulfills, practitioners can assess a team's capability to handle its work via archival performance appraisals or by observing the team in context. The information gathered during this process can be subsequently utilized to define which of a team's core functions fall under its dominion. Once this decision is made, it is important to inform teams about which of their functions are under their domain of control and to communicate the standards that must be achieved in order to be granted additional responsibilities for various functions. As the team grows and is increasingly capable, senior stakeholders can relinquish additional process control.

> **Best practice 6:** *Assess a team's capability to handle its functions and allocate authority accordingly*

The final characteristic of real teams is that they have a relatively stable membership, so stakeholders should strive to keep teams intact. Although macroeconomic conditions outside the control of any given organization can strongly affect team turnover, there are several steps concerned parties such as team leaders can take to maximize member retention. For example, organizational representatives that actively listen to team members' suggestions and take action on the basis of this advice can foster more trust and commitment to the team. Teams that have developed conflict resolution skills will also be more likely to have dyadic relationships that are characterized by mutual trust and respect. Finally, employment arrangements that include options such as flexitime, telecommuting, and distributed performance can immediately enhance the satisfaction of team members, reduce operating expenses in the mid-term, and over the long run help ameliorate the negative health and societal issues associated with rush hour travel and transcontinental flights (Stagl *et al.*, 2007).

> ***Best practice 7:*** *Retain team members by benchmarking best practices such as flexitime, telecommuting, and distributed performance arrangements*
> *Visioning a Compelling Direction*

According to Hackman (2002), direction is compelling when it is challenging, clear, and consequential. When the direction a team is given is compelling, it energizes, orients, and engages a team's talents. Those stakeholders attempting to build more effective teams must define, communicate, and operationalize a vision for teams that is inspirational. If, however, a vision already exists but has largely failed to challenge the status quo, senior stakeholders should exercise their authority to change the direction for teams when necessary. The objective is to articulate a mission that balances the possible with the impossible (Welch and Welch, 2005) and thereby creates an impetus for teams to continually strive to achieve what would be clearly unattainable as individuals.

> ***Best practice 8:*** *Articulate and operationalize a compelling and valued vision but do not hesitate to modify it as situational contingencies arise*

A clear direction helps align a team's performance strategies with its purposes. Thus, the content of the direction provided to a team must be tailored to the particular contingencies of that given team. Stakeholders should proactively discuss a team's goals, objectives, and performance standards in order to clearly specify a team's desired end states but not the means of task accomplishment that team members utilize to realize their objectives. For example, the Ansari X Prize charged aviation teams vying for a $10-million dollar payout to reach 100 kilometers in altitude twice in a two-week time frame with what equates to three adults on board. The team designing SpaceShipOne, developed by Burt Rutan's team at Scaled Composites, and funded by Microsoft co-founder Paul Allen, knew their precise objectives and crafted a unique reusable air-launched suborbital spaceplane to accomplish the mission. In turn, the original vision articulated by the Ansari X Prize committee helped launch a new commercial industry as plans for SpaceShipTwo are already being implemented by Richard Branson at Virgin Galactic.

Best practice 9: *Identify targeted objectives but empower teams to help set and adapt the specific means of task accomplishment*

A consequential direction engages a team and its members by instilling collective aspirations to accomplish a common mission. Stakeholders can help foster a consequential direction by making explicit the linkages between each team members' self-concept and the actions each member undertakes on behalf of his or her team. Moreover, team member roles can be defined in terms of ideological values. When members internalize the collective as a core part of their self-concept, they will reactively use the word "we" instead of "I" to discuss their performance processes. Over time, some members will come to internalize the core values of their team and their actions will be guided by a set of implicit assumptions that include notions about the benefits of teamwork.

Best practice 10: *Define member roles in terms of overarching core values*
Establishing an Enabling Structure

The third condition that must be established to foster more effective teams is an enabling structure. An enabling structure consists of three components, the design of a team's work, the establishment and enforcement of norms of conduct, and the manner in which teams are staffed or composed (Hackman, 2002). The first (i.e., the design of a team's work) and last (i.e., staffing solutions) would be depicted as team interventions in Tannenbaum and colleagues' (1992) framework. Norms of conduct are included in the team effectiveness framework as a work structure variable.

A team's work should be designed to promote self-regulation and self-reward. In regards to this issue, job characteristics theory (Hackman and Oldham, 1980) suggests stakeholders can take several steps to help ensure teams have meaningful work to do and that they ultimately feel responsible for completing their work in a timely, effective manner. For example, teams should be provided with some measure of authority over their work. Combining tasks and establishing direct team-to-client relationships creates a context where collectives and their representatives must draw upon a variety of skills to fulfill their objectives. Task identity and task significance can be created by forming natural work units and by combining tasks. A fourth component, autonomy, is fostered when teams are empowered to handle responsibilities traditionally relegated to management. Finally, open channels of communication need to be created throughout the organization to provide feedback.

Best practice 11: *Provide teams with meaningful work and a sense of responsibility for that work by combining tasks, opening channels of communication, and forging direct team-to-client relationships*

Norms of conduct are common expectations that regulate and regularize a team's behavior. When norms are established, they serve to reinforce desired behaviors and sanction inappropriate ones. Thus, a team should have norms for how it scans its environment for opportunities and what must and cannot be done to seize opportunities (Hackman, 2002). Effective teams also have internal norms which shape dyadic interactions and team level exchanges. Team leaders and other concerned parties must actively monitor and control these external and internal norms, lest informal norms arise within a collective that are at odds with those that support an organization's objectives.

Best practice 12: *Establish within team norms that govern the dyadic exchanges team members engage in by reinforcing desirable behaviors and sanctioning inappropriate ones*

The final facet that comprises an enabling structure is a team's composition. In regard to this issue, effective teams should have an optimal number and mix of personnel. Accumulated evidence suggests teams should be staffed with the fewest number of members possible to accomplish a task (Wageman, 1995). This is because the introduction of each additional member creates new coordination demands, the potential for conflict, and an additional drain on an already limited corporate resource pool. For all of the reasons, slack human capital resources in teams can ultimately lead to process losses or performance decrements. Prior research findings suggest that teams should typically be staffed with four to seven members (Kameda *et al.*, 1992; Wageman, 1995).

Stakeholders charged with building more effective teams must also actively manage a team's diversity of talent or mixture of KSAOs. In regard to this issue, concerned parties should keep in mind that more of a characteristic (e.g., extraversion, deliberation) is not always desirable. For example, in some conceptualizations of the structure of human personality, one facet of the personality factor conscientious is deliberation (Costa and McCrae, 1992). More cautious individuals have the tendency to reflect over all of the facts available in a diligent, sometimes painstaking manner before making a decision. It is easy to imagine a team largely composed of cautious members suffering from analysis paralysis and thereby failing to seize emerging opportunities in a timely manner (Stagl *et al.*, 2002). Similarly, a team staffed with all highly extroverted members may spend far too much time socializing to accomplish anything meaningful. These examples illustrate why the builders of effective teams must leverage an organization's human capital systems to proactively hire or fire members, develop existing members, or secure the services of ad hoc members, in order to manage and blend a team's talents, tendencies, and social networks (Kozlowski and Bell, 2003).

Best practice 13: *Lean towards assigning too few members to accomplish a team's objectives rather than too many*

Best practice 14: *Actively manage a team's capabilities and characteristics Fostering a Supportive Organizational Context*

The fourth condition required to build more effective teams is a supportive organizational context; this consists of establishing a reward system, an information system, and an educational system that promote team performance (Hackman, 2002). Reward systems are depicted as an organizational characteristic in Tannenbaum *et al.*'s (1992) team effectiveness framework. Traditionally, the allocation of rewards in most organizations has been geared towards reinforcing individual performance. Increasingly, however, stakeholders have made efforts to tweak their individually-geared reward systems to facilitate team performance. Most organizations making this shift have implemented multitiered reward systems by phasing in team performance as a distinct facet of each team member's performance appraisal. This is an important practice, because it creates the expectancy that coordination, cooperation, and communication are instrumental in achieving valued financial and interpersonal rewards.

Best practice 15: *Phase in teamwork as a distinct facet of members' performance appraisals*

An information system serves to provide teams with the near real-time input they need to plan, execute, and monitor their activities. Teams can be more adaptive and efficient when they have performance-targeted information, so it is important for stakeholders attempting to build more effective teams to manage the type and flow of information a team receives. To institute a useful information system requires working closely with both internal systems designers and/or outside vendors during its development to ensure that teams receive actionable information rather than just copious amounts of data. Moreover, concerned stakeholders may also need to negotiate with senior management to secure access to sensitive information when it is useful for a team's planning and execution of performance processes. Mission critical information can also be generated by creating tighter coupling between teams.

Best practice 16: *Manage the type and flow of information a team receives*

The final component of a supportive organizational context is an educational system. To build more effective teams, stakeholders must provide or secure developmental opportunities for them. Teams of experts need to be developed because they often lack all of the competencies needed to perform as expert teams. Furthermore, what competencies teams and their members do possess, can quickly become outmoded in the increasingly dynamic marketplace that characterizes the operational environment of most mid-sized to large businesses. Newly formed teams can also benefit from developmental opportunities by accruing the capacities that mature teams leverage to be effective during their ongoing activities.

In order to provide teams with the requisite resources they need to conduct their operations, stakeholders should schedule formal training for teams as a planned intervention to enhance the direct determinants of performance including job knowledge, skill, and volitional choice behavior (Campbell and Kuncel, 2002). Formal training programs consist of theoretically grounded tools and methodologies, which are combined with a set of competencies and training objectives to form an instructional strategy (Salas and Cannon-Bowers, 1997). For example, cross-training is a strategy that can be used to train each of several members in the tasks, roles, and responsibilities of their teammates. By providing team members with either insight into, or direct practice with, their teammates' tasks and roles, cross-training serves to impart interpositional knowledge within the team, a specific type of team-interaction mental model. In turn, this shared cognitive state facilitates the timely delivery of teamwork processes such as backup behavior and peer leadership. Prior research has identified twenty best practices for cross-training teams; these practices are advanced in Table 7.3 (Stagl, Salas and Fiore, in press).

Best practice 17: *Use instructional strategies such as cross-training as a surrogate for the experiences that teams accrue naturally over time*

Although many different types of training programs exist, a commonality of all these techniques is their reliance upon one of three methods for conveying instructional material (i.e., information-based, demonstration-based, practice-based) (Salas and Cannon-Bowers, 2000). Information-based methods utilize lectures, handbooks, advanced organizers, and slide-shows to convey facts, concepts, and tips. Demonstration-based methods depict behaviors, actions, and/or strategies via video or multimedia-based information technologies. Practice-based methods provide trainee team members and teams with hands on rehearsal and ongoing feedback via role-play exercises, moderate fidelity desktop-based computer simulations, or high fidelity virtual reality simulations. Many training programs combine these three methods (Stagl *et al.*, in press).

Table 7.3 Best practices in cross training (adapted from Stagl, Salas and Fiore, in press)

• **Best practice 1:**	Blend scientifically grounded tools, methodologies, competencies, and training objectives to create training programs
• **Best practice 2:**	Design training to leverage information-based, demonstration-based, and/or practice-based methods
• **Best practice 3:**	Begin by training team members then move on to teams
• **Best practice 4:**	Conduct training evaluation to gauge horizontal transfer and vertical transfer
• **Best practice 5:**	Include both formative and summative aspects in training evaluation efforts
• **Best practice 6:**	Estimate the return on investment from training programs
• **Best practice 7:**	Think twice before utilizing traditional team training programs to impart or change knowledge structures
• **Best practice 8:**	Use cross-training to impart interpositional knowledge, a specific type of shared team-interaction mental model
• **Best practice 9:**	Consider the pros and cons associated with each of the three cross-training techniques in light of growth objectives and contextual constraints
• **Best practice 10:**	Use positional clarification cross-training to impart shared team-interaction mental models
• **Best practice 11:**	Conceptualize and measure the proximal effects of positional clarification cross-training to gauge its impact
• **Best practice 12:**	Take into account the additional ambiguities inherent to distributed performance arrangements when choosing between positional clarification and more intensive forms of cross-training
• **Best practice 13:**	Use positional modeling cross-training to impart to impart shared team-interaction mental models
• **Best practice 14:**	Use positional modeling cross-training to impart performance processes such as leadership, backup behavior, and situation assessment
• **Best practice 15:**	Use positional rotation cross-training to promote emergent cognitive states such as IPK and team performance processes such as leadership
• **Best practice 16:**	Revise performance measurement systems to account for the nuanced effects of cross-training on team inputs and processes
• **Best practice 17:**	Use positional rotation cross-training to reduce the latency with which targeted team performance outcomes are realized
• **Best practice 18:**	Consider the workload typically experienced by a team, as positional rotation cross-training is most effective when tasks are demanding
• **Best practice 19:**	Train intact teams via experiential positional rotation cross-training to minimize the performance decrements that result from turnover
• **Best practice 20:**	Use positional rotation cross-training to foster team processes such as coordination and thereby valued team performance outcomes

Best practice 18: *Utilize information-based, demonstration-based, and practice-based methods to convey team-based instructional content*

Whenever possible, leaders or senior stakeholders should seek to arrange for opportunities to train entire intact teams after team members have been individually prepared to promote the development of performance-enhancing team level resources. Stakeholders should also stimulate experiential learning via an action-learning process whereby teams work on, reflect on, and learn from their projects in the context of substantive business problems (Conger, Spreitzer and Lawler, 1999). A number of other interventions exist which can be utilized to enhance the development of teams (see Day and Halpin, 2001). Irregardless of which of the many mechanisms leaders or other organizational representatives leverage to develop teams, perhaps the single most important point to be emphasized is the need to shift away from the mindset of growth and learning as gained from any single event towards viewing it as a continuous process that occurs through a variety of mechanisms over a lifetime.

Best practice 19: *Reinforce formal training with team-based action learning projects that arise naturally as part of a team's ongoing operations*

Providing Expert Coaching

The final condition required to foster more effective teams is the provision of expert coaching. Team coaching has been conceptualized as a "direct interaction with a team intended to help members make coordinated and task-appropriate use of their collective resources in accomplishing the team's work" (Hackman and Wageman, 2005, p. 269). Coaching consists of the activities leaders and other stakeholders engage in to facilitate the performance of, and to develop, teams and their members before, during, and after performance episodes.

When coaching is delivered prior to performance, it is often motivational in nature (Hackman, 2002). Coaches can use the beginnings of a performance episode to conduct pre-briefs and thereby instill shared affect and cognition. As previously noted, shared affective (e.g., psychological safety, team potency, task-specific team efficacy) and cognitive states (e.g., team mental models, team situation awareness) are leverage used by teams as they enact taskwork and teamwork processes during performance episodes. Coaches can help foster these shared states by communicating a shared mission and belief in the team's capability to execute that mission successfully. One means of helping to create a comfortable, confident environment is to utilize a questioning approach that encourages discussion and suggestions. For example, coaches should provide informal reinforcements when suggestions or questions are raised and offer supportive, non-defensive responses to those questions. This type of interaction encourages team members to feel safe in sharing their thoughts, questions, and concerns prior to engaging in performance.

> **Best practice 20:** *Encourage questions, thoughts, and concerns at the beginnings of task performance by providing informal reinforcements when issues are raised and supportive, non-defensive responses*

The midpoints of task performance can be utilized to provide novel task performance strategies that may ultimately make better use of a team's resources during subsequent performance episodes (Hackman, 2002). For example, coaches can provide a situation assessment update on how a team is doing relative to its goals. During this discussion, coaches can review the performance strategies which have been employed by a team during its prior performance phases, as well as present approaches that are a better fit given current operational constraints. It is important to identify the new challenges that have arisen in a team's context that could change its goals and to specify how new approaches differ from a team's current activities. Stakeholders should also encourage members to continue monitoring their environment for significant challenges that may require a team to further adapt its performance processes to meet contextual demands.

> **Best practice 21:** *Identify significant challenges that have arisen at the midpoints of performance and discuss how those challenges can be addressed by modifications or innovations in a team's actions or structures*

The endings of task performance present a unique opportunity to educate a team and its members. At the conclusion of a performance episode, a sufficient block of time should be set aside for learning with an emphasis on fostering future performance improvements. A core aspect of this process is a two-way discussion to generate lessons learned and discussion of how they can be utilized to address upcoming challenges. A wide variety of stakeholders should be encouraged to share their observations of a team's processes and performance outcomes. Once concerned parties have had the opportunity to voice their opinions, coaches should question team members' understanding of why they engaged in particular actions and prompt members to generate explanations for their own, and their team's, performance.

Prior research with military teams suggests that in order to maximize the value of this post-process discussion, coaches should provide a self-critique early in the review, avoid person-oriented feedback, provide specific constructive suggestions, discuss both teamwork and taskwork processes, make reference to lessons learned from prior performance episodes, and recognize and

Table 7.4 Best practices in building effective teams

• **Best practice 1:**	Conduct a team task analysis
• **Best practice 2:**	Create complementary and clear roles and responsibilities
• **Best practice 3:**	Set mutually agreed upon, specific, and increasingly difficult team-based goals for teams and their members
• **Best practice 4:**	Deliver feedback about both team member and team performance
• **Best practice 5:**	Reinforce mutual accountabilities with preliminary meetings, membership rosters, and team web pages
• **Best practice 6:**	Assess a team's capability to handle its functions and allocate authority accordingly
• **Best practice 7:**	Retain team members by benchmarking best practices such as flexitime, telecommuting, and distributed performance arrangements
• **Best practice 8:**	Articulate and operationalize a compelling and valued vision but do not hesitate to modify it as situational contingencies arise
• **Best practice 9:**	Identify targeted objectives but empower teams to help set and adapt the specific means of task accomplishment
• **Best practice 10:**	Define member roles in terms of overarching core values
• **Best practice 11:**	Provide teams with meaningful work and a sense of responsibility for that work by combining tasks, opening channels of communication, and forging direct team-to-client relationships
• **Best practice 12:**	Establish within team norms that govern the dyadic exchanges team members engage in by reinforcing desirable behaviors and sanctioning inappropriate ones
• **Best practice 13:**	Lean towards assigning too few members to accomplish a team's objectives rather than too many
• **Best practice 14:**	Actively manage a team's capabilities and characteristics
• **Best practice 15:**	Phase in teamwork as a distinct facet of members' performance appraisals
• **Best practice 16:**	Manage the type and flow of information a team receives
• **Best practice 17:**	Use instructional strategies such as cross-training as a surrogate for the experiences that teams accrue naturally over time
• **Best practice 18:**	Utilize information-based, demonstration-based, and practice-based methods to convey team-based instructional content
• **Best practice 19:**	Reinforce formal training with team-based action learning projects that arise naturally as part of a team's ongoing operations
• **Best practice 20:**	Encourage questions, thoughts, and concerns at the beginnings of task performance by providing informal reinforcements when issues are raised and supportive, non-defensive responses
• **Best practice 21:**	Identify significant challenges that have arisen at the midpoints of performance and discuss how those challenges can be addressed by modifications or innovations in a team's actions or structures
• **Best practice 22:**	Dedicate a block of time at the endings of task performance in order to critique a team's work, set the stage for future improvements, and reward effective performance

reinforce the spontaneous displays of effective team processes (Tannenbaum, Smith-Jentsch and Behson, 1998). Coaches that engage in these behaviors will be more likely to create a context characterized by psychological safety, or the shared belief that a team is safe for advancing ideas and taking interpersonal risks (e.g., pointing out failures) (Edmondson, 1999). This approach also helps foster shared mental models of a team's tasks, equipment, members, and interaction processes.

> **Best practice 22:** *Dedicate a block of time at the endings of task performance to critique a team's work, set the stage for future improvements, and reward effective performance*

Conclusion

Teams have been used to humankind's advantage since the first tribes organized hunting parties millennia ago. Throughout the course of history, it has become abundantly clear that teams can swiftly and triumphantly navigate the most-complex challenges conceived. Equally evident is the fact that teamwork comes at a price, and that most organizations' half-hearted attempt to pay that price ends with team failure and the disillusionment of senior stakeholders. Fortunately, a science of teams has evolved over the past century which offers much in terms of maximizing the synergies teams offer, while minimizing the performance decrements inherent to coordination. This body of theory, applied research findings, techniques, and tools can be leveraged to help ensure teams of experts continue to evolve into expert teams.

This chapter drew upon team theory and practice to discuss what it takes to build more effective teams. We began by defining the nature of teams, teamwork, team performance, and team effectiveness. These core constructs served as platform for identifying levers of change for building more-effective teams. The position advanced herein suggested that leaders and other organizational stakeholders influence the attainment of objectives by instituting and sustaining five conditions including: (1) establishing a real team (2) that has a compelling direction, (3) an enabling structure, (4) a supportive context, and (5) access to expert coaching. Concerned parties that establish and maintain these five conditions will help ensure their teams are more effective in the wild. When feasible, these five conditions were linked to a comprehensive team effectiveness framework. Moreover, twenty-two best practices were advanced that can be leveraged by stakeholders in their efforts to build more effective teams (see Table 7.4).

Acknowledgements

This work was partially supported by funding from the Army Research Laboratory's Advanced Decision Architecture Collaborative Technology Alliance (Cooperative Agreement DAAD19-01-2-0009). This work was also partially supported by the DOD Multidisciplinary University Research Initiative (MURI) program administered by the Army Research Office under grant DAAD19-01-0621. All opinions expressed in this paper are those of the authors and do not necessarily reflect the official opinion or position of the University of Central Florida, the U.S. Army Research Laboratory, or the Department of Defense.

REFERENCES

Bowers, C. A., Braun, C. C. and Morgan, B. B., Jr. (1997) Team workload: Its meaning and measurement. In M. T. Brannick, E. Salas and C. Prince (eds.), *Team performance and measurement: Theory, methods, and applications,* 85–108. Mahwah: Erlbaum Associates.

Burke, C. S. (2005) Team task analysis. In N. Stanton, A. Hedge, K. Brookhuis, E. Salas and H. Hendrick (eds.), *Handbook of human factors and ergonomics methods.* London: CRC Press.

Burke, C. S., Stagl, K. C., Klein, C., Goodwin, G. F., Salas, E. and Halpin, S. (2006) What types of leader behaviors are functional in teams?: A meta-analytic integration. *Leadership Quarterly, 17,* 288–307.

Burke, C. S., Stagl, K. C., Salas, E., Pierce, L. and Kendall, D. L. (2006) Understanding team adaptation: A conceptual analysis and model. *Journal of Applied Psychology, 91*(6), 1189–1207.

Cannon-Bowers, J. A., Tannenbaum, S. I., Salas, E. and Volpe, C. E. (1995) Defining team competencies and establishing team training requirements. In R. Guzzo, E. Salas and Associates (eds.), *Team effectiveness and decision making in organizations* (pp. 333–80). San Francisco: Jossey-Bass.

Campbell, J. P. and Kuncel, N. R. (2002) Individual and team training. In N. Anderson, D. S. Ones, H. K. Sinangil and C. Viswesvaran (eds.), *Handbook of industrial, work and organizational psychology.* London: Sage.

Conger, J. A., Spreitzer, G. M. and Lawler, E. E. (1999) Take-away lessons: What we know and where we need to go. In J. A. Conger, G. M. Spreitzer, E. E. Lawler and Associates (eds.), *The leader's change handbook.* San Francisco: Jossey-Bass.

Costa, P. T. and McCrae, R. R. (1992) *Revised NEO personality inventory (NEO PI-R): Professional manual.* Odessa: Psychological Assessment Resources.

Day, D. V. and Halpin, S. M. (2001) *Leadership development: A review of industry best practices* (Technical Report Number 1111). Alexandria, VA: US Army Research Institute for the Behavioral and Social Sciences.

DeShon, R. P., Kozlowski, S. W. J., Schmidt, A. M., Milner, K. R. and Wiechmann, D. (2004) A multiple goal, multilevel model of feedback effects on the regulation of individual and team performance in training. *Journal of Applied Psychology*, *85*(6), 1035–56.

Edmondson, A. (1999) Psychological safety and learning behavior in work teams. *Administrative Science Quarterly*, *44*, 350–83.

Fleishman, E. A. and Quaintance, M. K. (1984) *Taxonomies of human performance*. Orlando: Academic Press.

Fleishman, E. A. and Zaccaro, S. J. (1992) Toward a taxonomy of team performance functions. In R. W. Swezey and E. Salas (eds.), *Teams: Their training and performance*. Norwood: Ablex.

Hackman, J. R. (1987) The design of work teams. In J. Lorsch (ed.), *Handbook of Organizational Behavior*. Englewood Cliffs: Prentice Hall.

Hackman, J. R. (1992) Group influences on individuals in organizations. In. M. D. Dunnette and L. M. Hough (eds.), *Handbook of Industrial and Organizational Psychology* (Vol. 3). Palo Alto: Consulting Psychologists Press.

Hackman, J. R. (2002) *Leading teams: Setting the stage for great performances*. Boston: HBS Press.

Hackman, J. R. and Oldham, G. R. (1980) *Work redesign*. Reading: Addison-Wesley.

Hackman, J. R. and Wageman, R. (2005) A theory of team coaching. *Academy of Management Review*, *30*, 269–87.

Kameda, T., Stasson, M. F., Davis, J. H., Parks, C. D. and Zimmerman, S. K. (1992) Social dilemmas, subgroups, and motivation loss in task-oriented groups: In search of an "optimal" team size in division of work. *Social Psychology Quarterly*, *55*, 47–56.

Kozlowski, S. W. J. and Bell, B. S. (2003) Work groups and teams in organizations. In W. C. Borman, D. R. Ilgen and R. J. Klimoski (eds.), *Handbook of psychology: Industrial and organizational psychology*, Vol. 12. Chichester: Wiley and Sons.

Kozlowski, S. W. J., Gully, S. M., Salas, E. and Cannon-Bowers, J. A. (1996) Team leadership and development: Theory, principles, and guidelines for training leaders and teams. In M. Beyerlein, S. Beyerlein and D. Johnson (eds.), *Advances in interdisciplinary studies of work teams: Team leadership*, Vol. 3. Greenwich: JAI Press.

Locke, E. A. and Latham, G. P. (1990) A theory of goal setting and performance. Englewood Cliffs: Prentice Hall.

Marks, M. A., Mathieu, J. E. and Zaccaro, S. J. (2001) A temporally based framework and taxonomy of team process. *Academy of Management Review*, *26*, 356–76.

Orasanu, J. and Salas, E. (1993) Team decision making in complex environments. In G. Klein, J. Orasanu, R. Calderwood and C. E. Zsambok (eds.), *Decision making in action: Models and methods* (pp. 327–45). Norwood: Ablex Publishing.

Rutkowski, K. A. and Steelman, L. A. (2005) Testing a path model for anteceedents of accountability. *Journal of Management Development*, *24*, 473–86.

Salas, E. and Cannon-Bowers, J. A. (1997) A framework for developing team performance measures in training. In M. T. Brannick, E. Salas and C. Prince (eds.), *Team performance assessment and measurement: Theory, methods, and applications*. Mahwah: Erlbaum Associates.

Salas, E. and Cannon-Bowers, J. A. (2000) The anatomy of team training. In S. Tobias and J. D. Fletcher (eds.), *Training & Retraining: A Handbook for Business, Industry, Government, and the Military*. New York: Macmillan.

Salas, E., Cannon-Bowers, J. A. and Johnston, J. H. (1997) How can you turn a team of experts into an expert team?: Emerging training strategies. In C. E. Zsambok and G. Klein (eds.), *Naturalistic decision making* (pp. 359–70). Mahwah: Erlbaum Associates.

Salas, E., Dickinson, T. L., Converse, S. A. and Tannenbaum, S. I. (1992) Toward and understanding of team performance and team training. In R. W. Swezey and E. Salas (eds.), *Teams: Their Training and Performance*. Norwood: Ablex Publishing.

Salas, E., Stagl, K. C., Burke, C. S. and Goodwin, G. F. (in press) Fostering team effectiveness in organizations: Toward an integrative theoretical framework of team performance. In J. W. Shuart, W. Spaulding and J. Poland (eds.), *Modeling complex systems: Motivation, cognition and social processes, Nebraska symposium on motivation, 51*, Lincoln, NE: University of Nebraska Press.

Smith-Jentsch, K. A., Zeisig, R. L., Acton, B. and McPherson, J. A. (1998) Team dimensional training: A strategy for guided team self-correction. In J. A. Cannon-Bowers and E. Salas (eds.), Making decisions under stress: Implications for individual and team training. Washington: APA Press.

Stagl, K. C., Burke, C. S., Salas, E. and Pierce, L. (2006) Team adaptation: Realizing team synergy. In C. S. Burke, L. Pierce and E. Salas (eds.), *Understanding adaptability: A prerequisite for effective performance within complex environments*. Oxford: Elsevier Science.

Stagl, K. C., Fowlkes, J., Burke, C. S. and Salas, E. (2002, March). Team member conscientiousness and adaptive team performance. Presentation conducted at the 23rd Annual Industrial Organizational and Organizational Behavior Conference, Tampa.

Stagl, K. C., Salas, E. and Burke, C. S. (2007) Best practices in team leadership: What team leaders do to facilitate team effectiveness. In J. A. Conger and R. E. Riggio (eds.), *The practice of leadership: Developing the next generation of leaders*. San Francisco: Jossey-Boss.

Stagl, K. C., Salas, E. and Fiore, S. M. (in press). Best practices in cross training teams. In D. A. Nembhard (ed.), *Workforce cross training handbook*. Boca Raton: CRC Press.

Stagl, K. C., Salas, E., Rosen, M., Priest, H. A., Burke, C. S., Goodwin, G. F. and Johnston, J. H. (2007). Distributed team performance: A multilevel review of distribution, diversity, and decision-making. In F. Yammarino and F. Dansereau (eds.) *Multilevel issues in organizations*, Amsterdam: Elsevier.

Tannenbaum, S. I., Beard, R. L. and Salas, E. (1992) Team building and its influence on team effectiveness: An examination of conceptual and empirical developments. In K. Kelley (ed.), *Issue, theory, and research in industrial/organizational psychology*. Amsterdam: Elsevier.

Tannenbaum, S. I., Smith-Jentsch, K. A. and Behson, S. J. (1998) Training team leaders to facilitate team learning and performance. In J. A. Cannon-Bowers and E. Salas (eds.), *Making decisions under stress: Implications for individual and team training*. Washington: APA.

Wageman, R. (1995) Interdependence and group effectiveness. *Administrative Science Quarterly, 40*, 145–80.

Welch, J. and Welch, S. (2005) *Winning*. New York: Harper Collins.

Yukl, G. (2007) Best practices in the use of proactive influence tactics by leaders. In J. A. Conger and R. E. Riggio (eds.), *The Practice of Leadership*. San Francisco: Jossey-Bass.

Yukl, G. and Van Fleet, D. (1992) Theory and research on leadership in organizations. In M. D. Dunnette and L. M. Hough (eds.), *Handbook of industrial and organizational psychology*, 2nd edn. Palo Alto: Consulting Psychologists Press.

8 Career development processes in organizations

Yehuda Baruch and Sherry E. Sullivan

Traditionally, organizational career management programs have been based on the premise that the organization was comprised of individuals who planned to spend their entire worklife within that same workplace. This premise stemmed from early career stage models that depicted workers as being focused on upward movement within a clear and stable structure with one or two employers over their life spans (e.g., Super, 1957). Such traditional models suggested that paternalistic employers offer resources to its employees to enable these individuals to repeatedly win rounds in the career tournament (see Ng *et al.*, 2005 for a review; Nicholson and De Waal-Andrew, 2005; Rosenbaum, 1979). Likewise, emphasis was placed on how certain factors, such as having a mentor (Kram, 1985; Forret and de Janasz, 2005), could enhance career outcomes, especially salary and rate of promotion (Feldman, 1990; Sullivan and Arthur, 2006).

However, over the last twenty-five years, the work landscape has dramatically changed (Baruch, 2004; Hall, 2002). Demographic shifts (Bureau of Labor Statistics, 2004a&b), increased globalization (Bartlett and Ghoshal, 1989), the increased rate of technological advances (e.g., Friedman, 2005; Kanter, 2001) changes in the psychological employment contract (Rousseau, 1989; Rousseau and Wade-Benzoni, 1995; Conway and Briner, 2005), and the fundamental uncertainty of the career environment have called into question assumptions about traditional linear careers (Arthur and Rousseau, 1996; Cappelli, 1999; Hall, 1996; Osterman, 1996; Weick, 1996). Careers are no longer viewed as bounded by a single organization, industry, profession or even country (Arthur and Rousseau, 1996; Peiperl and Baruch, 1997; Sullivan and Arthur, 2006; Weick, 1996) nor are they solely characterized by upward advancement (Baruch, 2004; Cappelli, 1999) or extrinsic rewards (Gunz and Heslin, 2005; Heslin, 2005).

The psychological contract whereby workers exchanged organizational loyalty for job security was violated as firms laid off employees en-masse, including an unprecedented number of white collar professionals. A new contract was being enacted whereby workers gained learning opportunities, with no promise of long-term employment, and in return gave firms high quality performance, with no promise of organizational loyalty beyond the current work assignment (see Sullivan, 1999 for a review). Unlike employees in the traditional, multi-layered firms, workers under this new psychological contract changed jobs more frequently (Arthur and Rousseau, 1996; Cascio, 2000; Weick, 1996) and increasingly sought intrinsic sources of satisfaction in addition to extrinsic rewards (Hall, 1996, 2002, 2004). Career management, once viewed as the firm's responsibility to its long-term employees, gradually became viewed as the responsibility of the individual (Baruch, 2004, 2006a). Careers, and subsequently career management practices, were no longer defined solely within the context of the firm as illustrated by Hall's (2002, p. 12) definition of the modern careers as "the individually perceived sequence of attitudes and behaviors associated with work-related experiences and activities over the span of the person's life."

Given the fundamental changes that have occurred in the workplace, the domain of career management has also changed. The purpose of this chapter is to examine these changes, tracing how career management systems have evolved from the practices designed for traditional organizational systems to meet the needs of traditional, linear careerists to programs designed to meet the needs of individuals with multidirectional career paths. Specially, this chapter begins by reviewing traditional career management practices which are based on the linear career stage models. Next, a model of changing career patterns is used to depict how organizations may develop career management practices in response to the needs of workers with nontraditional, multidirectional careers patterns. Then, we detail a new model of careers and how organizations can use this model to develop the next generation of career management programs and practices. We close the chapter by discussing the continuing evolution of the workforce and what challenges are ahead for future career management practices and research.

The past: traditional careers and traditional career management

Traditional linear career models, as typified by the research of Donald Super (Super, 1957; Super, Thompson and Lindeman, 1988), emphasize upward movement within one or two organizations over an individual's lifetime. Even though linear models may not have accurately represented many of the careers of that time, it was still portrayed as the ideal, desired career type. Linear

Table 8.1 Example career management programs based on linear career stage models

Career stage	Traditional programs
Exploration	• Opportunities for young adults to gain work experience • Internships
Establishment	• Recruiting with the use of realistic job previews • Organizational orientation, socialization and training programs • Tuition reimbursement • Learning how to be a protégé as part of firm's formal mentoring program • Employee handbook and other written company information
Maintenance	• Updating of skills, especially those related to changes in technology • Learning how to be a mentor as part of the firm's formal mentoring program • Engaging in an international assignment • Health-related programs such as stress management • Use of assessment centers
Disengagement	• Retirement preparation programs

models tend to emphasize the attainment of extrinsic rewards including a high salary, quick rates of promotion, and job perks (e.g., the corner office, an expense account, the company car). Super (1957) articulated a model by which individuals expressed their self-concept as summarized by four career stages. In each stage, the individual strived to complete certain tasks in order to develop, mature, and successfully move onto the next stage. Super's (1957) four stages are:

1. Exploration, a period of engaging in self-examination, schooling, and the study of different career options;
2. Establishment, a period of becoming employed and finding a niche;
3. Maintenance, a period of holding on to one's position and up-dating skills; and
4. Disengagement, a time to phase into retirement.

Given the assumption that individuals generally progress through these stages in a linear and uniform fashion, organizations designed career management programs to assist their employees in successfully completing the tasks associated with each stage of development. Examples of these traditional career management programs are summarized in Table 8.1.

In the exploration stage, firms offer young adults internships which allow them the chance to gain work experience and discover what they like and dislike about work situations. Likewise, companies use these internships as a selection tool to get actual work samples from potential employees, often utilizing these internships as one long interview for a full-time position (see Sullivan and Arthur, 2006 for a review of early career processes).

For employees in the establishment stage, the firm's career management programs focused on organizational entry and socialization into the company's culture and norms. Although many firms still use seduction methods, (i.e., painting a glowing but unrealistic picture of the firm), to recruit new employees, some more progressive firms use Realistic Job Previews (RJPs) to provide job applicants with a balanced view of the positives and negatives of working for the firm (Blenkinsopp and Zdunczyk, 2005; Wanous, 1992).

Those in the establishment stage usually go through an orientation program, in which the employee handbook is distributed, key organizational players are introduced, basic information about the company's mission, goals and policies are reviewed, and necessary training is provided. The purpose of the orientation and socialization process is to effectively transform the newcomer to an insider. With the support of tenured members of the organization, newcomers can be more quickly socialized, increasing their organizational commitment and sense of belonging (Reichers, 1987).

For employees in the later career stages of maintenance and disengagement, relatively few opportunities for training and development are provided by firms (Sullivan and Duplaga, 1997). Most of the training offered at this stage focuses on the updating of skills, especially computer and other technological skills. Individuals in the maintenance stage may also learn how to mentor less-tenured employees (Levinson, 1978), be prepared for an international assignment, or may learn about health-related issues (e.g., stress reduction) in an effort to stem increasing health care costs (see Crocitto, 2006 for a review of midcareer). Likewise, employees in the disengagement stage may be offered information on how to be a better mentor or assist in the firm's long-range planning process. With the collapse of many pension plans in the UK, rising health care costs in the US, and increased downsizing in western countries, there are more of the so-called "gray-hair" employees who must continue to work because of insufficient funds. Given these workplace changes as well as the varying ages of potential retirees (e.g., young retirees of 50 to older retirees of 70 plus) and those older workers who voluntarily seek a second career or desire to remain employed beyond the traditional retirement age, more forward-thinking firms are already going beyond just the financial aspects of retirement planning to include other issues such as work after retirement (e.g., part-time work, phased retirement), personal relationships, and mental health issues, especially for those employees facing forced retirement or redundancy.

In sum, traditional organizational career management programs have largely been based on the developmental tasks depicted in the linear stage based models. These programs tend to be lock-step, with special training offered only to certain groups, such as those on the fast-track (London and Stumpf, 1982). For the most part, development is not tailored to the individual's needs as it is assumed that most employees will enter the firm at an early age, become socialized into the firm's culture, receive necessary training to fulfill their firm-specific jobs, and then be readied for retirement.

In one of the few attempts to systematically capture the organizational career management practices actually implemented by firms, Baruch (2006a) compared the career management practices of high tech firms in Israel and the UK (Baruch, 1996) to large US firms (Gutteridge, Leibowitz and Shore, 1993). His review, which captures career management practices of the 1990s, is summarized in Table 8.2.

As expected, a high percentage of organizations made use of traditional career management programs such as orientation and socialization, formal education, counseling by managers and HR specialists, succession planning, internal job postings (which are believed to encourage organizational tenure) and performance appraisal as a career planning tool. Surprisingly, although a relatively large percentage of the high tech firms (90% in Israel; 78% in the UK) reported the use of pre-retirement programs, only 5% of the US firms reported their use. Likewise, the high tech firms reported a greater use of assessment centers (69% in Israel; 67% in UK) compared to the US firms (23%). Despite the academic literature on the benefits of mentoring (e.g., Allen *et al.*, 2004), just a little more than 40% of the firms in these three countries had formal mentoring programs. It may be that these organizations encourage employees to develop informal mentoring relationships rather than formalizing these developmental experiences.

Baruch (2006a) found that the use of newer career management practices was less common than more traditional approaches. Only 13 percent of the US firms had any sort of programs related to issues such as dual-career couples or women and minorities in the workplace. Similarly, a relatively small percentage of Israeli and US firms offered skills and self-development workshops (14%, 24% respectively; 44% of nine UK firms).

As can be seen by Baruch's (2006a) review, organizations still tend to focus on providing traditional career management programs. Moreover, there is a pattern to how companies implement career practices; they tend to apply them in clusters, for example, starting with a set of basic functions, next moving to more developmental practices or to practices relating to planning, and

Table 8.2 Organizational use of career management practices (in percentages; Adopted from Baruch, 2006b)

Career Practices	High tech firms in Israel (n = 51)	High tech firms in UK (n = 9)	Large US firms (n = 256)
Orientation and socialization programs	NA	NA	78
Formal education	100	100	78
Training programs for managers	75	44	30
Skill and self-development workshops	14	44	24
Pre-retirement programs	90	78	5
Special need programs (e.g., women, minorities)	NA	NA	13
Career information (e.g., booklets)	22	33	19
Lateral moves or job rotation	NA	NA	60
Succession planning	63	33	69
Internal job postings	55	89	68
Fixed, common-career paths	67	56	NA
Non-managerial ladder for tech employees	75	44	34
Counseling by manager	59	89	97
Counseling by HR	41	56	67
Performance appraisal as career planning tool	82	89	NA
Assessment center	69	67	23
Formal mentoring	43	44	44
Written, individual career plans	14	33	NA

NA = not available. Because information provided in this table was drawn from two different studies by different researchers, not all the same career management practices were examined by each team.

then implementing more innovative practices (Baruch and Peiperl, 2000). The clusters might vary in different countries (Baruch and Budhwar, 2006), and is a topic deserving more empirical study.

Overall, there are still many organizations with traditional structures that focus primarily on hiring and maintaining traditional employees. Likewise, there are a growing number of organizations that have some employees with traditional careers and other employees with a variety of nontraditional career patterns. For those not enacting a traditional career, the paternalistic career management programs typically offered by companies may not provide the necessary learning opportunities needed to remain marketable in a post-corporate career (Baruch, 2004; Pieperl and Baruch, 1997). In the next section, we discuss the rise of the nonlinear career pattern and detail how organizations can respond to the career management needs of employees with different career values and patterns.

The growth of nontraditional careers

Environmental changes, such as the unprecedented downsizing of white collar and highly educated workers in the 1980s and 1990s, as well as the impact of increased globalization and technological advancement (Cappelli, 1999), has caused an increase in the physical (e.g., number and speed of moves across industries, professionals, organizations and countries) and psychological (e.g., recognition of opportunities and alternative career options) mobility of individuals (Arthur and Rousseau, 1996; Sullivan and Arthur, 2006). In the past, only certain industries were characterized by this level of high mobility and turnover. Saxenian (1996), for example, provided a case study of how social networks supported the high rates of job mobility and continuous learning among professionals in the Silicon Valley. She detailed how the region's open labor markets made job hopping the norm and encouraged loyalty based on professional relationships rather than organizational membership. Similarly, Jones (1996), using case studies and prior literature, examined project networks in the film industry. She described how individuals with portable skills moved from one movie project to another, gaining skills and building a reputation that would ensure their continued employability.

No longer is such movement limited to those in the Silicon Valley or the entertainment industry. A growing number of professionals are taking themselves off the fast-track (Ibarra, 2003), redefining career success (Gunz and Heslin, 2005; Sturges, 1999), or are opting-out of corporations to open small businesses (Buttner and Moore, 1997; Mainiero and Sullivan, 2005), to find more challenging and authentic work, or to focus on nonwork issues (Mainiero and Sullivan, 2006). Many have proclaimed the traditional career to be dead (Hall, 1996; Pink, 2002) and have called for the development of new models to guide a firm's management of a workforce characterized by increasingly diverse career patterns (Sullivan, Carden and Martin, 1998).

Despite these environmental changes, much research is still based on the linear career models (Arthur *et al.*, 2005). Concerns have been raised, however, about the validity of the traditional models (Sullivan, 1999; Baruch, 2004), with many scholars questioning whether an uninterrupted career progression depicts reality (Mirvis and Hall, 1996; Schneer and Reitman, 1993, 1997, 2002), how cultural norms impact the way careers unfold (for a review see Sullivan and Crocitto, in press), whether these linear models are applicable to the careers of both men and women (Gallos, 1989; Powell and Mainiero, 1992, 1993; Sullivan, 1999) and across different generations (Catalyst, 2001; Mainiero and Sullivan, 2005, 2006). Dissatisfaction with the traditional, linear age-based career models have encouraged the development of nontraditional career models including "Boundaryless" (Arthur and Rousseau, 1996), "Protean" (Hall, 1996; Briscoe, Hall and DeMuth, 2006), "Multidirectional" (Baruch, 2004), "Customized" (Valcour, Bailyn and Quijada, 2005), and "Kaleidoscope" (Mainiero and Sullivan, 2005) careers. These newer career paths are nonlinear (Baruch, 2004; Brousseau et al., 1996; Driver, 1979, 1982; Driver and Combs, 1983), and include taking time out from work to balance work and nonwork demands (Powell and Mainiero, 1992, 1993), as well as recycling to early career concerns in order to change career course (Power and Rothausen, 2003; Sullivan et al., 2004). Nontraditional careers are often based on project work (DeFillipi and Jones, 1996; Jones, 1996), portable skills (Saxenian, 1996; Sullivan, Carden and Martin, 1998), career interruptions (Schneer and Reitman, 1997), free agency (Peiperl and Baruch, 1997), and part-time job assignments (Feldman, 1990). Individuals with nontraditional careers often are more committed to their profession than their employer (Arthur and Rousseau, 1996). The differences between traditional and nontraditional careers are summarized in Table 8.3.

The present: nontraditional careers and changes in career management

Today's firms are comprised of many different types of workers – full-time, part-time, core employees, contingency employees, project workers, temps – and these workers have different career aspirations and needs, thus requiring varying training and career development schemes. The cookie-cutter, "one size fits all" career management programs of the past are no longer viable. Organizations need to rethink career management systems in order to address the needs of workers with diverse career patterns and goals. To provide guidance to organizations on how such a redesign of career management processes can be accomplished, we recommend the use of Sullivan et al.'s (1998) "Career Grid."

The Career Grid, as depicted in Figure 8.1, suggests four major career archetypes based on the intersection of two continua: the level of an individual's portability of career capital (e.g., the level by which an individual's

Table 8.3 Comparison of traditional and nontraditional careers (adopted from Baruch, 2004)

Aspect	Traditional	Nontraditional
Environment	Stable	Dynamic, sometimes chaotic
Career choice being made	At an early age, often influenced by parents	Repeatedly, sometimes cyclical, throughout the lifespan
Main responsibility for career management lies with	The organization	The individual
Employment	With one or two firms	With several firms, perhaps across several industries, occupations, and even countries
Career planning	Long term	Short term
Scope of individual change	Incremental as dictated by the organization	Often transformational as dictated by the individual's need to grow and remain employable
Psychological contract	Employer gives job security in return for employee's organizational commitment	Employer gives learning opportunities in return for high quality work

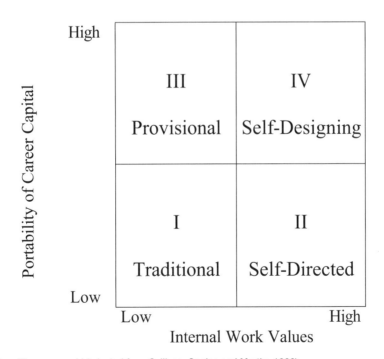

Figure 8.1   The career grid (adopted from Sullivan, Carden and Martin, 1998)

knowledge, skills and abilities is organizationally bound), and the level of an individual's internal work values (i.e., level of emphasis on intrinsic rewards, meaningfully, fulfilling and challenging work). Organizations can construct programs to help meet the needs of diverse employees bearing in mind these archetypes (see Sullivan *et al.*, 1998 for more details).

To begin, employees with a traditional career (Quadrant I, low portability of career capital, low internal work values) will desire traditional career management programs. These individuals may make up the firm's core employees. As long-term employees, they posses extensive organizational knowledge and are highly loyal to the firm or remain with the firm due to earlier investments (see the "Side-bets theory," Becker, 1960). Firms need to provide these traditional employees with extensive orientation, socialization and training because these individuals are likely to remain with the firm for long periods of time, perhaps even to retirement. Formal mentoring programs would also be useful and could enhance organizational commitment. Traditional practices such as promotion from within as well as the use of seniority, tenure, and other factors to reward employees and reinforce the commitment of high quality personnel are still appropriate. The value of non-monetary rewards, such as praise for a job well done and developmental feedback, should not be underestimated.

In contrast, organizations employing those with nontraditional careers – the self-directed, self-designing and provisional careerists – will need a different, adjustable portfolio of career management programs. The self-directed careers (Quadrant II, low portability of career capital, high internal work values) may also be long-time, core employees of the organization. Like traditional careerists, they will benefit from traditional career management efforts such as extensive orientation, socialization, and mentoring. Because self-directed careerists are more focused on internal work motivations and alliances with those in professional associations than traditional careerists, firms wishing to retain high performance self-directed careerists must be sure to design work so that it is intrinsically satisfying and meaningful (e.g., enabling telecommuting and other alternative work arrangements). Firms should encourage self-directed employees' interaction with others in their profession, or by the use of secondments (see Baruch 2006a). Self-directed careerists may also value a company that is socially responsible (e.g., uses environmentally sound practices, donates money to worthy causes) and that encourages employee growth within the boundaries of the firm (e.g., intrapreneurship, whereby employees are encouraged to be entrepreneurs within the firm, sometimes generating satellite companies).

A growing number of the labor force in western countries are provisional workers (Quadrant III, high portability of career capital, low internal work values). These longer-term temps or part-time employees need a quick orientation so they can rapidly contribute to the workplace. Such orientation and socialization programs should be tailored to the time the individual will be with the firm and the required tasks to be assigned. The use of videos and computer-assisted instruction, many of which are now internet-based, may be especially helpful. Provisional employees may also require training on any issues specific to the job at hand. They should be offered extrinsic rewards to maintain their motivation.

The last group, those with self-designing careers (Quadrant IV, high portability of career capital, high internal work values) may work for an organization for a short period of time (e.g., a few months to a year) as a project worker or consultant or may prefer to work in a team-based environment that encourages self-fulfillment and group empowerment. Companies must provide quick, short orientation and training to these employees so that they rapidly understand the cultural and norms of the environment in which they will be working. They may be assigned a "developer" to help ease their transition into the workplace. Self-designing careerists should be offered highly challenging tasks as they seek to increase their knowledge and skills in order to enhance their marketability. They should be proactive in seeking out mentors within their professions to enhance their career capital.

Given the growing number of nontraditional careerists in the workforce, firms should rethink traditional career management programs and the notion that "up is the only way" (Kaye, 2002). Firms need to consider using newer career management strategies including: colearning between junior and senior employees and team members (Hall, 1996b; Kram, 1986), action learning (Mirvis and Hall, 1996), developmental assignments, on-the-job learning (McCall, Lombardo and Morrison, 1988; White, 1992), learning through self-reflection (Seibert, 1996), and just-in-time on-line internet training and career assessment (Howard, 1995). Firms should encourage their employees to be more *proactive* participants in their own career planning (see Power, 2006 and Seibert *et al.*, 2001). Firms, however, must still provide more traditional career counseling and learning programs (e.g., tuition reimbursement programs; see Benson, Finegold and Mohrman, 2004, Cappelli, 2000; 2004) to their core employees.

The Career Grid is not a static model; some individuals will move between the different quadrants and may need assistance in making these transitions. For example, companies that downsize traditional and self-directed careerists will need to provide outplacement programs that recognize the changing work landscape. Managers will need to adopt a new mindset, focusing on "career empowerment" (Baruch, 2004). To successfully manage nontraditional careerists, organizations must continue to invest in people and offer multidirectional career paths which recognize flexibility and the employees' need to balance work and family demands (Baruch, 2004; Mainiero and Sullivan, 2005). Firms will need to train their managers on how to motivate and lead nontraditional careerists who, unlike the traditional careerists, may not have a strong attachment to, or in-depth knowledge of, the firm (Sullivan, *et al.*, 1998).

Unfortunately, many organizations have failed to recognize the need for an integrative career management system that effectively contributes to the learning of employees with diverse career paths. In an exploratory examination of the learning of individuals both in and outside organizational boundaries, Mallon and Walton (2005) found that less learning was occurring than would be expected. While individuals agreed in principle that workers were responsible for their own career development and intended to engage in learning activities, they were unsure how to do this. Those within organizational boundaries were perhaps afraid to try new things fearing that a mistake could derail their upward career progression. They were passive about their career development and seemed not to recognize the importance of informal learning to their own growth.

Although both those traditional and nontraditional careerists in Mallon and Walton's (2005) study recognized the importance of life-long learning, their good intentions about engaging in developmental activities didn't translate into actual behaviors. This suggests that organizations cannot divorce themselves from the career management process – even when dealing with nontraditional careerists.

In sum, the old psychological contract must be replaced by a new, open partnership between organizations and employees. HR departments must disregard traditional assumptions that training is only for those full-time, long-time, core employees of the organization and extend training to those with nontraditional careers. Although nontraditional careerists have broken away from the physical boundaries of an organization, they still may be psychologically trapped in the traditional career paradigm and may need guidance to make the transition from traditional to nontraditional careerists. The Career Grid (Sullivan, *et al.*, 1998) provides an important bridge between the traditional linear career models and newer, nonlinear models (e.g., protean, boundaryless) and can be used by organizations to help manage employees making the transition from traditional to nontraditional careers. In the next section, we discuss how organizations can use a new career model, the Kaleidoscope Career Model, (KCM), to develop the next generation of career management programs to meet the evolving needs of employees in the contemporary workplace.

The future: organizational career management programs and kaleidoscope careers

Although more organizations are reconsidering their career management programs in an effort to recognize workers with different types of career patterns, the rapid pace of change and increased complexities of the contemporary work environments calls for an even greater redefinition of the firm's role in workers' careers. In place of the linear career stage models that still guide many career and HRM programs, we suggest the use of the kaleidoscope career model (Mainiero and Sullivan, 2005 and 2006) as the basis for developing organizational programs to better guide the increasingly complex careers of a progressively more diverse workforce.

The kaleidoscope career model

Using a multi-method approach (e.g., interviews, focus groups, and three extensive surveys) with a sample of over 3,000 individuals, Mainiero and Sullivan (2005 and 2006) developed a new model of careers, called the Kaleidoscope Career Model (KCM), to better represent the contemporary careers of women and men given the context of rapid change. Using the metaphor of a kaleidoscope, Mainiero and Sullivan suggest that: "Like a kaleidoscope that produces changing patterns when the tube is rotated and its glass chips fall into new arrangements, [individuals] shift the pattern of their careers by rotating different aspects of their lives to arrange roles and relationships in new ways" (Mainiero and Sullivan, 2005, p. 111).

Just as a kaleidoscope uses three mirrors to create infinite patterns, the Kaleidoscope Career Model has three "mirrors" or parameters which combine in different ways throughout a person's life, reflecting the unique patterns of his/her career. To use an artistic metaphor, the colors of the kaleidoscope are reflected in these three parameters, shaping an individual's decisions as one aspect of the kaleidoscope, or color, takes on greater intensity as a decision parameter at different points of the life span. Over the course of the life span, as a person searches for the best fit that matches the character and context of his/her life, the colors of the kaleidoscope shift in response, with one color (parameter) moving to the foreground and intensifying in color as that parameter takes priority at that time in his/her life. The other two colors (parameters) lessen in intensity and recede to the background, but are still present and active as all aspects are necessary to create the current pattern of his/her life/career.

These three parameters of the KCM shift over the course of an individual's life span to create different patterns. All three parameters are always present and always interacting but take on different levels of importance based on what is occurring in an individual's life at that point in time and the fit between the person's life and his/her career. The three parameters are:

1. Authenticity – defined as being true to oneself in the midst of the constant interplay between personal development and work and nonwork issues.
2. Balance – defined as making decisions so that the different aspects of one's life, both work and nonwork, form a coherent whole.
3. Challenge – defined as engaging in activities that permit the individual to demonstrate responsibility, control, and autonomy while learning and growing.

In their research, Mainiero and Sullivan (2006) found that gender plays a major role here, as men typically follow the pattern of pursing challenge then authenticity then balance (C–A–B) over the course of their life spans. Women, though, tend to pursue a C–B–A (challenge, balance, authenticity) pattern. Age is yet another factor; many younger men (Gen X and Y) have career patterns more similar to women. Therefore, unlike the males of the Baby Boom and Greatest Generation, younger men may also desire more organizational programs that promote alternative career paths and more work-life balance.

In sum, the KCM suggests that each of these parameters – authenticity, balance, and challenge – are active as signposts throughout an individual's career. Certain issues predominate at different points in the life span, becoming the parameter that caused a pivot in the person's decision making about his/her career. The remaining aspects, still active, are not irrelevant but take on a secondary role at that point in time (see Mainiero and Sullivan, 2005 for more details). In the next section, we discuss how organizations can apply the KCM to create the next generation of innovative career management programs.

Organizational use of the KCM to guide career management processes

What implications does the Kaleidoscope Career Model have for organizational career management programs?[1] First, the KCM suggests that organizations need to rethink the way work is done and consider how the use of technology can assist their employees in achieving better integration of work and life. Some firms, such as Sun Microsystems, have permitted more flexibility in scheduling and measure performance based on work outcomes rather than face time. For example, 95 percent of Sun Microsystems' employees are on flexible schedules (Mainiero and Sullivan, 2006). Such forward-thinking firms recognize that workers have a "dual-agenda" whereby both work and family are valued. These firms listen to employees' suggestions on how work can be better designed to increase productivity while permitting individuals to devote quality time to their family, friends, and community. Firms may encourage their employees to engage in socially responsible community projects that not only spread goodwill and permit employees to spend time contributing to their communities, but help employees grow and learn. Lessons learned through these community service projects and other new experiences (e.g., volunteer fundraising, Peace Corps) are brought back to the job and contribute to employee effectiveness and positive work attitudes.

Second, firms need to realize that for many, the linear career is dead and career interruptions and time-outs are the new norm, especially for women. Individuals need to be able to take time off of work to handle different aspects of their lives (e.g., childcare, care of the elderly, personal and spiritual development), without the penalty of losing their jobs. Such "on and off ramps" can take the form of part-time downscaling, a leave of absence, paid and unpaid sabbaticals, and "boomerang" programs whereby former employees are re-admitted to the firm after taking a career interruption or working for another firm. To succeed, such programs need to rely on a corporate culture that provides those on leave with continued training and development opportunities, job banks that give first priority to the hiring of alumni, and human resource support for those on varying work schedules (e.g., benefits for part-time workers).

Third, many organizations, intentionally or unintentionally, still prevent women and other minorities from reaching the ranks of top management (Altman *et al.*, 2005). More efforts must be made to help women and disadvantaged populations break through the glass ceiling and obtain work experience characterized by the criticality, visibility, and breadth of responsibility. These individuals must be placed in roles along career paths that provide the experience needed to assume top organizational positions. Firms can begin this process by measuring whether the workplace population at the various levels throughout the organization represents the population of the community. Next, companies can benchmark the best practices of other organizations that have a fair representation of women and minorities in the upper echelons. Firms must monitor the number of women and minorities in the pipeline positions, and hold senior-level management accountable for their advancement at all levels. These efforts need to be carried out in an equitable manner so as to prevent backlash from white males. Fair representation of women and minorities in the upper echelons is good business because such diversity has a positive impact on the organization's bottom line (Harel, Tzafrir and Baruch, 2003).

Fourth, outdated evaluation and reward systems must be replaced by systems that support career development and encourage workers to achieve authenticity, balance and challenge. Emphasis should be placed on flexible project based work that pay for outcomes rather than hours worked. Benefit systems need to be revised and based on expanding definitions of what composes a family. Initiatives that firms should consider include: extending health care coverage and inheritance of pensions to include a domestic partner, parents, and adult children; giving employees an allowance to be spent on benefits of their choice rather than imposing "one size-fits all" programs that may be of little use to some workers (e.g., value of childcare programs to single employees without children); and eliminating biases in reward systems that pay married employees, especially men, greater salaries regardless of performance.

Fifth, firms must realize that some programs, once considered perks, are now necessary in order to attract and maintain high quality workers. Some of these quality work–life programs include: guaranteed job return for individuals; maternity or paternity leave or for those taking care of elderly relatives; time banks of paid leave for meeting personal and family needs; reduced hour careers; job-sharing opportunities; reduction in the number of hours in the paid workweek; increasing paid vacation time; and creating more quality part-time jobs with prorated benefits and pension plans. Table 8.4 summarizes some of the career management programs that are suggested by the use of the KCM.

In sum, firms can use the KCM to guide the development and implementation of organizational career management programs that meet the needs of an increasingly diverse and changing workforce. Organizations must develop and reinforce a culture that encourages the continued growth of all its employees – those with traditional and nontraditional career paths, especially in meeting individuals' needs for authenticity, balance and challenge.

Future challenges and conclusions

This chapter has summarized the evolution of organizational career management systems. In the traditional, tall, pyramid-structured organizations of the

Table 8.4 Examples of career management programs based on the kaleidoscope career model

Three parameters	Possible programs
Authenticity	Involvement in meaningful community projects
	Opportunities for self-assessment
	Activities that encourage self-reflection and growth, such as formal career coaching
Balance	Flexible work schedules with training on the best use of technology and how to manage work relationships remotely
	Career counseling focusing on stress management and how to manage the increased blurred boundaries between work and nonwork
Challenge	Job rotation and other programs to increase job variety and learning
	International assignments
	Rich feedback and opportunities to reflect on daily on-the-job learning experiences

manufacturing era, the linear career stage models were used to guide the development of career management practices. Organizations designed programs to meet the needs of the traditional, linear careerists, typically a man whose homemaker wife cared for the children and coordinated the couple's social life, thereby permitting the male worker to be career focused. Although there are still organizations and industries that are more traditionally structured, there are an increasing number of organizations that have dynamic and fluid structures. Because of the growing number of women and dual-career couples in the workforce, the man as the sole breadwinner of the family is no longer the norm in western countries. Thus, in addition to organizational programs that meet the needs of traditional careerists, organizations need to develop programs for nontraditional careerists. We discussed the Career Grid as a framework for bridging the transition from traditional and nontraditional careers. As suggested by the Career Grid, organizations should continue to provide traditional career management programs for those employees who follow a more traditional, linear career path while also introducing newer programs to enhance the work performance of self-directed, self-designing, and provisional careerists. Although requiring more variation in programs and procedures, tailoring career management programs to meet the specific needs of employees with different career types will help the organization attract, motivate and retain high quality workers.

As organizational forms and careers continue to evolve, firms will need to remain proactive. They will need to keep refining and improving their career management systems to meet the needs of an increasingly diverse workforce. To remain responsive and to gain a competitive advantage through the effective use of human capital, we suggest that organizations employ the Kaleidoscope Career Model (KCM) as a framework for developing the next generation of career management systems.

In addition to serving as the foundation for organizational development of innovative career management systems, the KCM may also be useful in helping organizations to navigate emerging challenges.[2] One major challenge currently facing organizations is the effective management of careers across national borders. Numerous multinational corporations (MNC) have already encountered the struggle of meeting the expectations and needs of employees with very diverse cultural backgrounds within diverse political, economic, and social contexts (e.g., Bartlett and Ghoshal, 1989; Guzzo, Nooman and Elron, 1994; Harvey, 1997). MNCs with diverse operations in different countries have the difficult task of maintaining and reinforcing their overall corporate culture and general strategy while overseeing the career management of employees in different local systems.

There may be sharp contrasts in the strategies employed by different organizations and some integration and compromises may be required to recognize contextual differences (Baruch and Altman, 2002). Moreover, much of what is known about career management systems is based on the research conducted in western countries; the career systems in other countries may vary greatly and are sometimes less well-developed due to political and societal factors (e.g., the former lack of free enterprise in the Soviet Union, Eastern Europe and China). Also, despite the fact that career management programs related to the expatriation and repatriation of organizational employees have received much research attention, little research has been done on other career and human resource issues such as the working relationship between team members who may be in different countries and time zones; mentoring and knowledge transfer between different organizational locations throughout the world (Baugh and Sullivan, 2005; Crocitto, Sullivan and Carraher, 2005); and even how people throughout the world define, understand and experience careers.

Another major challenge that organizations face in regard to career management is how to effectively use technology to enhance training and performance as well as how technology can support the use of alternative work schedules, telecommuting, and other innovative work arrangements. Technology can also be used to provide online career assessment measures, career coaching and counseling, networking opportunities, and a host of other career-related programs. Firms are just beginning to recognize and use the technology to enhance human capital and future research on such applications needs to be conducted.

Finally, human resource managers who direct organizational career systems face the continuing challenge of assuming a more-strategic role within their organizations. Human resource managers must become more adept in quantifying the positive outcomes of training efforts as well as other career programs (e.g., use of human resource accounting methods). Additionally, while outsourcing may provide short-term cost savings, the outsourcing of key human resource functions may, in the long term, result in more costs than benefits. Such outsourcing carries the risk of poor service and quality (e.g., Cooke, Shen and McBride 2005); the development of career systems that don't match the particular culture of the organization or meet the needs of the firm's employees, both core employees as well as the growing number of contingency, project and part-time workers; and the loss of the competencies, knowledge, and potential impact that comes from having human resource management experts within the organization (see Greer, Youngblood and Gray, 1999).

REFERENCES

Allen, T. D., Eby, L. T., Poteet, M. L., Lentz, E. and Lima, L. (2004) Career benefits associated with mentoring for protégés: A meta-analysis. *Journal of Applied Psychology*, *89*; 127–36.

Altman, Y., Simpson, R., Baruch, Y. and Burke, R. J. (2005) Reframing the 'glass ceiling' debate. In R. J. Burke and M. C. Mattis, (eds.) Supporting Women's Career Advancement: Challenges and Opportunities. pp. 58–81, Cheltenham: Edward Elgar.

Arthur, M. B., Khapova, S. N. and Wilderom, C. P. M. (2005) Career success in a boundaryless career world. *Journal of Vocational Behavior*, *26*(*2*), 177–202.

Arthur, M. B. and Rousseau, D. M. (1996) The boundaryless career as a new employment principle. In M. G. Arthur and D. M. Rousseau (eds.), *The boundaryless career.* New York: Oxford University Press.

Bartlett, C. A. and Ghoshal, S. (1989) *Managing Across Borders. The Transnational Solution.* Boston: Harvard Business School Press.

Baruch, Y. (1996) Career planning and managing techniques in use *Career Development International*, *1*(*1*): 43–52.

Baruch, Y. (2004) Transforming careers from linear to multidirectional career paths: Organizational and individual perspectives. *Career Development International*, *9*(*1*), 57–73.

Baruch, Y. (2006a) Organizational career management. In J. Greenhaus and G. A. Callanan (eds.) *Encyclopedia of Career Development.* Thousand Oaks: Sage.

Baruch, Y. (2006b). Careers and career development in organizations. *Human Resource Management Review*, *16*(*2*), 125–38.

Baruch, Y. and Altman, Y. (2002) Expatriation and repatriation in MNC: A taxonomy. *Human Resource Management*, *41*, 239–59.

Baruch, Y. and Budhwar, P. (2006) Career practices: Comparing India vs UK, *International Business Review*, *15*(*1*), 84–101.

Baruch, Y. and Hall, D. T. (2004) The academic career: A model for future careers in other sectors? *Journal of Vocational Behavior, 64*(2), 241–62.

Baruch, Y. and Peiperl, M. A. (2000) Career management practices: An empirical survey and theoretical implications. *Human Resource Management* (US), *39*(4), 347–66.

Baugh, S. G. and Sullivan, S. E. (2005) Mentoring and career development. *Career Development International, 10*(6/7), 425–28.

Becker, H. S. (1960) Notes on the concept of commitment. *American Journal of Sociology, 66,* 32–40.

Benson, G. S., Finegold, D. and Mohrman, S. A. (2004) You paid for the skills, now keep them: Tuition-reimbursement and voluntary turnover. *Academy of Management Journal, 47*(3), 315–31.

Blenkinsopp, J. and Zdunczyk, K. (2005) Making sense of mistakes in managerial careers. *Career Development International, 10*(5), 359–74.

Briscoe, J. P., Hall, D. T. and DeMuth, R. L. F. (2006) Protean and boundaryless careers: An empirical exploration. *Journal of Vocational Behavior, 69*(1), 30–47.

Brousseau, K. R., Driver, M. J., Eneroth, K. and Larsson, R. (1996) Career pandemonium: realigning organizations and individuals *Academy of Management Executive.* Vol 10, No 4, 52–65.

Bureau of Labor Statistics, (2004a, April 20) *Employment Characteristics of Families Survey,* USDL04–719, www.bls.gov.

Bureau of Labor Statistics, (2004b, May 24) *Contingent and Alternative Employment Arrangements,* USDL 010153, www.bls.gov.

Buttner, E. H. and Moore, D. P. (1997) Women's organizational exodus to entrepreneurship: Self-reported motivations and correlates with success. *Journal of Small Business Management, 35*(1), 34–47.

Cappelli, P. (1999) *The new deal at work.* Boston: Harvard Business School Press.
  (2000) A market-driven approach to retaining talent. *Harvard Business Review, 78*:1, 103–11.
  (2004) Why do employers pay for college? *Journal of Econometrics, 121,* 213–41.

Cascio, W. F. (2000) New workplaces. In Jean M. Kummerow (ed.), *New Directions in Career Planning and the Workplace* (2nd edn.), Palo Alto: Davies-Black Publishing.

Catalyst (2001, Dec 11) *The next generation: Today's professionals, tomorrow's leaders.* Catalyst-women.org Press Release.

Cooke, F. L., Shen, J. and McBride A. (2005) Outsourcing HR as a competitive strategy? A literature review and an assessment of implications. *Human Resource Management 44/4,* 413–32.

Conway, N. and Briner, R. B. (2005) *Understanding Psychological Contracts at Work.* Oxford: Oxford University Press.

Crittenden, A. (2001) *The Price of Motherhood.* New York: Henry Holt and Company.

Crocitto, M. (2006) Middle career stages. In J. Greenaus and G. A. Callanan (eds.): *Encyclopedia of Career Development.* Thousand Oaks: Sage.

Crocitto, M., Sullivan, S. E. and Carraher, S. M. (2005) Global mentoring as a means of career development and knowledge creation: A learning based framework and agenda for future research. *Career Development International, 10*(6/7), 522–35.

DeFillipi, R. A., and Jones, C. (1996) Back to the future in film: Combining industry and self knowledge to meet career challenges of the 21st century. *Academy of Management Executive,* Vol. 10, No. 4.

Driver, M. J. (1979) Career concepts and career management in organizations. In C. L. Cooper (ed.), *Behavioral Problems in Organizations*: Englewood Cliffs: Prentice Hall.

Driver, M. J. (1982) Career concepts – a new approach to career research. In R. Katz (ed.), *Career Issues in Human Resource Management*. Englewood Cliffs: Prentice Hall.

Driver, M. J. and Combs, M. W. (1983) Fit between career concepts, corporate culture, and engineering productivity and morale. *Enhancing Engineering Careers*, (Conference Record of the IEEE Conference on Careers) 12–22. Palo Alto: The Institute of Electrical and Electronics Engineers.

Feldman, D. (1990) Reconceptualization: The nature and consequences of part-time work. *Academy of Management Review*, *15*, 103–12.

Forret, M. and de Janasz, S. (2005) Perceptions of an organization's culture for work and family: Do mentors make a difference? *Career Development International*, *10*, 6/7, 478–92.

Friedman, T. (2005) *The world is flat: A brief history of the 21st century*. New York: Farrar, Strauss, Giroux.

Friedman, S. D. and Greenhaus, J. H. (2000) *Work and family – Allies or enemies? What happens when business professionals confront life choices*. New York: Oxford University Press.

Gallos, J. V. (1989) Exploring women's development: Implications for career theory, practice and research. In M. B. Arthur, D. T. Hall and B. S. Lawrence (eds.), *Handbook of career theory*. New York: Cambridge University Press.

Greer, C. R., Youngblood, S. A. and Gray, D. A. (1999) Human resource management outsourcing: The make or buy decision, *Academy of Management Executive*, *13/3*, 85–96.

Gunz, H. P. and Heslin, P. A. (2005) Reconceptualizing career success. *Journal of Organizational Behavior*, *26*, 105–111.

Guzzo, R. A. Nooman, K. A. and Elron, E. (1994) Expatriate managers and the psychological contract. *Journal of Applied Psychology*, *79*, 617–26.

Hall, D. T. (1996) *The career is dead – long live the career*. San Francisco: Jossey-Bass.

Hall, D. T. (2002) *Careers in and out of organizations*. Thousand Oaks: Sage Publications.

Hall, D. T. (2004) The protean career: A quarter-century journey. *Journal of Vocational Behavior*, *65*, 1–13.

Hall, D. T. and Mirvis, P. H. (1996) The new protean career: Psychological success and the path with a heart. In D. T. Hall (ed.) *The career is dead, long live the career*. San Francisco: Jossey-Bass.

Harel, G., Tzafrir, S. and Baruch, Y. (2003) Achieving organizational effectiveness through promotion of women into managerial positions: HRM practice focus. *The International Journal of Human Resource Management*, *14(2)*: 247–63.

Harvey, M. (1997) Dual-career expatriates: expectations, adjustment and satisfaction with international relocation, *Journal of International Business Studies*, *28(3)*, 627–58.

Heslin, P. A. (2005) Conceptualizing and evaluating career success. *Journal of Organizational Behavior*, *26*, 113–36.

Howard, A. (1995) *The changing nature of work*. San Francisco: Jossey-Bass.

Ibarra, H. (2003) *Working identity: Unconventional strategies for reinventing your career*. Boston: Harvard Business School Press.

Jones, C. (1996) Careers in project networks: The case of the film industry. In M. A. Arthur and D. M. Rousseau (eds.). *The boundaryless career*. Oxford: Oxford University Press.

Kanter, R. M. (2001) *Evolve! Succeeding in the digital culture of tomorrow*. Boston: Harvard Business School Press.

Kaye, B (2002) *Up is not the only way.* Palo Alto: Davies-Black Publishing.

Konrad, A. M., Goldberg, C., Sullivan, S. E. and Yang, Y. (2006) Preferences for job attributes associated with work and family: A longitudinal study. *Sex Roles, 53(5/6)*, 303–15.

Konrad, A. M., Ritchie, J. E., Liebe, P. and Corrigall, E. (2000) Sex differences and similarities in job attributes preferences: A meta-analysis. *Psychological Bulletin, 126*, 593–641.

Kram K. E. (1985) *Mentoring in the work,* Glenvie: Scott, Foresman.

    (1986) Mentoring in the workplace. In D. T. Hall and Associates (eds.), *Career development in organizations.* San Francisco: Jossey-Bass.

Landers, R. M., Rebitzer, J. B. and Taylor, L. J. (1996) Human resources practices and the demographic transformation of professional labor markets. In P. Osterman (ed.), *Broken Ladders,* 215–45. New York: Oxford University Press.

Levinson, D. (1978) *The seasons of a man's life.* New York: Knopf.

London M. and Stumpf, S. A. (1982) *Managing careers.* Reading: Adisson-Wesley.

Maier, M. (1999) On the gendered substructure of organization: Dimensions and dilemmas of corporate masculinity. In G. N. Powell, (ed.), *Handbook of gender and work.* Thousand Oaks: Sage Publications.

Mainiero, L. A. and Sullivan, S. E. (2005) Kaleidoscope careers: An alternative explanation for the opt-out revolution. *Academy of Management Executive, 19(1)*, 106–23.

    (2006) *The opt-out revolt: Why people are leaving companies to create kaleidoscope careers.* Palo Alto: Davies-Black Publishing.

Mallon, M. and Walton, S. (2005) Career and learning: The ins and the outs of it. *Career Development International, 34(4)*, 468–87.

McCall, M. W., Lombardo, M. M. and Morrison, A. (1988) *The lessons of experience: how successful executives develop on the job.* New York: Lexington Books.

Mirvis, P. H. and Hall, D. T. (1996) New organizational forms and the new career. In D. T. Hall and Associates (eds.), *The career is dead-Long live the career.* San Francisco: Jossey-Bass.

Ng, T. W. H., Eby, L. T., Sorensen, K. L. and Feldman, D. C. (2005) Predictors of objective and subjective career success: A meta-analysis. *Personnel Psychology, 58*, 367–408.

Nicholson, N. and De Waal-Andrews, W. (2005) Playing to win: Biological imperatives self-regulation, and trade-offs in the game of career success. *Journal of Organizational Behavior, 26*, 137–54.

Osterman, R. (1996) *Broken ladders.* New York: Oxford University Press.

Peiperl, M. and Baruch, Y. (1997) Back to square zero: The post-corporate career. *Organizational Dynamics, 25(4)*, 6–22.

Pink, D. (2002) *Free agent nation: The future of working for yourself.* New York: Warner Business Books.

Powell, G. N. and Mainiero, L. A. (1992) Cross-currents in the river of time: Conceptualizing the complexities of women's careers. *Journal of Management, 18*, 215–37.

    (1993) Getting ahead – in career and life. In G. N. Powell (ed.) *Women and Men in Management* (pp. 186–224). Newbury Park: Sage Publications.

Power, S. J. (2006) *The Midcareer Success Guide, Planning the Second Half of Your Working Life* Westport: Greenwood Publishing Group.

Power, S. J. and Rothausen, T. J. (2003) The work-oriented midcareer development model: An extension of Super's maintenance stage. *The Counseling Psychologist, 31(2)*, 157–97.

Reichers, A. E. (1987) An interactionist perspective on newcomer socialization rates. *Academy of Management Review*, *12*(*2*), 278–88.

Rosenbaum, J. (1979) Tournament mobility: Career patterns in a corporation. *Administrative Science Quarterly*, *24*(*6*), 220–41.

Rousseau, D. M. (1989) Psychological and implied contracts in organizations. *Employee Responsibility and Rights Journal*, *2*(*2*), 121–39.

Rousseau, D. M. and Wade-Benzoni, K. A. (1995) Changing individual-organization attachments: A two-way street. In A. Howard (ed.), *The Changing Nature of Work*. San Francisco: Jossey-Bass.

Saxenian, A. L. (1996) Beyond boundaries: Open labor markets and learning in Silicon Valley. In M. B. Arthur and D. M. Rousseau (eds.), *The boundaryless career*. New York: Oxford University Press.

Schneer, J. A. and Reitman, F. (1993) Effects of alternative family structures on managerial career paths. *Academy of Management Journal*, *36*, 830–43.

Schneer, J. A. and Reitman. F. (1997) The interrupted managerial career path: A longitudinal study of MBAs. *Journal of Vocational Behavior*, *51*(*3*), 411–34.

Schneer, J. A. and Reitman, F. (2002) Managerial life without a wife: Family structure and managerial career success. *Journal of Business Ethics*, *37*, 25–38.

Seibert, K. (1996) Experience is the best teacher, if you can learn from it: real-time reflection and development In D. T. Hall and Associates (eds.), *The Career is Dead-Long Live the Career*. San Francisco: Jossey-Bass.

Seibert, S. E., Kraimer, M. L. and Crant, J. M. (2001) What do proactive people do? A longitudinal model linking proactive personality and career success. *Personnel Psychology*, *54*, 845–74.

Sturges, J. (1999) What it means to succeed: Personal conceptions of career success held by male and female managers at different ages. *British Journal of Management*, *10*, 239–52.

Sullivan, S. E. (1999) The changing nature of careers: A review and research agenda. *Journal of Management*, *25*, 457–84.

Sullivan, S. E. and Arthur, M. B. (2003) The physical and psychological passages and potential limitations of boundaryless careers. Presentation at the *Academy of Management Meetings*, Seattle.

(2006) The evolution of the boundaryless career concept: Examining physical and psychological mobility. *Journal of Vocational Behavior*, *69*, 19–29.

Sullivan, S. E., Carden, W. A. and Martin, D. F. (1998) Careers in the next millennium: A reconceptualization of traditional career theory. *Human Resource Management Review*, *8*, 165–85.

Sullivan, S. E. and Crocitto, M. (2007) Process theories of careers. In *Handbook of Career Studies*, M. Peiperl and H. Gunz (eds.). New York: Sage Publications.

Sullivan, S. E. and Duplaga, E. (1997) Recruiting and retaining older workers for the new millennium, *Business Horizons*, *40*(*6*), 65–9.

Sullivan, S. E., Martin, D. F., Carden, W. A. and Mainiero, L. A. (2004) The road less traveled: How to manage the recycling career stage. *Journal of Leadership and Organization Studies*, *10*(*2*), 34–42.

Super, D. (1957) *Psychology of Careers*. New York: Harper & Collins.

Super, D., Thompson, A. and Lindeman, R. (1988) *Adult Career Concerns Inventory: Manual for Research and Exploratory Use in Counseling*. Palo Alto: Consulting Psychologists Press.

Valcour, M., Bailyn, L. and Quijada M.A. (2007) Customized Careers. In *Handbook of Career Studies*, M. Peiperl and H. Gunz (eds.). New York: Sage Publication.

Waldfogel, J. (1998) Understanding the "family gap" in pay for women with children. *Journal of Economics Perspectives, 12,* 137–56.

Wanous, J. P. (1992) *Organizational Entry: Recruitment, Selection, Orientation and Socialization of Newcomers.* Reading: Addison-Wesley.

Weick, K. (1996) Enactment and the boundaryless career: Organizing as we work. In M. B. Arthur & D. M. Rousseau (eds.) *The boundaryless career: A new employment principle for a new organizational era* (pp 40–57). Oxford: Oxford University Press.

White, R. P. (1992) *Career development: Theory and practice.* Springfield: Charles Erlbaum.

Winkler, A. E. (2002) Measuring time use in households with more than one person. *Monthly Labor Review, 125(2),* 45–54.

NOTES

1. These five points are adopted from Mainiero and Sullivan's (2005) *Academy of Management Executive* article, "Kaleidoscope careers: An alternative explanation for the opt-out revolution." Mainiero and Sullivan have also developed the Kaleidoscope Career Self-Assessment Inventory which organizations can use to assist in the career development of its employees. For more information go to www.theoptoutrevolt.com.

2. We wish to acknowledge that one chapter is too short to do justice to the subject of career management. Many important issues, including the impact of stress on careers, entrepreneurial careers, career differences across different industry sectors, and the influence of mentors on career outcomes could not be adequately addressed. We recommend the following sources for additional reading:

   Arnold, J. (1997) *Managing careers into the 21st century.* London: Paul Chapman.

   Baruch, Y. (2004) *Managing careers: Theory and practice.* Harlow: FT-Prentice Hall/Pearson.

   Greenhaus J. H. and Callanan G. A. (eds.) (2006) *Encyclopedia of career management,* Sage.

   Greenhaus, J. H., Callanan, G. A. and Godshalk V. M. (2000) *Career management* 3rd edn. Fort Worth, TX: The Dryden Press.

   Gutteridge, T. G., Leibowitz, Z. B. and Shore, J. E. (1993) *Organizational career development.* San Francisco: Jossey-Bass.

   Peiperl, M., A., M., Goffee, R. and Anand, N. (eds.) (2002) *Career creativity: Exploration in the remaking of work.* Oxford: Oxford University Press.

9 Fostering organizational learning

Creating and maintaining a learning culture

Silvia Salas and Mary Ann Von Glinow

> Successful companies are those that consistently create new knowledge, disseminate it widely throughout the organizations, and quickly embody it in new technologies and products.

(Nonaka, 1991:96)

Introduction

Regardless of size and industry, the majority of organizations devote considerable time and resources to developing unique, profitable competencies. Many researchers and organizations look to knowledge to provide this competitive advantage (Crossan, Lane and White, 1999; Van de Ven, 2005), with the expectation that knowledge can be made to contribute to a firm's performance (Watson and Hewitt, 2006) when it is efficiently integrated with existing intellectual capital, and converted into unique, revenue-generating products or services (Appelbaum and Gallagher, 2000; Teare and Rayner, 2002; Turner and Makhija, 2006; Van de Ven, 2005). As Nonaka emphasized (1991: 96), "one sure source of lasting competitive advantage is knowledge".

But why are some organizations better at achieving "competitive advantage" through organizational learning than others? To better understand this question, we delve back into the basics on organizational learning and outline the necessary steps an organization should take to implement organizational learning.

There is general consensus in the research literature and the popular press that several key factors are needed to implement and embed "organizational learning" into the fabric of an organization (Figure 9.1): (1) the influence of leadership on individual and organization culture; (2) creating a culture conducive to organizational learning; (3) improving the quality of knowledge the individual acquires, while facilitating the sharing of that knowledge with

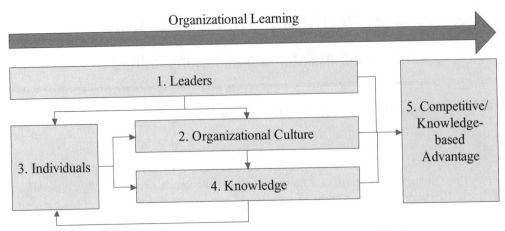

Figure 9.1   Key factors for achieving a competitive advantage through organizational learning.

others in the organization; (4) generating new, actionable knowledge as a result of the knowledge shared or transferred within the organization; and (5) developing a competitive advantage with the newly, generated knowledge (a knowledge-based advantage).

Arguably, one can add a sixth step – reintroduction of the new knowledge into the organization, and thereby, beginning the process once again, much like a feedback loop (Crossan *et al.*, 1999). If anything, this last step demonstrates that 'organizational learning' is not a single event; rather it should be an iterative process that is institutionalized, so that as new information is added to the organization, the dynamic system becomes a more robust source of knowledge and competencies.

However, even when organizations know what the right path to successful organizational learning is, it appears to us that they do not always know how to execute this process. As many organizations have demonstrated, it is not enough to have a working formula – the key to a successful implementation necessitates *organizational transformation.*

The purpose of this chapter is to provide an understanding of how organizational learning can be a strategic tool that allows organizations to develop core competencies that will result in competitive advantage. In the following sections, we will consider how organizations can take a proactive approach to organizational learning. We start with revolutionizing the organization's culture, such that it can be transformed it into a 'learning culture'. Then, we look at how leaders foster an environment that is suitable for the creation and sharing of knowledge (not just information). Following that, we consider how crucial individual learning is to the organization's interests, and we examine how the generation of new knowledge and the reframing of existing knowledge contributes to an organization's competitive advantage – one that can be considered a 'knowledge-based advantage'.

Organizational learning

Taken at face value, organizational learning or "learning by the collective organization" should potentially involve the replication and storage of individual learning, with access to the disseminated information throughout the organization. Although several organizations have tried this straightforward approach in the past, their methods did not always succeed (Crossan *et al.*, 1999; Kim, 1993; Yeo, 2002). By only looking at knowledge replication and storage, organizations overlook individual roles, existing organizational culture and the interaction between the different actors involved. As Yeung *et al.* (1999) noted, all organizations are made up of multiple actors, with diverse goals and methods of accomplishing those goals, and organizational learning plays an important role in the achievement of these goals.

What is organizational learning?

When we review the literature on organizational learning, there is a plethora of research that uses the terms "organizational learning" and "learning organization" interchangeably. However, as Easterby-Smith and Lyles argue, there are significant distinctions between the two; organizational learning "refers to the study of the learning processes of and within organizations", whereas a learning organization "is seen as an entity, an ideal type of organization, which has the capacity to learn effectively, and hence to prosper" (2003: 2).

In this chapter, we are concerned with both interpretations; how an organization can foster an "organizational learning" culture (putting structure and change in place) so that they can become a dynamic, "learning organization".

Organizational learning styles

Even without including related areas of research such as organizational knowledge and knowledge management (Easterby-Smith and Lyles, 2003), the study of organizational learning is vast and voluminous. In fact, the research can be divided into two substantive areas: organizational learning styles and organizational learning processes.

Single-loop versus double loop

In the past, organizational learning has been classified as cursory. In this context, Chris Argyris is perhaps most well known for distinguishing between single-loop learning and double-loop learning. According to Argyris, single-loop learning refers to learning by correcting errors, solving problems and decision making without changing the fundamental values of the organization. On the other hand, double-loop learning requires that the organization change its values as part of the learning process (Argyris, 2003). Similarly, Yeung *et al.* (1999) discussed learning as occurring on a continuum from superficial to substantial.

This chapter focuses on double-loop, substantial learning that changes the organization's values, and leads to the development of core competencies for a competitive advantage.

Exploration versus exploitation

Another distinction in the organizational learning research is that of exploration versus exploitation (Grant and Baden-Fuller, 2004; Yeung *et al.*, 1999). Exploration is defined as organizations seeking to acquire knowledge that does not already exist within the organization, and can be in the form of new products or services, access to new industries, etc. Exploitation refers to the process of looking at existing knowledge and resources from a different angle (reframing), with the intent of reusing that knowledge in a heretofore uncharted way.

From the organization's perspective, exploration can be seen as organizational learning through "processes by which organizations create variety in experience through *experimentation*, trialing and free association", and exploitation as "processes by which organizations create reliability in experience through *refinement*" and "focused attention" (Holmqvist, 2004: 70). Therefore, we can consider that exploration is "learning by experimenting" and exploitation is "learning from making and correcting mistakes".

In their book on organizational learning capabilities, Yeung and colleagues (1999) developed a model that defined how learning sources (i.e., *learning directly* from experience or from *experience of others*) impact the choice of *exploration* or *exploitation*, and what relative outcomes could be expected. According to the authors' learning capability profiles, organizations learn in four ways: through experimentation (exploration/direct learning), competency acquisition (exploration/learn from others), bench-marking (exploitation/learn from others) and continuous improvement (exploitation/direct learning).

Experimentation refers to organizations that have a high tendency for explo-ration and learning from direct experience. Their knowledge can come from customers, employees or through controlled experiments. *Competency acqui-sition* refers to knowledge that is brought in from the outside in the forms of recruitment, investments or alliances, and the exploration is attained by deriving new competencies. *Benchmarking* is another strategy that incorpo-rates knowledge from outside the organization, but the primary source is existing standards (i.e., industry, etc.) or expertise (exploitation). Finally, in *continuous improvement*, the organization depends on employees dynamically adding to the existing knowledge base (Yeung *et al.*, 1999).

Organizational learning processes

After decades of research and application of strategies, the majority of the approaches posit that for organizational learning to be successful, several things needs to happen (Figure 9.2): (1) knowledge needs to be generated (captured or acquired, and generally by individuals or groups) (Inkpen, 1998; Teare and Rayner, 2002; Wensley and Verwijk-O'Sullivan, 2000); (2) knowl-edge needs to be transferred to others in the organization (Szulanski, Cappetta and Jensen, 2004; Watson and Hewitt, 2006); (3) knowledge is applied and integrated into the organization's shared memory (Grant, 2000; Grant and Baden-Fuller, 2004); (4) application of knowledge creates a unique capabil-ity or core competence that results in a competitive advantage (Grant and Baden-Fuller, 2004); and (5) the newly generated organizational knowledge circulates back to the individuals and groups, and the process repeats. This dynamic approach to organizational learning has been described by many researchers (Alavi and Tiwana, 2003; Cohen and Levinthal, 1990; Crossan *et al.*, 1999; Nonaka, Toyama and Nagata, 2000; Schulz, 2001).

As Garvin characterizes, for an organization to learn, it needs to be "skilled at creating, acquiring, and transferring knowledge, and at modifying its behavior to reflect new knowledge and insights" (1993: 80).

Although we have approached organizational learning at the macro level (how organizations learn), it is important to look at the micro level com-ponents (what organizations learn) as well. In a nutshell, for organizational learning to take place, an exchange of information and/or knowledge needs to

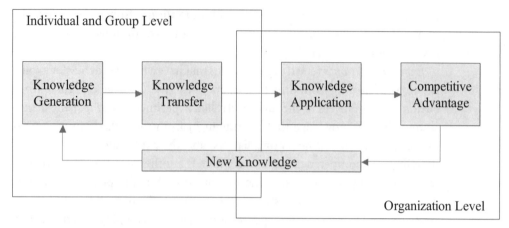

Figure 9.2   Key factors in the organizational learning process.

occur. Therefore, it is important to understand the role of knowledge in the organization and as a factor of organizational learning.

Knowledge types

Even though most researchers use the generic term 'knowledge' for specialized information that has been processed at some level, knowledge can manifest in different ways; in essence, all knowledge is not the same. The simplest distinction to be made is that of explicit versus tacit knowledge. Explicit knowledge refers to information that has been encoded and can be "shared formally and systematically" (Becerra-Fernandez, Gonzalez and Sabherwal, 2004: 19). For example, a report or drawing exists formally, and can be easily transferred to others. On the other hand, tacit knowledge refers to information that is based on experience (i.e., learning by doing) and insights, and since it is hard to encode and formalize, it can be difficult to share or transfer (Miller, Zhao and Calantone, 2006).

As Grant and Baden-Fuller explain, "different types of knowledge vary in their transferability: explicit knowledge can be articulated and easily communicated between individuals and organizations; tacit knowledge (skills, know-how, and contextual knowledge) is manifest[ed] only in its application – transferring it from one individual to another is costly and slow" (2004: 66).

Knowledge generation

According to Robert Grant (2000), knowledge generation has three distinct dimensions: knowledge creation, learning by doing (experience) and the acquisition of external knowledge. Alavi and Tiwana define knowledge creation as the "development of 'new' organizational know-how and capability" (2003: 106). Generating knowledge through observation or practice (i.e., on the job experience) is a common method for individuals to capture and create knowledge within an organization (Becerra-Fernandez *et al.*, 2004). Despres and Chauvel describe this form of learning as "addressing the problem of unknown ignorance by learning from experience and action" (2000: 65). Organizations that lack the skills or structure to create their own knowledge find it essential to acquire knowledge outside the firm. Knowledge acquisition can be accomplished through exploration, through the purchase of the knowledge or company that owns the knowledge, through licensing arrangements, and through strategic alliances (Grant, 2000).

Knowledge transfer

Knowledge transfer is vital if the organization is to benefit and develop a competency. As Ulrich *et al.* found, "learning cannot occur unless ideas are shared across any one of a number of boundaries: time, vertical, horizontal, external or geographic" (1993: 60). For example, if an individual acquires a new skill or expertise but does not share it with coworkers who can also benefit from the knowledge, the information never becomes actionable knowledge within the organization. Therefore, sharing or transferring the know-how between individuals and groups is necessary. As Schultz contends: "knowledge production by individuals or subunits is of limited value if they do not share the resulting knowledge with other parts of the organization" (2001: 661).

It is important to note that knowledge transfer is not always possible or desired. In cases where knowledge is very specific and cannot be generalized, knowledge transfer should not take place. Other factors which can affect valuable knowledge transfer include causal ambiguity (knowledge that is difficult to codify and transfer), reliability of the source providing the knowledge; and inability of the recipient understanding the knowledge even if transferred (Argote and Ingram, 2000; Szulanski, 2000).

Knowledge application

At the macro level, once the knowledge has been created and shared, the value increases through its application to problem solving, decision making or product development (Alavi and Tiwana, 2003). The application of knowledge is a complex process that requires input from various individuals or groups, and is then evolved into new knowledge or product by other individuals or groups (Grant and Baden-Fuller, 2004). Similarly, Chakravarthy *et al.* found that applying existing or newly acquired knowledge across the organization allows the business "to maximize the return on that knowledge", and "accelerate the knowledge articulation process, by providing more application opportunities" (2003: 314).

Competitive advantage

Throughout this chapter, we allude to "competitive advantage" and "knowledge-based advantage" as the desired end-goal for all organizations that want to compete in the ever-expanding global economy (Drucker, 2005; Grant, 1996; McEvily and Chakravarthy, 2002; Zollo and Winter, 2002). But what exactly is competitive advantage, and how does knowledge and organizational learning fit into the equation?

According to Hoskisson *et al.* (2004: 101), "a sustainable competitive advantage is developed when firms use the strategic management process to implement strategies that uniquely use a firm's resources, capabilities and core competencies". Core competencies are characterized as (1) valuable (value creating); (2) unique (or rare); (3) difficult to imitate; and (4) not easily substitutable.

Within the organizational learning context, King and Zeithaml (2003: 764) note that "knowledge resources have distinctive properties that help create and sustain competitive advantage", and Turner and Makhija (2006: 197) suggest that "building [a] competitive advantage involves creating and acquiring new knowledge, disseminating it to appropriate parts of the firm, interpreting and integrating it with existing knowledge, and, ultimately, using it to achieve superior performance".

Although the literature suggests that organizations should secure as many of the four characteristics (i.e., value-creating, unique, difficult to imitate and hard to substitute) as possible, some organizations have developed a competitive advantage based on one or two core competencies (i.e., branding, technology, etc.). Unfortunately, this type of advantage is rarely sustainable in the long run (Hoskisson *et al.*, 2004). Therefore, developing and maintaining a learning culture and applying organizational learning as a competitive advantage needs to be a dynamic process if it is to be sustainable and enduring.

There are several frameworks that demonstrate a similar pattern of developing an advantage by integrating multilevel processes within the organization, and they include the 4I organizational learning framework by Crossan *et al.* (1999) and the organizational learning capabilities by Yeung *et al.* (1999).

Examples of organizational learning frameworks

Crossan *et al.* (1999) developed the 4I organizational learning framework, where they observed that learning is associated with four processes (intuiting, interpreting, integrating, and institutionalizing) across three different levels (individual, groups and organization). Based on their framework, individuals capture knowledge through the processes of intuiting and interpreting, they share or transfer the knowledge to others in their sphere through integrating, and then applying that knowledge at the organizational level by institutionalizing. Likewise, Yeung *et al.* (1999) determined that for an organization to develop a "learning capability", managers needed to generate ideas (knowledge generation) with impact, and then generalize those ideas (knowledge transfer and application) across multiple boundaries including space, time, geography, etc.

Transforming the organization

Cummings and Worley define transformational change as "reshaping the organization's culture," and characterize the changes as systemic and revolutionary since the "entire nature of the organization [would be] altered fundamentally" (2005: 480).

In applying this strategy to organizational learning, one can see that it is necessary to reshape the organization's culture and transform it into an atmosphere where learning and knowledge are valued as investments in the organization's sustainability, and not seen as a liability or a drain on the organization's resources. By encouraging systemic and revolutionary change, the organization is sending a clear and consistent message to employees, associates and vendors that learning matters. As Ulrich and colleagues emphasize, learning "matters [to] managers who are charged with articulating and implementing ever-evolving strategies" and learning "matters [to] employees who are required to upgrade current skills or acquire new ones" (1993: 55). And finally, for an organization to fundamentally alter its nature, learning needs to become a core belief and strategy; the organization needs to embody a 'learning culture'.

All of this implies change. We considered the organizational change literature for suggestions on implementing transformational, organizational learning, and the recommended strategies centered on: (1) modification of an organization's culture; (2) influence of leadership; and (3) behavior modification of the individuals. We now address these three strategies.

Organizational culture

Organizational culture is described as a set of shared beliefs (Ravasi and Schultz, 2006) and tacit assumptions (Aguinis and Henle, 2003) that establish individual and group perceptions, thoughts, feelings and behavior (Schein, 1996). Similarly, Moorehead and Griffin define organizational culture as a "set of shared values, often taken for granted, that help people in an organization understand which actions are considered acceptable and which are considered unacceptable" (2004: 496).

Several studies have found that organizational culture has a significant impact on a firm's ability to learn and perform. For example, regardless of how much a leader wants to improve organizational learning or how much funding is provided, if the environment is not conducive to cooperation and collaboration, efforts will be largely ineffectual (Hopkins, Hopkins and Mallette, 2005; Popper and Lipshitz, 2000b). As part of a *learning culture*, leaders and employees should reframe their values and beliefs (Berg, 1993), overcome existing barriers to knowledge creation and knowledge transfer (Beer and Eisenstat, 2000; Seo, 2003), and create an association between their values and the organization's real objectives (Appelbaum and Goransson, 1997; Kim, 1993).

Many researchers have examined characteristics that make up "best practices in organizational learning", and they emphasize the impact organizational culture has on the organizational learning process (Denton, 1998); specifically, the necessity of having a flexible structure, and an intelligent failure/experimentation culture as part of the process.

Flexible structure

In a flexible structure, Denton advises that organizations needed to do away with "rigid job descriptions, strict hierarchy and excessive bureaucracy", and that allowing for cross-functional teamwork would improve the knowledge flow between departments (1998: 92). Whether the changes implemented were radical or incremental, the organization had to adopt flexibility to successfully compete in the marketplace (Englehardt and Simmons, 2002). As Englehardt and Simmons stated, "change is often relentless and rapid, and successful adaptation is an important part of success in today's business world" (2002: 113). In addition to a flexible organization, Bass *et al.* (2003) went so far as to say that a new type of leader was needed: an adaptive leader. They found that adaptive and flexible leaders were best suited to understanding the "rapidly changing environment" and "then appropriately responding to those challenges" (Bass *et al.*, 2003: 207).

Intelligent failure and experimentation

As part of a blame-free culture, researchers have reasoned that individuals were going to make mistakes as part of any learning process (i.e., intelligent failures) and that individuals should be encouraged to share them with others as this would provide additional learning opportunities (Denton, 1998; Yeung *et al.*, 1999). Early on, Argyris stated that organizational learning was "the process of detecting and correcting error" and that errors were "any feature of knowledge or knowing that inhibits learning" (1977: 116). His philosophy, which put the onus on leaders and managers, advocated that superficial learning (single-loop) was not enough to create sustainable, organization success. Instead, leaders needed to reconsider the organization's beliefs and values – double-loop learning (Argyris, 1977) – in order to achieve lasting 'organizational learning'.

This emphasis on changing the firm's culture has been echoed repeatedly throughout the years in the organizational learning literature and elsewhere. For example, Ulrich *et al.* make a distinction between first-order and second-order learning. The authors define first-order learning as "learning without significant change in the firm's basic assumptions", while second-order learning reevaluates the "nature of objectives and the values and beliefs underlying them", and "involves changing the organization's culture" (1993: 53). Engle-hardt and Simmons (2002) advocate the creation of an "organizational space", where a culture of sharing and experimentation could develop. Berg (1993) applies a reframing strategy, which involves looking at familiar processes and beliefs in a new way.

Similarly, Carroll *et al.* point to psychological safety as the environment that encourages "organization members to ask questions, explore, listen and learn" (2003: 581), and Ulrich *et al.*, found that "when managers build a culture focused on learning capability, they are able to encourage individuals to share ideas across boundaries" (1993: 64). In addition, Holmqvist (2004) argues that organizational learning could be derived from taking risks, learning by experimenting (exploration), and learning from mistakes (exploitation).

Obviously experimentation and innovation are not foreign concepts to organizational learning strategists; organizations and individuals have been learning through the creation of new products and services (trial and error) for centuries.

Leadership

When considering organizational change, past literature and research suggest that lasting change begins with the modification of the organization's culture (Bartlett and Ghoshal, 1998; Bennis and Nanus, 1985; Bierly, Kessler and Christensen, 2000; Martiny, 1998), an area where leaders have direct and indirect control (Mahoney, 2000; Popper and Lipshitz, 2000a; Wah, 1999). Leaders, "setting the cultural tone" in an organization, play a critical role when profound change is needed to transform an organization from mainstream into a knowledge-based organization through implementing organizational learning (Cooksey, 2003).

Within the organizational transformation literature, there are numerous approaches that leaders can take to effect enduring change. Various recommendations stand out as being particularly helpful in fostering organizational learning. For example, leaders need to motivate change in their employees, and they can do this by nurturing employee support and exercising influence over their employees. Once change has been created, leaders will need to carefully manage the transition period, and put in place strategic plans that will help to sustain the momentum started (Cummings and Worley, 2005).

Motivating change

By communicating the critical factors of organizational transformation, leaders can motivate and prepare employees for changes within the organization. Research has demonstrated that individuals, and some organizations, are happy with the status quo. If the organization has been performing well, very few people would arguably be interested in changes to the formula (i.e., processes, products, philosophy, etc.) that helped them achieve success in the first place. However, many organizations are realizing that success is more closely defined by organizational agility and continuous improvement rather than past achievements. Therefore, one of the most important roles that leaders must play is that of coach and change agent.

Communication

In this section, we emphasize that leaders need to communicate effectively while demonstrating empathy for the difficulties employees may experience during the change and transition phases. As part of their study, Beer and Eisenstat (2000) found that the quality of the information and communication flowing from the leaders to the followers could have a significant impact on whether an organization would (or could) learn. Employees need to have current and up-to-date information on why the company is changing, the goals and objectives leaders want to accomplish, and the plan to get them there. If the communication is poor or the message is unclear and conflicting, employees would have a difficult time perceiving how to best align their activities to the organization's goals. Finally, in addition to encouragement and communication, leaders should make an effort to get employee buy-in or participation. When employees are involved in the problem-solving and solution-generating stages, the likelihood that they will resist change diminishes (Cummings and Worley, 2005). Therefore, establishing good communication and effectively outlining how the organization's values and beliefs tie into the company's performance is fundamental (Wilhelm, 2006).

Creating a vision

Although leaders have many roles in which they must excel, creating a vision and transforming that vision into strategy is central to their position (Bass *et al.*, 2003; Vera and Crossan, 2004). Vision is important because it is necessary to have a clearly defined road map (core values and purpose) for a company to achieve competitive advantage. As Jack Welch asserts, "good business leaders create a vision, articulate the vision, passionately own the vision, and relentlessly drive it to completion" (Seijts, 2006: 64).

However, vision by itself is not enough; the leader will have the added task of selling the long-term objectives and strategy to the employees that can directly affect a change (Denton, 1998). This is where enthusiasm and confidence in the vision is imperative. Whether the plan is presented as a large package ("we are going to transform the organization") or as feasible objectives ("we need to share knowledge across departments"), the message should be positioned in a positive light, and the employees need to know where the organization is headed (desired end state). As Bass and associates contend, transformational "leaders are expected to enhance the performance capacity of their followers by setting higher expectations and generating a greater willingness to address more difficult challenges" (2003: 209).

Developing support

Once a leader has a vision and strategy in mind, they can use influence and power to ensure that followers adhere (Drucker, 2005). It has become essential for leaders to understand how they can proactively use their power to institutionalize organizational learning and create knowledge-based value for the firm in today's global, dynamic business environment (Grojean *et al.*, 2004; Hult *et al.*, 2000; Ingelgard *et al.*, 2002; Teare, 1997; Vera and Crossan, 2004).

Through virtue of their executive position, access to resources and the ability to influence the direction in which an organization heads, leaders can draw on several power sources (i.e., legitimate, reward, and expert) to carry out learning strategies and decisions (Hughes, Ginnett and Curphy, 2002).

However, even though leaders and managers are credited with influencing the behaviors and outcomes of individual employees, research into leadership influence on organizational learning continues to lag (Vera and Crossan, 2004). Much of the research on organizational learning focuses on program development and the mechanics of implementing a "learning system"; few studies address how leaders, at every level of the organization, have the power and opportunity to create, support and influence organizational learning (Vera and Crossan, 2004). Yet, as O'Keefe argues, "the leader who effectively harnesses the collective ingenuity of his employees will simply blow the competition away" (2005: 776).

Managing the transition

Drucker contends that an effective leader sets the goals, priorities, and maintains the standards; the transition phase is precisely about setting goals, priorities and standards. Managing the transition from a previous state to the desired end-state requires that the leader and his/her supporters function on multiple levels, affecting change from the organizational level through to the group and individual levels. Having a vision and abstract goals served the purpose of motivating individuals and developing buy-in; the transition phase requires planning, actionable goals, and subtle shifts in the processes that had been in place to the new course of action that will move the organization to its desired end-state (i.e., learning organization).

In addition to setting the plan in motion, leaders must establish monitoring (i.e., scorecard) and controlling (i.e., making adjustments as needed) measures, such as an iterative feedback process that indicates whether the changes are helping the organization achieve its goals or hindering progress, and alert the individuals that can correct the direction.

From a learning perspective, this new strategy can be a radical departure from the traditional way of doing business. If the company has not previously experienced the "desired" end-state, it may be hard to tell that the transition is affecting beneficial outcomes, particularly since everything in the middle of any process change seems messy. Since the desire to institutionalize organizational learning aims for positive transference (when the right kinds of knowledge are being shared), not negative transference (when bad knowledge or processes are being perpetuated), monitoring and controlling are crucial (Turner and Makhija, 2006).

Sustaining momentum

The most difficult phase of successful organizational transformation is making the desired changes continue and endure – until they are firmly embedded into the fabric of the organization. However, organizations, like people, forget to reinforce the new skills and competencies promoted during the implementation. This negligence makes it possible for the individuals and the organization to revert back to prior, comfortable habits.

Sustaining the momentum created by the organizational transformation requires that new factors be considered, such as providing resources to maintain the change, altering systems and structures to accomplish changes, facilitating the development of new competencies and skills, and reinforcing new behaviors. Changes in the organization can require new or different resources than those utilized in the past. For example, if an organizational learning system did not exist in the past, additional resources will be needed to maintain the new system once it is implemented. New systems and/or structures may be requisite in order to make the transition to a learning organization. This may also require the services or skills of learning facilitators to help make changes last. Cutting off funding and support once an implementation is finished, can ultimately lead to the undoing of all the changes and transformation if those changes have not been firmly embedded in the organization's systems, structures, processes and people. So many organizations fail to make changes last simply because they throw too little support into the process, quit before they're finished and don't reinforce the new transformation.

Another key factor produced with new systems or processes is the development of new competencies and skills at all levels. Management research has demonstrated that the resources (human, technical and financial) needed during an implementation are different than those considered necessary during the day-to-day maintenance.

Along with the organization, leaders, individuals and change agents will need to make their own personal transitions in order to flourish under the new structure (Earl and Scott, 2000). This new structure will most likely require that everyone develop new competencies and skills (Cummings and Worley, 2005), and organizations need to be sensitive to these new requirements. For example, to encourage a learning culture, individuals, teams that are colocated, and even virtual teams (Grant, 2000) can meet for brainstorm sessions or knowledge transfer/problem-solving sessions. The organization needs to take these requirements into consideration, and ensure that those involved have the venues necessary to meet, access to the information needed for the session, and even a facilitator to maximize the utility of the process. In some cases, individuals may require additional training to gain skills (i.e., training on coaching, leadership, facilitation, brainstorm, etc.).

Individual learning

Many researchers argue that organizational learning begins with the individuals acquiring new information or skills. As DeTienne *et al.* note, individuals "are the creators, transferors, and users of knowledge" (2004: 27). In this context, we refer to individual learning as the solitary acquisition of skills, data or information.

As part of the larger organizational learning strategies, employees play a key role (Elkjaer, 2001; Fiol, 1994; Kim, 1993; Teare and Rayner, 2002): they acquire knowledge by learning and enhancing their own individual skills and knowledge, they share their knowledge (know-how) with others in the organization, and they absorb the new, resulting knowledge that is generated as a consequence of the collective knowledge processing that takes place at the organizational level.

However, organizational learning based on individual learning alone presents a problem if the knowledge is not disseminated to the rest of the organization (Elkjaer, 2003). If an individual hoards knowledge or learning (until the employee can use it to his or her advantage) or they take that knowledge with them when they leave (i.e., deep smarts), the organization does not benefit from the individual learning. For example, organizations often lose insights from expatriate managers who exit upon repatriation.

One way that individual learning can be elevated to organizational learning is through the application of social learning theory (Elkjaer, 2003). "Learning is that which enables actors to modify their relations to others while contributing to the shared activity" (Elkjaer, 2003: 44). In this new context, we incorporate additional methods of learning such as through interaction with others in the organization as well as participation.

Therefore, the transfer of knowledge from the individual to the organization, as a whole, has to be firmly established if the organization is to augment its collective learning. As Yeung *et al.* (1999) point out, when new knowledge or ideas are created but not generalized (shared across boundaries), organizational learning does not occur.

Although an emphasis is placed on "knowledge", as a tangible commodity, the primary contributor to "knowledge" is the human factor. In the past, importance was placed on the use of technology as a way to enhance the circulation of actionable information throughout the organization (Chen, Lee, Zhang and Zhang, 2003). But most organizations quickly discovered that it is the *individual* that transforms information into knowledge (DeTienne *et al.*, 2004; Ruiz-Mercader, Merono-Cerdan and Sabater-Sanchez, 2006).

In effect, organizational learning is not just about learning and knowledge; it is also about the actors being receptive to the acquisition and integration of knowledge, with the goal and purpose of improving an organization's performance (i.e., competitive advantage). Consequently, it behooves us to better understand what knowledge really is, and how it moves around the organization via individual and organizational learning.

Summary

Denton maintained that "in an organization with a learning strategy, learning is no longer a discrete activity, but a part of each individual's and each team's full-time job" (1998: 92).

Many studies in the last twenty years indicate that when organizations effectively transfer knowledge between individual, group and the organization levels, they gain a competitive advantage over their rivals and competitors (Argote, McEvily and Reagans, 2003; Szulanski *et al.*, 2004). For organizations actively pursuing the creation, retention and dissemination of knowledge as a value proposition, leaders need to pursue a deliberate plan that will effect a positive change in this direction (Zollo and Winter, 2002). However, in addition to capturing and disseminating knowledge efficiently, leaders need to understand that effective organizational learning is not a one-time endeavor. For organizational learning and knowledge to become a competitive advantage, it must be pervasive, continuous, and institutionalized (Popper and Lipshitz, 2000a; Yeo, 2005), and this is where leadership and organizational culture can enhance and facilitate the processes (Yeo, 2005). As Wilhelm states, "to create a true learning organization," the organization "must believe in the value of continuous learning" (2006: 17). Thus to return to our original question as to why some organizations are better at achieving "competitive advantage" through organizational learning than others, we emphasize the important link between *continuous* organizational learning and knowledge. Absent the *continuous* aspect of learning, organizations will likely fail in degree if not entirety.

REFERENCES

Aguinis, H. and Henle, C. A. (2003) The search of universals in cross-cultural organizational behavior. In J. Greenberg (ed.), *Organizational behavior: The state of the science* (2nd edn). Mahwah: Erlbaum Associates.

Alavi, M. and Tiwana, A. (2003) Knowledge management: The information technology dimension. In M. Easterby-Smith and M. A. Lyles (eds.), *The Blackwell handbook of organizational learning and knowledge management*. Oxford: Blackwell Publishing.

Appelbaum, S. H. and Gallagher, J. (2000) The competitive advantage of organizational learning. *Journal of Workplace Learning*, *12(2)*, 40.

Argote, L. and Ingram, P. (2000) Knowledge transfer: A basis for competitive advantage in firms. *Organizational Behavior and Human Decision Processes*, *82(1)*, 150–69.

Argote, L., McEvily, B. and Reagans, R. (2003) Managing knowledge in organizations: An integrative framework and review of emerging themes. *Management Science*, *49(4)*, 571.

Argyris, C. (1977) Double loop learning in organizations. *Harvard Business Review*, *55(5)*, 115.

Argyris, C. (2003) A life full of learning. *Organization Studies*, *24(7)*, 1178.

Bartlett, C. A. and Ghoshal, S. (1998) Beyond strategic planning to organization learning: Lifeblood of the individualized corporation. *Strategy & Leadership*, *26(1)*, 34.

Bass, B. M., Avolio, B. J., Jung, D. I. and Benson, Y. (2003) Predicting unit performance by assessing transformational and transactional leadership. *Journal of Applied Psychology*, *88(2)*, 207–18.

Becerra-Fernandez, I., Gonzalez, A. and Sabherwal, R. (2004) *Knowledge management: Challenges, solutions and technologies*. Upper Saddle River: Prentice Hall.

Beer, M. and Eisenstat, R. A. (2000) The silent killers of strategy implementation and learning. *Sloan Management Review*, *41(4)*, 29.

Bennis, W. and Nanus, B. (1985) Organizational learning: The management of the collective self. *New Management*, *3(1)*, 6.

Bierly, P. E., III, Kessler, E. H. and Christensen, E. W. (2000) Organizational learning, knowledge and wisdom. *Journal of Organizational Change Management*, *13(6)*, 595.

Carroll, J. S., Rudolph, J. W. and Hatakenaka, S. (2003) Learning from organizational experience. In M. Easterby-Smith and M. A. Lyles (eds.), *The Blackwell handbook of organizational learning and knowledge management*. Oxford: Blackwell Publishing.

Chakravarthy, B., McEvily, S., Doz, Y. and Rau, D. (2003) Knowledge management and competitive advantage. In M. Easterby-Smith and M. A. Lyles (eds.), *The Blackwell handbook of organizational learning and knowledge management*. Oxford: Blackwell Publishing.

Chen, J. Q., Lee, T. E., Zhang, R. and Zhang, Y. J. (2003) Systems requirements for organizational learning. *Association for Computing Machinery. Communications of the ACM*, *46(12)*, 73.

Cohen, W. M. and Levinthal, D. A. (1990) Absorptive capacity: A new perspective on learning and innovation. *Administrative Science Quarterly*, *35(1)*, 128.

Cooksey, R. W. (2003) "Learnership" in complex organisational textures. *Leadership & Organization Development Journal*, *24(4)*, 204.

Crossan, M. M., Lane, H. W. and White, R. E. (1999) An organizational learning framework: From intuition to institution. *Academy of Management. The Academy of Management Review*, 24(3), 522.

Cummings, T. G. and Worley, C. G. (2005) *Organization development and change* (8th edn). Mason: South-Western.

Denton, J. (1998) *Organisational learning and effectiveness.* London: Routledge.

Despres, C. and Chauvel, D. (2000) A thematic analysis of the thinking in knowledge management. In C. Despres & D. Chauvel (eds.), *Knowledge Horizons: The present and the promise of knowledge management.* Woburn: Butterworth-Heinemann.

DeTienne, K. B., Dyer, G., Hoopes, C. and Harris, S. (2004) Toward a model of effective knowledge management and directions for future research: Culture, leadership, and CKOs. *Journal of Leadership & Organizational Studies*, 10(4), 26.

Drucker, P. F. (2005) *The essential Drucker.* New York: Collins Business.

Earl, M. J. and Scott, I. A. (2000) What do we know about CKOs? In C. Despres and D. Chauvel (eds.), *Knowledge horizons: The present and the promise of knowledge management.* Woburn: Butterworth-Heinemann.

Easterby-Smith, M. and Lyles, M. A. (2003) Watersheds of organizational learning and knowledge mangement. In M. Easterby-Smith and M. A. Lyles (eds.), *The Blackwell handbook of organizational learning and knowledge management.* Oxford: Blackwell Publishing.

Elkjaer, B. (2001) The learning organization: An undelivered promise. *Management Learning*, 32(4), 437.

Elkjaer, B. (2003) Social learning theory: Learning as participation in social process. In M. Easterby-Smith and M. A. Lyles (eds.), *The Blackwell handbook of organizational learning and knowledge management.* Oxford: Blackwell Publishing.

Englehardt, C. S. and Simmons, P. R. (2002) Organizational flexibility for a changing world. *Leadership & Organization Development Journal*, 23(3), 113–21.

Fiol, C. M. (1994) Consensus, diversity, and learning in organizations. *Organization Science*, 5(3), 403.

Garvin, D. A. (1993) Building a learning organization. *Harvard Business Review*, 71/(4), 78–91.

Grant, R. M. (1996) Prospering in dynamically-competitive environments: Organizational capability as knowledge integration. *Organization Science*, 7(4), 375.

Grant, R. M. (2000) Shifts in the world economy: The drivers of knowledge management. In C. Despres and D. Chauvel (eds.), *Knowledge horizons: The present and the promise of knowledge management.* Woburn: Butterworth-Heinemann.

Grant, R. M. and Baden-Fuller, C. (2004) A knowledge assessing theory of strategic alliances. *The Journal of Management Studies*, 41(1), 61.

Grojean, M. W., Resick, C. J., Dickson, M. W. and Smith, D. B. (2004) Leaders, values, and organizational climate: Examining leadership strategies for establishing an organizational climate regarding ethics. *Journal of Business Ethics*, 55(3), 223.

Holmqvist, M. (2004) Experiential learning processes of exploitation and exploration within and between organizations: An empirical study of product development. *Organization Science*, 15(1), 70.

Hopkins, W. E., Hopkins, S. A. and Mallette, P. (2005) *Aligning organizational subcultures for competitive advantage.* New York: Basic Books.

Hoskisson, R. E., Hitt, M. A. and Ireland, R. D. (2004) *Competing for advantage*. Mason: South-Western.

Hughes, R. L., Ginnett, R. C. and Curphy, G. J. (2002) *Leadership: enhancing the lessons of experience*. Boston: McGraw-Hill/Irwin.

Hult, G. T. M., Hurley, R. F., Giunipero, L. C. and Nichols, E. L., Jr. (2000) Organizational learning in global purchasing: A model and test of internal users and corporate buyers. *Decision Sciences*, 31(2), 293.

Ingelgard, A., Roth, J., Shani, A. B. and Styhre, A. (2002) Dynamic learning capability and actionable knowledge creation: Clinical R&D in a pharmaceutical company. *The Learning Organization*, 9(2), 65.

Inkpen, A. (1998) Learning, knowledge acquisition, and strategic alliances. *European Management Journal*, 16(2), 223.

Kim, D. H. (1993) The link between individual and organizational learning. *Sloan Management Review*, 35(1), 37.

King, A. W. and Zeithaml, C. P. (2003) Measuring organizational knowledge: a conceptual and methodological framework. *Strategic Management Journal*, 24(8), 763–72.

Mahoney, R. (2000) Leadership and learning organisations. *The Learning Organization*, 7(5), 241.

Martiny, M. (1998) Knowledge management at HP consulting. *Organizational Dynamics*, 27(2), 71.

McEvily, S. K. and Chakravarthy, B. (2002) The persistence of knowledge-based advantage: An empirical test for product performance and technological knowledge. *Strategic Management Journal*, 23, 285–305.

Miller, K. D., Zhao, M. and Calantone, R. J. (2006) Adding interpersonal learning and tacit knowledge to March's exploration-exploitation model. *Academy of Management Journal*, 49(4), 709.

Moorhead, G. and Griffin, R. W. (2004) *Organizational behavior: Managing people and organizations*. Boston: Houghton Mifflin Company.

Nonaka, I. (1991) The Knowledge-Creating Company. *Harvard Business Review*, 69(6), 96–104.

Nonaka, I., Toyama, R. and Nagata, A. (2000) A firm as a knowledge-creating entity: A new perspective on the theory of the firm. *Industrial and Corporate Change*, 9(1), 1.

O'Keeffe, T. (2005) Towards zero management learning organisations: A honey-bee perspective. *Journal of European Industrial Training*, 29(8/9), 764.

Popper, M. and Lipshitz, R. (2000a) Installing mechanisms and instilling values: the role of leaders in organizational learning. *The Learning Organization*, 7(3), 135.

(2000b). Organizational learning: Mechanisms, culture, and feasibility. *Management Learning*, 31(2), 181.

Ravasi, D. and Schultz, M. (2006) Responding to organizational identity threats: Exploring the role of organizational culture. *Academy of Management Journal*, 49(3).

Ruiz-Mercader, J., Merono-Cerdan, A. L. and Sabater-Sanchez, R. (2006) Information technology and learning: Their relationship and impact on organisational performance in small businesses. *International Journal of Information Management*, 26(1), 16.

Schein, E. H. (1996) Three cultures of management: The key to organizational learning. *Sloan Management Review*, 38(1).

Schulz, M. (2001) The uncertain relevance of newness: Organizational learning and knowledge flows. *Academy of Management Journal*, 44(4), 661.

Seijts, G. H. (2006) *Cases in organizational behavior.* Thousand Oaks: Sage Publications.

Szulanski, G. (2000) The process of knowledge transfer: A diachronic analysis of stickiness. *Organizational Behavior and Human Decision Processes*, 82(1), 9–27.

Szulanski, G., Cappetta, R. and Jensen, R. J. (2004) When and how trustworthiness matters: Knowledge transfer and the moderating effect of causal ambiguity. *Organization Science*, 15(5), 600.

Teare, R. (1997) Enabling organizational learning. *International Journal of Contemporary Hospitality Management*, 9(7), 315.

Teare, R. and Rayner, C. (2002) Capturing organizational learning. *International Journal of Contemporary Hospitality Management*, 14(7), 354.

Turner, K. L. and Makhija, M. V. (2006) The role of organizational controls in managing knowledge. *Academy of Management Review*, 31(1), 197–217.

Ulrich, D., Von Glinow, M. A. and Jick, T. (1993) High-impact learning: Building and diffusing learning capability. *Organizational Dynamics*, 22(2), 52.

Van de Ven, A. H. (2005) Running in packs to develop knowledge-intensive technologies 1. *MIS Quarterly*, 29(2), 365.

Vera, D. and Crossan, M. (2004) Strategic leadership and organizational learning. *The Academy of Management Review*, 29(2), 222.

Wah, L. (1999) Making knowledge stick. *Management Review*, 88(5), 24.

Watson, S. and Hewitt, K. (2006) A multi-theoretical model of knowledge transfer in organizations: Determinants of knowledge contribution and knowledge reuse. *The Journal of Management Studies*, 43(2), 141.

Wensley, A. K. P. and Verwijk-O'Sullivan, A. (2000) Tools for knowledge management. In C. Despres and D. Chauvel (eds.), *Knowledge horizons: The present and the promise of knowledge management.* Woburn: Butterworth-Heinemann.

Wilhelm, W. (2006) Learning organizations. *Leadership Excellence*, 23(3), 17.

Yeo, R. K. (2002) From individual to team learning: Practical perspectives on the learning organisation. *Team Performance Management*, 8(7/8), 157.

Yeo, R. K. (2005) Learning: The secret to the art of war. *Management Research News*, 28(8), 27.

Yeung, A. K., Ulrich, D. O., Nason, S. W. and Glinow, M. A. V. (1999) *Organizational learning capability.* New York: Oxford University Press.

Zollo, M. and Winter, S. G. (2002) Deliberate learning and the evolution of dynamic capabilities. *Organization Science*, 13(3), 339.

10 Work–life balance, best practices and healthy organisations

A European perspective

Christina Purcell, Suzan Lewis, Janet Smithson and Sue Caton

Introduction

Managing paid work and family life is a major challenge for many European workers. Growing numbers of women with children are remaining in paid employment albeit with a diverse range of working time regimes and different levels of state support across Europe for reconciling work and family (Fagnani, Houriet-Ségard and Bédouin, 2004). In addition, with changing family structures more men want to or need to be involved in family care. The European Commission, driven by the twin concerns of gender equality and the demographic challenges of the twenty-first century, has encouraged the participation of both women in the workforce and men in family life. Gender equality has historically been constructed by the EC in relation to the position of women in the labour market, leading first to an emphasis on equal pay and, more recently, to a commitment to combat the structural barriers to equality in the workplace through the promotion of a "level playing field" in which women can compete fairly alongside their male counterparts (Lewis, 2001). This has involved promoting policies which take account of the position of women as primary childcarers in the family and of the impact this has on the career progression and wages of women. This coincides with the recent preoccupation in Western Europe with "ageing societies" (OECD, 2006) and the need to encourage the labour market activity of sections of the working age population that are traditionally less active, such as women with children. Consequently, "work–life reconciliation" is increasingly becoming an issue in Europe.[1]

This development in European social policy has important implications for employing organisations. Organisations operate within a changing regulative environment as European countries adopt policies that are consciously more favourable to the employment conditions of parents (Fagnani *et al.*, 2004). At the same time, employing organisations themselves have an interest in attracting and retaining a skilled workforce in a context of increased global competition. This includes skilled women, many of whom will at some point make the transition to parenthood. Meanwhile, in Northern European countries, small but increasing numbers of fathers are taking time off paid work or working flexibly for childcare reasons, and workplaces and policymakers are increasingly reconsidering the role of fathers in the family (Smithson *et al.*, 2004).

This chapter draws on a cross-national European study[2] – TRANSITIONS: Gender, Parenthood and the Changing European Workplace – which examined perceptions of organisational best practices for supporting work–life balance, from the perspectives of employed parents and their managers, working in private and public sector organisations in seven European countries. The study involved eleven case studies carried out in: one public sector (social services) and one private sector (primarily finance) organisation in Bulgaria, Norway, Portugal, and the UK; a private sector (finance) organisation in the Netherlands and Slovenia and a public sector (social services) organisation in Sweden. Methods of data collection used in the case studies included document analysis, well-being questionnaires, interviews with managers, focus groups with parents of young children and follow-up biographical interviews with some of the employed parents and their partners.[3]

In this chapter we first critically examine the notion of "best" practice and emphasise the context-specific nature of perceived best practice that emerged from our study. We then propose an alternative framework for establishing core principles which can facilitate work–life reconciliation for employed parents – that of healthy organisations. We draw upon focus group and interview data collected in our study to identify some of these core principles. Finally we examine the specific practices that parents in the TRANSITIONS study identified as facilitating the negotiation of work–family boundaries within specific national, workplace and family contexts.

Issues in defining best practice

Context matters

Best practice in the workplace is generally understood as a set of practices or actions which results in optimum outcomes, ideally benefiting both employees and the employing organisation. The aim of identifying best practice is to set a standard to which organisations can aspire. However, the TRANSITIONS cross-national and cross-sector investigation into paid work and family reconciliation shows that this can be problematic for a number of reasons. In particular, context needs to be taken into account. What works in one setting is not necessarily applicable in others. What constitutes best practice in one country, or for one organisation, may even be perceived as bad practice in another.

At a national level, not only is workplace best practice interpreted differently from country to country, but it is also perceived as largely irrelevant in some countries. In some cases this is due to a long tradition of mainstreaming gender equity in both policy and society which has given rise to a workplace context regarded as relatively supportive for parents. In such a context workplace best practice may not be regarded as an issue. This is the prevailing view in the Swedish public sector organisation in the TRANSITIONS study, although in practice there is often an implementation gap between espoused organisational and societal values on the one hand and workplace practice on the other. In other cases, best practices are considered irrelevant because certain issues are more pressing for employees. Parents in Bulgaria, for example, were too concerned about job insecurity and low wages to consider specific workplace practices which would facilitate their negotiation of work–family boundaries. In addition, Bulgarian parents in the private sector considered the concept of best practice unhelpful and unrealistic since they could not imagine a private company – based on market logic – improving workplace practice unless obliged to do so by regulation at the state level:

According to me, the employer should be obliged [to provide family support], otherwise no employer would show sympathy. Without an obligation, there is no sympathy. I just can't imagine it, it is absurd. (Bulgarian mother, private sector)

Private employers will never take your responsibilities as a mother seriously. There is work to be done. If you are not fit, then go away. There are people waiting to take your job. (Bulgarian mother, private sector)

This view was also found amongst managers:

There is no private employer caring for his employees. The state is one thing, the employer is another. (Bulgarian manager, private sector)

There appears to be no conception amongst these interviewees that practices supporting employees' work and personal life have the potential to have a positive impact on organisational performance.

Perceptions of best practices are highly subjective and influenced by the support parents feel entitled to expect. National and cultural contexts shape employees' sense of entitlement to workplace support for the reconciliation of paid work and family life (Lewis and Smithson, 2001). This works in a variety of ways. For example, cultural attitudes to the needs of young children shape perceptions of best practice. Portuguese interviewees in our study stressed the importance of the role of the mother in childcare in the early years, whilst Norwegian interviewees stressed the role of parents – both mothers and fathers – in the early years of childhood. Best practice in these countries tends to focus more on either long maternity leave or parental leave respectively. Attitudes to gender equality and related social policies also influence perceived best practice. In countries with a strong tradition of promoting gender equality, best practices identified by both parents and managers tended to be those that encourage a more-equal participation of women in the labour market and fathers in the family. Whilst egalitarian gender ideology and policy at the state or workplace level are not necessarily experienced by parents as sufficiently influencing practice, they do appear to have raised expectations of support for employed mothers and fathers. This Norwegian mother sums up her frustration with what she sees as a gap between discourse and practice, which contrasts with the much-lower expectations of support for gender equality in some of the other countries:

[the organisation] has many fine words on paper on many things, among others, gender equality and consideration for the life situation of employees. Maybe they could get even better at following up what they have on paper? That would make this company even better for everybody. (Norwegian mother, private sector)

Sense of entitlement to support also varies across sectors. In all the countries, public sector workers tended to have higher expectations of best practices than those working in the private sector.

The effect of social comparison on perceptions of best practice

Employees in the TRANSITIONS study often compared their conditions with others in similar situations and this influenced the way they evaluated their own employer's practices. Social comparison operates on different levels, both within and between sectors and countries. In some cases, social comparison contributed to parents' acceptance of bad practices in the belief that conditions would be worse elsewhere. The parents quoted below are grateful to be working in the public sector due to their bad experiences, or the experiences of parents they know, in the private sector. Thus their aspirations for best practices are relatively limited:

I think that working in Social Care is better than working in another sphere. A private employer might exploit me and demand that I work more than 8 hours a day. (i. Bulgarian mother, public sector)

Here, they try to follow legislation. I remember . . . I can give you a comparison: when I had my first child, the first year of his life, I was working in a private company and he was 11 or 12 hours in the crèche. This is too much for a baby in his first year! And I see, since the moment I came here, I can balance things in another way . . . and with my second child, I will have some facilities which in a private company would be impossible! However, it is the same law! But we know the way we are seen and treated is completely different." (Portuguese parent, public sector)

On the other hand, social comparisons made with practices in countries thought of as having more gender equitable solutions to work–family challenges played a role in raising expectations of what could be achieved by establishing better working practices (and legislation). For example, while some British participants were pleased with new regulations on parental leave, others realised that these still compared unfavourably with policies in other countries.

. . . you get better maternity rights and flexible hours for parents . . . overseas – Scandinavia. Things could be better. (UK father, private sector)

Different perspectives on best practices

Individual factors such as status in the organisation, gender and family structure and responsibilities also contribute to different perspectives on what might constitute best practices. Managers in our case studies tended to report more best practices than non-managerial employees. In many cases, managers perceived their organisation as "family-friendly" in terms of both formal organisational policy and equitable implementation of that policy. However, the day-to-day experience of some of the new parents conflicted with management accounts. This discrepancy was greatest where managers perceived employee and employer needs as more mutually exclusive than mutually advantageous. In the Dutch private sector, organisation managers tended to perceive the organisation as a caring and "social" employer, however the following quotes illustrate the contested nature of this claim:

The managers in the management team understand there must be time for the family. But not at any price, that's what we agreed on. You're here with a business interest; we have a contract that concerns duties and privileges for all parties. If you want to stay a healthy and professional organisation, it's necessary to watch that carefully. Especially when it concerns a multi national. (Dutch manager, private sector)

4x9, [working four nine hour days] some people have that because of the free day, but as a manager I am not very happy with it. Nothing really is done in the ninth hour, it's not a productive hour, it just costs money. I discourage that. It's also quite a burden for people. All these work patterns make it harder to make arrangements for the management. (Dutch manager, private sector)

Both managers here frame family-friendly policies in terms of their negative effects on the organisation, although the first does acknowledge the need for some level of organisational practice sensitive to parental responsibility. This contrasts with the views of some of the employees in the same company, focusing as they do on the mutual gains of work–life balance:

My commitment increases when I have more freedom at my work and my willingness to do things on my day off also increases. So in a sense it becomes an interaction. Only the times shift, get more interchangeable: work and private life. (Dutch mother, private sector)

What is good for your private life is also good for your work. In that sense is it beneficial for the employer when it is taken good care of. (Dutch father, private sector)

Perceptions of best practice were also highly gendered in our study, with women being more conscious than men of the need for supportive practices. Mothers and fathers also often articulated different needs. For example, in the UK private sector and in the Netherlands, mothers were more likely to want to reduce their overall working hours with fathers preferring flexible full-time hours, whilst fathers whose partners had left the labour market to be full-time carers of their young children were less concerned with best practice. Perceptions of best practices also tend to be different in single and two-parent families because of their different support needs. The variety of preferences demonstrate the difficulty in establishing a definite set of best practices.

The double-edged nature of "best" practice

An additional complication in identifying best practice arises from the double-edged nature of many of the contemporary practices that are generally considered to be helpful to parents in the workplace. This has become particularly apparent in the context of intensification of work (Burchell *et al.*, 1999; Burchell, Lapido and Wilkinson, 2002; Brannen and Moss, 1998; Green and McIntosh, 2001; Green, 2001; Green, 2002). Flexible working, for example, is frequently presented as a positive practice for employees with multiple roles. However, it can also have negative consequences, such as "allowing" employees to work longer hours to manage intense workloads, in return for more flexibility. The TRANSITIONS study showed that many parents seemed to accept these negative aspects of flexibility in return for having some freedom in organising their working hours (Nilsen and Brannen, 2005), so whilst this may be mutually advantageous in the short term, its impact on long-term sustainability is questionable.

These examples of the way in which best practice can be experienced negatively in certain contexts undermine the very premise on which best practice is based: identifying optimum practices or a set of practices that can be applied across a variety of contexts.

Healthy organisations and work–life balance

Given the complexity of the notion of best practices we suggest an alternative concept – that of the healthy organisation – as a more useful way of examining the effect of organisational practices on work–life balance. The notion of the "healthy organisation" is a relatively recent development in academic literature and is based on the enticing idea that organisational effectiveness is enhanced by fair, ethical and effective management (Newell, 2002). We propose two dimensions to healthy organisations in relation to "work–life balance": mutual advantage and social sustainability. A "healthy organisation" is one that values the role of its employees in sustaining and increasing its economic health. It therefore recognises the interdependence of individual and organisational health (McHugh and Brotherton, 2000; Černigoj-Sadar, 2005) and the mutual advantage of workplace practices that pursue a "dual agenda" (Rapoport *et al.*, 2002) of workplace effectiveness and employee well-being, including work–life balance.

A Norwegian mother working in a private sector organisation articulates this view in the following extract from the interview study:

*If you take the employer's point of view, if you only hire people without children . . . you'll miss a lot of the workforce. So the employers should give flexible arrangements. Because it has a lot to do with well-being, **if you like being at work you'll do a better job**. (Norwegian mother, private sector)*

Indeed, the findings of the organisational case studies carried out in the TRANSITIONS project show that for many parents – and managers – best practices are regarded as those based on mutual advantage. Nevertheless this remains counterintuitive in some organisations or specific departments where organisational and employee needs are perceived as conflicting (das Dores Guerreiro, Abrantes and Pereira, 2004).

Again, the intensification of work reported in all the case studies poses a potential conflict of interest. While some employees thrive on the challenge of intense workloads, particularly if combined with autonomy and interesting work, this can present particular difficulties at certain life course phases, especially during early parenthood.

Sometimes I'm so tired that I don't have much patience for my children. In the tough periods we work long hours and we even work Saturdays. It is so absorbent that we sometimes can't think about anything else except work matters. (Portuguese father, private sector)

How sustainable is this for employees, their families, and employing organisations? Taking a longer-term perspective, the second dimension of healthy organisations relates to the emerging concept of socially sustainable working practices (Webster, 2004; Brewster, 2004). As Juliet Webster argues, "we now have to broaden our concerns to consider the impact of the organisation of work on the wider sphere of life beyond paid employment – for the individual, for communities, for society at large. In other words, our concern must now be with enhancing the broader social sustainability of working life" (2004: 62–3).

The sustainability of current forms of paid work is in question for a number of reasons. Firstly, rising levels of stress and sickness absence (Bäck-Wiklund and Plantin, (in press); Geurts, Kompier and Gründemann, 2000) threatens the sustainability of people and organisations (Lewis and Cooper, 1999). Secondly, birth rates are declining in Europe and throughout much of the industrialised world. This raises issues of population sustainability and related concerns about a crisis of caring as populations age, as well as the sustainability of workforces and future consumers. Fertility changes in Europe have been linked with persistent gendered employment experiences, exacerbated by current forms of work (Fagnani, forthcoming; Hašková, forthcoming) which underestimate the importance of social reproduction for national economies as well as quality of life. Considering work–life issues within a social sustainability framework highlights the need to consider both business and social imperatives.

While there is empirical evidence that work practices meeting the dual agenda of employee well-being and workplace effectiveness can have very positive outcomes, research indicates that maximum benefits accrue, in the long term, if both agendas are given equal consideration to maximise (Rapoport *et al.*, 2002; Lewis and Cooper, 2005). Very often the business perspective is privileged. Our study, by focusing on the experiences of parents in organisations, privileges the voice of the employee within this dual agenda.

Principles underpinning "good" or "best" workplace practices

Despite the caveats surrounding the concept of best practice, the organisational case studies highlighted some basic principles that underpin parents' perspectives on best practices for sustainable and effective work–life balance.

Implementing statutory entitlements – with attention to culture and practice change

Best practice at its most basic level is regarded as simply implementing statutory policy. Some employees in Portugal emphasised how important it was to be able to use the full range of statutory rights available to them, which suggests that these rights, though universal in theory, are not universal in practice. In fact, implementation of statutory policy often varied according to organisational context and sector.

In Bulgaria, whilst both public and private sector managers and employees stressed the role of the state in regulating organisational practice, significant differences were reported between the private and the public sector, with the Labour Code being adhered to more strictly in the public sector.

Indeed, our study revealed that organisational culture is an important factor in whether parents are able to make use of the full range of statutory rights that are available to them, regardless of the national welfare regime. Many employees in all the countries felt that state policies needed to be complemented by positive workplace culture and practice:

Interviewer: "What do you think an employer could contribute in a context like Norway? A: "The culture and the attitudes, in addition to the rights." L: "Yes, that you don't get ostracised if you make use of your rights" (Norwegian mothers, private sector)

This view was reinforced by the experience of a Norwegian father who, being one of the few fathers in Norway taking full advantage of the leave policies aimed at men, felt that he was perceived as lacking commitment to his work. If in a country such as Norway, with a high commitment to gender equality and supporting work–life balance, organisational culture can make it difficult for fathers to take up all their entitlements, the barriers fathers face in other countries are likely to be extensive.

Implementation of statutory rights also depends on the communication of those rights within the organisational context. Some parents in our study were not aware of their entitlements to leave or to be able to request flexible working following the transition to parenthood, which hampered their efforts to reconcile work and family. In a fast-changing legislative context relating to a very specific phase in the life course, it may not always be easy for employees and managers to be fully aware of national statutory policy when negotiating working conditions. In some cases, however, employees felt that organisations were less than forthcoming about communicating information concerning parental rights in the workplace:

My sister-in-law works for [name of organisation]. When they learnt about these changes in legislation, they were very open with all their employees and told everyone and thought, well, we'll just have to see what happens. Whereas our company has kept it all quiet. (UK mother, private sector)

Statutory rights such as maternity/paternity/parental leave and leave to care for sick children are essential to sustainable family practices in a context of an increasing incidence of modified breadwinner models and even dual bread-winner models (Fagnani *et al.*, 2004). Whilst employers and managers may perceive generous state entitlements as a source of logistical problems for organisations in the short term, our study showed that organisations can benefit from increased commitment and performance in the long term:

"We're a so called 'inclusive workplace'. We have a very conscious policy towards sick leave. We care for our employees. If they have a good personal life they're likely to function well at work too." (Norwegian manager, private sector)

Management support

Line managers emerged as crucial in shaping the experience of parents in the organisations. Management attitudes to the specific needs of parents were found to impact considerably on workplace practices.

"It depends on what kind of person your superior is. You may apply for sick leave because you have a sick child at home and you won't hear a word of criticism from him and all your work will be done. My experience is positive." (Slovenian mother, private sector)

"I think it's very important to have a supportive manager. I mean . . . a manager's decision, which directly affects the workplace practice . . . policies are only ambitions." (Swedish manager, public sector)

The emphasis that the parents in our study placed on the role of management illustrates the way in which national and workplace policies are mediated through day-to-day negotiations at a local level. Management was identified as one of the main loci of power in determining and carrying out workplace policies and practices (das Dores Guerreiro *et al.*, 2004)), although the impact of management discretion on the experience of parents depended on the specific national and local context in which labour conditions are defined. The degree of tightness or vagueness of the state regulatory framework had, respectively, a moderating or aggravating effect on the influence of line managers. Despite this, parents in all countries underline the importance of supportive management.

Management consistency

One of the consequences of the pre-eminence of management discretion (Dick and Hyde, 2006) was management inconsistency, which was experienced particularly negatively and often led to demoralisation. Lack of equitable treatment seemed to be particularly prevalent in the UK public and private sector organisations.

"I think they mean well, but they need to sort out the management and they need to get some consistency, because there are some really good, fair managers there, but there's some really bad ones as well." (*UK mother, private sector*)

"My manager was very unsupportive and made it very clear that she didn't agree with four days a week, although there were other people in the same position as me, working four days a week. Somebody else asked to go four days a week, to the same manager, and she got it and I got turned down." (*UK mother, private sector*)

The effect of inconsistency on employee morale and commitment can be considerable. In the UK finance sector organistaion, it was one of a number of negative experiences which led to employees looking for work elsewhere. These negative consequences are compounded if organisations have a stated commitment to work–life balance which is unevenly implemented throughout the organisation.

Trust and mutual understanding

Management discretion worked best in a context of trust and mutual understanding. This was crucial where work–life reconciliation depended largely on informal practices, for example in the UK private sector case, where there was a shift from formal (recorded) methods of flexitime to a more informal trust-based system of flexibility.

Trust and mutual understanding was also considered essential by Bulgarian interviewees in the public sector who stressed that without it *"things just won't work"*. Parents in other countries also refer to the importance of empathy.

"My supervisor has children of her own. So when you knock at her door and you tell her 'my child is sick', she knows what you are talking about." (Dutch mother, private sector)

"I know the manager and I know the supervisor I'm more than likely going to be working for, so I know they'll be flexible if I need it. And the same with me as well, if they need me to be flexible I will be as much as I can obviously." (UK mother, private sector)

"Because my manager certainly here gives me a lot of flexibility . . . if I come in a little later there's never been any major issues around that . . . if there's been a problem then it just means that I work, you know for, for an extra half hour . . . ." (UK mother, public sector)

These examples highlight the importance of manager support, and also illustrate the two-way process of mutual understanding in the workplace which can contribute to the achievement of organisational objectives whilst taking account of the family responsibilities of employees with young children.

The role of colleagues

Whilst management attitudes dominate most workplace environments, the role of colleagues in determining whether parents feel confident in asserting their rights was frequently referred to in the in-depth interviews. Many parents referred to colleague solidarity and reciprocal arrangements which were vital to the day-to-day planning of the work–family interface. In some instances colleague solidarity was linked to a workplace environment that encouraged a climate of supportive team spirit. As with management support, trust was a key factor in facilitating the negotiation of informal reciprocal arrangements.

Reciprocal arrangements were in some cases resolved amongst members of work teams without recourse to managers. This was particularly true for the Swedish public sector organisation, where colleague solidarity and reciprocal relations played an important role in dealing with absences due to family responsibilities. Some of the interviewees even argued that the role of colleagues in relation to work–life balance was greater than that of managers:

"Yes, it is important to deal with your colleagues because when you are away, they are the ones that have to do your job. It's not the manager. The manager doesn't do anything in this respect." (Porter, Swedish public organisation)

"I used to plan my visits to the doctor at times of the day when I know we have less to do in the kitchen. I negotiate and plan it with my colleagues. And then I stand by my colleagues another time." (*Cook, Swedish public organisation*)

There is a danger however that positive team dynamics and equity can be undermined when there is a combination of intense workloads alongside work–life policies that do not take the whole team into consideration. Intense workloads can result in parents being unwilling to make use of flexible policies or practices, for example, to take time off if a child is ill, because they know that if they do so their colleagues will be even more overloaded.

Employees in the Slovenian public sector, reported that although they can generally take sick leave for childcare when necessary, in contrast with employees in the Slovenian private sector, they felt uneasy about doing so, due to co-workers having to work more. They dealt with this by taking annual leave instead, thereby voluntarily limiting their entitlements.

Colleague solidarity can also be undermined if parents in the workplace are perceived to be receiving too many entitlements or special treatment, which can lead to resentment from other colleagues.

"They're scared of the people without children feeling discriminated against. So unless they can offer all these facilities to everyone, all this new legislation is not really having that much effect in our company." (*UK mother, private sector*)

One Dutch team dealt with this danger of a "backlash" by restricting colleague mutual flexibility to the parents in the team. While this way of resolving problems associated with unexpected family emergencies may make parents feel less anxious about family problems encroaching on work, there is a risk that parents will become overburdened.

Negative perceptions of preferential treatment are not necessarily confined to the parent/non-parent divide. In the UK public sector, one of the fathers felt that it was fathers in particular that got a raw deal in contrast to mothers, whilst some employers and supervisors felt that senior managers who are mothers are given preferential treatment. This points to a need to mainstream policies and practices such as flexible working arrangements which may be currently limited to parents. Indeed work–life balance discourse, whilst primarily a discourse aimed at reconciling work with family life has increasingly evolved into a more inclusive discourse (Wise and Bond, 2003). Mainstreaming work–life balance policies arguably has the potential to be mutually advantageous and socially sustainable: allowing all employees to move closer to their preferred working time arrangements creates equity in the workplace which has the potential to enhance employee/management and employee/employee relations.

Realistic workloads

As discussed above, the negative impact of heavy workloads on best practices should not be underestimated. The growing intensification of work that was experienced by parents in our study is an issue for all employees, but is particularly problematic for new parents. Many of the organisations had experienced downsizing, leading to increased workloads. One of the consequences of this has been a tendency to work long hours to meet organisational objectives, leading to stress amongst many of the parents (das Dores Guerreiro *et al.*, 2004).

Flexibility to manage unrealistic workloads, such as working from home after work, whilst it was appreciated by parents in the study, is not a sustainable solution, as it will not reduce workplace-related stress (and may even increase it), and therefore can have negative consequences for both workplace effectiveness and family life. This leads to a mutually disadvantageous situation.

Collaborative agreements

The sometimes arbitrary and inconsistent support employees receive in the workplace highlights the importance of collaborative agreements or similar processes that involve employees in decisions regarding best practice in the workplace (Rapoport *et al.*, 2002; Lewis and Cooper, 2005). Involving employees in decision making could also be positive in the sense that it would open up debates in organisations on issues such as work–family reconciliation, creating the possibility for exploration of the concept and its practical application within the organisational context. Our study also suggests that employees are well placed to understand the logistical problems associated with their family-based needs, hence the willingness of some parents to voluntarily limit their entitlements. Group problem-solving, involving the insight of employees working on the ground could have potential to find innovative solutions within a framework of mutual advantage.

Gender equity

It was overwhelmingly women in our study who made use of practices aimed at reconciling paid work and family life, from flexible working to leave for family illnesses. The assumption that work–family policies are an issue mainly for mothers of young children was rarely contested by the parents or managers.

Consequently, despite the increased role that women play in the labour market and the increasing numbers of fathers demonstrating some willingness to take on more of a caring role (Rostgaard, 2002; Hobson, 2002), the role of women as the primary child-carer appears to be perpetuated, reinforced either by leave policies based on this gendered assumption or by the gendered application of policies, or both.

If women reduce their working hours they are often held back in their careers following the transition to parenthood. We found that there was a common pattern of women being demoted when they moved to part-time working, particularly in the UK. Additionally, a recurrent theme identified in our study was the perceived incompatibility between the tasks of management and parenthood, or more specifically, involved motherhood. Rather than seeking innovative ways to redefine professional job characteristics, it appeared that a number of the organisations in the study were adopting short-term solutions by regrading high status women who chose to work less on their return from maternity leave. This inevitably underutilises skills acquired over many years in the labour market and can create resentment and frustration. As one Bulgarian mother in the private sector stated, daring to "be absent for two years"[4] signalled the end of a woman's career.

Gendered assumptions regarding parenting roles also affected fathers, who were less likely than women to make use of policies and practices aimed at work–family reconciliation, even when they expressed a desire to do so. By hindering more involved fatherhood, organisations are also losing the chance to gain from the relational skills learnt through more hands-on parenting, skills that could be transferable to the workplace. At the same time, fathers, children and society as whole, are unable to benefit from the positive personal and social impacts of the increased presence and involvement of fathers in the family unit (Gregg and Washbrook, 2003; Lamb, 2004; Lamb and Lewis, 2004).

Positive workplace practices in different contexts

The principles outlined above touch on issues of organisational culture and how this can facilitate, hinder or support work–family reconciliation. We now turn to the specific practices that parents in the TRANSITIONS study identified as most useful, bearing in mind the context-specificity of the way employees perceive best practice.

Overwhelmingly, flexible working practices were identified as a major resource enabling parents to organise their work more effectively around child-care responsibilities. Flexibility operated in a wide variety of ways, depending on the different national, organisational and individual contexts. The different examples given below illustrate the various contexts in which various types of flexible working practices can successfully lead to mutually advantageous and socially sustainable solutions.

What types of helpful flexible working practices do parents identify?

Reducing contracted hours

Having the option to work less than the standard working week on returning to work after maternity leave was popular among a significant proportion of the women interviewed in our study. However, these women tended to be concentrated amongst high household income, two-parent families in the wealthier countries in the study (UK, Netherlands, Norway and Sweden). In low-wage economies this was unlikely to be a viable option. In Bulgaria, for example, none of the interviewees had taken up the part-time possibilities allowed for in the labour code. Similarly, single mothers in low-wage jobs in the various national contexts rarely found part-time working financially sustainable, despite being the parents most in need of reducing their hours. A number of the fathers talked about wanting to work less, but most did not feel comfortable asking for this.

In Portugal where part-time work is rare, the issue of reducing working hours takes on a different form due to the prevalence of split shifts – a working practice that prolongs the working day. Portuguese mothers expressed a desire to reduce the length of their working day by taking shorter lunch breaks.

For mothers who were able to take advantage of opportunities to reduce their working hours, this was a key factor influencing attitudes to returning to work and contributing to increased job commitment. However, negative aspects of part-time working were also identified: being moved to less demanding positions, or workloads not being proportionately reduced.

"It can be quite negative when you've promised x, y, z to somebody ... people forget that you only work three days." (*UK mother, private sector*)

"I'm here every day but stop work at 14:30 and now, suddenly, people expect me to work 100% or to do as much as all the others do. So it's not only the manager but also my colleagues – they ... expect me to do as much as they do." (*Swedish manager, recently moved from 50% to 75% working time, public sector*)

Compressed hours

Where part-time working was impractical for parents, compressed hours were sometimes used as a way of organising the working week more effectively. This was particularly prevalent in the Netherlands, where in some cases employees are working longer daily hours over four days rather than five. This has been facilitated by a reduction in the working week in the banking sector, from forty hours to thirty-six hours, which came into force in the 1980s as part of a collective agreement for the sector. Taking one day off per week, without loss of salary or job status, was seen by some to be a viable strategy, enabling them to spend more time with their family and cutting down on commuting time. The downside for parents was that the working days are very long, leaving little time in the evening for the family on working days. It worked best where two parents could find a way of organising drop-offs and pick-ups at crèches around crèche opening times. There is also a danger for the organisation, articulated by one Dutch manager, that productivity may be negatively affected if the working day is extended. Hence the mutually advantageous nature of compressed hours is questionable. It may be that it works in only very specific cases.

Flexible working hours – with autonomy

Flexible working hours clearly help parents to organise work and childcare arrangements. Whilst the degree of flexibility desired or possible can vary in different contexts, most parents in our study regarded some flexibility in working hours as essential. A shift to a focus on outputs rather than the number of hours spent at work was one of the ways in which mutual flexibility was conceived by parents:

"It is all very flexible, and my team is output oriented." (*Dutch manager, private sector*)

". . . I can work more one day and less the next, depending on the situation. But I'm flexible too so if I have a day off and there's an important meeting, I will make time for going into work anyway." (*Norwegian mother, private sector*)

Some managers believe that flexibility is more difficult to arrange in certain jobs, for example in front-line public services or more client-based positions. In some situations, this would evidently present operational problems for organisations. However, perceived restrictions on flexible working can be overcome by creative and innovative problem-solving, or by self-managed teams, which worked well in some of the organisations. In Sweden, social services managers described how they endeavoured to organise the work in such a way "that allows people to suddenly leave for different missions". Unit managers also described how they tried to meet individual needs, negotiating agreements such as excluding some employees from evening work, or from working schedules which demanded staffing until 4:30 in the afternoon. Other projects have also demonstrated how a radical rethinking of the human resource allocation has successfully met the challenge of providing both sufficient cover for front-line services and flexibility for employees.[5]

All parents considered that some autonomy and control over work is important, and that this could have positive effects on attitudes to, and quality of, work.[6] In a Slovenian private sector organisation a flexitime system in one department allowed employees to organise their work in a relatively autonomous way. This was experienced as an example of best practice in contrast to the rest of the organisation's more rigid practices. The positive impact of control over working practices is expressed by this Portuguese parent:

I have technical autonomy in here. I have a certain freedom of expression. No one tells me that I have to be twenty minutes with this client and five minutes with that one. I have to manage my time and provide a quality service. (Portuguese mother, public sector)

These examples show that organisational objectives and parents' needs are not inevitably contradictory. Mutual flexibility means that organisational practices which permit a less-stressful organisation of working life, can engender a workplace environment in which parents are willing to be flexible in return.

Working from home

Enabling employees to deal with some tasks at home by using email and providing access to employers' servers can open up a variety of ways in which time can be used more efficiently: avoiding the rush hour, working from home on certain days of the week, cutting down on weekly commuting time or working from home during family emergencies.

As with other forms of flexibility, home-working is not a viable solution for all types of work. It is not just service and front-line staff that are unable to make use of home-working, other considerations can also render home-working inoperable. In less affluent countries or in areas where housing is very expensive, parents may be living with their own parents and/or there is often not enough space to work from home. This was the case for some of our parents in Bulgaria and Slovenia. For the Norwegian social workers in the study, home-working was not considered an option due to confidentiality issues.

In the Norwegian private sector, parents welcomed any commitment to enable more staff to work from home. However, where home-working is a viable option it is not a panacea for work–life balance. There is a danger that boundaries between paid work and family life will be blurred when home doubles up as the workplace (Sullivan and Lewis, 2001). Unless such hurdles are overcome (by adopting strategies such as establishing times when home-based employees are off-line and unavailable), work-family interface stress can be increased with palpable negative effects for both areas of life.

Arrangements for dealing with family emergencies

New parents inevitably experience periods of childhood illness. Statutory rights to take leave – paid or unpaid – to care for a sick child exist in all the countries in the TRANSITIONS study (Fagnani *et al.*, 2004). The most generous entitlements are to be found in Bulgaria with paid sick leave for up to sixty days per year. Workplace practices that enable parents to deal with such emergencies without reproach or feelings of guilt are considered by the parents in the study to be a basic requirement of best practice. However, catching up on workloads on return to work following absence due to family illnesses or other crises can put stress on parents and limit their effectiveness in the workplace, due to intense workloads and lack of cover during their absences.

Conclusion

We have argued that there is no one best practice or set of best practices applicable in all contexts for overcoming the complex problems facing employed parents as they try to negotiate paid work and family in contemporary society. Rather there are principles which employers, managers and employees can refer to in order to seek innovative solutions for specific contexts. There are two fundamental problems with the concept of best practice: the context-specificity of what constitutes best practice and the lack of enforceability of those practices that are found to work in specific contexts, often leading to an implementation gap between policy and practice.

Whether best practices will be well-implemented in organisations will largely depend on workplace culture. Although government policy has a major role to play in facilitating the work-family interface in the European context (Lewis and Smithson, 2006), statutory policies designed to reconcile paid work and family life also need to be accompanied by cultural shifts at the organisation level. In particular it is important to question the assumption that ideal workers do not have family demands (Gambles, Lewis and Rapoport, 2006).

In many instances employees in our study had difficulty in merely accessing the statutory rights to which they were entitled. This suggests that there is a perceived conflict of interest between the needs of employees and the needs of the organisation, rather than a focus on mutual flexibility. Instead of finding ways to implement a dual agenda of enhanced effectiveness, organisations are frequently driven by imperatives that engender socially unsustainable working practices, focusing as they do on productivity and profitability, considered crucial in a period of intense international competition, rather than *in addition* to employee needs. Such a focus tends to be narrow and short term in the context of rapidly changing market conditions; employee well-being can be threatened in the process (das Dores Guerreiro *et al.*, 2004; Nilsen and Brannen, 2005). Longer-term considerations which take into account wider, societal issues that go beyond the logic of organisational imperatives can be overlooked. The ability of parents engaged in paid work to ensure a healthy family environment – desirable on a variety of levels: individual, family, organisational and societal – is one such issue which is frequently excluded from organisational agendas.[7]

Appeals to "mutual advantage" which emphasise positive outcomes for both business and employees can, to some extent, play a role in encouraging businesses to be more "socially responsible" and to adopt workplace practices which engender "healthy organisations", since workplace practices to reconcile parenthood and paid work can also benefit organisations in terms of retention, productivity and commitment. The difficulty lies in businesses being able to go beyond the immediate rationales which determine their business practices (Dickens, 1999).

It is also important to recognise that the preferences that parents expressed in this study are shaped by a complex interaction of multiple factors (Hantrais and Ackers, 2005; Tomlinson, 2006). Parents make choices within the constraints of their socio-economic status within different national welfare state frameworks. Moreover, a discourse of choice can also often be used as a rhetorical device to encourage the acceptance of procedures that are, in practice, double-edged. This was evident in the UK public sector organisation, where the discourse of "choice" to work more flexibly was an important factor used by management in gaining employee acceptance of the outsourcing of work in an elderly persons' home. The notion of flexibility seemed attractive at the time, particularly for those with young children; however, employees lost out in the long run due to a re-negotiated and less favourable pension scheme that was the result of outsourcing.

Finally, the significance of context should not be overlooked. The context within which parents negotiate the reconciliation of paid work and family is multivarious: national context, socio-economic status, access to various resources and support networks, position within the organisation. All these factors contribute to the ways in which workplace practices are experienced and how relevant and effective "family-friendly" practices are. Gender – and cultural attitudes to gendered parenting roles – greatly influence perceptions of best practice and the sense of entitlement to different types of practices related to paid work and family (Lewis and Smithson, 2001). From this flows the emphasis on principles of best practice presented here, rather than best practice *per se*. The European study on which this chapter is based suggests that these principles, based on a need to establish workplace practices which meet the dual agenda and are socially sustainable, may provide a framework within which employees and their representatives can negotiate work and family solutions in their workplace organisations. The positive workplace practices identified in this chapter offer some possible solutions to organisations and the employees that work in them; however, they are not a blueprint for facilitating paid work and family reconciliation, and there is much scope for innovation in the future.

REFERENCES

Bäck-Wiklund, M. and Plantin, M. (in press) The workplace as an area for negotiating the work-family boundary. A case study of two Swedish social services agencies. In R. Crompton, S. Lewis and C. Lyonette (eds.), *Women, men, work and family in Europe*. London: Palgrave.

Brannen, J. and Moss, P. (1998) The polarisation and intensification of parental employment in Britain: consequences for children, families and the community. *Community, Work and Family*, 1(3), 229–48.

Brewster, J. (2004) Working and living in the European knowledge society: The policy implications of developments in working life and their effects on social relations. Report for the project 'Infowork'. Department of Sociology, Trinity College, Dublin.

Burchell, B. J., Day, D., Hudson, M., Lapido, D., Mankelow, J. P., Nolan, H. R., Wichert, I. and Wilkinson, F. (1999) *Job insecurity and work intensification: flexibility and the changing boundaries of work*. York: Joseph Rowntree Foundation.

Burchell, B. J., Lapido, D. and Wilkinson, F. (eds.) (2002) *Job insecurity and work intensification*. London: Routledge.

Černigoj-Sadar, N. (2005) *Transitions Research Report No. 10: Report on well-being*. Report for the EU Framework 5 funded study 'Gender, parenthood and the changing European workplace'. Manchester: Manchester Metropolitan University: Research Institute for Health and Social Change.

das Dores Guerreiro, M., Abrantes, P. and Pereira, I. (2004) *Transitions Research Report No. 3: Case studies*. Report for the EU Framework 5 funded study 'Gender, parenthood and the changing European workplace'. Manchester: Manchester Metropolitan University: Research Institute for Health and Social Change.

den Dulk, L., Peper, B. and van Doorne-Huiskes, A. (2004) *Transitions Research Report No. 2: Literature Review.* Report for the EU Framework 5 funded study 'Gender, parenthood and the changing European workplace'. Manchester: Manchester Metropolitan University: Research Institute for Health and Social Change.

Dick, P. and Hyde, R. (2006) Line manager involvement in work–life balance and career development: Can't manage, won't manage? *British Journal of Guidance and Counselling,* *34(3),* 345–64.

Dickens, L. (1999) Beyond the business case: A three-pronged approach to equality action, *Human Resources Journal, 9(1),* 9–19.

Fagnani, J., Houriet-Ségard G. and Bédouin, S. (2004) *Transitions Research Report No. 1: Context Mapping.* Report for the EU Framework 5 funded study 'Gender, parenthood and the changing European workplace'. Manchester: Manchester Metropolitan University: Research Institute for Health and Social Change.

Fagnani, J. (forthcoming). Fertility rates and mothers' employment behaviour in comparative perspective: similarities and differences in six European countries. In R. Crompton, S. Lewis and C. Lyonette (eds.) *Women, men, work and family in Europe.* London: Palgrave.

Gambles, R., Lewis, S. and Rapoport, R. (2006) *The myth of work–life balance; The challenge of our time for men, women and societies.* Chichester: John Wiley.

Geurts, S., Kompier, M. and Gründemann, R. (2000) Curing the Dutch disease? Sickness absence and work disability in the Netherlands. *International Social Security Review, 53(4),* 79–103.

Green, F. (2001) It's been a hard day's night: the concentration and intensification of work in late 20th century Britain. *British Journal of Industrial Relations, 39(1),* 53–80.

(2002) *Why has work effort become more intense?* University of Kent, Department of Economics, Discussion Paper 0207.

Green, F and Tsitsianis, N. (2004) *Can the changing nature of jobs account for national trends in job satisfaction?* UKC Discussion Papers in Economics, 2004, 04/06.

Green, F. and S. Mcintosh (2001) The intensification of work in Europe. *Labour Economics,* *8(2),* 291–308.

Gregg, P. and Washbrook, E. (2003) *The effects of early maternal employment on child development in the UK.* University of Bristol: CMPO Working Paper Series.

Guest, D. and Peccei, R (2001) Partnership at work: Mutuality and the balance of advantage. *British Journal of Industrial Relations, 39(2),* 207–36.

Hantrais, L. and Ackers, P. (2005) Women's choice in Europe: Striking the work–life balance. *European Journal of Industrial Relations, 11(2),*197–212.

Hardy, S. and Adnett, N. (2002) The parental leave directive: Towards a "family-friendly" social Europe? *European Journal of Industrial Relations, 8(2),* 157–72.

Hašková, H. (forthcoming) Fertility decline, the postponement of childbearing and the increase in childlessness in Central and Eastern Europe: a gender equity approach. In R. Crompton, S. Lewis and C. Lyonette (eds.) *Women, men, work and family in Europe.* London: Palgrave.

Hobson, B. (2002) *Making Men into fathers: Men, masculinities, and the social politics of fatherhood.* Cambridge: Cambridge University Press.

Lamb, M. E. and Lewis, C. (2004) The development and significance of father-child relationships in two parent families. In R. D. Day and M. E. Lamb (eds.), *Conceptualising and measuring father involvement*. Mahwah: Erlbaum Associates.

Lamb M. E. (ed.) (2004) *The role of the father in child development*, 4th edn. New York: John Wiley and Sons.

Lewis, J. (2001) *Reconciling adaptability and equal opportunities in European workplaces*. Report for the DG-Employment of the European Commission.

Lewis, S. and Cooper, C. (1999) The work–family research agenda in changing contexts. *Journal of Occupational Health Psychology*, *4*(4), 382–93.

   (2005) *Work–Life Integration: Case studies of organizational change*. Chichester: John Wiley and Sons Ltd.

Lewis, S. and Smithson, J. (2001) Sense of entitlement to support for the reconciliation of employment and family life. *Human Relations*, *55*, 1455–81.

Lewis, S. and Smithson, J. (2006) *Transitions Research Report No. 11: Final report on the transitions project*. Report for the EU Framework 5 funded study 'Gender, parenthood and the changing European workplace'. Manchester: Manchester Metropolitan University: Research Institute for Health and Social Change.

McHugh, M. and Brotherton, C. (2000) Health is wealth: Organisational utopia or myopia? *Journal of Managerial Psychology*, *15*(8), 744–70.

Newell, S. (2002) *Creating the healthy organisation*. London: Thomson Learning.

Nilsen, A. and Brannen, J. (2005) *Transitions Research Report No. 8: Negotiating parenthood: consolidated interview study report*. Report for the EU Framework 5 funded study 'Gender, parenthood and the changing European workplace'. Manchester: Manchester Metropolitan University: Research Institute for Health and Social Change.

Rapoport, R., Bailyn, L., Fletcher, J. K., and Pruitt, B. H. (2002) *Beyond work–family balance: advancing gender equity and workplace performance*. San Francisco: Jossey Bass.

Rostgaard, T. (2002), Setting time aside for the father: father's leave in Scandanavia, *Community Work and Family 5(3)* 344–64.

Smithson, J., Lewis, S., Haworth, J and Brannen, J. (2004) UK literature review. In *Transitions Research Report No. 2: Literature Review*. Report for the EU Framework 5 funded study 'Gender, parenthood and the changing European workplace'. Manchester: Manchester Metropolitan University: Research Institute for Health and Social Change.

Sullivan, C. and Lewis, S. (2001) Home-based telework, gender, and the synchronization of work and family: Perspectives of teleworkers and their co-residents. *Gender, Work and Organizations*, *8*(2), 123–45.

Tomlinson, J. (2006) Women's work–life balance trajectories in the UK: Reformulating choice and constraint in transitions through part-time work across the life-course, *British Journal of Guidance and Counselling*, *34*(3), 365–82.

Webster, J. (2004) *Working and living in the European knowledge society: the policy implications of developments in working life and their effects on social relations*. Report for the 'Infowork: Social Cohesion, the organisation of work and information and communication technologies: drawing out the lessons of the TSER research programme and the Key Action on Socio-economic Research. Brussels.

Wise, S. and Bond, S. (2003) Work–life policy: Does it do exactly what it says on the tin? *Women in Management Review*, *18*(1/2), 20–31.

NOTES

1. This is illustrated by both the 2000 Lisbon Agenda of the European Council, which stressed the need to facilitate the reconciliation of working life and family life in order to improve equality between women and men and to increase the employment rate of women and the 2002 EU Employment Guidelines which called on "Member states and social partners to design, promote and implement a wide-range of family-friendly working arrangements" (Hardy and Adnett, 2002).

2. The authors would like to acknowledge the contribution of the other members of the TRAN-SITIONS team: Julia Brannen and Michaela Brockmann, Thomas Coram Research Unit, Institute of Education, University of London; Ann Nilsen, Sevil Sumer and Lise Granlund, University of Bergen; Margareta Bäck-Wiklund and Lars Plantin, University of Goteborg; Nevenka Cernigoj-Sadar, Jana Nadoh and Polona Kersnik, University of Ljubljana; Anneke van Doorne-Huiskes, Laura den Dulk, Bram Peper and Marijke Veldhoen-van Blitterswijk, Utrecht University; Siyka Kovacheva and Atanas Matev, Paissii Hilendarski State University; Jeanne Fagnani, MATISSE, University of Paris 1-CNRS; Maria das Dores Guerreiro, Pedro Abrantes and Inês Pereira, CIES/ISCTE. See the TRANSITIONS website for more details of the study and its findings www.workliferesearch.org/transitions.

3. See Nilsen and Brannen (2005) and Lewis and Smithson (2006) for more details of the methods used.

4. In Bulgaria, it is possible to take statutory parental leave until the second birthday of the child (Fagnani *et al.*, 2004).

5. For an exemplary model of human resource allocation based on flexible working arrangements for all the workforce, refer to the Bristol City Council *Time of Our Lives* project. www.tuc.org.uk/changingtimes/casestudies_bristol.htm

6. See Green (2004), Can the changing nature of jobs account for trends in job satisfaction? UKC Discussion Paper in Economics, for a recent discussion of factors relating to job satisfaction.

7. Employers' organisations are often resistant to increased rights to "family-friendly" or employee-led flexibility. However, research in the UK has pointed to the positive effects of such policies in terms of staff retention and motivation: www.cipd.co.uk/pressoffice/_articles12092005151417.htm?IsSrchRes=1.

11 Diversity management practices in leading edge firms

Val Singh

Introduction

Diversity management is an important and popular tool to manage the various individual differences (such as sex, race, ethnicity, religion, disability, age, parental status and so on) that people bring into the workforce, so that the employer can draw on their diversity as an organisational resource, to access new markets, to enhance creativity and improve decision making and to recruit from a wider talent pool (Cox and Blake, 1991). In some contexts, such as the USA, this new diversity discourse which is focused on individual differences appears to be replacing the affirmative action discourse about the need for special treatment for disadvantaged groups such as women and racial minorities (Kirby and Harter, 2003). In the UK, the business case for diversity tends to sit alongside the fairness case of equal opportunities (Liff, 1999), as employers want to be seen as good places for women and other minority groups to work, as well as endorsing the business case for diversity. To address this challenge of competing discourses with their focus on individual and/or group level differences, diversity is increasingly being associated with policies concerned with inclusion. There are a number of excellent practitioner texts on how to implement diversity management, particularly the book by Kandola and Fullerton (1998) drawing on the 'diversity as mosaic' metaphor. However, there is no golden rule for guaranteed success, nor is there a single initiative that can deliver sustainable results. But diversity experts and new diversity managers can learn through the experience and creativity of other organisations about what is likely to work best in their own contexts.

The purpose of this chapter is to highlight some of the latest diversity and inclusion management initiatives from leading edge firms. After a brief look at some relevant research literature, it will show how leading companies set their agenda for strategic change and how they engage managers in the process.

A number of directors and diversity managers of global firms were interviewed for this chapter in mid-2006, contributing their experiences of new diversity management programmes. Other examples have been drawn from recent award-winning diversity initiatives. The chapter highlights a number of initiatives dealing with diversity and careers, including recruitment, development and role modelling within global companies. It then considers diversity and inclusion programmes. An innovative reverse mentoring scheme is presented that shows how the leaders of a global firm are engaging with younger diverse talented individuals who lead the mentoring relationship, providing unique insight for the chief executive and top team into how things really are lower down the firm. Next we see how some firms have gone about setting up structures and processes such as corporate diversity networks, initiatives for respecting religious diversity needs, and some creative diversity events. The chapter then moves on to examine some innovative flexible working initiatives and how these feed back into better inclusion, retention and wellness of the workforce. Moving on to an outwards-facing aspect of diversity management, the chapter explores some diversity partnering initiatives that help build inclusion internally but also build corporate reputation. It is really important to know whether progress is happening, and so some examples of diversity performance measurement are included. Drawing together the experiences of these leading firms, the chapter concludes with an inspiring comment on inclusion by Mother Teresa.

Diversity management research

So what does diversity management mean? First, the construct of diversity itself is 'slippery', with multiple meanings (Ragins and Gonzalez, 2003). It can be defined at an individual level as all the ways people are or can be perceived as similar and different from one another, based on visible or less visible differences, which in turn may be primary and fixed (such as sex) or secondary and more fluid (e.g., political persuasion or parental status). However, diversity can also be seen as a group level construct, relating to groups of people with those particular characteristics. At a macro level, diversity can be seen as a cultural issue within a social system, and as a phenomenon associated with the power, status and resources of some groups to decide who belongs and who does not – who is defined as 'other'. Ragins and Gonzalez consider a number of theories that give insight into the construct of diversity, with social identity theory being particularly relevant for understanding the organisational dynamics in dealing with difference and inclusion. Further investigation into the construct of diversity can be found in *The Handbook of Workplace Diversity* (Konrad, Prasad and Pringle, 2006), which provides an excellent overview of the research on workplace diversity, including critical and postcolonial perspectives which are seldom reported in the practitioner press. A number of measures for research into diversity, inclusion and climate are included in the book. The chapter by Kossek, Lobel and Brown (2006) on human resource strategies to manage workforce diversity is particularly relevant to this current paper. Kossek *et al.* draw attention to a number of studies that show a positive impact of formalised HRM strategies on workforce diversity, but comment that retaining diverse talent is still a challenge. Several studies indicate that the greater the demographic diversity in teams, the lower the social cohesion, although diverse groups could outperform homogenous groups in brainstorming. Elvira and Cohen (2001) reported that the fewer women employed at a particular job level, the more likely the women were to leave, indicating the importance of organisational demography for women's careers. For a multinational enterprise perspective on managing diversity, see Florkowski (1998).

Diversity management is said to bring business benefits to the organisation, by increasing the numerical representation of minority groups to reflect the composition of the marketplace, so that sales and services can be improved; by introducing diverse perspectives into the decision-making process, so that team performance is enhanced and by accessing new talent (Cox and Blake, 1991; Richard, 2000). But diversity is a complex issue, and whilst the discourse of diversity management is presented as a business imperative that is likely to be more acceptable than equal opportunities or affirmative action to those in power, its critics are concerned that it takes away the focus on the need to deal with the inequalities based on group attributes which are so persistent for women, for racial and ethnic minorities, for disabled people and other disempowered groups (Lorbiecki and Jack, 2000; Litvin, 2006). Hence diversity management presents a challenge for practitioners in its underpinning philosophy of diversity as a business resource – should they adopt the new discourse, and if they decide that it is right for their organisation, how do they ensure that fairness and equality concerns about group-level inequalities are not forgotten?

Up to now, the business case is still unproven in monetary terms. Research has not yet identified clear effects on the bottom line, although after a major five-year study, the Bold Initiative led by Kochan and colleagues (2003) suggests that gender diversity may have a positive impact at the team level. However, racial diversity is only likely to enhance performance when it is proactively managed in an innovative climate, otherwise conflict and withdrawal may result in lower performance (Richard *et al.*, 2004). Kochan comments that the business case may or may not bring financial benefits, but it is important to recognise that diversity is a fact in today's workforce. Successful companies are those that facilitate learning, hence managing diversity provides an opportunity for organisational learning at all levels. This can be achieved by attention to inclusion and cooperation, so that diverse individuals are empowered to make their contribution to the organisation's future success, whatever their personal diverse characteristics.

Dass and Parker (1999) have identified a framework of proactive, accommodative, defensive or resistant strategies for managing diversity, which can be implemented episodically, as freestanding initiatives and as systemic integrated processes. Only the proactive systemic measures are likely to result in longer-term change. In a study of diversity statements located on careers and corporate values pages of large company websites across eight countries in Europe, Singh and Point (2004) found that most of the largest UK companies had texts indicating the proactive strategy of managing diversity for competitive advantage, whilst many European companies reported defensive strategies, still framing diversity as a problem to be managed. Kossek *et al.* (2006) reviewed research on HRM strategies to change individuals, such as mentoring and diversity training, and noted the difficulty with strategies for change at the group level, as is the case with networks based on diverse characteristics, where there may be backlash from the majority in power, or continued isolation of the diverse group from the main networks of the organisation. Kossek *et al.* recommend that strategies for change at the organisational level are focused on culture change with leadership commitment and integration with corporate objectives. In the next section, we shall see how some leading edge companies are dealing with this challenge.

Diversity and strategic change

Drivers for change at Pearson

Diversity initiatives can often be undertaken in a piecemeal manner that does not necessarily lead to sustainable change. The key is to integrate diversity into the business strategy of the organisation, as Pearson has done. The drivers for the initiative by Pearson were twofold. First was the desire to be a really good employer with fair and transparent people management processes. Note that Sir David Bell takes the title "Director for People", indicating a philosophy of service for people as individuals rather than the depersonalised and exploitable 'human resources' term more commonly used. Second was recognition that as the biggest educational publisher in the world, and as one of the largest publishers in the world, it was essential to reflect in management and leadership the diversity of the societies in which Pearson operates. That includes sixty-one countries, but within many of those countries, there is much diversity. For example in London, half of the schoolchildren are from non-UK backgrounds; in inner cities in the USA, most children are African-Americans or Hispanics, whilst Hong Kong or Singapore again have different ethnic mixes. These diverse children are important present and future customers of the global educational publishing business, and it is essential for everyone in the company to realise that diversity is an absolute and critical advantage for the business, and that one size doesn't fit all situations.

There is still often too much homogeneity in the candidates coming forward for selection, especially to managerial jobs. Head-hunters play an important role in who gets into the frame for consideration. Sir David advises firms to insist that recruitment agencies should submit diverse candidates on the slates for all positions and send the list back if it does not reflect diversity. The biggest diversity challenges for Pearson, according to Sir David, are finding new places where diverse talent is developing; getting people to recognise potential in diverse individuals as well as people like themselves; finding inspiring role models, and finding more female talent at mid-career level outside the more female-dominated areas of the firm. Getting people to say what they really think about diversity is another challenge.

The solution is to get people to meet lots of others with really different backgrounds to their own, and to get them to understand and accept the commercial business case that diversity is an integral and key part of the future of the firm. Sir David comments that Pearson still has a way to go. But in 2002, when they put into place their four-year diversity action plan, they were confident enough to put it onto the corporate website for all to see, with actions/achieved each year, and a plan for the current year. Such transparency is remarkable, given the usually slow pace of change on this issue in most organisations.

Reuters – Diversity review in the annual report

Another company making its diversity strategy transparent is Reuters, which now has a section on equality and diversity in its annual report, positioned within the Operating and Financial Review. Such a placing highlights the strategic importance of managing diversity well, communicating the message to a wide variety of stakeholders, both internal and external. Reuters established a Global Diversity Advisory Council in 2004, and both the chairman, Niall Fitzgerald, and the chief executive, Tom Glocer, are visible and vocal champions of diversity. Indeed, there are several women on the corporate board and the top team, as well as the first UK black director of a FTSE 100 company. The annual review reveals the 2006 CSR objectives: to develop a diversity code for their suppliers, and to roll out a reverse mentoring programme (which is reported below). Reuters report that their annual survey of employee engagement revealed very high support for the statement 'Reuters provides a working environment that is accepting of ethnic differences'. This is an achievement for a company that has employees of 115 nationalities in eighty-nine countries, and the foundation for carrying out their business practices, as they say, 'with independence, integrity and freedom from bias'.

Diversity awareness

Getting managers to engage in diversity management awareness courses in practice can be difficult, as most managers pride themselves on their sense of fairness and good practice. Hence the inequalities of systemic gendered or otherwise discriminatory processes are not apparent to them. The fact that managers above a certain level in their organisations are all white males, often middle class from similar backgrounds, does not surprise them or challenge their thinking – it is normal, and their view is that the playing field is level for all with the talent to be there. So how do you educate them? Here we see how some organisations have tackled the issue.

The British Airways experience

To address the lack of awareness amongst managers about the differences between the equal opportunities (EO) and the newer diversity management (DM) philosophy and implications for practice, many organisations are starting to develop diversity management awareness courses. British Airways decided to update its diversity training for its managerial tier of between three and four thousand people managers, many in specialist jobs including pilots, engineers and accountants. At British Airways, there had been an EO course in place since 1998, delivered by external consultants, but as training budgets got tighter, delivery moved in-house. The course had been designed around legislative requirements and the diversity team wanted to align with the newer values of Diversity and Inclusion. In addition, because it was designed to communicate the legislation on the various anti-discrimination acts, it didn't help managers to understand some of the more practical elements or how to best engage with managing diversity.

However, a new course would require new resources, and so a business case had to be prepared, which focused on Diversity and Inclusion and emphasised the importance of behaviour, attitudes and stereotypes. This was particularly relevant because of the forthcoming introduction of age legislation in the UK. Funding was granted for a pilot four-hour module for managers to be designed and delivered in-house. However it soon became clear that significantly more expertise in diversity training than was available in-house had to be acquired before the initiative really started to change managers' behaviours. So leading diversity consultants were called in, with the proviso that part of the training should be designed as e-learning. This was a challenge to the company's software systems, as well as a challenge for the designers, as there was little e-learning material available externally, and dealing with people and behavioural issues such as stereotyping was much more difficult than e-learning on technical subjects.

The new e-learning was a one-hour module, designed to communicate the importance of the business case for diversity, as well as helping managers to understand the impact of stereotyping, and providing them with sufficient understanding to get the most out of their workshop module in the classroom. Managers have to undertake the e-module before the classroom sessions, and prepare for a number of diversity scenarios designed to help them understand the impact of their own behaviour. These address issues such as management styles, first impressions, and being in a minority. In the classroom, managers engage in multi-brain scenarios, presenting live situations that they have to experience, understand and address, or observe others doing so. As they experience how they feel, and vicariously, how others feel, together they can talk through the meaning of diversity and inclusion, learning how to be more inclusive managers. This innovative intervention has been running for several months, on time and on budget. The whole managerial tier is scheduled to refresh their diversity training over a three-year period. Feedback has been very positive and managers report that not only did they learn but they also enjoyed the experience.

The content was excellent, very focused and they made every session count. There was no waffle, and the 'build 'throughout the day was cohesive and really worked. It created a shift in the room, and the participants were really engaged. The scenarios were sufficiently challenging to create good debate. (Managerial participant)

There is an evaluation on the day, and British Airways is evaluating the impact of the Diversity and Inclusion initiative on the business, undertaken by external consultants and university researchers. Diversity questions are also included in the usual employee surveys, so questions can be tailored to identify to what extent the new initiative is impacting the way staff feel. Diversity training is a key piece of the diversity strategy in British Airways as it supports one of the other key objectives of ensuring that diversity and inclusion are being integrated into the business across the whole company.

A better way to work: the Law Society of Scotland

A small organisation with a very different customer profile is the Law Society of Scotland, which provides services to the legal profession including training and professional development. It reveals in its on-line journal (lawscot.org.uk) that in implementing its three-year Equality and Diversity Strategy, it introduced the philosophy of diversity management to its council and committee members through a very simple exercise. Members were each asked to list ten key principles of good customer service, and the resulting concepts such as communication, politeness, friendliness, understanding and flexible and non-threatening behaviour were then discussed in relation to managing employee and customer diversity. It then became crystal clear that respect and equality of treatment were not only core to good service but also to individual relationships with the organisation. A message from the President of the organisation to its stakeholders comments that the profession is getting younger, more women than men are entering the profession and both men and women are seeking better work–life balance. Attention to diversity and equality is therefore essential, requiring a new dialogue with all concerned stakeholders. Their very simple exercise made the achievement of the diversity objectives more likely.

Diversity and recruitment

The PwC recruitment initiative

Increasingly employers in the US are seeking to attract well-educated candidates from diverse backgrounds, according to the *Wall Street Journal* (2006), which reported that PwC New York starts contact with potential employees as early as high school, running workshops and conferences, bringing young people into the firm during holidays and giving scholarships for tuition. The PwC vice president of recruiting reports that 85 percent of the interns are offered jobs, with a 90 percent acceptance rate, indicating the loyalty benefits and effectiveness of the initiative.

The Pearson ethnic diversity outreach programme

We now look in more depth at an example of an initiative to reach more young people from diverse ethnic backgrounds. This innovative outreach programme based in London identifies twenty-two young students from ethnic minority backgrounds and brings them into the company for six weeks. In the first two years, students were spread across the undergraduate years; they included both young women and men and came from a variety of ethnic backgrounds. Indeed, the programme has included several young Muslim women wearing burqas. The interns were identified via the "milk round" and careers fairs, where they were given a booklet about the programme, invited to send in their curriculum vitae, and eventually interviewed by the HR and diversity team. The diversity team works with managers across the business to identify a range of possible projects. Students are paid £1,000 per month, and depending upon their skills and interests, are allocated to specific projects on which they will be expected to report at the end of their stay. The interns are welcomed by David Bell, the Director for People, who is also Chairman of Pearson Inc. He emphasises how important diversity is to Pearson, and this is evident from his personal involvement in the programme. At the end of the internship, a development day is held. An appraisal takes place, students present their work on the specific projects, and both students and supervisors comment on the outcomes. Over lunch there are opportunities for everyone to meet the Director for People again and exchange views. Whilst feedback is generally very positive, there are of course some things that are not so good, but the open and honest dialogue helps to bring about suggestions for improvement. After two years, the Internship Programme has been reviewed by participants, managers and HR, and is undergoing some important changes. The focus will be on reaching those students most likely to be interested in being considered for future employment, and so students will be only offered internships in their third year. The programme name will also change to Diversity Internship, and will include other diverse characteristics, not just ethnicity. Thus future internships could be held by people who are disabled or older students who may be seeking employment in publishing.

Diversity and career management

Women's recruitment, development and retention at Shell

Ensuring a pipeline of female talent is not an easy task, and Shell has put into place a number of structures and systems to improve the attraction, development, progression and retention of women, including setting global targets, developing focused training programmes and monitoring the work environment through the global Shell People Surveys. Furthermore, Shell is determined to do more to accelerate the process. In 2004, the women's network in the Netherlands raised concerns that despite all current efforts, there was a perception that there were barriers affecting the retention and progression of women in that country. After some initial data gathering and the discovery of several parallel projects in other Shell units, it was decided to undertake a global study focusing on the Netherlands and the UK, leading to recommendations for global implementation. This project was a key project for Diversity and Inclusiveness, and was fully supported by the HR Executive Leadership and Talent Management teams, sponsored by the country chairs of the two countries, and championed by the Executive Director of Downstream Business.

The study used a combination of data sources. Firstly, Shell undertook a survey of all the women in the Netherlands and UK above a certain level, using an on-line questionnaire originally developed by Catalyst about barriers for women. There was a very good completion rate, with over 1,000 female employees responding. The quantitative inputs were then supplemented with more qualitative inputs from interviews with a number of current and former women employees to get a deeper understanding of the issues. The Diversity and Inclusiveness (D&I) team also examined the internal database for demographic composition and gender balance at recruitment, attrition, promotions, bonus awarding, potential assessment and other HR procedures. They tracked the changes over the past two to three years, so that they could identify any potential problems and the scale of them. Lastly, the responses by male and female employees in the biennial Shell People Survey were also analysed to assess the overall inclusive environment for women.

The survey results showed that the top perceived barrier was the lack of visible female role models, closely followed by women's commitment to personal and family responsibilities. The third major barrier was stereotyping and preconceptions about women's roles. Results from the internal database analysis showed no significant gender differences in any HR procedures. However, findings from interviews and data analysis revealed some areas where improvement actions could be made. For example, it was found that whilst men tend to leave at retirement, more women resign and they leave earlier than men.

Shell decided to take some action within the year to accelerate the retention and progression of women, and to have a strategic plan for longer-term change. Some examples of the actions are provided below. Women were to be put onto the majority of shortlists for managerial appointments in the UK, US and the Netherlands, and every senior female leader was asked by the directors to engage more actively in role modelling within the company. All senior executives need to include D&I in their annual performance discussions. Shell seeks to recruit more women at both graduate and mid-career hire level, particularly those with technical qualifications. Whilst there is a healthy proportion of women at junior management level, more needs to be done to develop them on the career ladder, so women at mid-levels with leadership potential will be targeted for career development. To assist the retention of women after maternity leave, ensuring top quartile childcare provisions in the market will be a target for action in the Netherlands, the UK and the US. Such an action plan requires particular expertise from leaders and HR and diversity professionals. Therefore, all senior managers are expected to attend a half-day gender culture difference engagement workshop to improve their awareness and develop action plans, and all HR practitioners above a certain level whose job requires D&I competence will attend a three-day D&I Awareness and Skills Seminar by the end of 2007.

Diverse role models

The lack of diverse role models is frequently listed as a major barrier, particularly for women and those from ethnic minorities. Singh, Vinnicombe and James (2006) identified how important role models were for young women aspiring to management positions, and how concerned they felt about the lack of women with children at the top of the business world. Gibson (2004) examines the construal of role models, identifying that people need role models for different purposes at different stages of their careers, whilst Sealy and Singh (2006) explores the importance of role models and corporate demographic composition for senior women. All of these studies indicate the symbolic value of having female leaders.

Active role modelling at IBM

There is a dearth of black role models in the UK business world. Recognising this, members of the ethnic minority network at IBM have given their own time to run an event for 160 ethnic minority children in a school in a less well-off area of London, forming a lasting bond with the particular school through mentoring of talented teenagers. Children responded to the event by saying that they had no idea that people with ethnic backgrounds similar to themselves could succeed in companies such as IBM. The role models take it upon themselves to inspire youngsters to want to work hard at school and university, and help make things easier inside the company by running the Ethnic Minority Network. Importantly, their efforts have been recognised both by the UK chief executive, and the European Federation of Black Women Business Owners.

Female role models at Shell

Shell has recognised that the lack of female role models continues to be an issue that hinders the recruitment and development of women into their still male-dominated sector of energy and petrochemicals. To redress this, Shell makes efforts to highlight many of the really outstanding women, particularly those in the technology side of the business. A number of women are profiled on the careers website, and they represent a truly international set of high achievers with different backgrounds, career paths and personal styles. Their job titles include executive director gas and power, executive VP chemicals, VP global IT infrastructure, executive VP global manufacturing, executive VP gas and power, global head of marine products, global technology manager, VP general counsel – these are significant positions in one of the world's leading companies. The encouraging thing about these women is that they are willing to acknowledge their own efforts to maintain a balance between career and personal lives, for example, managing high profile jobs and striving to be good mothers too. So often, high profile women only reveal their work personae, which means that young women seeking to combine career and family life in mid-career do not believe that it is possible to succeed unless they remain childless. One of the key benefits of women's corporate networks is that through the leadership and engagement of the top women, members can get to know that there are senior women who have young families or other personal circumstances similar to themselves, and still manage to achieve senior executive positions (Vinnicombe, Singh and Kumra, 2004). This leads to younger women maintaining their ambition and motivation to build careers within the firm.

Diversity and leadership commitment

Reuters valuing difference global reverse mentoring programme

Reverse mentoring is the reverse of the traditional model of mentoring where a senior manager takes a personal interest in the development of a more junior employee, with a view to helping the mentee prepare for a more senior post. In Reuters global reverse mentoring programme, very senior managers are paired with more junior mentors of diverse backgrounds, so that they can gain insight into what is happening and how people feel deeper in the organisation. The objective of this programme is to raise awareness of diversity and inclusion issues at the highest levels. The mentors are typically first- to middle-level managers, who are high performers and ideally who are co-located with the mentees, so that a more personal and informal relationship can develop, building up the trust needed to communicate on sensitive diversity issues. Following the success of a regional reverse mentoring programme in the USA, Reuters global programme pairs the CEO and his direct reports with senior women and Asians outside Asia, two groups that are underrepresented at the highest levels. Nominations for these mentors were made by HR and senior management, and candidates underwent a selection process to ascertain their suitability as mentors of global leaders in the company. Based on the positive experiences of participants in the US and global programmes, a third programme has been launched in the business. As is good practice for usual mentoring schemes, Reuters has developed a set of guidelines about the roles and responsibilities of the reverse mentoring pairs and provides guidance and coaching through regular check-ins with reverse mentors. The results should be illuminating for the global leaders, as well as being a developmental and rewarding experience for the participants. From their experiences, new methods and tools can be developed to improve the work environment and culture as well as contribute to business development. A key feature of the reverse mentoring programme is that it demonstrates the commitment of leadership and senior management to diversity by real-time engagement with diverse talented individuals.

Diversity and inclusion through corporate networks

The PwC people networks

PwC supports a number of internal corporate networks, run by volunteer teams and most are chaired by a client-facing partner. These include race (the ethnic forum), gender and sexual orientation (the award-winning PwC-women, and the GALE network for gay, lesbian, bisexual and transgender partners and staff), faith-based (PwC Muslims, PwC Christians, the Hindu network, the Jewish network), and carers' networks (the parents network and the special needs child support network for parents). There is also an accessibility team to focus on the needs of disabled employees and clients.

The networks are supported for two particular reasons. First is to provide accessible networking opportunities to minority individuals who feel the need to be connected to those in a similar position. Second is to enhance the business, by taking advantage of the diversity of network members to understand and build better links with diverse clients and other stakeholders. For example, PwCwomen held a 'Girlfriends in high places' event, where each member was asked to bring a female client along to a major department store. Through this kind of innovative event, professional women could socialise and build better relationships with female clients in a way that was much more suited to women's preferences than entertaining them in a pub or on the golf course, as is common amongst their male peers.

Affinity groups at Reuters

Reuters describe their diverse internal employee networks as affinity groups, which self-formed in the US to provide peer support and mentoring, share common experiences and discuss ways to address issues of concern to them. They provide an opportunity for dialogue at all levels of the company. There are affinity groups for women, for Asian members, for gay, lesbian, bisexual and transgender employees, for black employees and for Hispanic employees. These are set up in different geographical regions, such as the US and Europe, and in some cases by business. ReuBEN is the affinity group for black employees, recently addressed by Reuter's non-executive director, Ken Olisa, the only FTSE 100 director coming from a black UK background. Importantly, affinity groups are now seen as business partners, helping to develop not just their members but also the business. This is reflected in the direct engagement of the chief executive, Tom Glocer, speaking to the affinity groups and championing diversity. One particular event held by ReuBEN demonstrates the Board's willingness to get involved. ReuBEN was holding a BBQ in London and invited Tom Glocer along. The event happened to be the same day as a Board meeting and Tom ended up bringing the entire Board along – it had fantastic impact. Many other Board members have also been very involved. Lawton Fitt and Penny Hughes have both been very active attending dinners with senior Reuters women in both New York and London, helping to organise and participate in Reuters sponsored diversity events for the financial services industry and even informally mentoring some senior women in Reuters (all in the last year!). There is also, of course, the major influence of the chairman Niall Fitzgerald, who consistently and passionately raises the diversity topic in various forums and at all levels.

Through affinity groups, individuals have a voice as citizens of the corporation. This is great for increasing employee engagement and commitment. They can raise issues about their own experiences that can then be discussed in broader terms and referred at policy-making level to the appropriate internal departments in an atmosphere of trust. The affinity groups are a mechanism for consultation by those responsible for HR and development. The company provides support and guidance to those wishing to set up such a group, recommending that an executive leader should identified as early as possible, and that the aims of the group are established. These groups which have been set up around the world are asked to keep in regular communication to share best practice. New groups are set up as old ones fold – it is an evolutionary process that is responsive to employee needs and aspirations, to the benefit of both the company and its diverse employees. The Reuters affinity groups are in their formative stage at present, and the challenge is to maintain the momentum with continued engagement.

Shell women's networks

Shell sees corporate networks as an integral part of their Diversity and Inclusiveness strategy. By the end of 2005, Shell had twenty-two active employee networks, ten of which are women's networks based in the UK, the US, Germany, the Netherlands, Thailand, Singapore, Malaysia, Australia, Dubai and Nigeria. The senior leadership team in each country supports the networks, together with the Global D&I Practice. Shell believes that such networks help to leverage the full personal and professional potential of women and other diverse individuals, through active learning, self-development, mentoring and business engagement, at the same time contributing to corporate goals. Therefore Shell has identified eight more countries with a sufficiently sized population of female employees to encourage the formation of new women's networks.

Inclusion through diversity events

Pearson and the diversity week

To raise awareness in a more relaxed way, the Penguin division of Pearson introduced a diversity week in London, with a number of events and activities to promote good diversity relations. The canteens provided a variety of Afro-Caribbean food, accompanied by steel bands. A number of inspiring speakers from ethnic minority backgrounds were invited, attracting large audiences, and the speakers featured in the intranet news for wider circulation and awareness raising. There was a special movie-showing, and a new book launch to celebrate the former BBC journalist and war reporter Rageh Omaar's new book, *Only Half of Me: Being a Muslim in Britain.* The Diversity Week also introduced another art form, Jamaican dub poetry, spoken words over reggae rhythms and predominantly concerned with politics and social justice. The legendary dub poet Linton Kwesi Johnson took the audience through his work, from his early 1970s poetry to the turbulent 1980s where he commented on the Brixton riots of 1981 and finally to his most recent work of the 1990s. He also opened up the floor for questioning and answered a variety of challenging questions about equality and diversity today and talked about today's 'lost generation' of black youths. The Diversity Week was a fun event that engaged interest across the company, raising awareness and promoting inclusiveness and understanding. Two further diversity weeks are planned for other businesses within Pearson. For Pearson, the diversity weeks should be a reflection of the business's own and specific products and services. This is to underline that diversity is not only the right thing to do, but it also has a commercial benefit that flows through from those who work for the company into the products and services that they offer their customers. Managing diversity well is good for business as well as making a better place for people to work and develop their diverse talents.

Inclusion through respecting religious diversity

Some companies are working with faith groups to ensure that religious festivals across relevant faiths are celebrated in an inclusive way, so that Christian festivals such as Christmas and Easter are not the only festivals acknowledged by the firm. McDonalds had a diversity calendar that allowed them to develop location-specific actions to celebrate the religious festivals of the local communities. For example, in towns where there were many people of Indian origin, managers would be ready to organise special food products to offer over the Diwali holiday period. Similarly, the B&Q stores in the UK have a calendar of significant religious dates and festivals, developed in association with the Interfaith Network, so that managers are aware of the need for special consideration on those dates for customers and employees. Some companies provide prayer rooms for those whose religion requires prayers through the working day. However, dedicated rooms are often difficult to resource, and hence some companies made efforts to maintain some continuity of room allocation so that people could pray together. Goodwill is needed from both sides to incorporate such requests within the normal facilities and arrangements.

Diversity and flexibility

Diversity management is also about how best to deal with differences of responsibilities and interests held by employees outside work, whether childcare, eldercare or community activities such as school governing and local politics. Increasingly people want time for other activities such as education and sport, yet the demands of their working lives means that pressure to be at the office or workplace for ever longer hours combined with new technology connecting them to work in their non-work time leaves little space for other responsibilities and activities.

Many organisations struggle with the desire for more balanced working lives, coming increasingly from men as well as from women. When people feel in control of their lives, they are more productive, more focused and more satisfied. There are push and pull factors. In the UK, parents now have a right to ask for flexible hours when their children are very young, and although they do not have a right to work flexible hours, employers have to take such requests seriously. Some companies demand that employees work flexibly, especially now that technology has linked up the various time zones around the world. Others are faced with demands from employees for flexibility that they do not wish to contemplate – yet often this is a mind-set issue that requires lateral thinking rather than seeing such requests as an insolvable problem.

Some larger companies address some of the work–life balance issues by putting in place a number of services, such as crèches, emergency child care centres, concierge services to deal with dry-cleaning, tickets etc, and amenities such as on-site gyms, long hour coffee shops which provide a sense of community for those working non-standard hours, and health centres. Smaller firms offer childcare vouchers and subsidised gym membership, for example, rather than provide facilities on site. But employers need to consider to what extent it is essential that staff members work on site for fixed hours, and whether more flexible ways of working would not only make life easier for people but also make them more productive for the firm. Some good examples below show what can happen when employers take the flexible approach.

Flexible working at IBM

IBM celebrates the new way of working, drawing on the benefits of technology to free employees from the need to be at their desks for the whole of the working week. Now the majority of the IBM employees in the UK work flexibly, in what they call the on-demand workplace, using a mobile think-pad to connect to IBM. The result is that 83 percent of UK employees can keep in touch with the business when away from the office or on the move. More time is freed up to spend with clients, travel costs have been reduced, and less office space is needed at the corporate offices. This new way of working has meant that flexible working patterns have been introduced with relative ease to allow individuals to manage the balance that they seek between work and non-work responsibilities and aspirations. Whilst only 4 percent of IBM UK employees work reduced hours, almost 60 percent of the workforce work flexibly, whether job sharing, term-time working, compressed hours, and sabbaticals. Even at director level, flexible working really does work, according to Tim Shercliff, the IBM Global Services strategy and marketing director. He has worked in this way for four years, and says: 'Working reduced hours gives me more time for my family, but I also have more energy when I'm at work, which helps me focus and really add value.'

Flexible working at BT

The telecoms giant BT has 75 percent of its employees on some form of flexible working, allowing most employees control over the hours and location of their working day. This follows a major job redesign programme, with a shift towards output- or outcome-based performance, rather than how much time employees are present on site. The desire for work–life balance has been recognised and addressed by BT, and has moved on from the earlier presenteeism culture that exists in so many large companies. The flexible approach has provided a number of benefits, including massive savings in recruitment costs, as retention rates soared. Now 99 percent of women return from maternity leave, because they are in control of their hours and outputs, even during school holiday times through the annualised hours scheme. Across the UK, so many women are unable to continue their careers when they have to take responsibility for childcare during long school holidays, simply because of a rigid view of how jobs should be scoped and managed. BT has moved on from that fixed view, even for those at senior management level, and is now reaping the rewards as one of the UK's most forward-looking employers.

Flexible working at Centrica

The UK gas giant, Centrica has worked hard to improve flexible working offerings recently, as flexibility was identified as a key factor affecting both female and male employees. A new flexible working policy was launched, with reviews of individual working arrangements alongside investments in work infrastructure to allow employees to have more control over their lives, to improve productivity and quality of work and to encourage men and women to develop their careers within the company. The company also identified a need for managers to be trained to manage flexible workers within the new system. Centrica has already achieved awards for its diversity on the board and its commitment to developing women leaders. It is noted for having women holding 24 percent of senior positions and 28 percent of middle level posts, with a 34 percent female workforce of only. These figures may be improved further as flexible working allows more talented women to stay and fulfil their potential during and after periods of non-standard working hours.

Wellness at Goldman Sachs

Diversity and inclusion means treating all employees with respect, and in many companies this means consideration for their non-work as well as work responsibilities, because if people can manage those well, they are more likely to stay with the company and to enhance their commitment and contribution. A number of work–life initiatives have been put in place by Goldman Sachs, with health, work and family, fitness, nutrition, learning and recreation offerings bundled together as the Wellness Exchange, to provide facilities, services and resources to employees and their families. Knowing that such resources are available enables employees to manage their work and family commitments more flexibly, with less stress and the ability to make positive lifestyle choices. The company offers generous maternity leave, on and near-site child-care, resources for new parents, and consideration for those with elder care responsibilities. Goldman Sachs was one of the earliest firms to set up a special initiative for expectant and new mothers, through the joint efforts of the wellness group and the women's network. The maternity buddy programme provides an informal link during maternity leave between the new mother, a volunteer maternity mentor who has been through the same experience, and the manager. The manager is responsible for ensuring that the buddy and the employee understand the various support structures available, and that they keep in touch during the leave period. The buddies are trained to provide professional and personal support but also are expected to share their own experiences of going through the process and then returning to work as a new parent within Goldman Sachs. The programme is also open to employees going through adoption. Such programmes can make a real difference to post-maternity attrition rates, as valuable employees are retained and helped to manage the change and challenges of their newly structured lives.

Credit Suisse parents network pregnancy to pre-school group

As part of their wider diversity and inclusion programme, Credit Suisse set up a parents network in the UK. A subgroup of the network is the pregnancy to pre-school group. This initiative aims to support women going on and during maternity leave, as well as when they return to work. It also provides advice to parents of pre-school children. The rationale for the company is that many new mothers feel stressed and unable to balance work and the new challenges in their family lives, and may decide not to return to work. Others may return, but decide to be less involved, downscaling their ambition and reducing their commitment. These outcomes are likely to impact the bottom line, so Credit Suisse has taken action to facilitate the retention of women as part of their diversity and inclusion initiative. The programme involves the mentoring of women going on maternity leave by women who have recently gone through the same experience. Expectant mothers are provided with an information pack and the company sends congratulations cards and welcome back cards to all returning mothers. Special classes are held for first time fathers, as well as on-site antenatal classes. During their leave, women are invited to monthly meetings to provide informal support as well as discussions on particular themes. There are courses on helping children to read, as well as invaluable first aid courses. A children's Christmas party is also held. The success of the initiative is measured by the number of attendees at the monthly meetings, the number of registrants for the courses, the website hits and the number of mothers participating in the mentoring programme. The trends on uptake and the percentage of women returning from maternity leave will be monitored at a later date. Communication to managers about diversity programmes now emphasises the need for support rather than compliance with legal requirements. The Credit Suisse programme is an example of innovative best practice, which they believe has had a significant impact on the well-being and morale of new and returning mothers, allowing them to continue to develop their careers within the firm.

Work–life balance and the importance of leadership

It is clear from the practices described above that in these leading-edge organisations, their leaders are not only championing diversity and inclusion, but also personally engaging in enacting the valuing of diversity. It is not a responsibility to be taken lightly. Leaders are role models, particularly for those in middle and senior management who are watching and learning. Through their personal behaviour, leaders set an example to their followers. A leader in one of the companies commented on the fact that if he sent an email at 4 am on a Sunday because it suited him, the recipient might feel obliged to deal with it outside normal hours when there was really no need to do so. He said that even though they may feel very normal and ordinary, leaders are being watched all the time by many people for clues about how to behave, how to succeed and how to balance work and family. He stressed that it was important for leaders to communicate their expectations and pass the message down the line, and that managers should delegate, deputise and roster so that no-one should feel pressured to be on call 24 hours a day. Clearly this leader showed awareness of the responsibility that leaders have in setting a good example, particularly in a global business where communications continued around the clock.

Working with partners

PwC and partnering

In addition to the diversity activities within the firm, PwC takes a partnership approach with external bodies to help bring change within society. They support the Women Directors on Boards initiative with Cranfield School of Management, Shell and the Government. They sponsored the 2005 Diversity Conference with the Department of Trade & Industry and the Confederation of British Industry. They also sponsor the CityPink network for gay women, the Asian Women of Achievement Awards, the First Women Awards and the RADAR Human Rights Awards as well as being prominent members of various diversity institutions.

IBM and the diversity champions scheme

IBM was one of the first UK employers to include sexual orientation in its equal opportunities programme, and extended their consideration to gender identity and expression in 2002. The CEO of IBM UK, Larry Hirst, hosted the first gay, lesbian and bisexual, transgender career empowerment seminar for IBM employees in 2004, highlighting the corporate belief that people should not have to hide their sexual orientation at work. IBM became a founder member of the diversity champions scheme, which brings employers and Stonewall (a major charity dedicated to removing discrimination on grounds of sexual orientation) together to exchange and develop best practice, as well as to support initiatives such as the prevention of homophobic bullying in schools. Engaging in such activities affirms corporate values and develops the sense of belonging and inclusion regardless of diversity in sexual orientation. IBM UK has recently come second out of 150 major employers in the Stonewall Corporate Equality Index.

Enhancing diversity through procurement

The Mayor of London, Ken Livingstone, is a vocal champion of diversity. Concerned with the slow progress of women into leadership positions, he has started a number of initiatives within the administrative body for London, including flexible working, more childcare facilities and a link with the Learning and Skills Councils to ensure that women in London have better access to training. But there is more that can be done with a carrot rather than the proverbial stick. As London expands to meet the challenges of hosting the Olympics in 2012, many new business opportunities will arise within the control of the GLA. Livingstone's 'Diversity Works for London' policy for the London Development Agency is that diversity and inclusion can be enhanced not just internally but externally through procurement policies in the supply chain. Only those firms with acceptable diversity policies will be approved, and bids will be encouraged from small, minority and disabled people-owned businesses. To help suppliers move forward, a number of support systems are available, including an on-line diversity dividend diagnostic. Whilst this is a public sector body that is making changes, similar policies can be adopted by any organisation, spreading the message that diversity really does matter, and that there are business benefits too.

Diversity performance monitoring

Leading companies such as Pearson and Lloyds TSB back up their diversity strategies with key performance indicators (KPI), often as part of a balanced scorecard. Companies monitor gender, ethnic origin, age, employment status, level and disability of all employees, using monthly and annual surveys. Each area of the business has its own diversity action plan, with targets to meet specific priorities. Formal benchmarking with other leading organisations on diversity indicators provides external validation of progress, and results can be a useful driver for further action internally. Informal benchmarking can be undertaken by heads of diversity working with others in similar positions across organisations. For an example of how one leading company measures performance, the Pearson.com website includes their diversity targets, plans and KPIs.

The PricewaterhouseCoopers diversity indicator model

Tackling the supply of diverse talent requires a detailed understanding not only of sex and minority statistics by each level in the hierarchy, but also of the flow rates within the pipeline. PricewaterhouseCoopers LLP has a diversity indicator model that examines men and women's career progression from graduate entry to top team level. When the model was first run in 2005, the initial results indicated that at entry and junior to senior management levels, there was gender-balanced staff profile in terms of promotions, but at very senior levels, the proportion of promoted women tailed off. The model allows predictions to be made about future trends. If change is to be achieved within ten years, then the glass ceiling effect between middle and senior levels needs to be addressed by appropriate interventions to remove any inequalities in promotion rates. Having these data has allowed PwC to develop their new diversity initiatives from a firm baseline. Previously there was a general view that senior women were not progressing as well as their male peers, but there was no solid evidence of the scope of the problem. Interventions to address the blockage include mentoring, coaching and networking. A further round of data collection will be undertaken to identify the current trend, with more data gathered on specific issues. A similar exercise is planned to identify the promotion flow rates for people from ethnic minorities.

The Lloyds TSB equal pay initiative

An important issue for companies is how to tackle the issue of pay inequalities, particularly gender-based pay differences. The UK bank, Lloyds TSB has led the way in dealing with this, and the chief executive personally sponsored the audit process. The project team piloted an audit across three groups, developing their own database and analysis tool to establish where inequalities were located, by examining pay data across organisational sets (by grade, role, length of service, gender, etc) and across different pay structures (basic salary, bonuses, total earnings etc). Interestingly, inequalities emerged not just between men and women, but between men, and between women across the company. The review revealed that the overriding contributory factor to pay inequality was length of service, and the systemic nature of the problem led Lloyds TSB to introduce a single new salary structure the following year. Adjustments were made to individual staff salaries, and the organisation pledged that funding would not be a barrier to sorting out any inequalities identified. The rationale for the new system had to be communicated across the company, requiring a training course for the key HR staff and those responsible for setting pay levels. As a result of the new system, the gender pay gap has been reduced at almost every grade, with over 10 percent of staff receiving pay increases of over 8 percent, whilst 15 percent of staff remained on their present salaries. The new analysis tool allows the situation to be monitored and addressed more quickly and transparently, and the principles of pay equality are now implemented based explicitly on the individual contribution to the business. The company is not only making a difference inside the company. Through participation in equal pay forums across the UK, Lloyds TSB is providing guidance to other organisations about to undertake equal pay audits.

Conclusion

This chapter has reported a number of exemplary practices from some of the world's leading companies and organisations. They set a high standard, but are nonetheless still striving to improve their own diversity management practices, and are engaging to help others too. The message from these findings is that there are many different and sometimes very creative ways of addressing the diversity and inclusion issue. Leadership commitment is essential, as is qualitative as well as quantitative measurement of the effectiveness of diversity initiatives. Regular strategic reviews are needed of progress of diverse groups into all levels of management, as well as the focus on the individual. Diversity is now a fact in the US, the UK, Europe and across the world, and diversity management coupled with inclusion policies should bring about a more equitable, flexible and enjoyable work climate, hopefully getting over the critical views that diversity management can be a smokescreen that avoids the need to attend to persistent and systemic group level inequalities. If people have mutual respect for their diverse colleagues, at whatever level, in whatever job and work towards the same goals with the commitment that comes from inclusion, the employer will benefit as well as the individuals. Mother Teresa once said: 'Do not wait for leaders. Do it alone, person to person'. Good advice for diversity and inclusion management too.

Acknowledgements

Much of the advice and examples in this chapter have come from interviews with HR directors, diversity directors and managers. In particular I wish to thank Sir David Bell, Alison Young and Abu Bundu-Kamara at Pearson; Gail Sulkes at Reuters; Alison Dalton at British Airways; Shaminder Flora at PwC and Ida Yuan at Shell.

REFERENCES

Cox, T. H. and Blake, S. (1991) Managing cultural diversity: Implications for organizational competitiveness. *Academy of Management Review*, 5(3) 45–56.

Dass, P. and Parker, B. (1999) Strategies for managing human resource diversity: From resistance to learning. *Academy of Management Executive*, 13(2) 68–80.

Elvira, M. and Cohen, L. (2001) Location matters: A cross-level analysis of the effects of orgniza-tional sex composition on turnover. *Academy of Management Journal, 44,* 591–605.

Florkowski, G. (1998) Managing diversity within multinational firms for competitive advantage. In E. E. Kossek and S. A. Lobel (eds.), *Managing diversity: Human resource strategies for transforming the workplace.* Cambridge, MA: Blackwell.

Gibson, D. E. (2004) Role models in career development: New directions for theory and research. *Journal of Vocational Behavior, 65,* 134–56.

Kandola, R. and Fullerton, J. (1998) *Diversity in action: Managing the mosaic* (2nd edn.) London: Chartered Institute of Personnel and Development.

Kirby, E. L. and Harter, L. M. (2003) Speaking the language of the bottom line: the metaphor of 'managing diversity' *Journal of Business Communication, 40(1),* 28–49.

Kochan, T., Bezrukova, K., Ely, R., Jackson, S., Joshi, A., Jehn, K., Leonard, J., Levine, D. and Thomas, D. (2003) The effects of diversity on business performance: Report of the Diversity Research Network. *Human Resource Management, 42,* 1, 3–21.

Konrad, A., Prasad, P. and Pringle, J. K. (eds.) (2006) *Handbook of workplace diversity.* London: Sage.

Kossek, E. E., Lobel, S. A. and Brown, J. (2006) Human resource strategies to manage workforce diversity: Examining 'the business case'. In A. M. Konrad, P. Prasad and J. K. Pringle (eds.) *Handbook of workplace diversity.* London: Sage.

Liff, S. (1999) Diversity and equal opportunities: Room for a constructive compromise. *Human Resource Management Journal, 9(1),* 65–75.

Litvin, D. R. (2006) Diversity: Making space for a better case. In A. M. Konrad, P. Prasad and J. K. Pringle (eds.), *Handbook of workplace diversity.* London: Sage.

Lorbiecki, A. and Jack, G. (2000) Critical turns in the evolution of diversity management. *British Journal of Management,* 11, Special issue S17–S31.

Ragins, B. R. and Gonzalez, J. A. (2003) Understanding diversity in organizations: Getting a grip on a slippery construct. In J. Greenberg (ed.) *Organizational behavior: The state of the science* 2nd edn., Mahwah: Erlbaum Associates.

Richard, O. C. (2000) Racial diversity, business strategy and firm performance: A resource-based view. *Academy of Management Journal, 43(2),* 164–77.

Richard, O. C., Barnett, T., Dwyer, S. and Chadwick, K. (2004) Cultural diversity in management, firm performance and the moderating role of entrepreneurial orientation dimensions. *Academy of Management Journal, 47(5)* 255–66.

Sealy, R. and Singh, V. (2006) Role models, work identity and senior women's career progression – Why are role models important? *Best Papers Proceedings of Academy of Management Annual Meeting,* Atlanta, GA, August.

Singh, V. and Point, S. (2004) Strategic responses by European companies to the diversity challenge: An on-line comparison. *Long Range Planning, 3/4,* 295–318.

Singh, V., Vinnicombe, S. and James, K. (2006) Constructing a professional identity: How young female managers use role models. *Women in Management Review, 21(1)* 67–81.

Vinnicombe, S., Singh, V. and Kumra, S. (2004) *Making good connections: Best practice for women's corporate networks,* London: Opportunity Now.

Wall Street Journal (2006, 15 August). US firms zero in on potential employees early. *The Wall Street Journal,* p. 30.

Part IV

Transforming organizations

12 Making it better – achieving outstanding performance in manufacturing organizations

John Bessant and Dave Francis

The manufacturing challenge

Say the word "manufacturing" to most people and the chances are that they will conjure up images of belching smokestacks, urban sprawl, lines of unfriendly looking machinery – all with a uniform colour scheme based on very drab grey! As for the way people fit into this puzzle that image is probably best captured by the immortal shot in "Modern Times" where Charlie Chaplin literally becomes a cog in the giant industrial machine.

The reality is, needless to say, somewhat different. Manufacturing has come a long way from the Industrial Revolution days when elements of the above picture could be seen. Visit the new BMW factory in Leipzig, for example, and you find a building designed by an award-winning architect with spacious halls, glass almost everywhere and the car assembly track weaving its aerial way in and out of the office space. Customers are invited to enjoy the experience of seeing their cars being made as well as owning and driving them. And the product itself has come a long way form Henry Ford's famous limited choice – one Model T design with two or four doors and "any colour you like – as long as it's black!" Prospective BMW owners begin by sitting with sales staff in a "design suite" in which they together configure their particular and personalised choice from the thousands of permutations of model, engine, interior trim, exterior features and add-on extras – and only when they are happy with the virtual design is it committed to physical production.

Whether it is making cars, carpets, cookers or cardboard boxes the *process* of manufacturing remains the same – a sequence of operations which bridge design with physical production and configuration before final distribution to end-users. What has changed are the ways in which this is carried out – Table 12.1 gives some examples of the major shifts which have taken place in recent years.

Table 12.1 The changing face of manufacturing

Dimensions	Changes
Location	Increasingly mobile, both in terms of shifting to locations with favourable wage or energy costs but also where there is proximity to knowledge sources or clusters.
Operations	Moves from direct physical manufacturing and assembly of components to an extended network of activities ranging from design, through various physical processes and out into distribution and after-sales service and support. The emerging picture is less one of 'making' than 'design/make/serve'.
Number and arrangement of players	Increasingly requires a number of specialist suppliers of ideas, goods and services which need to be configured and co-ordinated. Moves from vertical integration to organizing and managing extended and often globally distributed networks.
Drivers	Increasing role of non-price factors like design, choice, delivery speed and after-sales service, although price remains a key competitiveness factor
Technology	Shift from direct physical tools to increasing integration and sophisticated use of automation technologies across design, make and serve activities.

All of this impacts on the way we organize and manage manufacturing. One obvious area is in the sheer numbers of people involved; in most advanced economies the proportion of people employed in manufacturing has been steadily falling and typically accounts for less than 20 percent. Even in countries associated with a manufacturing boom – such as China – there is evidence that the absolute level of employment is stabilising and may even be starting to fall. This is not a reflection on the decline of manufacturing *activity* but rather on the ways it is carried out – with continuing substitution of capital for labour via the use of advanced process equipment. And that highlights a second key trend – the rising skill levels which have accompanied this overall decline in employment numbers. We may see fewer people in our factories but those who remain are highly and often multi-skilled, reflecting a shift in knowledge intensity.

This chapter looks at some of the aspects of organizing for effective manufacturing in the twenty-first century. How do successful manufacturers manage key shifts in the underlying pattern – such as the shift to knowledge-based competitiveness or the demands for higher levels of agility?

From craft production to agile manufacturing

Typical of the products available at the turn of the twentieth century – and in many ways a symbol of the whole era – was Henry Ford's Model T. A car for Everyman, its manufacture required a new pattern of production technology and organisation, based on innovations which reduced the need for skilled labour, mechanised much of the assembly process, integrated preparation and manufacturing operations and systemised the entire process. The new approach had a dramatic impact on productivity; for example, the first assembly line, installed in 1913 for flywheel assembly, cut the assembly time from twenty man minutes to five.

Arguably, Ford's model represented the most efficient response to the market environment of its time. But by the 1920s what had begun as a winning formula began gradually to represent a major obstacle to change. The game shifted away from trying to offer the customer low cost personal transportation and Ford was increasingly forced to add features to the ageing Model T. A new model was needed and production of the Model T stopped in 1927 – but changing over involved crippling investments of time and money since the blueprint for the highly integrated factories was only designed to make one model well. In the process Ford lost $200m and was forced to lay off thousands of workers – 60,000 in Detroit alone. 15,000 machine tools were scrapped and a further 25,000 had to be rebuilt – and even though the Model A eventually became competitive, Ford lost its market leadership to General Motors (Abernathy, 1977).

This highlights a key lesson in manufacturing – nothing stays the same for ever! Flexibility in the face of shifting market conditions is a key challenge. These days customers can demand better levels of service, better quality products, better delivery and support and greater specificity in what they buy. And *when* they get it. Supply and distribution chain management now involves cutting out buffer stocks and inventory holding 'just in case' of problems; instead the move is now to producing and delivering 'just in time' for something to be used. Even the products themselves cannot be taken for granted. Whereas the life of a typical product might once have been measured in years, the life cycle of many products today is down to months. Some consumer products – like television sets or mobile phones – go through several changes every year. The effect of this is to challenge the idea that industries go through phases, moving from being new young and innovative sectors associated with new products to mature industries in which the product and the way in which it is made are well established. Pressure for shorter product life cycles means that industries now need to find ways of constant renewal.

All of this poses enormous challenges for manufacturers – and takes them a long way from the kind of world in which Henry Ford was operating. Today the expectation is not for trade-offs (e.g., quality vs price, or delivery reliability vs variety) but rather for 'bundles' of 'order winning' factors. And this puts pressure on manufacturers to develop much higher levels of *agility* – being able to switch between, and reconfigure these quickly (Bessant *et al.*, 2002).

Lewin's famous change model suggests that change occurs in the movement from one frozen state to another via a period of unfreezing. (Lewin, 1947). But in an 'agile' world there is no frozen or unfrozen state, but a constant blend of both. The firm is constantly re-inventing itself and needs the "organisational flexibility to adopt for each project the managerial vehicle that will yield the great competitive advantage". (Goldman and Nagel, 1993)

Towards high involvement innovation

The word manufacture comes from the Latin – meaning to make by hand. But in a rapidly mechanising world, people were increasingly consigned to low skill 'machine minding' roles. Emphasis on 'scientific management' meant that skilled specialists were able to analyze and devise 'best' manufacturing systems in which a few skilled specialists handled co-ordination and decision making. Given this rise in indirect activity and a separation between doing and thinking/deciding, it wasn't surprising to hear Henry Ford complain *"how come when I want a pair of hands I get a human being as well?"* But with manufacturing facing a range of challenges it needs all the creative ideas it can get – and maybe needs to rethink this approach (Boer *et al.*, 1999).

The idea that people can contribute to innovation through suggesting and implementing their ideas isn't new. Attempts to utilise this approach in a formal way can be traced back to the eighteenth century, when the eighth shogun Yoshimune Tokugawa introduced the suggestion box in Japan. In 1871 Denny's shipyard in Dumbarton, Scotland employed a programme of incentives to encourage suggestions about productivity-improving techniques; they sought to draw out *"any change by which work is rendered either superior in quality or more economical in cost"*. In 1894 the National Cash Register company made considerable efforts to mobilise the "hundred-headed brain" which their staff represented, whilst the Lincoln Electric Company started implementing an "incentive management system" in 1915. Joseph Juran, one of the pioneers of the quality movement, pointed out the significance of "the gold in the mine" suggesting that each worker in a factory could potentially contribute a valuable and continuing stream of improvements – provided they were enabled to do so (Juran, 1951).

This simple principle was neglected in much Western manufacturing until the last part of the twentieth century. But in post-war Japan it became a powerful engine for innovation. Firms like Kawasaki Heavy Engineering, Nissan, Toshiba and Toyota regularly report the number of ideas contributed by their workforce in millions, with the bulk of these being implemented. But it took a long time before the lessons which the Japanese had worked so hard at learning migrated to the rest of the world.

These days most organizations have attempted to implement some form of employee involvement and the gains from doing so are becoming increasingly apparent. For example, *"more than 30 studies carried out in the UK and US since the early 1990s leave no room to doubt that there is a correlation between people management and business performance, that the relationship is positive, and that it is cumulative: and the more effective the practices, the better the result . . ."* (Caulkin, 2001).

Analysis of the national UK Workplace Employee Relations Survey suggests a link between the use of more advanced HR practices and a range of positive outcomes, including greater employee involvement, satisfaction and commitment, productivity and better financial performance. (Guest *et al.*, 2000). Another study concludes that *"Practices that encourage workers to think and interact to improve the production process are strongly linked to increased productivity"* (Stern and Sommerblad, 1999) – a conclusion drawn by several other researchers (Huselid, 1995; Pfeffer and Veiga, 1999).

How can organizations develop and sustain a higher level of involvement of their workforce in innovation? Research suggests it's not a single action but a journey, progressing in terms of the development of systems and capability to involve people but also progressing in terms of the bottom line benefits which can be expected (Bessant, 2003).

The first stage is characterised by little, if any, innovative involvement going on and when it does happen it is essentially random in nature and occasional in frequency. People do help to solve problems from time to time – for example, they will pull together to iron out problems with a new system or working procedure, or getting the bugs out of a new product. But there is no formal attempt to mobilise or build on this activity, and many organisations may actively restrict the opportunities for it to take place.

The next level involves setting up a formal process for finding and solving problems in a structured and systematic way – and training and encouraging people to use it. Supporting this will be some form of reward/recognition arrangement to motivate and encourage continued participation. Ideas will be managed through some form of system for processing and progressing as many as possible and handling those which cannot be implemented. Underpinning this is an infrastructure of appropriate mechanisms (teams, task forces or whatever) facilitators and some form of steering group to enable it to take place and to monitor and adjust its operation over time.

Capability at this level contributes improvements but these may lack focus and are often concentrated at a local level, having minimal impact on more strategic concerns of the organisation. Level 3 involves coupling high involvement innovation to the strategic goals of the organisation such that all the various local level improvement activities of teams and individuals can be aligned. In order to do this two key behaviours need to be added to the basic suite – those of strategy deployment and of monitoring and measuring. Strategy (or policy) deployment involves communicating the overall strategy of the organisation and breaking it down into manageable objectives towards which activities in different areas can be targeted. Linked to this is the need to learn to monitor and measure the performance of a process and use this to drive the continuous improvement cycle.

One of the limits of level 3 is that the direction of activity is still largely set by management and within prescribed limits. Activities may take place at different levels, from individuals through small groups to cross-functional teams, but they are still largely responsive and steered externally. The move to level 4 introduces a new element – that of "empowerment" of individuals and groups to experiment and innovate on their own initiative.

Table 12.2 illustrates the key elements in each stage:

From physical to virtual manufacturing

Increasingly the ways in which manufactured objects are made real involves an extended excursion into the virtual world. Enabled by information and communications technology, we are seeing an acceleration of three broad and converging trends which have shaped the evolution of manufacturing:

- Mechanisation – where the physical effort is increasingly taken over by machinery.
- Automation – where the decision-making component of the skilled and experienced craftsman is replaced by some form of machine intelligence.
- Integration – where different operations become linked together and simplified, reducing both the need for physical and skilled inputs.

Table 12.2 Stages in the evolution of high involvement innovation (HII) capability

Stage of development	Typical characteristics
(1) 'Natural'/background HII	Problem-solving random No formal efforts or structure Occasional bursts punctuated by inactivity and non-participation Dominant mode of problem-solving is by specialists Short-term benefits No strategic impact
(2) Structured HII	Formal attempts to create and sustain HII Use of a formal problem-solving process Use of participation Training in basic HII tools Structured idea management system Recognition system Often parallel system to operations
(3) Goal oriented HII	All of the above, plus formal deployment of strategic goals Monitoring and measurement of HII against these goals In-line system
(4) Proactive/empowered HII	All of the above, plus responsibility for mechanisms, timing, etc., devolved to problem-solving unit Internally-directed rather than externally-directed HII High levels of experimentation

These trends have been around for a long time – for example, the radical nature of the Industrial Revolution was about accelerating mechanisation fuelled by new power sources (water and steam), integration (with the design of increasingly complex multi-stage machinery) and automation through the use of cams and punched cards in industries like textiles. But the arrival of the computer on the scene triggered a step-change in, and convergence between, these lines of development. "computer-integrated manufacturing" involved the coming together of design, co-ordination, distribution and other activities around the physical making core. The implications of this trend for manufacturing organization are clear – a shift from direct physical engagement to indirect and highly skilled support.

Early experience with implementing CIM highlighted the importance of these organizational changes. Expectations of radical improvement were often disappointed; closer examination of the problem suggested that investment

Table 12.3 Summarises the key dimensions of such changes

Dimensions of change

(1)	Work organisation
(i)	From single skill to multi-skill developments
(ii)	From high division of labour to integrated tasks
(iii)	From long skill life cycle to short skill life cycle
(iv)	From skill life = employee life to skill life < employee life
(v)	From individual work/accountability to team work/accountability
(vi)	From payment by results to alternative payment systems
(vii)	From supervisor controlled to supervisor supported
(viii)	From low work discretion to increased flexibility/autonomy
(2)	Changes in management organisation
(ix)	From sharp line staff boundary to blurred boundaries
(x)	From steep pyramid to flat structure
(xi)	From vertical communication to network communication
(xii)	From formal control to 'holographic adjustment'
(xiii)	From functional structures to product/ project/customer-based
(xiv)	From status differentiated to single status
(xv)	From rigid and non-participative to flexible-participative
(3)	Inter-organisation relationships
(xvi)	From tight boundaries between firms to blurred boundaries
(xvii)	From 'arm's-length dealing' to co-operative relations
(xviii)	From short-term to long-term relationships
(xix)	From confrontational to co-operative relationships/partnerships
(xx)	Lack of customer involvement to 'customer is king'

was unlikely to succeed unless it was accompanied by relevant parallel organisational change (Bessant, 1994; Ettlie, 1988; Voss, 1988).

This should not have come as a surprise; after all the principle that radical technological change requires some form of concomitant organisational change was at the heart of the 1960s work by the Tavistock Centre researchers which led to the development of the concept of "socio-technical systems design"; in turn, this work built upon a much earlier foundation of research and theory (Miller and Rice, 1967). It's clear that technologies which span more than one functional boundary are likely to pose problems of organisational integration; for example, one of the major requirements in effective computer-aided design and manufacture (CAD/CAM) utilisation is the organisation of a multi-disciplinary, multi-functional design process to enable close co-operation and integration.

From solo act to networks

No man is an island – and these days few businesses are either. Companies operate in a complex web involving a host of different players – suppliers, customers, competitors, regulators, collaborators and many others. The challenge is no longer how to manage the business but how to manage it in the wider context of networking.

For example, Dell's business model for creating a world class computer business owes less to high tech manufacturing techniques than in sophisticated use of a network model to allow fast and customized procurement, configuration and support for its growing market. At the other end of the scale, Italian firms continue to dominate the export league table for furniture – their edge coming from premium priced products which emphasize design and other non-price factors. Yet the average firm size in this sector is less than twenty people. They achieve their success, not by being individually strong, but by working together, sharing key resources and collaborating in order to compete externally. Studies of such "collective efficiency" have shown that its use is widespread – not just confined to parts of Italy, Spain and Germany but diffused around the world – and under certain conditions, extremely effective. (Best, 2001; Humphrey and Schmitz, 1996; Nadvi, 1997; Piore and Sabel, 1982) For example, one town (Salkot) in Pakistan plays a dominant role in the world market for specialist surgical instruments made of stainless steel. From a core group of 300 small firms, supported by 1,500 even smaller suppliers, 90 percent of production (1996) was exported and took a 20 percent share of the world market, second only to Germany. In another case the Sinos valley in Brazil contains around 500 small firm manufacturers of specialist high quality leather shoes. between 1970 and 1990 their share of the world market rose from 0.3 to 12.5 percent and they now export some 70 percent of total production. In each case the gains are seen as resulting from close interdependence in a co-operative network.

It is not simply a matter of regional co-operation – networking can also operate at the level of sectors or supply chains. Amongst examples of such arrangements in operation is the case of Toyota where an active supplier association has been responsible for sustained learning and development over an extended period of time (Dyer and Nobeoka, 2000). Hines reports on other examples of supplier associations which have contributed to sustainable growth and development in a number of sectors particularly engineering and automotive (Hines, 1994). Case studies in industries as diverse as food and wine, construction and aerospace provide further examples of different modes of learning networks organised around supply chains (AFFA, 2000; Bessant, Kaplinsky and Lamming, 2003; Fearne and Hughes, 1999; Marsh and Shaw, 2000).

But how do we set up and run effective manufacturing networks? We have enough difficulties trying to manage within the boundaries of a typical business. The challenges include:

- how to manage something we don't own or control;
- how to see system level effects not narrow self-interests;
- how to build trust and shared risk taking without tying the process up in contractual red tape;
- how to avoid "free riders" and information "spillovers."

It's a new game and one in which, once again, a new set of management skills becomes important. The key issues here are about trying to establish some core operating processes about which there is support and agreement. These need to deal with:

- network boundary management – how the membership of the network is defined and maintained;
- decision-making – how (where, when, who) decisions get taken at the network level;
- conflict resolution – how conflicts are resolved effectively;
- information processing – how information flows among members and is managed;
- knowledge management – how knowledge is created, captured, shared and used across the network;
- motivation – how members are motivated to join/remain within the network;
- risk/benefit sharing – how the risks and rewards are allocated across members of the network;
- co-ordination – how the operations of the network are integrated and co-ordinated.

Conclusion

Manufacturing is constantly changing – nowadays it's no more like the images in Chaplin's "Modern Times" or belching smokestacks than they were like the medieval craft workshops. The pace of change may be accelerating but, as we've seen in this chapter, the underlying trends are long-running. They may be enabled by technology but fundamentally they pose the challenge that they always did – how to find and develop an effective way of organizing and managing the process of manufacturing. And although automation may take increasing numbers of people off the direct factory floor the day of the automated manufacturing business remains a long way off. Instead we've seen major shifts in the composition and distribution of the workforce with a growing emphasis on high skills and high flexibility and an increase in networking. We are also seeing a shift in mind-set in more advanced economies where the recognition is that remaining in the manufacturing game requires a different view of how the process works. Whereas in the old model people were essentially an adjunct to technological systems, a necessary expense which future developments tried to marginalise and distance, the new one is increasingly dependent upon human intervention to provide flexibility, creativity and the ability to capture, retain and pass on knowledge.

REFERENCES

Abernathy, W. (1977) *The productivity dilemma: Roadblock to innovation in the automobile Industry.* Baltimore: Johns Hopkins University Press.

AFFA. (2000) *Supply chain Learning: Chain reversal and shared Learning for global competitiveness* (Report). Canberra: Department of Agriculture, Fisheries and Forestry – Australia (AFFA).

Bessant, J. (1994) Towards total integrated manufacturing. *International Journal of Production Economics, 34,* 237–51.

Bessant, J. (2003) *High involvement innovation.* Chichester: John Wiley & Sons.

Bessant, J., Brown, S., Francis, D., Kaplinsky, R., and Meredith, S. (2002) Developing manufacturing agility. *International Journal of Technology Management, 22(2/3).*

Bessant, J., Kaplinsky, R. and Lamming, R. (2003) Putting supply chain learning into practice. *International Journal of Operations and Production Management, 23(2),* 167–84.

Best, M. (2001) *The new competitive advantage.* Oxford: Oxford University Press.

Boer, H., Berger, A., Chapman, R. and Gertsen, F. (1999) *CI changes: From Suggestion Box to the Learning Organisation.* Aldershot: Ashgate.

Caulkin, S. (2001) *Performance through people.* London: Chartered Institute of Personnel and Development.

Dyer, J. and Nobeoka, K. (2000) Creating and managing a high-performance knowledge-sharing network: The Toyota case. *Strategic Management Journal, 21(3),* 345–67.

Ettlie, J. (1988) *Taking Charge of Manufacturing.* San Francisco: Jossey-Bass.

Fearne, A. and Hughes, D. (1999) Success factors in the fresh produce supply chain; insights from the UK. *Supply Management, 4(3).*

Goldman, S. and Nagel, R. (1993) Management technology and agility; the emergence of a new era in manufacturing. *International Journal of Technology Management, 8(1/2).*

Guest, D., Michie, J., Sheehan, M. and Conway, N. (2000) *Employment relations, HRM and business performance: An anlysis of the 1998 Workplace Employee Relations Survey.* London: CIPD.

Hines, P. (1994) *Creating world class suppliers: Unlocking mutual competitive advantage.* London: Pitman.

Humphrey, J. and Schmitz, H. (1996) The Triple C approach to local industrial policy. *World Development, 24(12),* 1859–77.

Huselid, M. (1995) The impact of human resource management practices on turnover, productivity and corporate financial performance. *Academy of Management Journal, 38,* 647–56.

Juran, J. (1951) *Quality control handbook.* New York: McGraw-Hill.

Lewin, K. (1947) Frontiers in group dynamics: Concept, method and reality in the social sciences. *Human Relations, 1(1),* 5–41.

Marsh, I. and Shaw, B. (2000) *Australia's wine industry. Collaboration and learning as causes of competitive success, Working paper.* Melbourne: Australian Graduate School of Management.

Miller, E. and Rice, A. (1967) *Systems of organisation.* London: Tavistock.

Nadvi, K. (1997) *The cutting edge: Collective efficiency and international competitiveness in Pakistan* (Discussion Paper No. 360): Institute of Development Studies.

Pfeffer, J. and Veiga, J. (1999) Putting people first for organizational success. *Academy of Management Executive, 13(2),* 37–48.

Piore, M. and Sabel, C. (1982) *The second industrial divide.* New York: Basic Books.

Stern, E. and Sommerblad, E. (1999) *Workplace learning, culture and performance.* London: Chartered Institute of Personnel and Development.

Voss, C. (1988) Success and failure in AMT. *International Journal of Technology Management, 3(3),* 285–97.

13 Culture change in a financial services organisation[1]

Emma Preece

Introduction

This chapter presents a case study of culture change in a large financial services organisation. The organisation under discussion is the second largest mutual[2] building society in the UK, Britannia Building Society. Founded in 1856, Britannia employs in excess of 5,000 people, has over 3 million members and a network of over 250 branches.

In 2003 Britannia embarked upon a journey of organisational cultural change. This case study describes the approach and strategies adopted by Britannia in achieving cultural change and provides an overview of the implementation process. Although evaluation of the cultural change is in its infancy and is beyond the scope of this chapter, an outline of associated employee outcomes, in the form of employee satisfaction survey results, is provided.

Context for change

Unlike large-scale corporate change programmes, the rationale for culture change at Britannia was not rooted in a commercial crisis. Rather, there was recognition that the changes reshaping the financial services sector demanded a different type of organisation. The financial services sector was already experiencing far-reaching change. This included, for example, intensifying competition, new domestic and overseas competitors, and increasing product innovation.

Thus it was recognised that the culture and ethos of Britannia that had stood it in good stead for 147 years was now no longer appropriate. Success now required an organisation that was more flexible and better equipped to deal with structural market change.

Understanding the existing culture

It is widely acknowledged that achieving cultural change requires an understanding of the existing organisational culture (e.g., Cockman, Evans and Reynolds, 1999). Britannia Building Society carried out research to elicit the features of the prevailing culture. Some of the key findings were

- there was no clear people strategy;
- there existed a lack of understanding and agreement about the *purpose* of the organisation amongst employees;
- there was a perceived trust in Britannia as an employer, regardless of restructuring or efficiency savings;
- poor performance was unchallenged and without consequence;
- internal networks were prioritised over customer relationships;
- there was an absence of open communication systems;
- problem-solving was symptom rather than solution focused;
- there were limited performance standards and measurement;
- decision making was not made in the context of a 'running a business'.

Organisational culture and change

These findings highlight the human process elements of organisational culture change. Whilst the task and systems components of an organisation are important levels of analysis, the human process issues within an organisation are instrumental in both the understanding and change of organisational culture (e.g., Cockman, Evans and Reynolds, 1999).

More specifically, the change process requires employees at both an individual and group level to develop new patterns of thinking and to learn new behaviours. Thus a sole focus on task, technology and other procedural components of change is not sufficient to aid change.

In addition, sustainable change needs to incorporate communication, participation and involvement in decision making, purposeful training and development and participative management (Cockman, Evans and Reynolds, 1999). Change is only deemed effective when there is permanence, when the effects become self-sustaining (Burnes, 1998) and when it becomes 'part of the way we do things around here' (Clarke, 1994 as cited in Burnes, 1998).

Case study methodology

The study of organisational culture and change is fraught with methodological issues (e.g., Schein, 1990). Various methods have been articulated in the literature. The approach adopted in this case study utilises a multi-method approach, eliciting information from stakeholder interviews, company and policy documentation and employee satisfaction surveys.

Stakeholder interviews

Nine semi-structured interviews were carried out with key stakeholders across the organisation. The Chief Executive and Director of Organisational Development were interviewed to elicit their views on how they embarked upon the journey of organisational culture change. An additional seven employees were subsequently interviewed from various levels across the organisation in order to gain a deeper insight into the cultural change initiatives from the perspective of the employees.

The questions for the seven employee interviews were formulated based on findings from the approach described by the Director of Organisational Development and the Chief Executive and from a review of company and policy documentation. However, recognising that the understanding of organisational culture is best achieved when no assumptions are made (e.g., Schein, 1990), the questions were open ended and guided by the participant responses. Examples of the questions asked were

- How do you feel Britannia has changed over the last three years?
- How effective do you feel communication is at Britannia?
- What role do you feel the Chief Executive and Directors have played in the process of cultural change?

Company and policy documentation

A review of written policies/guidelines and company documentation since the cultural change process began was undertaken. This included, for example, policies relating to flexible working practices, internal magazine for employees, website articles and other relevant internal documents.

Employee satisfaction surveys

As part of the change process, Britannia commissioned an external consultancy to conduct two employee satisfaction surveys each year. The survey process and findings were used to provide an indication of the impact of the culture change process on employee perceptions.

Underlying approach and strategies adopted

Various approaches to organisational culture change exist, but it is acknowledged that there is no one correct approach (Arnold, Cooper and Robertson, 1998). Unlike other culture change programmes, Britannia did not embark upon a series of large scale 'off-the shelf' interventions; change became more about the *ways in which things were done.* Furthermore, in a bid to achieve sustainable change it was recognised and clearly communicated that culture change is a medium-term 'journey' rather than an overnight or short-term process.

This section describes the underlying approach and the strategies that were adopted by Britannia in bringing about culture change.

People at the heart of cultural change

"People are at the heart of the strategy." *(Karen Moir, Director of Organisational Development)*

The underlying principle of Britannia's approach to culture change is a focus on people. For example, the Chief Executive held the view that the better the "people capability" is in a business then the better the organisation will be equipped in identifying and dealing with change.

"If your strategy is built around people, the development of the people . . . then you are developing people who will spot changes and tell you how to react." (Neville Richardson, Chief Executive)

Moreover, people issues were not viewed as the sole responsibility of the human resources department.

"It's about business and how we run the business not about a Human Resources Department. The Human Resources team may give advice but solutions are devised from a fully integrated approach to people." (Neville Richardson, Chief Executive)

The view that the development of an effective organisation is one in which its people are valued, listened to and developed was evidenced across all sources of information utilised in this case study. This belief is implicit in all the strategies outlined below.

Organisational values and strategy

Preceding the recognition of the need for change, Britannia lacked agreement on the purpose of its business. A soccer-pitch analogy was made in which it felt like a whole series of different games were being played on one pitch.

Thus a starting point for those at the top of the organisation was to ask, "What is the purpose of Britannia Building Society?" Following extensive consultation with key stakeholders, the Chief Executive and Executive Board clarified its purpose: "We are dedicated to helping our members achieve their goals" and developed the mission "To be known as Britain's best mutual – a great organisation to which our members and our people are proud to belong". From this, six "givens" were generated: an essential description of the key aspects for the achievement of its core purpose:

• remaining mutual and acting in the membership's best interests;
• being financially strong;
• being ethical, socially responsible and a model of compliance;
• being a great place to grow and develop;
• rewarding members through our loyalty scheme;
• maintaining an extensive branch network.

In addition, the core values generated that underlined the strategy were clearly stated; the organisation's enduring features. These, together with the givens, remain stable despite any changes in business practices and strategies. Britannia's values are:

• Putting our customers first.
• Being easy to do business with.
• Being excellent at communications.
• Taking personal responsibility.
• Being faster, cheaper, better.

Research demonstrates the importance of values for overall organisational effectiveness including employee development and the 'bottom line' (Collins and Porras, 2005; Fassel, Monroy and Monroy, 2000). An organisation's values have been shown to influence how employees interact with each other, how managers communicate and how general business decisions are made (Murphy and Cooper, 2000).

The articulation of organisational values is a relatively straightforward task. However, effective organisations are those that achieve alignment between values and subsequent behaviour. In practice this manifests itself in all levels of decision-making behaviour across all levels in the organisation, in recruitment and training and in the overall way in which 'things are done around here'.

The key elements of Britannia's approach are how the values have been utilised as a framework for behavioural change. Internally, this was phrased as 'Living the Values' and it was recognised that this starts at the top of the organisation. There was a clear understanding of the importance of leadership commitment to organisational values and the ensuing behaviours. In particular it was recognised how the alignment between 'what is said and what is done' is fundamental in encouraging employees to buy into the approach and to behave in similar ways.

The Chief Executive and Executive Board were unhesitating in applying the values to their own practices. The need for those at the top of the organisation to consistently demonstrate the values in their own practices was explicit; 'saying one thing and doing another' was not an option. Consequently, some senior employees whose practices were in conflict with the values exited the organisation. The implications of this for other employees in the organisation cannot be overstated. The approach was viewed favourably by employees and delivered a powerful message that there must be consistency between values and behaviour at all levels within the organisation:

"He [Neville Richardson, Chief Executive] was very clear that we all had to go in the same direction. The decision made to part company with some senior members that weren't evidencing the strategy sends a very powerful message."

"If you don't fit you stand out a mile. If you don't fit it's not going to work for either party."

The findings from the employee interviews reinforce the belief that senior managers consistently model and 'live' the values. Several other examples were given of how the Board members' behaviour was aligned with the values, including for example, taking personal responsibility to attend road shows, listening to employees' feedback and promoting products that put the customer first.

It is clear that this approach has filtered down through all levels of the organisation and has become implicit within day-to-day business practice. Clarifying the values has provided employees with a sense of direction and a framework to work within that had previously been absent.

During the interviews, employees described how the values were starting to become "engrained" in their thinking and how they affect not only the way they interact with customers but also their colleagues. For example, preceding the introduction of values, inter-departmental working was rare. However the values have now provided all departments with common goals and ways of working which has fostered a culture of working together.

They have also been responsible for the introduction of a performance management culture in which the values have been used as a criterion against which to judge performance. This is evident in the monthly "desk reviews" for employees, reward systems, formal appraisals and promotion avenues.

The company documentation, (e.g., written policies/guidelines and internal communication briefings) illustrates an alignment between the organisation's values and decision making about the businesses. It also evidences how the framework has been applied across all organisational practices including values-based recruitment and training for new employees.

Authenticity

In a comprehensive analysis of 18 organisations, researchers studied the key features of "visionary companies."[3] In addition to having a core set of values, it was also found that the authenticity of the approach was essential, and very often more important than the content of the ideology and values (Collins and Porras, 2005).

The authenticity of the approach adopted by the Chief Executive and the Directors at Britannia has been instrumental in the culture-change process.

"It's quite evident that the CEO *truly believes in the values and givens . . .*
He's passionate about them and the way he behaves shows this."

Employees have recognised this and in turn this has reinforced similar thoughts and behaviours in others. For example, one employee stated *"I'm a huge advocate of what we've achieved. I speak from the heart; before it was a corporate message, now I believe it."*

In another example, one employee spoke about the personal expression of gratitude that she and colleagues were given for the completion of a difficult piece of work. She reported that this approach demonstrated a genuineness that could not have been conveyed through written correspondence.

The authenticity demonstrated at senior level has filtered throughout the organisation. Departmental managers have become more "emotion" focused, listening to employees' views and responding to feedback.

Communication and consultation

In seeking to apply the approach described above, it was recognised that effective communication was a key ingredient in the whole culture-change process and a central component of every employee's role regardless of their level within the organisation.

The preceding culture had been characterised by a command-and-control approach whereby there was limited consultation and involvement of employees in decision making. In a bid to create a culture in which employee views count and where communication across all levels of the organisation was open, several methods were put in place to widen the communication channels and to reinforce the new strategy:

- employee road shows and workshops;
- written communication;
- increased visibility;
- active listening.

Employee road shows and workshops. Britannia took the decision to communicate the purpose, mission, values and givens face-to-face before providing written copies of each. The rationale for this approach was that verbal communication could enhance the authenticity of the message and give employees the opportunity to voice their views. The new strategy encompassing the purpose, mission, givens and values was launched at a conference in which various levels of employee from across the organisation attended (previously this had been restricted to managers). In addition, 37 road shows around the UK were facilitated to communicate the purpose, mission, values and givens to all employees. Since the launch of the new strategy, a total of 80 road shows have been facilitated. The key features of the road shows were that equal time was allocated to providing information and for listening to employees' views. The Chief Executive led all the road shows and where points of concern were raised, a Director was available to respond and to provide immediate feedback. These elements of good practice have been powerful in reinforcing the authenticity of the approach. They also demonstrated alignment between the value of 'personal responsibility' and subsequent behaviour.

"*He [Neville Richardson, Chief Executive] took personal responsibility by himself attending over 80 road shows that were resource intensive.*"

In addition to the road shows, a series of 'values workshops' were facilitated in which every team spent time outside the organisation understanding the framework. The aim of these workshops was to consider what the values meant for each team/department and each individual's role within the teams.

Written communication. The positive effects of the road shows have been maintained through a constant written reminder of the values and strategy. This has been achieved through monthly briefings on key aspects of the business and articles published in '*Hometruths*' magazine (for Britannia employees).

Increased visibility. In addition to the more formal methods of communication described above, there has been increased visibility of the Chief Executive and Directors across all levels of the organisation. This has included presence at employee briefings and visiting different departments. This has also served to reinforce the authenticity of those at the top of the organisation.

Listening to employee views. Since the launch of the new strategy, active listening and feedback have become a key element of Britannia's organisational culture. An environment has been fostered in which employees' views are listened to and responded to regardless of level within the organisation. The philosophy behind this approach is that perception is reality, with the Chief Executive stating, "If that's what it seems then that's what is real".

Employees' views are taken seriously and participation in decision making is actively encouraged at both a team and organisational level. For example, across most departments daily 'huddles' are held where issues can be raised and discussed as a team. These also provide an opportunity for verbal reinforcement of the organisation's values.

Britannia values the evaluations that employees make of their work environment and recognises how these perceptions influence behaviour. Therefore, employees are invited to feed back their views on organisational issues in the format of an employee satisfaction survey, which is sent to all employees twice annually.

The survey of employee satisfaction is not a new idea. However, the distinguishing feature of Britannia's approach is *what is done with the results*. It is not unusual for organisations to survey employees but not communicate the results. At Britannia the survey results are analysed across each of the businesses and for the organisation as a whole. The organisational development team then distribute reports summarising the findings to business leaders and managers. More detailed results and reports are also accessible from an electronic portal that managers can access. Within each business area, managers run focus groups and team meetings to address any concerns from the survey and to formulate an action plan. The action plans from these sessions are then collated into directorate reports, which are then fed back to the directors so that the progress can be monitored.

The findings of the employee satisfaction survey influence the business planning and decision-making practices within the organisation. Research shows that effective surveys are those that integrate results of employee surveys with business planning (e.g., Griffin, Hart and Wilson-Evered, 2000; Fassel, Monroy and Monroy, 2000). It is this alignment between staff perceptions and subsequent management decision making that differentiates Britannia from other organisations that survey without acting on the results.

"The whole point of Viewpoint [the employee satisfaction survey] is to give us a snapshot of the satisfaction of our people, so that we can understand and then improve it." (Hometruths. The magazine for the People of the Britannia Group, February 2006).

Leadership style

The strategies described above are all underpinned by a commitment to change at the top of the organisation. In addition, the leadership style of the Chief Executive is characterised by a desire to facilitate employees to be the best they can. Principally, this is achieved through the Chief Executive's focus on strategy and creation of a culture of effective communication.

"I can't do things on behalf of everybody, but the one thing I can do is create an environment where people can do it themselves." (Neville Richardson, Chief Executive)

"What I decided at the start was that I had two key roles. One was strategy and one was communication." (Neville Richardson, Chief Executive)

The link between leadership style and effective organisational practices is well articulated in the literature (e.g., Collins, 2001; Goleman, 2000). The practices evidenced at Britannia, and described above, attest to the significance of the approach adopted by the Chief Executive in bringing about cultural change. Indeed, the personal qualities, behaviours and style of leadership exhibited by the Chief Executive are akin to the description of emotional intelligence described by Goleman (2005). These include, for example, commitment to people and a cause, taking responsibility for actions and inspiring motivation.

Diversity and flexible working practices

Attention to work–life balance and recognition of diversity was seen as essential in the culture change process and in achieving alignment with the given "A great place to work, grow and develop". Diversity principles have become part of the fabric of the organisation rather than being seen as resource dependent or the responsibility of one department or employee.

In 2004, a framework of flexible working arrangements (internally known as 'Mutual Preferences') was introduced. This framework goes beyond a description of employees' legal rights, to include other flexible working arrangements offered to all employees. An accessible document is made available to all employees with a comprehensive overview of the flexible working arrangements offered by Britannia. Since the introduction of this policy there has been a growing increase in the number of employees on a flexible working arrangement. The proportion of employees with a flexible working arrangement is approximately one-third of the employee population at Britannia (with 20% of these being male).

An 'Enhancing Diversity programme' was also introduced to ensure that all employees were aware of diversity issues. The programme comprised an employee handbook and mandatory training for all employees.

Training

As with the majority of organisational change programmes, Britannia invested resources into employee training and development. A guiding philosophy was that training to assist culture change needed to be more than just about imparting skills and knowledge. Indeed, training about the organisation's ideologies, history and norms is recognised as a feature of visionary companies (Collins and Porras, 2005).

The roadshows described above became the starting point for this approach. This was later followed by 'The role of the manager' training which aimed to contextualise the strategies and values for middle managers in the organisation.

"All we were doing was raising awareness about the strategy." (Karen Moir, Director of Organisational Development)

"It was a three-year journey where raising awareness was achievement." (Neville Richardson, Chief Executive)

The process of culture change: implementation of strategies

Figure 13.1 illustrates the implementation process for the culture change strategies. It also highlights the key elements of best practice that were applied by Britannia.

As can be seen, the change process commenced with the development of a cohesive management structure at the top of the organisation. This was achieved through a variety of team assessment and development events. This created a climate appropriate for an examination of the purpose of Britannia, formulation of a strategy and the articulation of the values and givens. Subsequently, Britannia's purpose, mission, values and givens were communicated to all employees on a large scale through road shows and workshops.

Senior members then began to demonstrate these values in their behaviours and business practice alongside a widening of communication channels within the organisation. These latter two strategies have been consistently applied and are now integral features of the organisation in a bid to achieve sustainable change. Employee satisfaction surveys were introduced to the process to ensure not only a measurement of impact but also as a method for listening to employees' views, identifying areas of concern (hot spots) and informing subsequent business practice.

Outcomes

A full consideration of the outcomes of the culture change process at Britannia is beyond the scope of this case study. However, an overview of the impact of the process at an employee and organisational level is outlined.

Employee outcomes

Employee satisfaction survey. In addition to providing a method for employees to feed back their views on the organisation, the findings from the employee satisfaction survey can provide a measure of the impact of change.

The survey comprises 120 items over eight categories: leadership and direction; corporate strategy and values; supervision and management; role and responsibilities; involvement and participation; putting my customer first; taking personal responsibility; communications. Responses are rated on a 4-point scale, where 1 equals 'strongly agree' and 4 equals 'strongly disagree'.

Table 13.1 illustrates some of the findings from the May 2006 survey. It can be seen that a high percentage of employees either agreed or strongly agreed with a variety of statements about Britannia's values/givens and the

PROCESS

KEY ELEMENTS OF BEST PRACTICE

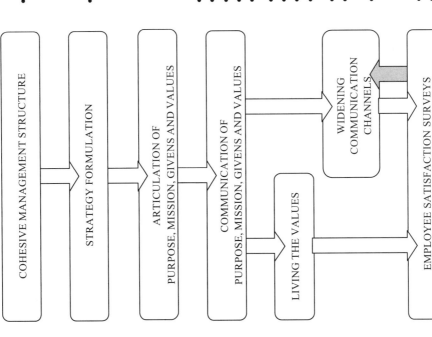

COHESIVE MANAGEMENT STRUCTURE

- Team development to encourage 'working together'

STRATEGY FORMULATION

- Consultation with key stakeholders

ARTICULATION OF PURPOSE, MISSION, GIVENS AND VALUES

COMMUNICATION OF PURPOSE, MISSION, GIVENS AND VALUES

- Chief Executive and Director presence
- Authenticity
- Active listening
- Face-to-face communication
- Consistently reinforced

LIVING THE VALUES

- Role modelling at the top of the organisation
- Permeates all business practice e.g. recruitment, performance management.
- Authenticity and consistency in modelling
- Applies at all levels in the organisation

WIDENING COMMUNICATION CHANNELS

- Active listening
- Written communication supported through increased visibility and face-to-face contact
- Participative approach with emphasis on employee feedback

EMPLOYEE SATISFACTION SURVEYS

- Results communicated to employees
- Results inform business practice
- Hot-spot focus groups

Figure 13.1 Implementation process and key elements of best practice.

Table 13.1 Employee satisfaction survey results

Item description	Percentage of employees who 'strongly agree' or 'agree'
Directors and senior managers actively demonstrate the appropriate Britannia group values and behaviours in the way they work	91
I feel the issues I raised in previous surveys are being addressed	80
I understand our Givens and Values	99
I am clear on what I can do differently to live the values	94
My immediate manager listens to my ideas	91
I believe the people I work with take personal responsibility	86
I am kept informed of why things are happening in the Britannia Group	87

communication processes. This would seem to suggest that the change has had a positive impact on the perceptions of its employees.

Culture survey. In addition to the employee satisfaction survey, a 'culture survey' has been administered annually as a method for measuring employee feelings and perceptions of relevant organisational behaviours. The survey comprises items generated from company documents and consultation with key stakeholders as to the positive and negative organisational behaviours required by Britannia. It requires employees to rate eight statements that describe feelings about the organisation on a 4-point rating scale, from 'strongly agree' to 'strongly disagree'. In addition, employees are asked to rate the observations of a series of negative and positive organisational behaviours utilising a 7-point frequency based rating scale where a rating of 1 refers to 'Never', 2 'Rarely', 3 'Infrequently', 4 'Sometimes', 5 'Frequently', 6 'Mostly' and 7 'Always'. For example, *"Managers are role models for our Values and preferred way of behaving" (positive behaviour), "In this organisation people put their own interests first" (negative behaviour)*. Table 13.2a illustrates the results from a selection of items from the 'feelings' section of the survey. Table 13.2b illustrates the results for a selection of items from the 'behaviours' section of the survey. Both sets of data are from the November 2005 survey.

As can be seen from Table 13.2a, a high percentage of employees either agreed or strongly agreed with some of the feelings statements from the culture survey. Table 13.2b lists items from the survey that relate to the strategies adopted by Britannia in bringing about cultural change (e.g.,

Table 13.2a Employee culture survey results: Feelings about the Britannia Group

Item description	Percentage of employees who 'strongly agree' or 'agree'
I do what is required because it genuinely seems to fit with my own values and beliefs	93
The senior people I respect are role models for the Values	88
The managers I regularly interact with inspire me to live the Values	83

Table 13.2b Employee culture survey results: behaviours observed in the Britannia Group

Item description	Most frequently occurring response
Managers are role models for our Values and preferred way of behaving	Mostly
Managers are open and receptive to new ideas	Mostly
Managers make every effort to communicate the right things at the right time	Mostly
Managers are role models for taking personal responsibility	Mostly
People actively seek and use feedback to assess the effectiveness of their communication	Sometimes
Managers encourage their people to be creative and generate new ideas	Mostly
People are clear on when they should take personal responsibility and when they should seek help	Mostly

Note: Based on calculation of the mode for each item.

alignment of values with behaviour and effective communication). It can be seen that the most frequently rated response for these items was 'mostly' or 'sometimes'.

Whilst it is acknowledged that these results need further exploration and clarification, they provide a useful starting point for demonstrating the positive impact of the culture change process at Britannia on employees' perceptions.

Organisational outcomes

The impact of the culture change process at Britannia is also evidenced at an organisational level. These effects include:

- record business results;
- record business profits;
- record customer satisfaction ratings;
- successful acquisition of Bristol and West from the Bank of Ireland. For example, a major consultation exercise with employees was undertaken, focusing on organisational structure and roles and responsibilities. This method of working has been seen to be accountable for the achievement of a successful systems integration within a nine-month time frame – external consultants had advised this would take 18 months.

Conclusion

The evidence outlined in this case study suggests that culture change is facilitated when employees are at the forefront of the approach and implementation process. Furthermore, the articulation of purpose and organisational values and subsequent alignment with behaviour has been an instrumental feature of the approach adopted by Britannia. Key to implementation has been a commitment to the approach and process at a senior manager level as demonstrated in a variety of practices. The authenticity of the approach by senior managers has filtered through the organisation and embedded new behaviours and learning in employee behaviour.

Effective communication and alignment of the values-driven approach with business practice has aided the change process and served to reinforce the approach. This has been evidenced across all levels of the organisation and is a key element of best practice.

Finally, it is argued that in addition to creating sustainable organisational change, the elements of best practice described in this case study aid the creation of a high involvement work organisation (Lawler, as cited in Murphy and Cooper, 2000).

REFERENCES

Burnes, B. (1998) Understanding organisational change. In Arnold, J., Cooper, C. L. and Robertson, I. T. (eds.) *Work psychology: Understanding human behaviour in the workplace.* Harlow: Pearson Education.

Cockman, P., Evans, B. and Reynolds, P. (1999) *Consulting for real people: A client-centred approach for change agents and leaders.* London: McGraw-Hill.

Collins, J. (2001) *Good to great: Why some companies make the leap and others don't.* London: Random House Business Books.

Collins, J. and Porras, J. I. (2005) *Built to last: successful habits of visionary companies.* 10th Anniversary Edition. London: Random House Business Books.

Fassel, D., Monroy, J. and Monroy, M. (2000) Improving organisational effectiveness through integration of core values. In L. R. Murphy and C. L. Cooper (eds.) *Healthy and productive work: An international perspective.* London: Taylor and Francis.

Goleman, D. (2000) *Working with emotional intelligence.* New York: Bantam Books.

(2005) *Emotional intelligence: Why it can matter more than IQ.* 10th Anniversary Edition. New York: Bantam Books.

Griffin, M. A., Hart, P. M. and Wilson-Evered, E. (2000) Using employee opinion surveys to improve organisational health. In L. R. Murphy and C. L. Cooper (eds.) *Healthy and productive work: An international perspective.* London: Taylor and Francis.

Schein, E. H. (1990) Organisational culture. *American Psychologist*, 45(2), 109–19.

Murphy, L. R. and Cooper, C. L. (eds.) (2000) *Healthy and productive work: An international perspective.* London: Taylor and Francis.

NOTES

1. The author wishes to thank David Conway for his contribution to the case study.
2. A mutual organisation is one that is owned by its members. Any profits made are used to benefit customers, not outside shareholders.
3. "Visionary companies prosper over long periods of time, through multiple life cycles and multiple generations of leaders" (Collins and Porras, 2005, p. 2).

14 Building the sustainable organization through adaptive, creative coherence in the HR system

Barry Colbert, Elizabeth Kurucz and David Wheeler

Introduction

"Without the private sector, sustainable development will remain only a distant dream. We now understand that both business and society stand to benefit from working together. And more and more we are realizing that it is only by mobilizing the corporate sector that we can make significant progress. The corporate sector has the finances, the technology and the management to make all this happen. The corporate sector need not wait for governments to take decisions for them to take initiatives".

– Kofi Annan, UN Secretary General, 2002

"More and more now we're looking at the concept of global sustainability, and what that means for the fundamental global drivers that are going to change the nature of our business. What implications is that going to have on us and our businesses, and how will we go about doing our business, in terms of closed systems and re-circulation systems and other sorts of things? And how can we impact some of the social problems facing the planet?"

Canadian Manufacturing Executive, 2005

These words from United Nations Secretary General Kofi Annan and an executive from heavy manufacturing industry illustrate the growing alignment of global and organizational leaders regarding the potential for positive transformation in the relationship between business and society. Over the past decade, scholars in the field of organizational sustainability have identified significant opportunities for value creation by firms that pursue the goal of sustainable development (Hart 1997; Hart and Milstein 2003; Kurucz, Colbert and Wheeler 2008; Wheeler, Colbert and Freeman, 2003). While academic scholarship is growing in this area, the management literature in general lags behind the increasingly urgent calls issued by leading practitioners in progressive business organizations who assert the imperatives for adopting more sustainable business practices (Holliday, Schmidheiny and Watts, 2002; Anderson, 1998). The practical motivation for these individuals is encapsulated in numerous 'business case' examples of organizations that have benefited by adopting strategic approaches to environmental and social issues impacting their organizations and sectors.

A natural question following adoption of a sustainability vision is: how to bring that vision alive inside the organization? What conceptual frameworks of organization and internal processes, in particular the Human Resource Management processes, are required to help to guide the development of both theory and practice in realizing this new business imperative? In other words, *how* might the sustainable organization be built?

Growing concerns described by advocacy organizations such as the World Resources Institute (WRI 2002) and leading scientific evidence from all corners of the globe (United Nations Environment Program, 2005) suggest that social and eco-systems are bowing under the weight of pressures unleashed from two transformations unprecedented in human history. The first was the 100-year transformation to an industrial-based society. The second was the transformation to a globalized economy which occurred in a just a few decades, accelerated massively by technological, political and cultural forces (Homer-Dixon, 2006). Given the parallel trend of a fundamental shift in power away from governments, and towards an increasingly pervasive influence of the corporate sector, many world leaders have suggested that if there is to be any hope of delivering sustainable development, it is imperative that business becomes significantly more involved in sustainable business practices (Hart, 1999). Some of the ways in which organizations create sustainable value (Hart and Milstein 1999; 2003) are well documented. They include low-risk initiatives such as the pursuit of eco-efficiency (De Simone and Popoff, 1997), to more radical and higher potential innovations, such as reconsidering the role of the private sector in developing nations (Wheeler *et al.*, 2005). However, the organizational and leadership challenges of how to accomplish these proposals are not well understood (Hart, 2005).

Exacerbating this lack of clarity concerning how to build more sustainable organizations are the traditional models of how change happens that are rooted in evolutionary (systems-based) or dialectical (Marxian) thinking (Stacey, 2003; Wheatley, 1992). Adopting either incremental or revolutionary perspectives on change may not be helpful in conceptualizing the internal organizational processes that might enable sustainability in organizations. Indeed, they may actually serve to reinforce the scepticism that organizational sustainability and forces of globalization are compatible (Barnett, 2004). The perspective that we advance in this chapter is that these traditional mental models of global systems and organizational change are unhelpful for envisioning organizational sustainability in the contextual reality of the twenty-first century.

In order to develop new mental models consistent with a highly networked world, metaphors from complexity science have been engaged by organization scholars in order to spark new insight into how organizations interact with the broader systems in which they are embedded (Morgan, 1996; Stacey, 2003). These new metaphors may help us to understand how to build the sustainable organization by subverting our dependence on traditional modes of conceptualizing organizational change, and offer new provocations for how we might envision organizations behaving and emerging in a rapidly changing context.

The growing pressure on all elements of our economic, social and ecosystems is amplified by the increasingly networked and rapidly evolving technological economy that represents the new reality of globalization (Wheeler, 2003). Thus, in order for the 'sustainable organization' to emerge, we suggest that what is needed is a fundamental shift in the frames we use to explain how change happens and what approaches to building organizational systems are most effective. To navigate external complexity, new internal resources and capabilities are required that will serve to build sustained competitive advantage for the firm (Barney, 1991). The "complex resource-based view" (Colbert, 2004), a perspective that operationalizes the traditional resource-based view (RBV) through the application of living systems heuristics, will allow us to identify the HR principles that are required to build capacity in terms of *connectivity, commitments, culture* and *capabilities* of the sustainable organization (Wheeler, 2003).

This chapter will explore the particular value that a complexity based approach to viewing organizational systems will confer in building the sustainable organization. We do this by considering the elements of the sustainable organization, described by the "4 C's model" of organizational sustainability (Wheeler, 2003), as they relate to the living systems' heuristics and relevant HR principles outlined by Colbert (2004). We will then identify insights provoked by the Complex RBV perspective for strategic human resource management practices in the context of the sustainable organization, constructing the outline of a coherent, adaptive HR system, and advancing understanding for managers of sustainably relevant HR principles and practices.

Conceptualizing the sustainable organization: 4 C's and complex RBV

In the face of global challenges and mounting uncertainty, managers are required daily to act, to marshal resources towards collective organizational ends. Human Resource managers, who include all managers of people, are charged with an even more daunting task: to align intangible resources to an often shifting strategy in an increasingly uncertain environment, akin to hitting a moving target in the dark. This task is less daunting if we focus not on the end point, but on the processes of adaptation and creative invention. Here we introduce two complementary frameworks derived independently in some of our prior work, each of which is aimed at helping to navigate uncertainty and complexity and which, taken together, form a richer framework for describing key leverage points for the human resource function in the sustainable organization.

The Four C's model for organizational sustainability

Based on a review of the management literature and some theoretical reasoning Wheeler, Colbert and Freeman (2003) advanced four candidate characteristics of the 'sustainable organization'. These characteristics were all deemed essential for the optimal navigation of uncertainty in a dynamic, globalizing and rapidly changing world: *connectivity, commitments, culture* and *capabilities* – the 'four C's' of sustainable management.

Building organizational *connectivity* requires that managers bring a systems-based approach to cognitively and consciously situating the organization in the context of macro global drivers across political, economic, social and ecological spheres. The organization is conceived as an entity that exists at the societal level and, as such, must be responsive to a pluralism of stakeholder concerns across each of these realms. This connectivity is essential, both to avoid potential risk to the organization from unanticipated issues emerging from these areas, and also to ensure that latent needs from these different areas are identified as sources of potential value creation. Examples of organizations that have learned this truth the hard way include Royal Dutch Shell (through the Brent Spar and Ogoni incidents), Monsanto (through the genetic modification controversy) and Union Carbide (through the Bhopal disaster and its aftermath).

Second, a focus on sustainable organizational *commitments* demands that managers incorporate a holistic perspective into organizational mission and goal setting, reconciling the pluralism of concerns illuminated through a systems-based approach to the external context with a focus on value creation across these domains. This commitment to the creation of multi-dimensional value is realized in the missions, codes, strategies, objectives and measures that managers establish in dialogue with the firm's stakeholders. In outlining these commitments managers must establish a shared understanding of the purpose of the firm, identify in whose interests the firm is run and declare the organization's commitment to maximizing value. Organizations that have succeeded in effecting radical strategic re-invention in this way include DuPont (diversification away from cyclical, commodity-based and non-renewable resource-based products and markets towards more knowledge-intensive and higher value add products and markets) and GE (through adoption of strategic stakes in the energy industries of the future and corporate repositioning around the concept of 'eco-imagination' which is showcased and celebrated on the company's home page).

Culture for the sustainable organization requires that that senior managers and executive teams embrace those multiple perspectives that characterize a global mindset, with an awareness of diversity across cultures and markets and the ability to synthesize a range of stakeholder demands. A sustainable organizational culture in this model is characterized by a focus on value maximization through recognizing the synergies between value dimensions – social, economic, and environmental value, for example – rather than adopting a view of trading off or simply preserving existing value. The globally situated conception of the organization and its commitments must be consonant with and entrenched within the internal values. Pioneers of sustainability cultures might include firms like Denmark's Novo Nordisk (healthcare), Texas-based Whole Foods (organic foods) and California-based Patagonia (outdoor apparel).

Finally, the organizational *capabilities* most significant for sustainability are leadership, learning, stakeholder inclusion, and innovation. These are essential in that they allow managers and employees to adapt, comprehend and navigate the complexity of the global and organizational contexts in which they are embedded. Which of these capabilities are "core competencies" depends on the particular competitive strategy, but the sustainable organization would require some level of threshold competency in each of these capabilities. Organizations that work hard on building their capabilities for sustainability might include many of the aforementioned firms, but nowhere are the capabilities more

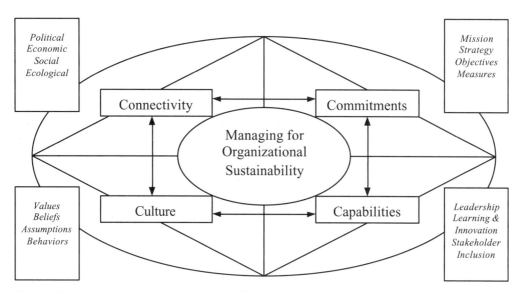

Figure 14.1 Managing for organizational sustainability.

important than in the extractive and natural resources industries where failure to build relationships with external constituencies results in direct denial of access to resources by communities and their advocates. Denver-based Newmont Mining's difficulties in expanding their gold mining operations in Peru are just one example of direct costs arising from difficult stakeholder relations. There are many other such examples from logging in British Columbia (MacMillan Blodel) to oil and gas extraction and transportation in Chad, Azerbaijan and Sakhalin, Russia (Exxon, BP and Shell). In contrast, firms that do build these capabilities tend to do well, for example Canadian oil and gas firms Suncor Energy and Nexen and Swedish/Finnish forestry firm Stora Enso.

Figure 14.1 depicts these '4 C's' of sustainable organizational management. Across all 4 C's, three commonalities emerge with regard to the role of managers in each of these aspects of organization. In order to simultaneously attend to these four domains, managers must be able to:

- adopt a systems-based perspective that allows for the recognition of pluralism;
- have the ability to synthesize a range of stakeholder interests to enable a holistic approach;
- promote a focus on value creation and value maximization on multiple fronts.

The complex resource-based view

If managing sustainably depends critically on building internal capacity and strategic resources with respect to managing organizational *connectivity, commitments, culture* and *capabilities*, the question arises: how is such sustainable strategic capacity developed, and what is the role for the HR system? In strategic management theory, it is the resource-based view (RBV) of the firm that attempts to describe how managers build strategic capabilities and compete 'from the inside out' (Barney, 1991, 1992), and the RBV serves as the most prevalent strategic perspective in research and theory in Strategic Human Resource Management (Barney and Wright, 1998; Snell, Yount and Wright, 1996; Wright, McMahan and McWilliams, 1994). The RBV has helped to build a productive theoretical bridge between the fields of strategy and HRM (Wright, Dunford and Snell, 2001), and serves as integrating ground on which much of SHRM theory and research is presented.

The resource-based view asserts that a firm develops competitive advantage by acquiring, developing, combining and effectively deploying its physical, human and organizational resources in ways that add unique value and are difficult for competitors to imitate (Barney, 1991). With the rise of the 'knowledge economy' over the past twenty-five years, the relative importance and value of human-based, intangible competitive resources such as knowledge, innovation, and learning, has risen proportionately. As such, most resource-based arguments are focused on human resources (the skills, knowledge, and behavior of employees) or organizational resources (control systems, routines, learning mechanisms), which are products of complex social structures built over time, and thus difficult to understand and imitate (Amit and Schoemaker, 1993; Conner, 1991; Mahoney and Pandian, 1992; Oliver, 1997; Peteraf, 1993). The RBV says that competitive advantage flows from *latent creative potential* and *idiosyncratic capabilities* (synchronous with the specific context), and that strategic resources must be valuable, rare, inimitable, and organizationally leveraged (Barney and Wright, 1998).

The resource-based view of firm strategy is a useful and simple way to conceptualize the contribution of firm resources, but it has been criticized for not being particularly useful to practicing managers, and for not offering much in the way of prescriptive advice on how to build strategically competitive resources. The development of intangible firm resources (such as a positive culture, or strong customer relationships) is *socially complex*, meaning that the phenomenon arises out of a myriad of complex, non-linear social interactions over time, and is *causally ambiguous* (Mosakowski, 1997). Thus it is hard to take apart and engineer, and moreover difficult to replicate.

The internal paradox of the RBV rests in the contention that in order to shield resources from scrutiny and imitation by competitors, and thereby protect and sustain competitive advantage, the nature and composition of the resource must remain causally ambiguous, to the degree that its origins may remain a mystery – even to the firm possessing it. Otherwise there is a danger of losing the advantage conferred by possession of the resource (Lippman and Rumelt, 1982). Put plainly: 'we are doing well, but we are not sure why, and if we examine and expose our source of advantage, we may lose it'. Therefore, while the RBV says that building deep capacity in strategic resources is critical, it also says that such resources emerge and typically are recognized only retrospectively. This is not a very useful idea for practising managers – who are ordinarily confined to operating in forward gear through the space-time continuum.

To resolve this logical conundrum, Colbert (2004) proposed an extension of the resource-based view in strategy by employing concepts from the science of complexity, and outlined the implications for strategic human resource management. Complexity is the study of linear and non-linear (stochastic) processes giving rise to emergent phenomena. Aspects of complexity are highly consonant with the critical but difficult aspects of the RBV. For example, four critical aspects of the RBV, as outlined in the extensive RBV strategy literature, are: (i) resources have adaptive potential as well as creative potential; (ii) strategic resources are causally ambiguous and emerge in complex, often inscrutable ways; (iii) they emerge over time depending on non-linear interactions (i.e., they are 'path-dependent'); and (iv) some resources are intangible and exist only at the system level, in relationships between things (like cooperation in the workforce, or a culture of knowledge sharing). These four aspects all make the RBV problematic, and they are all are central features of complex adaptive systems. Table 14.1 shows the alignment of the RBV and complexity; a focus on these features is termed *complex* RBV.

Complexity science involves the study of *complex adaptive systems* (CAS): systems characterized by networks of relationships that are independent, interdependent, and layered (Langton, 1989; Holland, 1975; Zimmerman, Lindberg and Plesk, 1998). Complex systems are generally characterized by two features: a *large number of interacting agents*, and the presence of stable, observable *emergent properties* – the appearance of patterns which are due to the collective behavior of the components of the system (Morel and Ramanujam,

Table 14.1 Complex-RBV: Critical-but-difficult features of the RBV and key features of complex systems (from Colbert 2004)

Key features	The resource-based view	Complexity
Creativity/adaptivity	• Competitive advantage grows from latent creative potential embedded in firm resources	• Complex adaptive systems learn and create new responses to their contextual environment
Complexity and ambiguity	• Inimitability arises from social complexity and causal ambiguity	• Living systems are comprised of complex interrelationships that are non-linear, non-deterministic, and unpredictable
Disequilibrium, dynamism, path dependence	• Complex relationships build over time, are historically dependent; disequilibrium is the creative state; dynamism, process issues are paramount.	• Systems thrive and create at far-from-equilibrium states; equilibrium leads to stagnation, decline, and death; history matters; paths unfold irreversibly through time
System-level resources	• Some key strategic resources are intangible, and exist only at the system-level, in relationship	• Some elements only exist at the system-level, in the dynamic relationships *between* things.

1999). Order emerges as the system under observation evolves and adapts with its context, although system boundaries are always somewhat arbitrarily drawn. Complex systems are 'living systems', which either continuously adapt and thrive, or die. Such living systems "are integrated wholes whose properties cannot be reduced to those of smaller parts. Their essential, or 'systemic', properties are properties of the whole, which none of the parts have. They arise from the 'organizing relations' of the parts – that is, from a configuration of ordered relationships that is characteristic of that particular class of organisms, or systems. Systemic properties are destroyed when a system is dissected into isolated elements" (Capra, 1996:36).

Kelly (1994) outlined a set of abstract principles for the growth of living systems, synthesized from diverse streams of complexity research. Seven of these principles are:

Distribute being: Allow that systems are not contained in discrete bodies; living systems are distributed over a multitude of smaller units. All the mysteries we find most interesting – life, intelligence, evolution – are found in the soil of large distributed systems.

Pursue multiple goals: Survival is a many-pointed goal. A complicated structure has many masters, and none of them can be served exclusively. An adaptive system must trade off between exploiting a known path of success (optimizing a current strategy), or diverting energy to exploring new paths (thereby wasting energy and reducing efficiency).

Maximize the fringes: A diverse, heterogeneous entity can adapt to the world in a thousand daily mini-revolutions, staying in a state of permanent, but never fatal, churning. In economic, ecological, evolutionary, and institutional models, a healthy fringe speeds adaptation, increases resilience, and is almost always the source of innovations.

Cultivate increasing returns: Each time you use an idea, a language, or a skill, you strengthen it, reinforce it, and make it more likely to be used again. That's known as positive feedback, or snowballing. Anything which alters its environment to increase production of itself is playing the game of increasing returns.

Control from the bottom up: When everything is connected to everything in a distributed network, wide and fast moving problems route around any central authority. Overall governance must arise from interdependent acts done locally in parallel, and not from a central command.

Grow by chunking: Allow complex systems to emerge out of the links among simple systems that work well and are capable of operating independently. Attempts to install highly complex organization, without growing it, inevitably lead to failure. Complexity is created by assembling it incrementally from simple modules that can operate independently.

Honour your errors: The process of going outside the usual method, game, or territory is indistinguishable from error. Even the most brilliant act of human genius is an act of trial and error. System evolution can be thought of as systematic error management.

Colbert (2004) combined the RBV and complexity by drafting HR management heuristics based on these *living system* principles, and offered one possible translation of such principles into the HR system architecture, flowing from more abstract to more concrete elements: HR principles to HR policies to HR practices. Application of these heuristics in concert can lend an overall coherence to the HR system and practices.

These heuristics characterize the behaviour of living systems that are adapting, creating, and thriving, and so are useful in thinking about the *connectivity, commitments, culture* and *capabilities* outlined by Wheeler (2003) as

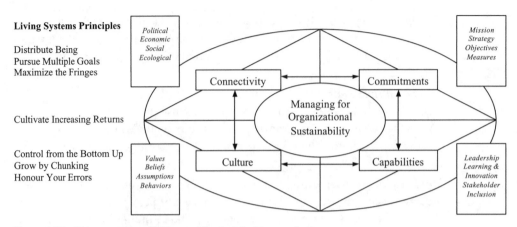

Figure 14.2 Living systems principles and the sustainable organization.

critical components of organizational sustainability. In the next section we combine the living systems principles for complex resource-based advantage with the four C's for organizational sustainability, in order to generate ideas for sustainable management through HR practices, and to offer some possible specifications for an HR architecture that is coherent and self-reinforcing.

The 4 C's model and HR processes with a living systems view

The living systems principles are broadly interpretable across organizational system boundaries. However, for our purposes we will consider the first three – *distribute being, pursue multiple goals,* and *maximize the fringes* – as they apply to the view outward from the organization, or to the top half of the 4 C's model, to *connectivity* and *commitments*. The latter three – *control from the bottom up, grow by chunking,* and *honour your errors,* we will consider with an internal organizational focus (the lower portion of the 4 C's model). The fourth principle, *cultivate increasing returns,* serves as a central credo to sustainable organizations, so we will consider that from both an inward and outward view. Figure 14.2 arrays these principles thus along the 4C's model, and Table 14.2 presents possible operational ideas and specifications across sixteen cells. These ideas are intended to be illustrative of the possibilities, and not exhaustive. Our aim is to elaborate ideas for developing capacity in each of the 4C's, while maintaining a coherent approach guided by some relevant living systems principles.

Table 14.2 Elaborating the 4 C's using living system principles – building coherence

	Four C's for managing for organizational sustainability (from Wheeler, 2003)	
Living system heuristics for complex RBV	**Connectivity**	**Commitments**
• with HR Principles (from Colbert 2004)	Societal level, systems-based view of the organization in global context	Create value on multiple fronts, install in mission and goals of the organization
Distribute being • Eradicate arbitrary borders • Build broad-based identity and capability	• Form connections across organizational boundaries • Build corporate identity and image in relation to the organization's role in society	• Develop shared goals with a range of stakeholder groups • Build identity through the development of a broad mission that extends beyond just organizational sustainability
Maximize the fringes • Embrace debate • Experiment	• Open generative dialogue with a wide range of stakeholders on the role of the organization in society • Experiment with stakeholders in opportunities for organizational value creation	• Encourage debate regarding the goals, codes and strategies of the organization • Advance commitments in a transparent manner and incorporate feedback in their evolution
Pursue multiple goals • Incorporate stakeholder perspectives aspirations • Tolerate multiple aims	• Embrace plurality in conversations with stakeholders • Create space for alternative methods for connecting to constituent groups and soliciting input to organizational direction • Link reputation to internal identity in virtuous cycle • Continuously relate organizational outcomes societal objectives	• Undertake collaborative goal setting in interaction with stakeholders, seeking win-win outcomes rather than tradeoffs • Develop an inclusive mission that will enable the creation of value on multiple fronts • Develop commitments that are strategic leverage points for the organization • Include stakeholders in the full-cycle planning processes for developing codes and strategies, from scanning to evaluation

(cont.)

Table 14.2 (*cont.*)

	Four C's for managing for organizational sustainability (from Wheeler, 2003)	
Cultivate increasing returns	**Culture**	**Capabilities**
• Seek opportunities to create positive reinforcement in the system • Be deliberate with language and symbols	Values, beliefs consistent with the organization's role in a globalized world • Seek integration on grounds of like values, create values-based networks • Create meanings around sustainability to develop mindsets for enabling innovation and change toward sustainability	Allow leaders to learn and navigate by incorporating multiple perspectives • Develop constantly evolving capabilities that are aligned with global organizational strategy • Reinforce and establish certain capabilities as core competencies over time through the deliberate use of language
Control from the bottom up • Feed information to all levels • Democratize the workplace	• Systematically include employees and business partners with different cultural and cognitive influences in policy setting • Create a culture of engagement, connecting the work of employees to the global role of the organization	• Develop strengths in stakeholder inclusion and network building that will feed information to all levels in the organization • Engage in meaningful partnerships with stakeholder groups (e.g., unions) to assist with democratization of the workplace
Grow by chunking • Encourage local innovation • Build learning capacity	• Provoke learning through local innovation inspired by cognitive diversity of organizational teams • Promote learning as a key organizational value	• Build leadership that legitimates a sustainability frame and gives permission for innovation towards more sustainable actions • Build capacity for continuous learning in a rapidly changing environment
Honour your errors • Encourage reflective practice	• Place an emphasis on reflective practice to inculcate a global mindset	• Focus on learning, adaptation and innovation, incorporating stakeholder interests to promote "creative destruction"

Connectivity: Relevant living systems principles

The principle of *cultivating increasing returns* is useful in thinking about the development of internal resources for *connectivity* in the sustainable organization. Opportunities for positive reinforcement can be encouraged through linking the organization's reputation with its internal identity in a virtuous cycle, by continuously relating organizational outcomes to societal objectives, and making adjustments for gaps between these two dimensions to build progress toward societal level sustainability. The growth and success of the Co-operative Bank in the UK and the Van City Credit Union in Canada provide good examples from the financial services industry of organizations that have leveraged well-established organizational identities in a highly active way through external campaigns and reputation building – especially with customers. In so doing, both have achieved unprecedented levels of stakeholder loyalty and consumer identification. *Distribute being* means nesting the organizational identity in institutions and relationships outside its borders, which requires managers to form connections across organizational boundaries and expand the scope of the firm beyond insular concerns. Taking a societal level systems-based perspective will allow for a broader range of perspectives to inform the approaches to risk reduction and value creation that the firm entertains. This approach to building broad-based identity and eradicating borders will enable the organization to build a corporate identity in relation to the organization's role in society, rather than being solely inwardly focused on a narrower range of organizational values and beliefs which can lead to a sub-optimal organizational narcissism. Whilst not advancing an explicit sustainability mission, firms like Google and Yahoo! and the opensource operating systems entity Linux represent bold, values-based, hyperinclusive business models that inspire a new vision for the role of business in society. Japanese automotive makers Toyota and Honda have demonstrated how sustainability values can be transported up and down the value chain just as effectively as quality management. This achieves supplier, firm, dealer and consumer alignment around a sustainability commitment made explicit by the manufacture and distribution of more environmentally efficient vehicles (including luxury brands like Lexus). Under *connectivity*, the heuristic of *maximizing the fringes* provides a provocation to managers to open generative dialogue with a wide range of stakeholders on the role of the organization in society and to experiment with stakeholders in identifying opportunities for organizational value creation. A plethora of 'fair trade' organizations have long pursued such a strategy through direct trading with distant producer communities in developing countries and effecting sales through northern-based solidarity networks. But now they are seeing their business models replicated by wholesale giants such as Nestlé and Starbucks and European retailers like Marks and Spencer and Sainsbury's. *Pursuing multiple goals* means embracing plurality and creating space for alternative methods of connecting with constituents in these conversations, which will enable the development of internal resources through and influence decisions about the organization's direction.

Connectivity: Leverage points in the HR system and processes

Table 14.3 outlines potential leverage points in the HR system to advance the development of connective capacity. Key processes identified here are organization development (OD), which is defined variously across organizations, but which typically includes process facilitation and functions of change management; Strategic human resource planning (HRP), which we take to include demand and supply forecasting of people requirements, along with succession management processes; Talent management (TM), including recruitment and selection and performance management processes and Training and development (T&D), which is included under talent management in some organizations, but which is a sufficiently important function to warrant separate consideration here. Again, this table is intended to be illustrative rather than exhaustive.

Connectivity, or a societal level, systems-based cognitive positioning of the organization within a globalized environment, can be enhanced by building business cases for change on a broad conception of the organization's role in society (OD); by foregrounding global ecological and social trends into the environmental scanning at the front end of HR planning processes (HRP); by arranging developmental secondments of high potential employees within stakeholder-responsive organizations – in not-for-profits, or in customer plants, for example (TM); and by inviting civil society representatives in as speakers in corporate training programs, to offer an outside, perhaps critical, view of the organization and to provoke reflection (T&D). Expanding mindsets and re-framing the conception of the organization is a critical component to building greater contextual connectivity, and there several key roles for HR in helping make that happen. Indeed, "[t]he ability to identify and help others discover their mind-sets and mental models, and the capability to change those mind-sets when necessary, are possibly

Table 14.3 Finding leverage points in the HR system to build a coherent approach to managing organizational sustainability

	Leverage points in the HR system for managing for organizational sustainability			
Leverage points in the HR system and processes	**Connectivity** Societal level, systems-based view of the organization in global context	**Commitments** Create value on multiple fronts, install in the mission and goals of the organization	**Culture** Values, beliefs consistent with the organization's role in a globalized world	**Capabilities** Allow leaders and employees to learn and navigate by incorporating multiple perspectives
Organization development/change management	• Build business cases for change on a broad conception of the organization in society • Facilitate generative dialogue with diverse stakeholders	• Frame change management deliverables along multi-dimensional value creation objectives • Design meaningful work and jobs that align with organizational objectives	• Foreground sustainability values in change management processes • Integrate sustainability based values (justice, respect) into organizational communication processes	• Foster and facilitate 'sustainability conversations' among senior leaders • Implement appreciative conflict resolution processes to include multiple perspectives
Strategic human resource planning	• Foreground global, economic, social and ecological trends in environment scanning for HR forecast modeling • Establish point people in new geographical markets	• Employ a Delphi forecasting technique drawing on diverse external stakeholders • Build in a requirement for broad exposure to diverse value creation fronts into leadership succession management	• Include soft skills such as learning, leadership and innovation in assessments of HR supply and demand • Reflect globally focused values in expatriate selection processes	• Develop a broad set of competencies for use in forecasting models • Include assessments of integrative thinking capacity in succession management readiness assessments

(cont.)

Table 14.3 (cont.)

	Leverage points in the HR system for managing for organizational sustainability		
Talent management/ performance management	• Integrate a socially connected view of the organization into recruitment messages • Arrange development secondments and exchanges with stakeholder organizations	• Include goals of multi-point value creation in upstream development of talent pools, e.g. funding to schools • Encourage unconventional developmental assignments across disciplines to maximize the fringes	• Include explicit values-based behavioural expectations in recruitment and in selection screens for applicants • Integrate 'values performance' in leadership assessments	• Recruit for integrative capacity at entry and leadership levels • Encourage reflection and learning from mistakes in performance evaluation and management processes
Training and development	• Include external civil society representatives as speakers in corporate training programs • Emphasize relational skills and global business acumen in T&D programs	• Include context on global positioning in all T&D programs • Integrate multi-dimensional organizational objectives into career development processes	• Provide training on methods of reflective practice • Provide training on organizational values and their interpretation	• Develop leadership capability for active stakeholder engagement • Employ pedagogical methods that include multiple perspectives

among the most critical capabilities an HR professional can have or acquire" (Pfeffer, 2005:125).

Commitments: Relevant living systems principles

Cultivating increasing returns provides some insight into how internal resources around *commitments* can be encouraged in the sustainable organization. This principle implies creating positive reinforcement through developing commitments that are strategic leverage points for the organization. Including stakeholders in the full cycle of planning processes for developing codes and strategies, from scanning to evaluation, will support this synergistic aim. Royal Dutch Shell's famed scenario planning would be one example of how strategy may be informed by the mobilization of external and internal stakeholders with opinions on the future. The heuristic of *distributing being* encourages the organization to eradicate arbitrary boundaries through developing shared goals with a range of stakeholder groups. The Body Shop International's experiments with social auditing in the early 1990s could be described as an attempt to develop and share goals iteratively with stakeholders. Broadening the scope of the firm means that organizational identity may be built through the development of a mission that extends beyond organizational level sustainability, one that is aimed toward creating value on multiple fronts. Through *maximizing the fringes*, debate may be encouraged within the organization regarding the commitments that are being advanced, encouraging a more robust set of goals, codes and strategies. Experimentation through advancing commitments in a transparent manner will enable feedback to be incorporated by the firm as to how effective these commitments are in encouraging movement towards the broader societal goals of sustainability. *Pursuing multiple goals* in the sustainable organization also translates to collaborative interaction with stakeholders in goal setting as a way to incorporate stakeholder perspectives and aspirations. Through developing an inclusive mission that represents diverse aims, the creation of value on multiple fronts will be made possible.

Commitments: Leverage points in the HR system and processes

Building capacity for making sustainable *commitments*, which means explicitly installing the aim of value creation on social, economic, and ecological fronts into the organizational 'meaning' architecture (mission, vision, goals), is a key role of the HR system. Organization design should follow the intended function of multi-front objectives (OD); succession management systems can deliberately expose developing leadership candidates to organizational functions that focus on different aspects of 'triple bottom line' (Elkington, 1998) value creation (HRP); upstream development of talent pools (e.g., funding information sessions to primary schools programs) can include awareness building on the need to create environmental and social value along with economic prosperity (TM); and career development processes can incorporate a broad conception of the organization to allow greater space for employees to 'find their passion' and get engaged in the business of value creation (T&D).

Culture: Relevant living systems principles

Building internal resources in the area of culture can be enlightened by the living systems principle of *cultivating increasing returns* by seeking integration on grounds of like values and creating value-based networks of communities of interest to accomplish this goal. In the sustainable organization, managers must work to create meanings around sustainability that will encourage mindsets enabling innovation and change towards more sustainable practices. Visionary business leaders like Ray Anderson (Interface Carpets) and Yvon Chouinard (Patagonia) are exemplars of such an approach and how it may lead to product innovation and enhanced value for customers. The heuristic of *control from the bottom up* illuminates the need for systematic inclusion of employees and business partners with different cultural and cognitive influences in policy setting in the organization. Unilever is one example of a global firm that attempts to embed cultural diversity in its operations through active local hiring and development. This enrichment of the workplace should encourage the flow of information between levels in the organization through developing a culture of engagement. The directive to *grow by chunking* in the culture of the sustainable organization promotes an emphasis on learning, where local innovation is inspired by the cognitive diversity embodied in organizational teams. An essential aspect of this focus on learning embraced in the culture of the sustainable organization is the principle *honour your errors*. An outcome of considering this living systems' heuristic in relation to the cultural component of the sustainable organization is an emphasis on reflective practice that will serve to inculcate a global mindset. This is characterized by a pluralistic approach where information systems that integrate feedback from a wide range of stakeholders are an essential component of the organization's culture.

Culture: Leverage points in the HR system and processes

Wright and Snell (2005) outline three challenges for HR professionals in the coming decade: intimately knowing the business they are supporting, demonstrating that their work is relevant to that business, and maintaining a focus on positive organizational values – and they warn of the dangers of over committing on the first two to get 'a seat at the table', then forgetting the third, at the expense of long-term organizational health. The HR function can help foster a sustainable culture by foregrounding positive values in change management and organizational communication processes (OD); by including consideration of softer, intangible skills like leadership and learning capacity in assessing HR supply and demand (HRP); by including values-screens in recruitment and selection processes through behavioural-based interviewing (TM); and by providing training on understanding and interpreting the values-in-action, and in their application to corporate policy.

Capabilities: Relevant living systems principles

In the area of capabilities, the sustainable organization can be directed to *cultivate increasing returns* by seeking to develop constantly evolving capabilities that are aligned with their global organizational strategy. This alignment will serve to create positive reinforcement between the evolving strategies and the dynamic capabilities that can help both to create and to realize these strategies. The deliberate use of language and symbols will assist to reinforce and establish certain capabilities over time as core competencies of the sustainable organization. The development of internal resources in the area of capabilities can be informed by the principle *control from the bottom up* through developing strengths in stakeholder inclusion and network building that will help to feed information to all levels in the organization. By engaging in meaningful partnerships with stakeholder groups, a democratization of the workplace may be encouraged. *Growing by chunking* encourages local innovation through developing leadership capabilities that legitimate a sustainability frame and give permission for innovating towards more sustainable practices. This heuristic illuminates the importance of building capacity for continuous learning for the sustainable organization in a rapidly changing environment. The

directive *honour your errors* when considered in relation to capabilities necessitates a focus on learning, adaptation and innovation through reflective
practice. By developing these capabilities through incorporating stakeholder
interests, "creative destruction" of the organization may be enabled, supporting the reinvention and competitive revitalization of the sustainable organization. Organizations with an explicit approach to capability-building for
sustainability are frequently those that show up in connectivity, commitments and culture domains, that is the sorts of companies listed throughout this chapter. Such organizations may also be observed in benchmark
associations such as the CEO-led World Business Council on Sustainable
Development which unites "180 international companies in a shared commitment to sustainable development through economic growth, ecological
balance and social progress". They may also be found as active members in
membership groups such as the UN Global Compact whose many hundreds
of business members are embraced by a mission which seeks "to promote
responsible corporate citizenship so that business can be part of the solution to the challenges of globalisation". It is often through these organizations and their many national counterparts that capabilities for leadership,
learning and stakeholder inclusivity are fostered at the most senior levels of
corporations.

Capabilities: Leverage points in the HR system and processes

Capabilities for sustainable organizational management include leadership,
learning, innovation and stakeholder inclusion, and the HR function is instrumental in building capacity in each of these areas. Fostering and facilitating 'sustainability conversations' among senior leaders can help to clarify
the various conceptions of sustainability at work within the organization,
and can lead to more concerted action (OD); up and coming leadership
candidates can be assessed for their capacity to think integratively regarding diverse stakeholder needs (HRP); performance evaluations can include
deliberate reflective practice, in which the person under evaluation considers what was learned from successes and disappointments over the past
period (TM); and leaders are groomed to be adept at engaging a variety
of stakeholders in different situations – employees on the job, community
constituents at a town hall meeting, or a meaningful customer interface
(T&D).

Conclusions

Deep challenges are facing the globe: environmental degradation, social injustice, and a growing disparity in the distribution of economic prosperity. Advancement towards global sustainability relies heavily on meaningful engagement of the business sector, which in turn depends on building effective, sustainable organizations. Creative, adaptive organizations are those that build and align intangible organizational resources in ways congruous with their operating environment. Since the global operating environment of most organizations is becoming increasingly complex, we contend that a complex process view of resource development is appropriate and helpful.

By combining the 4 C's of managing for organizational sustainability – *connectivity, commitments, culture* and *capabilities* – and living systems principles via Complex RBV – *distribute being, pursue multiple goals, maximize the fringes, cultivate increasing returns, control from the bottom up, grow by chunking,* and *honour your errors* – we open a wide array of ideas for bringing creative, adaptive coherence to the HR systems of would-be sustainable organizations. Managers of sustainable organizations must operate in forward gear in an increasingly complex global environment, and they must do more than simply hope that strategic resources emerge. The ideas offered here may allow managers to act coherently in constructing the conditions for the emergence of sustainable organizations, to implement adaptive HR policies, and to build organizations that work for their stakeholders and, more broadly, for the global human and ecological good.

REFERENCES

Amit, R. and P. J. H. Schoemaker (1993) "Strategic assets and organizational rent." *Strategic Management Journal 14(1)*: 33–46.

Anderson, R. (1998) *Mid-course correction.* Atlanta, GA: Chelsea-Green.

Barnett, M. L. (2004) "Are globalization and sustainability compatible?" *Organization and Environment 17(4)*: 523–32.

Barney, J. B. (1991) "Firm resources and sustained competitive advantage." *Journal of Management 17(1)*: 99–120.

(1992) Integrating organizational behavior and strategy formulation research: A resource-based analysis. In [P. Shrivastava, A. Huff and J. Dutton, (eds.)] *Advances in strategic management.* Greenwich, NJ: JAI Press.

Barney, J. B. and P. M. Wright (1998) "On becoming a strategic partner: the role of human resources in gaining competitive advantage." *Human Resource Management 37(1)*: 31–46.

Capra, F. (1996) *The web of life: A new scientific understanding of living systems.* New York: Anchor.

Colbert, B. A. (2004) "The complex resource-based view: Implications for theory and practice in strategic human resource management." *Academy of Management Review 29(3)*: 341–58.

Conner, K. R. (1991) "A historical comparison of resource-based theory and five schools of thought within industrial organization economics: Do we have a new theory of the firm?" *Journal of Management 17(1)*: 121–54.

De Simone, L. D. and F. Popoff (1997) *Eco-efficiency: The business link to sustainable development.* Cambridge, MA: MIT Press.

Elkington, J. (1998) *Cannibals with Forks.* Gabriola Island, B.C.: New Society.

Hart, S. L. (1997) "Beyond greening: strategies for a sustainable world." *Harvard Business Review 75(1)*: 66–76.

    (1999) Corporations as agents of global sustainability: Beyond competitive strategy. In *Organizational dimensions of global change: No limits to cooperation.* D. L. Cooperrider and J. E. Dutton (eds.). Thousand Oaks, CA: Sage 346–61.

Hart, S. (2005) *Capitalism at the crossroads: The unlimited business opportunities in solving the world's most difficult problems.* Upper Saddle River, NJ: Wharton School Publishing.

Hart, S. L. and M. B. Milstein (1999) "Global sustainability and the creative destruction of industries." *Sloan Management Review 41(1)*: 23–33.

Hart, S. L. and M. Milstein (2003) "Creating sustainable value." *Academy of Management Executive 17(2)*: 56–69.

Holland, J. H. (1975) *Adaptation in natural and artificial systems.* Ann Arbor, MI: University of Michigan Press.

Holliday, C. S. Schmidheiny and P. Watts (2002) *Walking the talk: The business case for sustainble development.* San Francisco, CA: Berrett-Koehler.

Homer-Dixon, T. (2006) *The upside of down: catastrophe, creativity, and the renewal of civilization.* Washington, D.C.: Island Press.

Kelly, K. (1994) *Out of control: The rise of neo-biological civilization.* Reading, MA: Addison-Wesley.

Kurucz, E., B. Colbert and Wheeler (2008) The business case for CSR. In *The Oxford handbook of corporate social responsibility.* D. Seigel, A. Crane, D. Matten, J. Moon and A. McWilliams (eds.) Oxford: Oxford University Press.

Langton, C. G., ed. (1989) *Artificial life: Santa Fe Institute Studies in the Sciences of Complexity.* Redwood City, CA: Addison-Wesley.

Lippman, S. and R. Rumelt (1982) "Uncertain imitability: An analysis of interfirm difference in efficiency under competition." *Bell Journal of Economics 13*: 418–38.

Mahoney, J. T. and R. J. Pandian (1992) "The resource-based view within the conversation of strategic management." *Strategic Management Journal 13(5)*: 363–80.

Morel, B. and R. Ramanujam (1999) "Through the looking glass of complexity: The dynamics of organizations as adaptive and evolving systems." *Organization Science 10(3)*: 278–93.

Morgan, G. (1996) *Images of organization.* Thousand Oaks, CA: Sage.

Mosakowski, E. (1997) "Strategy making under causal ambiguity: Conceptual issues and empirical evidence." *Organization Science 8(4)*: 414–42.

Oliver, C. (1990) "Determinants of interorganizational relationships: Integration and future directions." *Academy of Management Review 15(2)*: 241–65.

Peteraf, M. A. (1993) "The cornerstones of competitive advantage: A resource-based view." *Strategic Management Journal 14(3)*: 179–91.

Pfeffer, J. (2005) "Changing Mental Models: HR's Most Important Task." *Human Resource Management 44(2)*: 123–28.

Snell, S. A., Yount, M. A. and Wright, P. M. (1996) Establishing a framework for research in human resource management: Merging resource theory and organizational learning. *Research in Personnel and Human Resources Management, 14* 61–90.

Stacey, R. (2003) *Strategic management and organizational dynamics: The challenge of complexity.* Harlow, Essex: Pearson Education.

United Nations Environment Program (2005) *Living beyond our means: natural assets and human well-being (Statement of the MA Board).* Nairobi, Kenya: UNEP

Wheatley, M. J. (1992) *Leadership and the new science.* San Francisco, CA: Berrett-Koehler.

Wheeler, D. (2003) The successful navigation of uncertainty: Sustainability and the organization. In *Leading in turbulent times: Managing in the new world of work.* R. J. Burke and G. L. Cooper (eds.). London: Blackwell.

Wheeler, D., B. Colbert and Freeman (2003) "Focusing on Value: Reconciling Corporate Social Responsibility, Sustainability and a Stakeholder Approach in a Network World." *Journal of General Management 28(3)*: 1–28.

Wheeler, D., K. McKauge, J. Thomson, R. Davies, J. Medayle and M. Prada (2005) "Creating Sustainable Local Enterprise Networks." *MIT Sloan Management Review* Fall: 33–40.

WRI (2002) *Tomorrow's Markets: Global trends and their implications for business.* Washington, D. C., World Resources Institute.

Wright, P. M., G. C. McMahan and McWilliams (1994) "Human resources and sustained competitive advantage: a resource-based perspective." *International Journal of Human Resource Management 5(2)*: 301–26.

Wright, P. M., B. B. Dunford and Snell (2001) "Human resources and the resource based view of the firm." *Journal of Management* 27: 701–21.

Wright, P. M. and S. A. Snell (2005) "Partner or guardian? HR's challenge in balancing value and values." *Human Resource Management 44(2)*: 177–82.

Zimmerman, B. J., C. Lindberg and P. Plesk (1998) *Edgeware: Insights from complexity science for health care leaders.* Irving, TX: VHA, Inc.

15 Be in to Win – from absence to attendance in Royal Mail group

Stuart Kennedy and Tony McCarthy

'Be in to Win' was part of an innovative approach by Royal Mail Group to tackle the growing issue of chronic levels of unauthorised absence within the organisation. The approach involved a six-month scheme in which all employees with a 100 percent attendance record were entered into a draw to win one of thirty-seven brand new Ford cars. Initially seen by some in the media as a gimmick centered on bribery, the 'Be in to Win' incentive scheme increased attendance at Royal Mail by 18 percent, resulted in an average of 2,000 extra people at work per day and saved the business over £80 million in sick absence payments and lost time. Royal Mail's positive approach to absence management played a large part in helping the organisation return to profitability and record the highest levels of quality for over ten years.

Founded 360 years ago Royal Mail Group is one of the largest single employers in Europe, with over 185,000 people throughout the United Kingdom and 14,000 people in mainland Europe. Royal Mail's letters business delivers to over 27 million UK addresses and moves over 80 million items of mail every night. Post Office Limited, Royal Mail's retail arm, has over 14,000 outlets, 55,000 indirectly employed agents and 28 million customers per week, making it by far the UK's largest retail presence. In terms of the network, Royal Mail's fleet of 35,000 vehicles makes it second only in size in Europe to that of the Russian Army. The UK's most trusted brand, a £9 billion business and well respected globally, Royal Mail has traditionally been viewed a part of the fabric of UK society.

Despite its size and traditional profitability (driven by a monopoly status), by the end of the financial year 2002–03 Royal Mail was in serious financial trouble. From a position of long-term financial stability the business was now making substantial losses. In a little under two years Royal Mail had recorded losses of £1.7 billion – nearly £2 million per day. Quite some feat for a monopoly organisation. Quality of service had plummeted and targets for first class mail delivery hadn't been hit since 1992. In addition to all this the once trusted brand was slowly being eroded, not least because Royal Mail were managing to lose in excess of 28 million of its customers letters every year.

Culturally Royal Mail was facing significant difficulties. There had always been a deep-seated tradition of pride within the organisation but, whilst many still felt that pride, a number of issues had come together and helped create a somewhat demoralised workforce.

Pay was low. Temporary and casual staff were being recruited in unrestricted numbers with little or no attention being paid to quality of hire and willingness to work, undermining the permanent employee's view of the importance of their own role. Sixteen percent of people had experienced bullying and/or harassment in the previous twelve months. If you were a female worker on night duty this figure rose to an even more alarming 25 percent. The Equal Opportunities Commission, a body established within the UK to eliminate sex discrimination in the workplace, was planning to investigate the business because of a poor record on workplace diversity and an increasing number of high profile grievance cases. In terms of safety, Royal Mail's record was three times worse than the entire UK construction industry.

Union relations were extremely poor. The industrial relations climate had produced the UK's worst strike record. Fifty percent of all industrial action across the country involved Royal Mail. The Communication Workers Union (CWU) presented a significant challenge to the business. A strong union, the CWU favoured adversarial tactics and were not at all averse to using damaging unofficial action to make their point. Whilst in denial about the changing commercial environment, the union felt it was their right to veto any proposed changes to the business. Unfortunately, in the absence of strong frontline management, the union was often seen as the authority in certain units.

Poor training, poor health and safety, poor recruitment, poor quality of service, poor union relations and an increasingly poor workplace culture had seen a traditionally highly respected, continually profitable and trusted employer turn into a loss-making business with significant employee disengagement and an industrial relations climate more suited to the 1970s than the early part of the twenty-first century.

Placed within this context it is hardly surprising that unauthorised absence throughout this period could at best be described as 'chronic'. By 2003, unauthorised absence rates were running at an average of 7.5 percent. It is important to point out at this juncture that under-reporting of unauthorised absence and a lack of an effective and integrated HR IT system meant that the 7.5 percent figure was considerably lower than the actual unauthorised absence level. Regionally variations ranged from 4.9 percent unauthorised absence in the best performing units to well over 18 percent in the worst. In an organisation of 185,000 people absence cost the business approximately £350 million per year.

Attitudes to unauthorised absence very much reflected the old civil service mentality that was still present throughout many parts of the organisation. In many people's minds there was an allowable amount of sick days per year. If these sick days were not taken then they could be used unofficially to supplement annual leave. A large-scale lack of discretionary effort throughout the organisation meant that a blocked nose or a mild hangover was often likely to result in a day off work.

Why was it so bad?

High levels of bullying and/or harassment had meant that employee satisfaction was at an all time low. The drive to reduce the cost base throughout the business had cut discretionary spend and removed many of the things that had traditionally motivated people. Added to this, it was clear that managers simply were not managing unauthorised absence.

The management issue

The culture was such that when a frontline employee was sick his/her first call wasn't necessarily to the line manager. In fact it was more likely to be a call to the union representative or the member of administration staff whose job it was to record unauthorised absence. Consequently, the first a manager knew about a member of their team being absent was if a third party informed them. This meant that the manager/employee contact was lost from the outset.

Often those people on sick leave would just be left alone with little or no contact from their line manager. Indeed, any attempts by management to contact those on sick leave were seen as intrusive and over-bearing by the CWU. In many units the union representatives were pretty much in charge.

Things were no better when a team member returned from a period of sick leave. Rarely was a 'return to work' interview undertaken (as was required in Royal Mail policy) and very little attempt was made to do any root-cause analysis or investigate any underlying issues relating to an individual's absence. Put simply, all too often absence wasn't being taken seriously enough, procedures weren't being followed, contact with those on sick leave was limited and opposed by the union and there was laissez-faire attitude towards tackling underlying issues.

To compound the problems, unauthorised absence reporting was something of a hit and miss process. Different areas used different measures, metrics and source data and many of the calculations tended to under report the problem – this kept unauthorised absence off the radar of senior management and kept unit managers out of trouble. Furthermore, a number of frankly bizarre practices further skewed the figures. Firstly, when an employee had exceeded fourteen consecutive days or had had three separate instance of unauthorized leave, a warning was automatically generated by the HR system. The very fact that warnings were issued automatically and not by line management, meant that people were able to retrospectively convert unauthorised leave to annual leave to avoid disciplinary procedures. Second, because unauthorised absence was calculated by the finance department (a sure sign that the business saw the issue as a purely financial one rather than a cultural one) those individuals who were only receiving half pay, on account of length of time that they had been on sick leave, were only being counted as 'half absent' i.e., despite being on full sick leave the business only recorded half the lost time. Third, the business didn't include those that had been on sick leave for over twelve months in the figures at all!

Sixty-six percent of all absence was long-term (more than three consecutive weeks). Once someone was deemed long-term sick they were regularly referred to the Occupational Health Service (OHS) and forgotten about by their line manager. Exit from the business figures show that of those people absent for six months or more, 50 percent never returned to work. After twelve months 95 percent never returned to work. These people were rarely managed out of the business and stayed as Royal Mail employees for an average of three years.

Sickness absence in the UK

According to the latest CBI/AXA Insurance Absence Survey (CBI, 2006), the cost of absence to the UK was more than £13 billion in 2005 – the highest ever level. What is most surprising is that the actual number of days lost through absence actually fell to its lowest since 1987 – 164 million days. The rise in cost appears to show the greater appreciation UK employers have of the true cost of absence; the expense of short-term resource replacement, recruiting and training additional staff and the inevitable drop in quality of service and productivity that absence causes.

The Chartered Institute of Personnel and Development (CiPD) 2006 Absence Management Survey revealed that the average level of employee absence fell to 3.5 percent – the lowest ever recorded by that particular survey. The survey showed that average working time lost between 2003 and 2006 had fluctuated between 3.5 and 4 percent (2003, 3.9%, 2004, 4.0%, 2005, 3.7% and 2006, 3.5%). In 2006 the private sector working time lost through sickness absence stood at 3 percent, equating to 6.8 days per employee per year. In the public sector, despite a 0.2 percent drop, absence levels were still significantly higher at 4.3 percent of working time lost, 9.9 days per employee per year.

In 2004, at the time when Royal Mail first decided to attack the issue of rising unauthorised absence, the CiPD Employee Absence survey reported that the average level of sick absence in the 1,100 surveyed organisations (employing 2.9 million people) was 4.0 percent or 9.1 working days per employee. Public sector organisations had the highest level of sickness absence at 4.7 percent. Long-term absence was also highest in the public sector – 30 percent of all absence was deemed long-term (four weeks or more for this survey). The report also showed that the average days lost per employee per year for an organisation with 2,000 or more employees was 10.3 (all sectors).

Even by public sector standards (Royal Mail Group is a PLC with one shareholder – the UK government) the business was seriously adrift of the acceptable levels of unauthorised absence. By early 2004 the absence level was approximately 7.5 percent, although as previously stated this was almost certainly under reported. The average amount of days lost per employee per year was nearly fifteen days and as many as 10,000 people were failing to show up for work on any given day.

In terms of absence management, Royal Mail had a disengaged workforce, managers who failed to correctly apply unauthorised absence procedures (and even when they did apply the procedures they were often overly convoluted, complex and poorly understood), a culture of arms'-length contact with those who were sick, poor reporting channels, indecipherable sick absence calculation methods and no fit for purpose HR system to provide managers with even the most rudimentary, vaguely useful data and analysis about their people. Like the business as a whole, something urgent needed doing.

The approach

Jon Allen, Royal Mail Head of Employee Relations and the man charged with delivering the project to reduce absence, was able to see the bigger picture from the outset.

From the beginning it was clear that any absence management project was as much about cultural change as it was about absence, and that in order to be transformational and sustainable a long-term holistic approach would have to be taken.

Phase 1: March 2004 to March 2005

There was a need to identify what was happening in the operation. What were the barriers to absence being dealt with properly in terms of culture, systems, policies and processes? There was also a need to find out what best practice looked like both internally and externally. Then what was required were some 'fix solutions' that could be easily and quickly implemented to 'get a grip' on the issues, before deciding on the long-term plan.

The objectives of the absence management process were:

- Design a holistic and long-term solution to address barriers and cultural issues, whilst maintaining the balance between supporting employees and managing the impact of absence on our customers, quality and cost.
- Shift responsibilty from personnel teams back to the line and introduce a more adult relationship with our employees.
- Reduce unplanned absence.

A project board was established, headed by Jon Allen. Once this group had identified the size of the problem they were tasked with designing and implementing the solutions to combat it. A stakeholder-influencing group was also established to act as a two-way conduit between the project team and the business units. This team proved crucial in ensuring that appropriate influencing, information sharing and communications took place.

In addition, specialist subgroups were used to design, develop and implement the following:

- renegotiation of the attendance procedure;
- support package for managers;
- renegotiation of the occupational health service contract.

Aside from the from the obvious issues, Jon Allen found that the greatest issue was that of ownership:

The biggest barriers were the attitudes, the level of understanding and the capabilities of managers in effectively owning and managing absence. A failure to proactively manage absence resulted in a lack of contact between the employee and their manager. People went sick without speaking to their manager and there was often no subsequent discussion with them until they returned to work; and even then this was inconsistent and patchy.

Business renewal

In 2003, under new leadership, Royal Mail launched a recovery plan. The Royal Mail renewal plan would aim to halt the unsustainable losses and return the business to profitability. In addressing five key areas – capability (via people), performance management, procedures (production processes) structure and information processes Royal Mail began a course of action to transform a business on the brink of closure.

The focus of the recently appointed Royal Mail Chairman Allan Leighton was on three simple things – profitability, the recovery of quality of service levels and making the organisation a 'Great Place to Work'. For people and organisational development (P&OD) – the newly renamed HR department, a 'Great Place to Work' meant a much sharper focus on Royal Mail's people.

This presented a fantastic opportunity for P&OD. Prior to the renewal project the HR function was traditional, reactive and unsuited to meeting the challenge of business transformation. It was a costly function – £200 million per year and there were simply too many HR people. A headcount of 3,700 in the HR department meant that the HR to people ratio throughout the business was an astonishing 1:55. There was enormous duplication of effort as each area had its own personnel team. The impact of this was not only costly and unnecessary but it prevented line managers from dealing directly with their people. Weak management used HR as an excuse not to tackle issues or to have difficult conversations and good managers felt disempowered by the presence of so many 'local' HR people. The HR agenda was largely transactional, day-to-day and lacking a genuine strategic direction. In Royal Mail you traditionally gained credibility via your dealings with the unions, which in turn created more problems. Policies and procedures became overly prescriptive and unnecessarily complex due to the predilection of the HR teams and the CWU to negotiate over the slightest things. At the time of the renewal plan Royal Mail had 84 national agreements in place (some two inches thick) and in 2003/04 it lost 84,000 days through industrial action.

The history of HR suggests that it has evolved in four stages. Its origins were as a 'welfare function', next followed the more transactional 'personnel', then on to HR where for the first time people were seen as a resource and finally it has evolved into 'people/people and development'. In 2003, Royal Mail HR was somewhere between the paternalistic welfare approach and the day-to-day transactional activities of a personnel function. What Royal Mail required was a function capable of holding adult-to-adult conversations with its people and the ability to lead unprecedented change.

Transforming HR

The HR transformation formed part of the overall business renewal plan and helped create a climate where innovative and radical approaches to tackling big-ticket issues had a fighting chance of success. HR needed a clear end state and so the Ulrich 3-Box model approach was taken. Experts, business partners and shared services all to be delivered, beginning to end, in six months.

A number of factors enabled the transformation of the HR function into People and Organisational Development. Perhaps the most significant move was the injection of new talent into the organisation to create a critical mass of leaders in P&OD. For those remaining in the function a great deal of time and money was spent on their development. The Business Partners especially were assessed against a new competency framework. The intention was to drive value in Royal Mail through developing the capability of our P&OD Business Partners. A Business Partner profile was created which focused on the importance of business knowledge, the ability to utilize organisational development tools and processes in order to deliver business strategies (and not just HR strategies), the need for leading edge HR thinking/interventions, an understanding of consultancy techniques and the significance of personal credibility and emotional/intellectual intelligence.

The shared service function – People and Organisational Development Services (P&ODS) – was rationalised and its processes tightened. A new structure was put in place and all instances of duplication of effort were eradicated. In 2003 only 45 percent of those surveyed throughout the business felt the shared service offering responded to requests in a timely manner, a mere 55 percent felt that the quality of service was good or very good and only 38 percent agreed that the service showed 'business focus'. By 2005 this picture had changed dramatically, timeliness had risen to 75 percent, quality was up to 85 percent, business focus had increased to 85 percent and 75 percent of the people surveyed agreed with the statement 'P&ODS meets my needs.' P&ODS were able to drive cost out of the function and increase efficiency with such success that in November 2006 they were formally recognised as the UK's best shared service function.

By the end of the HR transformation the HR:People ratio had risen from 1:55 to 1:145. Headcount had fallen from 3,700 to a little over 2,000. P&OD people were beginning to reap the benefits of investment in their development. There were effective Business Partners facing off to other parts of the organisation and helping to embed change, a leading edge expert function and an efficient shared service offering. Operators were starting to own people decisions and calling on P&OD people for support rather than to deal with their people and their problems directly. The financial impact was significant, the transformation had taken nearly £60 million out of the function's cost base.

The result of the HR transformation was that it created a template for change that the rest of the business could follow. In changing so radically P&OD was configured to successfully undertake the changes that the business needed to make to survive. It also gave the function a good deal of credibility when it came to influencing the rest of the business to change, largely through the demonstrable effectiveness of its own transformation. Above all else, it gave the rest of the business the confidence to change too.

So when P&OD said 'let's improve unauthorised absence by giving away 37 cars!' most of the business, despite some resistance, felt it was worth a try.

Tackling the unauthorised absence problem

Against the backdrop of the organisational change, the likes of which Royal Mail had not experienced in its 360-year history, plans were drawn up to tackle the problem of chronic unauthorised absence. The first task was to regain control of the problem, starting with the basics.

An accessible 'Manager's Guide', online tools and information about further support were produced. Thirteen thousand managers were re-trained (or trained for the first time) on the basics of the attendance policy and the absence management procedures. 'Attendance coaches' were put in place, best practice was shared and absence was made a performance objective for all managers. There was also training for all second line managers on their role as coaches and the responsibility of the line manager to manage unauthorised absence.

There were new 'contact' standards introduced – people were now required to speak to their manager *first* if they were taking unauthorised leave. If the period of unauthorised leave was likely to exceed more than a few days, managers were required to keep in weekly contact. These contact standards reconnected the manager with the absent member of their team, allowing the manager the opportunity to offer the appropriate level of help and support. Those on sick leave were no longer left to fend for themselves.

In terms of those on long-term sick leave, meetings were arranged to discuss their progress and offer the relevant advice and support. The definition of 'long-term' was changed from three or more weeks to two or more weeks, and anyone deemed long-term sick was given a mandatory 'return to work' plan. Cases were now being monitored rather than left from one week to another.

Processes were improved and more closely adhered to. Auditing of return to work interviews identified the units where they were not being undertaken. Performance management became key. League tables of the best and worst performing areas were compiled, circulated and most importantly discussed at senior manager level, with directors contacting poor performing units on a weekly basis. The attendance procedure was changed, it became easier to use and the nature of the contract shifted from parent/child to adult to adult. One agreed definition of absence and one single source of data were used.

A new partnership was formed with Royal Mail's Occupational Health Service (OHS), so often in the past seen as a weak link in effectively managing people back to work. Telephone support was offered to referring managers on a 24/7 basis, OHS telephone triage was used in an attempt to reduce the number of wasted appointments due to failure to attend. Clear advice was offered to managers enabling them to make informed decisions about the various return to work options available to their people. The OHS offered a more 're-hab focused' service including Occupational Therapy and Physiotherapy (40 percent of all long-term absence was the result of musculo-skeletal injury and 40 percent was psychological or stress related). And, just as with operational managers, the OHS were given a KPI framework within which to work. This framework included an absence target.

We also said 'thank you', something that had rarely happened before, to managers with noticeable improvements in attendance by giving them additional funds to improve their units.

Once the basics were in place and the organisation had begun to take a grip of the unauthorised absence problem, it became clear that unauthorised absence and the impact it was having on the business needed a wider audience if it was to be effectively tackled. What the organisation needed was a way to get people talking about unauthorised absence and its effects in the same way as they had traditionally talked about quality of service and the importance of meeting financial targets. It needed an intervention to raise awareness of the benefits of effective attendance management, not only in financial terms but also for employee engagement and positive cultural change. What came out of this need was **'Be in to win'**.

Be in to win

The concept of 'Be in to win' was simple – a six-month scheme in which Royal Mail people with a 100 percent attendance record would be entered into a draw to win high value prizes. To create the biggest impact it was decided that the high value prizes should include thirty-seven brand new Ford cars, one per operational area of the UK and seventy-five £2,000 holiday vouchers, two per operational area, as runners up prizes. Employees who did not take time off sick during the period August 2004 to January 2005 would automatically be entered into the draw. All unauthorised absence related to pregnancy and illnesses that fell under the UK's Disability Discrimination Act was discounted.

Thirty-seven cars and seventy-five holiday vouchers certainly did a great deal to catch the attention of Royal Mail people and, significantly, the attention of the outside media. The reaction in the press was initially one of cynicism – here was a public sector organisation using tax payer's money to bribe its employees to do what they should already be doing – getting out of bed and doing an honest day's work. The organisation with one of the highest strike rate in the UK, that had not hit a performance target for first class mail for ten years now planned to give away not one but thirty-seven cars for turning up to work. Incentive? Desperation? Lunacy??

The UK press seized on the story with a good deal of the sensationalism for which they are famed. Under a six-inch headline 'Sick: posties bribed to turn up for work', popular British tabloid newspaper the *Daily Star* talked of Royal Mail using gimmicks to 'combat rampant absenteeism'. A day later, under the heading 'Prize chumps' the same tabloid claimed that a phone poll revealed that 'more than 85% of readers hit out at plans to give postal workers prizes for turning up to work.'

Writing an article in the *Daily Express* entitled 'Is bribery really the way to stop workers skiving?' Frank Furedi, Professor of Sociology at the University of Kent had this to say:

It [Royal Mail] is clearly desperate to find a way of managing its escalating problem of absenteeism. On any one day, 10 000 of its employees claim to be unfit for work. So instead of tightening up its procedures to cut down on workers skiving off, it has decided to opt for bribing them to show up.

The politically right-of-centre *Daily Mail* even lamented the demise of the Royal Mail itself. In the article 'Bribed to work' the newspaper questioned the organisation's values and management:

FREE cars, holiday vouchers, weekend breaks . . . how tempting the prizes are for postal staff who deign to turn up for duty. With absenteeism running at 10,000 a day, Royal Mail believes that they are the only way to ensure an honest day's work. Could there be a greater inversion of decent values or a more craven abdication of proper management when people have to be bribed not to take sickies? How sad that a once great institution should come to this.

With all the adverse press coverage it was hardly surprising that the CWU also took the opportunity to attack Be in to Win. The Deputy General Secretary dismissed the scheme, urging Royal Mail to be 'honest' and address the real causes of absenteeism.

Gimmicks won't offer a solution to low morale and stress levels resulting from the physical demands of the job and regimented management styles.

Despite the negative press that Be in to Win received when first launched, Dr Steve Boorman, Royal Mail Director of Corporate and Social Responsibility and Chief Medical Officer, has his own view on the media furore surrounding the initiative.

It was a positive approach. The scheme talked about attendance and not absence. In many ways it was a fun way of raising a serious issue, a PR exercise that enabled us to talk about sick absence in the workplace without the associated industrial relations issues conversations like that usually cause. It got the subject of sick absence into normal everyday workplace conversations.

For all the column inches that Be in to Win was generating in the outside media, the success of the scheme relied heavily on the effectiveness of the internal communications plan. The external media spotlight was likely to pass in a matter of days, but getting Royal Mail's people to take Be in to Win seriously would be the key to success.

Internal communications

Royal Mail internal communications took full advantage of their existing communications media. It was essential that the conversations took place at the local level, between managers and their people. The following were used to tell the Be in to Win story:

1. Work time listening and learning: Work time listening and learning (WTLL) is a weekly half-hour session in which teams discuss issues of local importance and find ways to improve their workplace. Its purpose is to get people involved in the workplace through regular dialogue, to focus on local issues

that are important to our people, and to sort out problems. It was an important vehicle for explaining the reasons for Be in to Win, the logistics surrounding it and importantly for countering the negative press.

2. Poster campaign: A creative company was brought in to design the Be in to Win visuals. Posters and leaflets were placed around operational sites and offices explaining the scheme and illustrating the prizes. Strap-lines such as 'Don't lose your Focus' (the thirty-seven cars were Ford Focus models), 'miss work, miss out' drove home the messages. The poster campaign was refreshed every couple of months. With four months to go a 'boiled egg' poster carried the heading 'Only four months to go – don't crack now!'

3. Effective internal communications: The well-established Royal Mail media was used to sell the story. *Courier*, the in-house newspaper, has a circulation of around 200,000 and so was a powerful tool for getting the message across.

4. High visibility strategy: A Ford Focus car toured the length and breadth of the country allowing people to see what they could win. The car was emblazed with the Be in to Win visuals and the phrase 'Win me' on the roof. People were invited to sit in the car and ask questions about the scheme. The purpose of this simple exercise was to prove to the cynics that the business was serious about giving away thirty-seven new cars, and to lend some authenticity to the scheme.

5. Simple information and Q&A's: With so much negative press surrounding the scheme it was essential that managers were given enough information to counter any questions that they might receive from their people. A full briefing pack was issued which dealt with the reasons why the business was running the scheme, the objectives of the scheme and some sample Q&A's regarding the more controversial aspects of giving away so many high value prizes.

Early wins

Whilst the publicity, both internally and externally, was growing surrounding Be in to Win the other less high profile interventions were paying dividends. The new OHS partnership was increasing turnaround times and giving the feel of a proactive rather a reactive consultancy. There was a noticeable difference in the amount of people failing to attend OHS appointments; failures to attend were dropping steadily.

By the time it came to reviewing the partnership with the OHS a number of dramatic changes had taken place. Average case closure was reduced for all services, saving approximately eight working days per case (a reduction of £640 per case). The telephone support to referring managers enabled fast clearance of a number of cases – the average clearance time for telephone cases fell to 3.2 days. The joint initiative with the rehabilitation specialists saw as much as a 5:1 return on investment in terms of the cost of the treatment against the money saved through a reduction in days lost. Failures to attend reduced markedly – 18 percent of wasted appointments to 5 percent in the space of one year.

31 January 2005 marked the end of the first Be in to Win scheme. The results of the scheme, combined with the other initiatives were impressive:

- unauthorised absence for the duration of the scheme averaged 5.7 percent, compared with 7.5 percent for the same period a year earlier;
- attendance levels had risen by 11 percent, meaning that approximately 1,000 more people were turning up for work on any given day;
- 92,000 people had managed to maintain a 100 percent attendance record during the six months of the scheme;
- £40 million had been saved.

The presentation of the cars to the winners gave Royal Mail its biggest exposure in the external media since the scheme was launched. The cars were presented to the winners in full view of the local and national media at locations around the country. The coverage of the scheme stretched as far as the Ukraine and China. The keys were handed over by leading members of the area management team to reinforce the message that the achievements of the winners had a positive impact at local and not just national level. This generated a real feel-good factor, especially when it was revealed that one of the winners was a 74 year-old outdoor delivery worker.

In addition to the cars and holiday vouchers, 92,000 people received a letter of thanks from the Chairman and a holiday voucher worth £150. This was an unexpected bonus for those who hadn't won one of the main prizes and went a long way to ensuring the long-term credibility of the Be in to Win scheme.

Corporate turnaround

By April 2005 Royal Mail had completed the biggest turnaround in UK corporate history. In the space of less than three years the business had gone from losing nearly £2 million per day to making an operating profit of £537 million. P&OD had played a significant role in the success of the renewal plan. It had successfully executed the change programme and redesigned 195,000 jobs. The amount of restrictive practices within the organisation had fallen from

1,271 to less than 200 (at the time of writing that figure is closer to forty five). Over 34,000 people had left the business voluntarily, a huge undertaking for P&ODS whose responsibility it was to administer all redundancy quotes and support the leavers through the entire exit process. The number of accidents had fallen by 40 percent, although that still made Royal Mail twice as bad as the construction industry. Relations with the CWU, although still difficult, had improved and 2005 saw a 92 percent reduction in the amount of industrial action that the organisation witnessed. Employee earnings, so often the cause of dissatisfaction, had increased by 18 percent and the unpopular six-day week had been scrapped in favour of a five-day week. In all, £1.5 billion of costs had been taken out of the business and the growth had been achieved with mail price increases below the level of inflation. Finally, the renewal plan delivered the best quality of service for nearly ten years.

The key success factors to the business and HR transformations had a great deal in common. In both cases things were kept simple – the business had three goals, profitability, quality of service and making the organisation a great place to work. P&OD had a clear end state, an injection of talent and an increase in business partner capabilities. For both transformations speed of execution was essential and both focussed purely on getting the basics right, a set of easily understood measures and clarity and consistency of message. If the business said that it was going to do something it did it. Our people knew the business needed transforming and HR people understood that the function was no longer fit for purpose and not able to lead major change programmes. In many ways the business transformation was very top down in its management approach. Due to the severity of the situation it was important that the leadership kept control during a period of unprecedented change. Changes in the business and in HR were driven in with or without agreement. If the leadership felt that it was the right thing to do then they did it. The approach was to be bold and not strive for perfection, whilst never underestimating the resistance to change.

With Royal Mail returned to profit, quality of service at the highest level in nearly ten years and employee satisfaction going in the right direction, albeit more slowly than the business would have liked, it was agreed that Royal Mail would launch Be in to Win 2. Along the same lines as before, Be in to Win 2 would be a twelve-month scheme. Starting in March 2005, the scheme again offered those with a perfect attendance record the chance to win a brand new car – this time there were thirty-nine Vauxhall Astra cars, each worth £10,000, on offer. To keep the interest levels high, a six-month draw would also take place, again for those with 100 percent attendance records, with the ten winners in each area winners receiving a £275 shopping voucher. A further prize of an additional five days annual leave was made available in response to feedback the business had received about the need for non-financial reward as well.

From absence to attendance

Be in to Win had initially been seen by some as a short-term gimmick. Six months later even the strongest of critics were forced to admit that Be in to Win, accompanied by a simplified absence procedure and an effective OHS, had more than justified the investment. By January 2005, 1,000 more people per day were turning up for work and the business had saved £40 million. Importantly, the issue of unauthorised absence was high on the business agenda and the positive message that improved attendance can help an ailing business was firmly embedded throughout the workplace.

By May 2006, the end of the second Be in to Win scheme, a clear picture of just how successful the approach to managing unauthorised absence had emerged:

- Unauthorised absence for the duration of the two schemes had fallen from approximately 7.5 percent in August 2004 to 5 percent in March 2006.
- Unauthorised absence for phase 2 of Be in to Win, March 2005 to March 2006, fell from 6.1 to 5 percent.
- The financial year 2005–06 saw attendance levels rise by 18 percent, with approximately 1,800–2,000 more people at work every day helping to deliver better quality to Royal Mail's customers.
- In total the approach saved the business £80 million per year in absence costs.
- The improved attendance rate has been a key factor in Royal Mail delivering record quality of service in 2005–06, when 94.1 percent of first class letters arrived the next working day, well above the 93 percent target level.

There were many operational benefits of the improved approach. Not only did it directly save the business millions in unauthorised absence costs, but it also meant that the operation no longer required a vast army of costly casual workers. This had a positive effect on morale and allowed the business to concentrate training spend on its directly employed people. A better trained, more stable workforce increased quality of service and helped to regain credibility in the eyes of the customer.

Aside from the obvious financial and quality of service impacts of the approach, there were a number indirect benefits. The various initiatives forced a bureaucratic and functionally silo'ed organisation to communicate. In order to solve the problem of unauthorised absence Employee Relations had to work with CSR who had to work with P&ODS who all had to work with the operation at local level. The approach helped thread the organisation together in a time of enormous change.

The spotlight on unauthorised absence helped shift the focus of operational managers away from quality of service targets alone. Dealing with unauthorised absence meant dealing with their people. The bottom line is that managers had a much wider awareness of the impact of unauthorised absence and the reasons for it. League tables and effective communications ensured that they knew where they stood and what was expected of them. Once managers were aware of what was expected of them they were able to contribute to the ongoing efforts to halt chronic levels of unauthorised absence. One unexpected benefit was that the business found that managers were beginning to raise issues around the approach. For example, it was as a result of manager feedback that it was discovered that the OHS was still not performing as well as it could do and remedial actions were taken.

Externally, the scheme is now recognised as a benchmark approach to absence management. Royal Mail is regularly approached by other organisations looking for advice and wishing to emulate the success of the initiatives.

Two things have summarised Royal Mail's approach to attendance management – control and reward:

Control through

- improved contact standards;
- better training and online/telephone support for managers;
- performance management in terms of attendance;
- improved support for those who were sick.

Reward through

- incentives and effective communications;
- good leadership;
- clear contracting with people;
- a climate where change is seen as the only option.

The success of the absence management approach was a further example of how P&OD had transformed itself into a function capable of delivering the kind of change interventions that impacted on Royal Mail's bottom line. P&OD transformed itself in order to facilitate change throughout the wider organisation, it was this change that created a climate in which Be in to Win was able to succeed.

The drive to improve unauthorised absence is a relentless one. At the time of writing, two years after the launch of the first Be in to Win scheme, the results are starting to plateau. The impact of the initiatives, and the improved processes has got the business to a certain level but now there is fresh impetus needed. With the Royal Mail facing an uncertain future due to the loss of its monopoly status in January 2006, P&OD must revisit, refresh and reinvigorate the absence management approach if the mistakes of the past are not to be repeated.

REFERENCES

Chartered Institute of Personnel and Development (2006) Absence Management, 3–22.
Chartered Institute of Personnel and Development (2005) Absence Management A Survey of Policy and Practice, 2–47.
Chartered Institute of Personnel and Development (2004) Employee Absence 2004, 2–5.
CBI/AXA Insurance, Absence and Labour Turnover Survey 2006, 1–4.

NOTES

1. Quality of Service in this case refers to the target of 93 percent of first class mail being delivered by the next working day.
2. 86,664 days lost to industrial action in 2003–04.
3. Unauthorised absence calculations in Royal Mail varied depending on whether the demonitators were full time equivalents (FTEs), Staff in post (SIP) or based on hours worked.
4. After Galbraith.
5. Royal Mail's P&OD capability programme was led by Professor Wayne Brockbank, University of Michigan, USA.
6. Personnel Today Award for Excellence in Outsourcing and Shared Service 2006 and Overall Winner.
7. Standardised absence calculation: Hours lost to sick leave and special leave divided by hours lost to contracted hours minus 10 percent for annual leave absence costs were calculated based on average hourly salary rates (direct cost of sickness) and a second figure which gave

the indirect cost of non-attendance (this included cost of additional overtime or replacement temporary staff, lost quality, cost through accidents).

8. Be in to Win was inspired by a visit to Sun Microsystems in 1999, where it was noted that in order to incentivise a recruitment drive the CEO was giving away a Ferrari.

9. *Daily Star* 06/08/2004 and 07/08/2004.

10. *Daily Express* 06/08/2004.

11. *Daily Mail* 06/08/2004.

12. *London Evening Standard*, 05/08/2004.

Transforming a company into a community

Philip Mirvis

At their second annual retreat, 250 leaders of the Asia region of a multi-national food business spent two to three days in ashrams, spiritual centers, micro-enterprises and charities in India to learn about community life. There they tended the needy, offered what help they could, and asked swamis, spiritual leaders, community entrepreneurs, and dabawhallas how they could accomplish so much with so few resources. These business leaders were learning what a true mission is and concluded that they needed to find a "higher purpose" for their business.

The intent of visiting these communities was for these Asian business leaders to experience communal living in its many forms and deepen their collective understanding of the ingredients of community life (McMillan and Chavis, 1986). The expectation was that as the leaders informed themselves about the people and circumstances of the communities they visited, they would also ponder the meaning and implications for their own leadership body and business.

The idea of running this company as a community had been an aim of the new chairman since he took over the region two years prior. To this point, the region had operated as a confederation of fifteen national operating companies with a strategic regional overlay and managing board. He wanted to connect the senior leaders of national companies together more closely and to include the next layers of country marketers, supply chain managers and staff in strategic discussions and operational reviews of regional business. Behind this was a perceived need and personal desire to build the capacity of this entire leadership body 250 plus, to think and feel together, that is, to operate as a community of leaders.

A proponent of using leadership events to drive action, the chairman applied many of the ideas advanced by those who study and lead large group interventions (see also, Bunker and Alban, 1997). The journey to India, like the ones that preceded it, brought the leaders of the whole of a relevant system together and engaged them in participatory fact-finding, visioning, and action planning. But guidance on building a spirit of community in this large group and increasing its capacities to function as a "single intelligence" came not from the large-scale group intervention field alone. Ideas were also drawn from theory and practices concerned with community building in large groups and with the use of dialogue in learning communities (Peck, 1987; Gozdz, 1996; Kofman and Senge, 1993).

As practitioners in these two loosely-defined arenas, Karen Ayas and I helped to organize and facilitate the trip to India and other learning journeys of the company. This chapter highlights some of the theory behind, and innovative practices employed in, building a leadership community. It begins with a review of key concepts behind this broad-based intervention and then develops them in the context of the learning journeys in this case.

Group dynamics in large group change

There is an extensive body of knowledge about group dynamics and facilitation that informs the work of many who conduct large group interventions (Beckhard and Harris, 1987; Bunker and Alban, 1992; Weisbord, 1992; Jacobs, 1994). The origins of much of this know-how – concerning the stages of group development, factors that help and hinder group communication and methods for facilitating group process – trace to the field of small group psychology and were developed initially in application to encounter groups or in human relations training (Bion, 1961; Bradford *et al.*, 1964). There are, of course, other theories of group development and dynamics (Smith and Berg, 1987; Sarason, 1974) that could be applied to large group interventions. Of interest here are the principles and practices of community building that have roots in laboratory education, but evolved in work with groups five-to-seven times that size (Peck, 1987).

The theories behind community building, which has people in a large circle open up about their lives and circumstances and speak from their heart about coming together with others present, certainly incorporate group dynamics, but they also reference trans-personal psychology and spirituality (Maslow, 1968; Wilbur, 1984; Harman, 1988). Dialogue, a related community-building practice, that has individuals speak to the "group as a whole" about matters of interest and simultaneously scan their feelings, assumptions, and reactions to the experience, also reflects ideas about the interconnection of human thought and energy (Bohm, 1986; Isaacs, 1999). A look at their conceptual foundations highlights the many similarities and some key differences between developmental stages of small groups versus larger ones (see Figure 16.1).

To begin, the generic model of group development, generalized from studies of therapy and encounter groups, involve stages of forming, storming, norming, and performing (Tuckman, 1965). In the formative phase, individuals have to deal with their purpose in coming together and form relationships with one another and with leaders. Schutz (1958) highlights how this raises issues of "inclusion" and begets questions about how much a person wants to be included and is inclined to include others. The group dynamic at this phase is more or less shaped by individuals' predilections and going-in assumptions.

In a larger group, the collective dynamic, what psychiatrist M. Scott Peck (1987) labels "pseudo-community," revolves around traditions at this early phase. Here, for instance, a new group often adopts a culturally comfortable form and rhythm that allows each individual to bring forth his or her needs, style, and ideas. In dialogue, this start-up period generally has people "talking nice" Scharmer (2004). The collective intent is to incorporate everyone, blur individual differences, and establish a common, familiar baseline of relating. On a larger scale, as people come together to establish a structure and achieve a purpose, this phase is marked by what Sarason (1974) refers to as utopian aspirations – everything is possible. It is a period marked by creativity and inventiveness as people contemplate the new.

In the next phase of group development, however, individual differences come to the fore and a group faces conflict and constraints – and begins to "storm." Group members have to deal with issues of control – how much to exert and how much to accept from others. In Freudian terms, the group moves from an "oral" phase, where individuals consider what nourishment or gratification they can get from a group, to its "anal" phase, where the group tries to master its internal processes and, figuratively, deal with the mess (Bennis and Shephard, 1956).

On a larger scale, this conflictual phase is called "chaos" in community building language and in dialogue has people "talking tough." Throughout this phase, boundaries are being set and a collective culture begins to take shape. There are of course structural as well as interpersonal conflicts between, say, leaders and followers, or between different members of a group, that have to be confronted. One common collective issue concerns a leadership crisis – who is in charge? Can a community lead itself?

This confrontation segues a group into "norming" and has it finding its own direction, setting rules and getting "organized." In practical settings, like group training and team building, this is sometimes facilitated and sped up

Human Relations **Piaget**	Motor Stage			Morality of Constraint		Morality of Cooperation
Interpersonal Dynamics **Schutz, Bennis & Shephard**	Oral–Inclusion		Anal–Control			Genital–intimacy
Group Dynamics **Bion**		Fight/Flight–	Dependency		–Pairing	
Group Development **Tuckman**	*Forming*	*Storming*		*Norming*		*Performing*
Group Dialogue **Isaacs, Scharmer**	Talking Nice	Talking Tough		Reflective Dialogue		Generative Dialogue
Community Building **Peck**	Pseudo-community	Chaos		Emptiness		Community
Social Structure/Setting **Sarason**	Creativity/Utopia	Leadership Crisis –Direction & Rules–Identity Crisis				Regression or Regeneration

Figure 16.1 Stages of development in human relations, groups, and social structure*

*Parts of this figure are adapted from material presented in Philip Slater, *Microcosm*, New York: Wiley, 1966.

through techniques like role negotiation, structured problem solving, goal setting, or conflict resolution interventions – common tools in a group facilitator's regimen. On a collective scale, it involves setting direction and defining rules for collective behavior.

Interestingly, methods for setting norms and addressing conflict take a different form in large groups involved in building community. In groups intending to form a learning community, for instance, conversation is directed not towards negotiation or problem solving but to what learning theorists characterize as collective "inquiry" (Argryis, 1982; 1985). Group members might, for example, be urged to reflect on themselves or the group to ponder how it is conversing. In the community building methodology, people are encouraged to talk personally about what's keeping them from connecting to the group and to witness one another do so. The rationale is that people progress towards community not by "working" issues but rather by "letting go" of thoughts, feelings, wishes, and everything else that gets in the way of being "fully present."

This entails personal vulnerability and the surrender of formal roles, agendas, and even goals. By "emptying" themselves, as in meditation or prayer or as one would in self-help groups or Quaker meetings, people open up to others present and comprehend their own lives and circumstances afresh. As this phase unfolds, self-awareness increases and feelings of empathy with others often emerge. A sense of community is born as people start then to see themselves in another and another in themselves (Mirvis, 2002).

Chaos in China: the Asian leadership community forms

Coming together for the first time as a leadership circle from fifteen different countries in Asia Pacific, the leaders of the food business's struggle with the process of opening up, talking together deeply, and making space for and including divergent points of view. The task at hand is to engage in a dialogue. A facilitator intones: "This is an effort to build a leadership community where everyone thinks and acts mindful of the whole. It is one based on shared understanding among people and deep communication, a community that values personal reflection, deep listening, and authentic conversation." Sitting in a circle, the 250 leaders present are asked to take a moment of silence, attend to their feelings and any discomfort, and heed when they are "moved to speak;" they are encouraged to speak up when they are so moved.

There is a long, awkward silence. The leaders sit on little benches, thinking and squirming, as a huge fire throws sparks into the blackness. The chairman finally begins to talk, by way of example. A few more speak up, with long stretches of nothing in between. There are genuine attempts at dialogue, but the bulk of the talk takes the form of stand-up speeches, filled with logical reasons to come together and occasional references to ancient wisdom or poetry on such matters, followed by polite applause, plus some quasi-debate. This format seems comfortable but there are many conversational gaps and no flow to the discussions. Importantly, most of the speakers are from central Asia – India and Pakistan – or with origins in Europe. One Chinese leader finally speaks directly to the chairman: It's hard to have a conversation with 200 people at a time.

There is impatient shifting and glancing around. One facilitator attempts to guide the group back to dialogue by encouraging members to express their feelings and urging them to reflect on being moved to speak. Another urges the soft-spoken South Asians to speak out loudly so that they can be heard. The group seems to be moving between comfort and chaos – individual agendas dominate, there is debate but not much listening or building on points. The talk winds down and the gathering ends in silence. Some leaders talk quietly in clusters of two or three. Most walk wordlessly away. Some participant reflections:

The evening "dialogue" was very frustrating, despite my own pitiful efforts at involvement. The whole exercise left a very sour taste in my mouth, and some anger as well, for forcing such an uncomfortable and culturally insensitive situation on us all. I felt so much empathy for my South Asian colleagues. I also come from a more publicly conservative culture, unlike our (European and Central Asian leaders). I went to bed feeling very pissed off.

How did I feel? I was so disappointed, because we were trying to go too far and pushing. Do we have to speak up? Do we have to always try to develop a dialogue?

Not everyone shares the same anguish and anger: "There are moments that things happen and moments when they don't," says a Pakistani leader. "I did feel a little let down when we failed to dialogue with each other but then I quickly used that opportunity to question my beliefs, the status quo, the easy and comfortable solutions." says another. Others continue to reflect and question more deeply why it was such a struggle:

Why was I not open and honest during that night when we tried to start-up up a dialogue? I believe there was a barrier of judgment, a barrier of "not giving" and a barrier of mind that were not letting me reach my heart. I was hiding myself in that darkness behind the barrier of self-centered and mind-driven judgment, resulting in neither giving or receiving, though my heart was forcing me to share.

I do need to admit however, that I was one of those who didn't stand up to talk during our outbreak. Why? Well, truthfully, I was scared. Nervous about standing up in front of 200 people to express how I feel. A bit wary of 'sharing' with a group of people I don't really know. Not knowing if I could trust them. It finally dawned on me that everything must come from the 'heart'. That is where it all begins.

That night when we were first asked to dialogue, the dead silence from the beginning really struck me. I sat there wondering why it was so easy for us to put our messages across but so difficult to listen to others' points and build on them. In fact, we had had several dialogues in pairs or in smaller groups that went very well; why did we struggle in this big group? I was not sure if this was arranged intentionally, but it really pushed my colleagues and me to the border of discomfort, so much that we exploded implicitly afterwards and explicitly the next day."

Facilitating large group dialogue

There are tradeoffs in how much to structure group experiences and always tensions between over- and under-structuring group work (Alderfer, 1980; Bunker and Alban, 1997). Even as community building and dialogue practitioners eschew many of the techniques that group facilitators and team builders use to structure conversation and speed a group into norming, they have their own brand of process facilitation. For instance, drawing from the tenets of humanistic psychology in the 1950s and 60s, group facilitators often stress the importance of dealing directly with "here and now" behavior and regard interpersonal feedback as key to the "helping relationship." By contrast, facilitators in the community building tradition instead urge participants to self-reflect, and be aware of their filtering and judgments – all in service of emptying oneself of what gets in the way of truly hearing another person. The idea, as expressed by Isaacs (1993) with reference to dialogue groups, is that by "observing the observer" and "listening to your listening," self-awareness of thoughts, feelings, and experiences, past and present, seep gently into consciousness.

In turn, the notion of offering feedback in a group – to help people see themselves more clearly through questioning or clarifying – is discouraged. In community building lingo, this equates to "fixing" – a worthy aspiration that has to be emptied in order to experience oneself and others more fully. Rather the focus is on collective dynamics and interpretive comments, if offered at all, are aimed at the group as a whole. Furthermore, the intent is not to "work through" tensions or conflicts by confronting them directly. Rather, the group serves as a "container" – to hold differences and conflicts up for ongoing exploration. This keeps "hot" conversation "cooled" sufficiently that people can see the "whole" of the group mind.

Facilitation tools in this tradition come not so much from human relations training but rather from spiritual counseling and emphasize reflection and "soul work" (Peck, 1993; Mirvis, 1997). Community building principles, for instance, are designed to set firm boundary conditions around group relations that support organic movement from chaos to community. At the start of community building or dialogue, expectations are set to speak personally, welcome diversity, deal with difficult issues, bridge differences with integrity, and relate with love and respect. At the same time, facilitators are admonished that they cannot "lead" a group to community. They and anyone else present can, however, share their own thoughts, call the group into silence, or merely slow the discussion down. The intended result is deep conversation among people or what Bohm (1989) likens to "superconductivity" in a group – where the elements of conversation move as a "whole" rather than as separate parts.

Unity in diversity

In this case, progressing dialogue across twenty different cultures was a challenge indeed. And the difficulty was not just about the mastery of the English language but also differences in communication styles and interpersonal orientations. Some participants came from cultures known as "reserved;" others from more "expressive" cultures. Some were relational in their interactions; others more transactional. Said one leader: "In an Asian culture, it's not easy to speak out, it's very risky. The risk is very high to stand up and say something. It must be the right thing."

Bridging the culture gap will take time. Some have never been exposed to any sustained group talk with peers and superiors from another culture. Some have difficulty following a conversation in English. But others are confident that dialogue and community feeling would develop. "We will build the bridge brick-by-brick," said one. "If we undermine diversity for this region, we are out. We have to respect individual cultures, individual characters. And we have to help each other. I'm Japanese and I'm Asian. I'd like to work together. I'd like to speak together."

The next day's dialogue begins in chaos. One leader challenges the chairman for seeming to question him about speaking up. At issue is the strength of his leadership. Several speak of their disgust with having "rules" for talking together and with the inefficiency of a whole group conversation. In some respects, this is akin to the "revolt" found in encounter groups where members turn against their leaders and the group begins to establish its own independent identity (Slater, 1966). The revolution is forestalled when a young female leader from Thailand speaks up and tells a personal story of experiencing fear. More stories then follow in sequence about personal adversities, trials, and even triumphs. In the community building vernacular, people begin to "empty."

It is likely that the emphasis on self-reflection and listening-to-your listening facilitated this process. Said a Philippino, "I know now that the experience of the previous night drove me and a colleague with whom I had never had a discussion with before to open up. We shared deeply our thoughts and difficulties and experience." "Whilst there were differences in our appearance, speech and food yet we were bonded by feeling of friendship and caring." said an Indian manager, "Sharing innermost feelings and fears so openly bonded us emotionally." The leaders also came to realize that intellect, wisdom and virtues were not the heritage or property of any particular nation or a group of people. Said one: "We all have different backgrounds, so I have to look into that deeply and I have to open my mind up and be big enough to accept each one of you in my heart. Then we can have some sort of understanding and then become more united together."

Sharing personal stories helped to lower cultural barriers and allowed the leaders to reflect on their differing reactions to one another and what they had in common:

This was difficult for me because it made me do things against my norms. However, I am grateful that I was forced to face it and reflect on myself, my future and my job.

Physical hugging might be a little embarrassing at our office in Japan. I still don't know why. But I discovered many touching stories and started to appreciate our diversity and richness of human being.

What makes the second day's dialogue fascinating is that nearly all the speakers are South Asian leaders (from Indonesia, Thailand, Malaysia, Vietnam, and China) who to this point have not spoken to the group as a whole. The more expressive English speakers from India and Pakistanis have seemingly emptied themselves of their need to speak. They are giving space to and welcoming the diversity of other voices. There is no applause. No speeches. People are standing up one at a time, as they are moved to speak, not competing for airtime but attentively listening and building on what is said. This is a glimmer of what true dialogue can be. Now that it has begun, what will the leaders talk about?

Inquiry into mission

Much of the writing and practice about large group intervention to date concerns applications to collective problem solving, futuring, work design, or simply information sharing. There are also well documented applications to business or organizational issues including mergers and acquisitions, cost reduction, and, broadly, culture change (Marks and Mirvis, 2000; Ulrich *et al.*, 2002; Axelrod, 2003). The case here is unique in that it shows the use of a large group intervention to aid business leaders in not only developing their internal processes but also inquiring into their very purpose for being together. The heart of their experience in India and talk together concerned the mission of their enterprise.

The idea that visions and missions can guide a business and provide meaning for its members and customers is well established. The importance of vision in business attracted widespread attention with publication of *In Search of Excellence* in the mid-1980s, which popularized the practice of defining a vision, connecting it to values, and communicating it inside and outside a company (Peters and Waterman, 1982). However, as the importance of short-term profitability increased in the years thereafter and the fortunes of several of the excellent companies declined, the "soft" aspects – vision and values – were called into question (Kanter and Mirvis, 1989). Publication of *Built to Last* (Collins and Porras, 1997) revived interest by demonstrating that successful companies could be differentiated from unsuccessful ones, in the same industry, on the basis of their "core ideology" and "vision of the future."

There are, needless to say, many definitions, concepts, and frameworks that have to do with vision and mission in companies and personal life.[1] Two things are generally agreed:

- clarifying and committing to one's own aspirations creates a strong personal sense of purpose; and

- a strong personal sense of purpose energizes participation with others to establish a shared vision and mission and make them more consequential.

Experiencing communities in India

On their next journey, the leaders assemble in India, divide into twenty-five groups, and then travel by train, bus, or car to self-study local communities. The sites include Mother Teresa's Missionaries of Charity, the Dalai Lama's monastery, the Sikh Golden Temple, the Brahma Kumaris in Mt Abu, Bah'ai Lotus Temple, as well as cloth spinning communes, the self-employed women's association (SEWA), ashrams, and so forth. The visits have elements of service learning in that the leaders were engaged in service to others, recorded observations, feelings, and insights about community practices and needs, and talked these over in informal and structured group reflections over several days thereafter.

The business leaders are asked to assume the role of an anthropologist for the visit, that is, to use their five senses – sight, hearing, smell, taste, and touch – to make sense of what was going on in the communities and to rely on their sixth sense – intuition or gut feel – to connect to the universal rhythms of human and community life. In so doing, they are urged to pay attention to preconceived cultural or intellectual assumptions; to be sensitive to their feelings and judgments and to open up to what they might experience during the visit. All are provided with workbooks to record thoughts on the physical environs they encountered, the social organization of the communities, the ties that seemed to bind people together, and their very purpose for being together.

Many are surprised at what they see and they find some aspects dispiriting and others delightful. Most connect deeply with people they met who were contributing what they could to humanity. Certainly the leaders deepen their understanding and appreciation of what it takes to live in a community. Their reactions vary as dramatically:

We were in 'The Art of Living' ashram for two days where we got an introduction to breathing techniques, meditation, yoga, offering *serva* (giving others service). The community was one big happy family all volunteering their services. Mastering the 'Art of Living' enables one to realize his full potential and live a fulfilling life. I am really impressed on how such a simple and basic concept can move millions into joining this movement.

Looking at how the **Sikh** community works, I cannot underestimate the power of common values in a community. People can simply work together in perfect harmony without a formal organization

We had that experience of visiting **Mother Teresa's** missionary sisters in Mombayasha. They didn't have a vision, I felt. They had a mission. And their mission was something that they, each and every nun could achieve on that day, which is really to give love. To really give love to the most unwanted, the most downtrodden individual whom they just take off the streets.

You go into their place and it is full of really sick and dying people, but the atmosphere is not that of misery but of joy and love. (My coworker) and I were told to massage some people who were just flesh and bones. And this volunteer who had been there for 14 years, a guy called Andy, came to us and said: 'Look, this is how you've got to do it.' It improves their blood circulation and bedsores. But most importantly, it's the human touch that they've missed for years, that you give them. So there's so much love and affection in that place. And you just get sucked in, and start doing things that you thought were impossible for you to do.

I admired the Buddhist monks in **Dharamshala** for debating and questioning everything in the philosophy as Buddha said, 'Do not believe it because I preached it – see and understand for yourself and live by it if you wish . . . ' This brings me back to the fact that everything we do in life is by choice – it is by choice that I have decided to be a leader. When you have a clear cause for life – choices become so apparent.

No question that, for many, a visit to these communities was a personal discovery. Said one who visited the charity of Mother Teresa: "The sisters and volunteers really inspired me with their humility, selflessness, courage, and mostly their faith. The energy they have to serve the poor, the disabled, the left-over really touched me and honestly I cried during the visit." Said another: "After the community experience, I have realized that I have been living my life without purpose. I have taken my life, my family, and society for granted for almost thirty-four years."

This, in turn, provoked broader considerations: "A new challenge arose for me: How could I be worried about my job and 'how much tea we sold last week' when thinking of all those that are giving their life to care for people for whom life seems to have been so unfair. This was a gap I could not bridge and I struggled with the rest of my group to see the link between those communities and our business-driven environment."

To bridge this gap, the two hundred leaders came to the conclusion that they would have to revise their mission and corporate purpose.

Redefining a company's mission

After their community visits, the 200 plus leaders reflected together over three days. In solo, in small groups, and as a community, they probed deeply into the existential questions of who am I?, who are we? and what are we here for? The result of their collective inquiry was a shared aspiration to make their work more meaningful and more relevant to the communities they serve in Asia. Said one, "I started getting the feeling that my work need not be confined to producing and selling as efficiently as possible but has a higher purpose of community service to the people of Asia. Maybe I can call it (a shift) from a mercenary to missionary view (of our business)."

Ongoing dialogue brought them closer to the conclusion that organizations have to be driven by their missions rather than by numbers and processes. "We should be able to serve the larger community by being relevant for them – not by just being providers of products," said one, "How else can organizations like Brahma Kumaris, Missionaries of Charities, etc. be managed without systems, procedures and controls and yet handle millions of dollars effectively?" The leaders also talked about what kind of an organization they would need to fulfil this aspiration; one where, in effect, people would be willing to "volunteer" their time and talents. One asked, "What can I contribute to the society and have I fulfilled my duty to mankind?" and then answered her own query, "we could all work towards leaving a legacy that transcends the borders and barriers of culture, religion, or race."

An imperative emerged: the leaders needed to put flesh into these caring aspirations and translate them into a mission and a way of life that would emphasize the healthy, nourishing aspects of food. Hear one of the statements:

We want to be responsible partners with the people of Asia, to provide health, vitality and the development of the children and families through better food and beverage. We can do this by earning the trust of people everywhere, having authentic standards for what is right food. We can do this by being at the leading edge of nutrition science and technology. We need to be actively involved in communities, to understand all their needs, especially the needs of the economically underprivileged, and children. We need to do so with humility, truth, and authenticity. That means we have to do what we say.

Another added, "With tremendous power and privilege comes responsibility. Our new mission, in whatever semantics it may finally be, will make our work more impactful. Our lives will take a route closer to the missions we have visited here in India."

An emerging sense of community

In its mature or performing phase, a group of whatever size dedicates more of its time and resources to its tasks – whatever they may be.[2] The interpersonal agenda has people asking how much to give of themselves to the task and how open and intimate to be to one another. A dialogue group asks "generative" questions about its tasks and about itself. To the extent a dialogue group takes on a life of its own, practices of self-management and self-organization are posited to emerge. And, in the community building vernacular, the mature group organizes in line with an "unseen" order that is both generative and healing. This transcendental state goes by many names. Spiritualists liken it to a state of grace (Peck, 1993); a recent research study gives it the prosaic label of "group magic" (Levi, 2003); and learning theorists describe it as "presencing" (Senge *et al.*, 2004).

On these matters, two Asian leaders reflected:

I realized that words like emotions, feeling, moods may not sound businesslike, however, once used in their best and sincere form have real consequences for getting work done. I began to understand that building a resonant culture, one where all of us can bring out the best in us, would bring us to greatness.

I feel very close to the Asia group. There was some weird sense of bonding that developed even though I didn't know more than half of the people. I really can't explain it well but it was a sense of oneness or being together. It is strange because I felt this when weren't even talking. It was a nice feeling. For the first time I experienced it outside my family. Maybe this is what we call community feeling.

A sense of community grew easily as the Asian leaders would strive to speak authentically, build on comments, challenge gracefully, and help new thoughts and intentions to emerge. The process was maturing to the point of collective thinking. Said one, "Initially it was hard, it was painful to talk so openly as we are so new to each other. Now it was great to see that words just poured out from everyone. We are starting to see the connections with each other." "When we talk about building this community, we are very serious about it" added another, "so it takes time for us to progress, to make it happen."

What helped this sense of community to emerge so strongly? More time together and familiarity were no doubt factors. So were practice with dialogue, experience in sharing personal stories and expressing vulnerability, and a degree of psychological safety established from past encounters. Furthermore, some of the norms of building community in a circle – speaking personally, listening thoughtfully, raising difficult issues, and talking from the heart – while originally "foreign" to these Asian leaders were proving agreeable.

Another factor was, in our view, the subject matter at hand. For one, there was the richness of unpacking the community visitations and reflecting on their emotional impact. Said a leader:

The India outbreak has brought about in me an increased awareness into the purpose and virtuous values of life. From the rich dialogues and sharing we had, I also got a much deeper understanding of the meaning of community and the journey. I feel that we, as a community, are well on our way.

Second, there was the conversation about applying the experiences and insights to the mission of the company.

I was struggling with the concept of community in a business corporation such as ours but the layers unpeeled over the days slowly. I feel it is a very powerful thought and I am still trying to soak it in. I saw a deeper meaning of life in all this. The real-life community program in the beginning of the program really touched me as I saw voluntary work, devotion, sacrifice, purity, truth, understanding, belonging, affiliation, caring, working together in a responsible and dedicated fashion like a family, a sense of fulfillment and so on. While family is so central to me in personal life, I feel that similar core thoughts need to be internalized and become a way of life in work life.

Or, as one leader put it simply, "I think a great community really happens when there is complete clarity of purpose."

Finally, there was the struggle of actually coming to terms with something so consequential. Some spoke of risks – "a heavy burden of responsibility" and a "fear of not living up to expectations;" others of doubts – the mission was "too idealistic, no connection to reality;" and still others of competing expectations: "We are obsessed by numbers and we are paid to maximize them. This is clear and will always be the case."

There was space in the circle to express these doubts and challenge prevailing sentiments. True community, in Peck's formulation, is born of inclusiveness and comes into being as a group transcends differences. Gardner (1995) terms this "wholeness incorporating diversity."

Fine words and uplifting sentiments, but the challenge facing the company is how to transform them into a way of life. In sharing their final thoughts and feelings on the challenge, some found the prospect to be daunting: "What still concerns me is how I will make this transition with my own selfish interests – of career growth, financial security, being in good books of my bosses, saying the politically acceptable things, taking short-cuts, putting myself ahead of others, etc.?" Said another: "This mission cannot co-exist with bad business performance or the absence of immediate action to bring it alive."

Others expressed their enthusiasm, and commitment: "I am excited with the idea of creating something magical and I am committed – realizing fully well the newly-found meaning of this word community – to making this happen."

Will they be able to deliver on their promise of their mission? As Sarason (1974), notes, events often shake the foundations of a community, creating an identity crisis that is resolved by regression – to a more-conventional mode of operations – or regeneration where a community redefines itself again. The company has not yet reached this crisis point. In practical terms, moreover, a shared aspiration and declaration of intent is not enough to bring the mission alive. Truly caring for the needy in Asia abounds with difficulties – it will take tough business decisions that might threaten the core business. Even so, the company has begun making major investments in children's nutrition and reaching out to the poorest-of-the-poor with inexpensive foods and community-based distribution systems (Prahalad and Hammond, 2002).

It is undeniable, however, that a community of leaders has formed and come to a new view of itself and its mission (Mirvis and Gunning 2000). It would take the experience of community life in India to help them rediscover their purpose. And while the power of this experience was significant to finding a new mission, it was the power of collective inquiry that helped to bring the mission to life. Building a community is very much a part of this. Gardner (1995) writes, "Where community exists it confers upon its members an identity, a sense of belonging, and a measure of security. It is in communities that the attributes that distinguish humans as social creatures are nourished. Communities are the ground level generators and preservers of values and ethical systems."

REFERENCES

Alderfer, C. P. (1980) Consulting to underbounded systems. In C. P. Alderfer and C. L. Cooper (eds.) *Advances in experiential social processes* (Vol. 2), pp. 267–95. New York: John Wiley.

Argyris, C. (1982) *Reasoning, learning, and action.* San Francisco: Jossey-Bass.

(1985) *Strategy, change, and defensive routines.* Cambridge: Ballinger.

Axelrod, R. H. (2003) *Terms of engagement: Changing the way we change organizations.* San Francisco: Berrett-Koehler.

Beckhard, R. and Harris, R. (1987) *Organizational transitions.* Reading, MA: Addison-Wesley.

Bennis, W. G. and Shephard, H. A. (1956) "A theory of group development," *Human Relations, 9*, 415–37.

Bion, W. R. (1961) *Experiences in Groups.* London: Tavistock Publications.

Bohm, D. (1986) *Wholeness and the implicate order.* London: Ark.

Bohm, D. (1989) *On dialogue,* David Bohm Seminars, Ojai, CA.

Bradford, L. P, Gibb, J. R. and Benne, K. W. (eds.), (1964) *T-group theory and laboratory method.* New York: Wiley.

Bunker, B. and Alban, B. (1992) What makes large group interventions effective? *Journal of Applied Behavioral Science 28(4).*

Bunker, B. and Alban, B. (1997) *Large group interventions: Engaging the whole system for rapid change.* San Francisco: Jossey-Bass.

Collins, J. C. and Porras, J. I. (1997) *Built to last: Successful habits of visionary companies.* New York: Harper-Business.

Gardner, J. (1995) *Building community.* Washington: Independent Sector.

Gozdz, K. (ed.) (1996) *Community building in business.* San Francisco: New Leaders Press.

Harman, W. (1988) *Global mind change.* New York: Warner.

Isaacs, W. (1999) *Dialogue and the art of thinking together: A pioneering approach to communicating in business and life.* New York: Doubleday.

Isaacs, W. N. (1993) "Dialogue: the power of collective thinking," *The Systems Thinker, 4,* 3.

Jacobs, R. W. (1994) *Real time strategic change.* San Francisco: Berrett-Koehler.

Kanter, D. L. and Mirvis, P. H. (1989) *The cynical Americans.* San Francisco: Jossey Bass.

Kofman, F. and Senge, P. (1993) "Communities of commitment: the heart of the learning organization," *Organization Dynamics,* Fall.

Levi, R. (2003) *Group Magic: An Inquiry into Experiences of Collective Resonance.* Doctoral dissertation summary. Self-published.

Marks, M. L. and P. H. Mirvis. (2000) Managing mergers, acquisitions, and alliances: Creating an effective transition structure. *Organizational Dynamics,* Winter, 35–47.

Maslow, A. H. (1968) *Toward a psychology of being.* New York: Van Nostrand.

McMillan, D. W. and Chavis, D. M. (1986) "Sense of community: A definition and theory," *Journal of Community Psychology, 14,* 6–23.

Mirvis, P. H. (2002) Community building in business. *Reflections, 3,3,* 45–51.

Mirvis, P. H. (1997) "'Soul work' in organizations". *Organization Science, 8,2,* 193–206.

Peck, M. S. (1987) *The different drum.* New York: Simon and Schuster.

Peck, M. S. (1993) *A world waiting to be born.* New York: Bantam.

Peters, T. J. and Waterman, R. H. Jr. (1982) *In search of excellence.* New York: Harper & Row.

Prahalad, C. K. and Hammond, A. (2002) Serving the world's poor, profitably, *Harvard Business Review.* September.

Sarason, S. (1974) *The psychological sense of community.* San Francisco: Jossey-Bass.

Scharmer, C. O. (2004) Theory U: Leading from the emerging future. www.ottoscharmer.com.

Schutz, W. (1958) *FIRO: A Three-dimensional theory of interpersonal behavior.* New York: Holt, Rinehart & Winston.

Senge, P. (1990) *The fifth discipline.* New York: Doubleday.

Senge, P., Scharmer, P. O., Jaworski, J. and Flowers, B. S. (2004) *Presence: Human purpose and the field of the future.* Cambridge: Society for Organizational Learning.

Slater, P. E. (1966) *Microcosm.* New York: Wiley Interscience.

Smith, K. and Berg, D. N. (1987) *Paradoxes of group life.* San Francisco: Jossey Bass.

Tuckman, B. W. (1965) "Developmental sequences in small groups," *Psychological Bulletin, 54,* 229–49.

Ulrich, D., Kerr, S., and Ashkenas, R. (2002) *The GE workout.* New York: McGraw-Hill.

Weisbord, M. (1992) *Discovering common ground.* San Francisco: Berrett-Koehler.

Wilbur, K. (1984) *Quantum questions,* Boston: Shambala.

NOTES

1. In *The Fifth Discipline,* Senge (1990) incorporates these concepts into a set of "governing ideas" for a business: (1) Vision is the 'What' – the picture of the future we seek to create; (2) Purpose is the 'Why' – the organization's answer to why we exist; and (3) Values are the 'How' – how do we act to achieve our vision.

2. This reminds me of key points about development of groups: First, progress through stages is by no means smooth or inevitable. On the contrary, people, small groups, and larger ones often seemingly get "stuck" at one or another phase and either do not face or fail to master more complex developmental challenges. Second, rather than a sequence, developmental stages might be better depicted as a spiral. Changes in setting and circumstances mean that individuals and groups must continuously cycle through activities involving forming, storming, norming, and performing. In the ideal, of course, new challenges can be managed more quickly and effectively by "mature" groups. In practice, however, many other factors can either increase progress or lead to regression.

Index